The Economy of Russia and Other Post-Soviet Countries

Authors:

Bulatov A.S. (units I and II);
Kvashnin A.D. (unit III);
Mamedova N.M. (units IV and V);
Zhdanov S.V. (unit VI).

Edited by A.S. Bulatov

Editor of the English version: M.A. Petrova

The Economy of Russia and Other Post-Soviet Countries

By

Alexander S. Bulatov,
Yury D. Kvashnin,
Nina M. Mamedova
and Sergei V. Zhdanov

Edited by Alexander S. Bulatov

Editor of the English version:
Marina A. Petrova

Cambridge
Scholars
Publishing

The Economy of Russia and Other Post-Soviet Countries

By Alexander S. Bulatov, Yury D. Kvashnin, Nina M. Mamedova
and Sergei V. Zhdanov

Edited by Alexander S. Bulatov

Editor of the English version: Marina A. Petrova

This book first published 2019

Cambridge Scholars Publishing

Lady Stephenson Library, Newcastle upon Tyne, NE6 2PA, UK

British Library Cataloguing in Publication Data
A catalogue record for this book is available from the British Library

ISBN (10): 1-5275-3276-3
ISBN (13): 978-1-5275-3276-2

MGIMO
UNIVERSITY

This study guide is aimed at introducing to its reader basic tendencies and problems of Russia and other post-Soviet countries along with the introduction of logics and analysis tools of the national economy.

In the first chapters of the unit II main features of Russian economic model, rates and proportions of Russian economy, investment and fixed assets, human capital, economic policy of modern Russia are considered. In other chapters real, financial, external, social sectors of Russian economy are analyzed.

In the other units (III-VI) of the guide other post-Soviet economies such as East European, Transcaucasian, Central Asian and the Baltics are described.

CONTENTS

INTRODUCTION

This study guide is aimed at introducing to its reader basic tendencies and problems of the post-Soviet countries along with the introduction of logics and analysis tools of the national economy (for that purpose the study guide begins from the unit I concentrated on analysis methods of a country economy).

Post-soviet countries are analyzed by regions (more definitely, by sub-regions), i.e. Russia (due to economic, demographic and geographic size it is analyzed as a separate economic region), the other three post-Soviet republics of Eastern Europe, Transcaucasia, Central Asia, and the Baltic states. Within each region (sub-region) there are a lot of differences between countries but a lot of economic similarities as well and that allows considering them together.

As for the whole post-Soviet territory, after the demise of the Soviet Union it is neither an economically nor politically integrated economic region of the world, which was the Soviet Union. It is rather a territory consisting of the separate sub-regions mentioned above. This point is justified by the Baltic countries that have already joined another economic region of the world – the European Union as well as Ukraine, Moldova and Georgia that are eager to join it.

In the meantime within the post-Soviet territory there are close economic ties growing into a formed economic integration between many other countries. This is the case for the Eurasian Economic Union, which has already united five countries (Russia, Belarus, Armenia, Kazakhstan, Kyrgyzstan), with a view of some other post-Soviet countries joining it.

Finally, it is useful to compare different post-Soviet countries (preferably of the same economic level, of course) with regard to their economic progress for the quarter of a century gone after the collapse of the USSR. Economic comparative studies provide a lot for the national economy analysis.

Authors hope that their book could help its readers to gain knowledge about the economy of Russia and the countries of the post-Soviet territory as well as to develop skills in the economic country analysis. Your feedback could be helpful for us, so please forward it to the e-mail: bulatov@mgimo.ru.

UNIT I

THE FOUNDATIONS OF ECONOMIC ANALYSIS BY COUNTRY

CHAPTER 1

THE ECONOMIC MODEL OF A COUNTRY

The Notion of a National Economy

The economy of a given country is an economy defined by national borders. So the Russian economy is that which exists within Russia's borders and, similarly, the economy of the Union of Soviet Socialist Republics (USSR) was that which existed within the borders of the now defunct USSR.

Talk of a country's economy might also need to take account of separate parts or territories of that country that enjoy economic autonomy and thus differ significantly from the economy of the country as a whole (e.g. Greenland in Denmark, Hong Kong in China). International economic organizations include such territories in the statistics they publish on the countries in question, explaining that by countries they mean not only states but some territories as well.

In addition, there are administrative-territorial entities that consider themselves to be states but which are not regarded as such by other countries around the world, but are seen merely as regions (e.g. Taiwan, which calls itself The Republic of China). Such entities also exist within the territory of the former Soviet Union. When analyzing such economies, it is better to proceed according to whether your own country recognizes the entity in question as a separate state or not. Thus, for example, Russia recognizes the independence of Abkhazia and South Ossetia, but considers Nagorno-Karabakh to be a territory of Azerbaijan, and Transdniestria to be a territory of Moldova.

The Typology of National Economies

Around two hundred national economies exist in the world today. These can be divided into the developed and the less developed. These groups can be regarded as two economic systems or as two subsystems if we regard the global international economy as a single system.

Developed (advanced) economies are characterized by high levels of economic development. The International Monetary Fund (IMF) identifies 39 advanced economies out of 193 member countries of the IMF:

	1	USA
Euro area	19	Austria, Belgium, Germany, Greece, Ireland, Spain, Italy, Cyprus, Luxembourg, Malta, the Netherlands, Portugal, Slovakia, Slovenia, Finland, France, Latvia, Lithuania, Estonia
	1	Japan
Other advanced economies	18	United Kingdom, Republic of Korea, Canada, Australia, Taiwan Province of China, Switzerland, Sweden, Singapore, Hong Kong SAR, Norway, Czech Republic, Israel, Denmark, New Zealand, Puerto Rico, Macao SAR, Iceland, San Marino

Other organizations offer different definitions of which countries qualify as developed. The Organisation for Economic Co-operation and Development (OECD) includes its 35 members (among them Hungary, Mexico, Poland, Turkey, and Chile). The United Nations (UN) excludes Israel and the newly industrialized Asian economies, but includes all members of the European Union (EU), some of whom — Bulgaria, Hungary, Poland, Romania, and Croatia — are less well developed.

All other economies across the world are regarded as less well developed or, by the IMF classification of countries, as emerging markets and developing economies. The World Bank classifies economies as low-income, lower-middle-income, upper-middle-income, or high-income (most of which are developed economies) based on gross national income per capita.

These are usually divided into two subgroups: developing countries (those with a forming market) and emerging economies. Over 130 economies belong to the first group, with around two dozen in the latter group; these are mainly countries transiting from socialist to market economies. This includes those former socialist countries of Central and Eastern Europe that do not qualify as developed, along with all the countries of the former Soviet Union (except the Baltic states) and Mongolia. China and Vietnam should in practice be seen as emerging economies, but their governments deny that capitalism is being formed there and so prefer to be classified as developing. Socialist Cuba and North Korea can be regarded as emerging.

Thus, in order to place a national economy in one or another group, it is necessary first to ascertain its level of economic development. This can be done by analysis of key economic indicators such as gross domestic product (GDP) or gross national income (GNI) per capita, and the structure of industrial output. Let us consider these indicators in more detail.

Gross Domestic Product and Gross National Income per capita

With the help of the added value method, GDP measures the quantity of goods and services produced within a country. By contrast, GNI shows the amount of income earned by the residents of a country along with their net primary income (that gained from output and property) with regard to their settlements with other countries. In most countries GDP is normally higher than GNI, but in some the reverse is true.

To make comparisons between different countries, GDP and GNI are usually expressed in US dollars, the most widely used currency. Even though our purpose here is to compare economic development of former Soviet countries, it would still be incorrect to convert figures in dollars to rubles — even at a nominal exchange rate — as exchange rates are exposed to fluctuations. Moreover, prices for goods and services differ from one country to another. To achieve an accurate comparison, a survey, the International Comparison Program, is carried out under the auspices of the UN every three years. This survey captures the prices of a basket of 3,000 named goods and services in different countries and compares the cost with the price of the same goods in the USA (corrected for differences in quality). Thus, by comparing the price of the basket of goods and services in one country with the USA, the value of that country's currency can be determined in relation to the dollar. This rate is called purchasing power parity (PPP). This PPP rate is a better indicator than a nominal rate in less developed countries as the prices for the majority of goods in these countries tend to be lower than in the USA.

In the years between surveys, national and international organizations extrapolate the PPP. The Federal State Statistics Service of the Russian Federation calculated Russian GDP PPP per capita in 2016 at US$23,163 (at an exchange rate of ₽25.33 to the dollar).

However, in many countries, the national statistical organizations do not carry out such calculations. So, for comparisons between countries, World Bank statistics are usually used. However, the World Bank often calculates the PPP using GNI rather than GDP and places a strong emphasis on average annual calculations, thus avoiding strong annual fluctuations that can be seen with GDP PPP as a result of changes in currency exchange rates. According to the Bank, Russia's GDP PPP per capita of US$24,451 in 2016 was at approximately the same level as countries at the bottom of the IMF list of developed countries, e.g. Lithuania (US$29,996), Estonia (US$29,365) and Latvia (US$26,031). Among the former Soviet countries, the lowest GDP PPP per capita was recorded in Kyrgyzstan (US$3,551) and Tajikistan (US$2,980), putting them close to countries in Africa.

Industrial Structure of Output

The contribution of different sectors to GDP changes as a country experiences economic development. The primary sector (agriculture, forestry, hunting, and fishing—often referred to simply as 'agriculture), which has dominated for hundreds of years, reduces in significance. The secondary sector (industry, construction, power, gas, and water supply—usually referred to as 'industry') which shot up during industrialization is now decreasing as the third sector (services) increases as the country transitions to a post-industrial model. There are, however, some variations in this pattern.

Primary sector production decreases in developed countries, firstly because demand of the sector's products sees slow growth in these countries due to high saturation in demand for food and improved performance from the use of industrial methods in the sector. The contribution to GDP of this sector ranges from 1% (USA, Germany) to 3% (Spain, Finland). In less developed countries this sector contributes more to GDP, except for the countries with a poor natural environment. For example, the primary sector contributes 4% of GDP in Russia, where there is no issue of high saturation of demand for food supplies and performance in this sector is not high—demonstrated by the fact that this sector accounts for 7% of national employment, but only contributes 4% to GDP. In the most developed former Soviet countries, these figures are broadly similar, and in the less developed countries they are much worse, especially in the central Asian republics. In Tajikistan, the primary sector accounts for 60% of employment but contributes just 30% of GDP.

The secondary sector has seen its contribution to GDP fall by 20–30% over the last decade, due to stronger growth in the tertiary sector and to the closing down of many industrial facilities. This latter phenomenon is often called 'deindustrialization'. In developed countries, it is seen mostly in 'simple' or 'dirty' sectors, such as mining. The economic losses of the process are partly mitigated by growth in advanced technological sectors.

There is significant diversification in the way this trend plays out in the former Soviet countries. The contribution of the secondary sector varies from 17–22% in Moldova and Tajikistan to 42–62% in industrial Belarus and oil and gas producing Azerbaijan. However, the contribution of the secondary sector to GDP is falling in the majority of former Soviet countries. Moreover, in many countries of the Commonwealth of Independent States (CIS), deindustrialization is characterized by deterioration in the structure of industry due to a reduction in high-technology sectors (especially engineering) and their replacement with the 'simple' and 'dirty' sectors like mining. Thus, in Russia, the contribution of the secondary sector to GDP went down to 36%, due less to growth in the tertiary sector than to reduced production in manufacturing, especially engineering, and in the consumer goods industry. (Some estimates suggest that, without the falling in manufacturing production, the contribution of the secondary sector would have fallen far less, remaining at around 46%.)

A majority of countries have a functioning tertiary sector. But the structure varies. In developed countries its structure is appropriate to a post-industrial economy: it includes branches such as education, medical care, financial, business and professional services. In the USA, 50% of people employed in services are involved in the latter categories (financial, business, and professional). More conventional industries, e.g. trade and transport, account for 24% of the services workforce. In less developed countries the picture is somewhat different. In Russia, 40% of those employed in services work in the former sectors (e.g. education and medical), due to only a small number of people working in financial services. Other branches of the services sector also account for around 40% of those employed, due in part to Russia has a larger proportion of the services sector workforce involved in trade than in the USA. Over the whole economy, Russia has 15% of people working in trade, compared with 14% in the USA.

The Notion of a National Economic Model

The next step in analyzing a national economy is to identify the characteristics of the country's economic model. A country's model is its specific economic mechanism that distinguishes it from its neighbors and from other countries at a similar level of economic development.

We need to clarify some of the specifics of this notion. Why is it important to compare a country's economic mechanism with that of its neighbors and with other countries at a similar level of economic development in order to identify its specific characteristics? We do this because of the way different objective laws operate at difference levels of development (e.g. rates of economic growth in developed countries are lower than in countries that are catching them up. But these latter countries will see lower levels of growth when they achieve the level of development seen in the most developed countries.) Comparison with neighboring countries can sometimes be inappropriate if two countries are at different levels of development. But such countries often have a number of features in common. This is why we often compare Russia with other former Soviet republics. Finally, the analysis also benefits from a comparison of the country in question with the leading economies around the world. It is also useful to compare economies of similar sizes.

How can we identify the specific character of the economic mechanisms in a country in order to define the national economic model? To achieve this, it is appropriate to focus our analysis, not just on a country's economic mechanisms, but also on its social, ethical, and political mechanisms as these have a noticeable influence on economic mechanisms.

Methods of Analyzing Specific Characteristics of a National Economic Model

To analyze specific characteristics of a country's economic mechanisms, we can select different economic indicators independently from national and international statistics. If looking for already prepared sets of indicators, one of the most useful is likely to be the *Global Competitiveness Report* produced annually by the World Economic Forum (WEF), an international non-governmental organization. The report is based on national statistics and interviews with local entrepreneurs in 140 countries. It gives each country an overall competitiveness score on a scale from 1 to 7. A total of 114 indicators are used to calculate the score. As well as the overall score, a further 12 sub-indices are produced giving greater insight into the individual characteristics of each country's economic structure.

To illustrate this, let us look at the example of Russia and compare Russia's sub-indices with those of other countries at a similar level of economic development.

Table 1.1 — Index of global competitiveness and its sub-indices in Russia and other countries with a similar level of economic development

	Russia	Poland	Turkey	Kazakhstan	*Memo:* USA
Index of global competitiveness (on a scale of 1 to 7, where 7 is the highest. The number in brackets gives the rank of a country on the list of 138 countries)	**4.6 (38)**	**4.6 (39)**	**4.4 (5.3)**	**4.3 (57)**	**5.9 (2)**
Institutions	3.7	3.8	3.8	4.0	5.3
Infrastructure	4.9	4.7	4.5	4.2	6.2
Macroeconomic environment	5.0	5.2	5.1	4.2	4.5
Health care and primary education	6.0	6.2	5.6	5.9	6.3
Higher education and training	5.1	5.0	4.8	4.6	6.1
Goods market efficiency	4.2	4.6	4.5	4.3	5.5
Labor market efficiency	4.3	4.1	3.4	4.6	5.6
Financial market development	3.4	4.2	3.8	3.3	5.7
Technological readiness	4.5	4.9	4.4	4.6	6.2
Market size	5.9	5.2	5.5	4.5	6.9
Business sophistication	4.0	4.1	4.0	3.6	5.8
Innovation	3.5	3.4	3.3	3.2	5.8

Source: The World Economic Forum. The Global Competitiveness Report 2017–2018; Geneva, 2017. pp. 164–303.

Table 1.1 shows the competitiveness score for a range of specific areas of the Russian economy. On the one hand, Russia stands out from other countries with similar levels of economic development for its good infrastructure (which could have been even better if the roads had been improved!), higher education and training, and market size. On the other hand, Russia's shortcomings can be seen in low scores for institutions, the macroeconomic environment, the efficiency of goods market, and financial market development.

More detailed analysis of the indictors and sub-indices enables us to draw a number of conclusions. The low score for institutions in Russia is the result of low rates in the indicators of e.g. property rights (on this Russia ranks 116th in the world), intellectual property protection (93rd), protection of minority shareholder interests (111th), the reliability of police services (98th), the independence of the judiciary (90th), irregular payments and bribery (76th), and the heavy burden of government regulation (79th).

Although Russia scores reasonably well for its macroeconomic environment (it ranks 6th for government debt), the picture is overwhelmed by high inflation for which the country ranks 112th, though in 2017 it was low (about 4%).

The low score for the efficiency of the goods market reflects weak local competition (where the country ranks 72nd), antimonopoly policies (83rd), high levels of tax (101st) coupled with weak tax incentives for investment (104th), and low levels of openness to foreign goods and services and foreign direct investment (FDI) (72nd–123rd).

Russia lags far behind in the index of financial market development due to poor scores for developing financial services that meet businesses' needs (rank 94th), difficulty in accessing loans (110th), and regulation of securities exchanges (112th).

Business Structure as an Element in the Analysis of the National Economic Model

The way business is structured in a country has an impact in determining specific features of a country's economic model. The term 'business structure' is used in different ways. In this book, we will use it to refer to small, medium, large, or public businesses or sectors. The business structure is an important element in the analysis of a country's economy and its individual sectors. Thus, if a country has a significant public sector, we can assume that it is a country with significant levels of government intervention. If large private businesses account for a high proportion of GDP, we can assume that the country has a heavily monopolized economy.

The main practical difficulty in analyzing the business structure of a country can be shortcomings in the available statistics. For example, the definition of a small business differs from country to country. In the USA, statistics define a company with less than 500 employees as 'small' and 500–1000 employees as 'medium.' Russian statistics use 'small' to mean a business with less than 100 employees (also included here are unincorporated individual entrepreneurs and farm households) and 'medium' to mean a business with no more than 250 employees. Moreover, the System of National Accounts (SNA) values products produced in private households, but does not include them in the statistics for small businesses on the assumption that such goods are produced for private consumption, rather than for the market. However, in some countries, a significant proportion of agricultural output is produced in precisely such households. In Russia, such private households produce 38% of the country's agricultural products and act as small businesses in the agricultural sector, while farm households produce only 11% of the country's agricultural products. Finally, it should be noted that the role of small businesses is underestimated in the statistics since a proportion of their activity happens outside the formal economy and is thus not picked up by official statistics. As a result, the definition of a small business in less developed economies needs to be treated carefully, as their true contribution may be underestimated in statistics.

In some cases, national statistics do not identify large private businesses as such. Their importance in the economy is measured as an implicit share of as many as 10 leading companies in a given sector, or of as many as 500 companies in the overall figure for GDP. In addition, it should be noted that, for a number of reasons relating to technology and other issues, concentration is high in the industrial and banking sectors, and lower in construction, agriculture, and in the majority of the services sector. Furthermore, countries that are major exporters of raw materials and thus have mining as a major contributor to GDP tend to have a small number of companies in the mining sector. So, when looking at the share of GDP of large companies, the sectoral context is important. In addition, when looking at large companies, it is important to note links between companies or groups of companies in the form of share participation or other traditional links. Careful analysis of such structures enables us to identify the true 'power centers' of an economy.

When looking at the role of the public sector in an economy, a number of specific factors should be taken into consideration. One clear indicator of a government's role in an economy is the quantity of assets that it owns. But the industrial structure of those assets should also be analyzed. Government-owned assets are often concentrated in transport and social infrastructure (roads, hospitals etc.). If the government owns a significant number of industrial assets, then it can be assumed to be playing a role in industrial output. Similarly, high levels of government ownership of banking assets will indicate direct governmental participation in the banking sector. In Russia, for example, more than 50% of bank assets belong to banks with public participation.

In addition, in emerging economies it is common for government and private businesses to share ownership of banks or companies. For example, the Russian government owns 52% of Gazprom, with the remaining 48% owned by private businesses. As a result, it can be difficult to accurately define the public sector's share of GDP. In Russia this share is estimated to be 20–25%. In Belarus, it is even higher.

The Influence of other Mechanisms on the Economic Model

The economic model of a country is heavily influenced by its social, political, and ethical structures (models).

Let's look first at the social model. This has the greatest influence on an economy such that, in many contexts, we refer not to a country's economic model, but to its social and economic model. This term is widely used in Russia. The main features of a country's social model are the level of living standards and quality of life enjoyed by the population. The UN Development Programme (UNDP) produces the Human Development Index (HDI) as a general indicator of levels of development. It is based on a range of indicators of living standards and is calculated as an arithmetic average of three sub-indices: life expectancy; level of education; and GDP PPP per capita. The ideal outcome is considered to be when every sub-index and the HDI itself reach 1, the highest value possible in current conditions.

According to the latest UNDP Human Development Report, in 2015, the top 51 places in the table of HDI (scoring from 0.949 to 0.800) were taken by the members of the EU (except for Bulgaria), other developed countries, and the Arab Gulf States (except for Oman), Brunei, Argentina, Montenegro, and Chile. Of the former Soviet countries, the Baltic states were in the last deciles (scoring 0.830–0.865) and Russia (0.804) occupied the 49th position in the leading group of 51 countries. Belarus and

Kazakhstan were further down the table (scoring 0.796 and 0,794 respectively). Other former Soviet countries scored badly: Ukraine, 0.743; Kyrgyzstan, 0.664; and Tajikistan, 0.627.

Table 1.2 — Russia and other countries of similar development level: some values of the social development level in 2015

	Russia	Poland	Turkey	Kazakhstan	*For reference:* the USA
Human Development Index (in points, where the highest value equals to 1, in brackets specified position of the country on the list of 187 countries)	**0.804 (49)**	**0.855 (36)**	**0.767 (71)**	**0.794 (56)**	**0.920 (10)**
including: Life expectancy (years)	70.3	77.6	75.5	69.6	79.2
Education level, incl. professional development and retraining (years)	12.0	11.9	7.9	11.7	13.2
GNI PPP per capita (dollars)	23,286	24,117	18,705	22,093	53,245
For reference: the Gini index (from 1 to 100 – maximal income differentiation) in 2010–2015	41.6	32.1	40.2	26.3	41.1

Source: UNDP. Human Development Report 2017; New York, 2016; pp. 200–202 and 208–209.

As Table 1.2 shows, Russia has a low life expectancy (1.3 years lower than the world average), a reasonable level of GDP PPP per capita (1.6 times the world average) and a high level of education (12 years in education per adult, compared with the world average of 8.3 years). An analysis of indicators made of sub-indices of healthcare and elementary education in the index of global competitiveness (see Table 1.1) does not suggest that Russian healthcare is lower than it should be for its general level of development. We may conclude that, by global standards, Russia is not a poor country, it has a reasonably well educated population, but a low life expectancy.

The political situation of a country also influences its economic development, first of all through its democratic institutions. There are various ratings that seek to measure the strength of democracy. According to the index published by the Economic Intelligence Unit (measures on a 10-point scale), among the former Soviet countries, the Baltic countries score the highest (7.48–7.74), while Tajikistan (2.37) and Turkmenistan (1.83) are near the bottom of the list.

Table 1.3 — Levels of democracy in selected countries, 2014 (10-point scale)

Russia	Poland	Turkey	Kazakhstan	*Memo:* the USA
3.39	7.47	5.20	3.17	8.11

Source:
http://www.eiu.com/public/topical_report.aspx?campaignid=Democracy0115

From this we can conclude that Russia has weak democratic institutions compared to other countries of a similar level of economic development. In Russia we see a wider gap between the interests of the ruling elite and the interests of the country as a whole, which produces significant poverty, limited independence of the judiciary, and widespread government intervention in the activities of companies.

The strength of the ethical framework in a country also influences the economic sphere through such aspects as the importance of the work ethic, commitment to ethical standards, integrity in public life, and compliance with the law. It is not easy to compare the work ethic of Russian citizens with that of citizens in other countries of a similar level of development, but levels of integrity and compliance with the law can be inferred from widely available statistics such as rates of crime and corruption. The Corruption Perception Index, prepared annually by Transparency International, a non-governmental organization, reflects the perceptions of business people and experts as to the level of corruption in the state apparatus. This shows a high level for Russia when compared to other similar countries. This is borne out in the indicator of ethical conduct among companies (taken from a sub-index of Economic institutions in the Global Competitive Index). The indicator for organized crime can be derived from the same sub-index.

Table 1.4 — Russia and the other countries of a similar level of development: indicators of corruption and organized crime in 2015

	Russia	Poland	Turkey	Kazakhstan	*Memo:* USA
The Corruption Perception Index (in points, where 100 would represent no corruption)	29	62	42	28	76
Ethical behavior of firms (country position on the list of 138 countries)	65	60	93	51	27
Organized crime (country position on the list of 138 countries)	85	51	77	53	70

Source: Transparency International; Corruption Perception Index (www.transparency.org); World Economic Forum. The Global Competitiveness Report 2016–2017. Geneva, 2016

On the basis of Table 1.4, we can conclude that corruption among state officials and non-ethical conduct by companies and organized crime have a negative impact on Russia's economic efficiency

The strategic concerns of a country

To sum up our analysis of economic models, it is useful to identify a country's strategic goals or targets. This can help clarify what a country needs to achieve successful economic development over the long term.

For example, in Russia, such targets are modernization, the development of the eastern and northern territories, economic reintegration with other former Soviet countries, overcoming the demographic crisis, improving the level of democracy, and an improvement in ethical standards (see Chapter 8).

Conclusion

We can draw three main conclusions from this chapter. Firstly, the economy of a country is defined by its national borders. There are around 200 national economies in the world, divided into two large social and economic groupings, developed and less developed countries.

Second, the level of economic development can be determined using a range of indicators, the most common being GDP (or GNI) per capita and the structure of a country's industrial output.

Third, an important stage in analyzing a country's economy is to determine its economic model, i.e., the characteristics of economic and social relations that are specific to the country and distinguish it from its neighbors and other countries at a similar level of economic development. To do this we analyze not just economic and social models but the political and ethical models of a country as well.

Questions

1. Why do we class Russia as a country with an emerging economy?
2. Is it a contradiction to say that Russia belongs to a group of countries with emerging markets?
3. What is the Human Development Index?
4. Define the economic model of a country (i.e. its national economic model).
5. How do political and ethical issues influence the economic and social models of a country?

Additional Sources of Information

World 2035. Global forecast. Edited by Dynkin A.A. Moscow, 2016, Ch.8 (in Russian).

National Economy. Textbook edited by Nureev R.M., Moscow, 2010, Ch.5 (in Russian)

Federal State Statistics Service. Russian Statistical Yearbook. Statistics digest (in Russian).

Federal State Statistics Service. Russia in Figures. Short statistics digest.

Interstate Statistical Committee of the Commonwealth of Independent States. Quick-reference book.

IMF. World Economic Outlook (www.imf.org)

IMF. International Financial Statistics (www.imf.org)

Transparency International. Global Corruption Report (www.transparency.org)

UNDP. Human Development Report (www.undp.org)

The World Bank. Indicators (www.worldbank.org)

The World Bank. World Development Report (www.worldbank.org)

World Economic Forum. World Competitiveness Report (www.weforum.org)

CHAPTER 2

THE PROPORTIONS OF A NATIONAL ECONOMY

There is a wide range of active agents participating in a nation's economy. Statisticians divide them into units, or institutional sectors as follows:

- households
- non-financial corporations (companies)
- financial corporations (primarily banks)
- non-profit institutions providing services for households (e.g. charitable organizations)
- government units (public institutions).

Economic theory traditionally divides the economy between two different levels: the microeconomic and the macroeconomic. Microeconomics describes activity at a micro or 'grassroots' level among households, corporations, industries and industrial markets. Macroeconomics refers to the national economy as a whole.

Naturally, any analysis of a national economy starts with the macro level. At this level activity among and between economic agents represents economic circulation. This is divided into the following phases:

- production
- income formation
- primary income distribution
- secondary income distribution (redistribution)
- consumption and saving
- capital formation (investment).

To analyze the interconnection between economic operators at the macro level, within phases of economic circulation, the System of National Accounts (SNA) is applied in almost all countries. To perform analysis at the micro level (specifically, at the level of industries), the input-output (inter-sectoral) balance—part of the SNA—is used.

In addition, the SNA is used to estimate the potential of a nation's economy, that is potential in the narrow sense of the volume of goods and services produced. Potential in the broader sense would be a calculation of an economy's resources.

Finally, the SNA is the main source of information about the dynamics and the proportional sizes of different parts of the economy. Let us look first at the questions of proportions.

The SNA as a data source for analysis of macroeconomic proportions

The SNA is a system of interconnected indicators that are used to describe and analyze the macroeconomic processes that occur at the different phases of economic circulation. The SNA is updated periodically; the 2008 standard has replaced the 1993 standard. Russian statistics have been using the SNA since 1992.

The SNA's calculation of production output (i.e. goods and services produced) is based strictly on value added, i.e., intermediate consumption charge-off. Thus, GDP, which is the main SNA indicator, is calculated on the basis of value added.

The SNA uses two types of price, market and basic (the latter only rarely). Market prices (the price paid by the end consumer) include all taxes, both direct (taxes on profits, property, mineral extraction etc.) and indirect (value added tax, sales tax, excise duties etc.). These are all referred to as taxes on products in the SNA. Basic prices include only direct taxes. Finally, the term 'net taxes' is used to mean taxes less subsidies on products.

The SNA works alongside another important statistical indicator that describes a country's external economic links, the balance of payments, which gives the external context of the SNA (see Chapter 13).

The SNA is made up of a number of statistics and tables. Let us demonstrate this by looking at the example of Russia.

Table 2.1 — Russia: The Goods and Services Account in 2015 (at current prices in ₽ bn)

Resources		Uses	
Output at basic prices*	141,036	Intermediate consumption	68,671
Imports of goods and services**	17,136	Final consumption expenditure	59,067
Taxes on products***	8,739	Gross capital formation	16,761
Subsidies on products****	(-)299	Exports of goods and services**	23,863
		Statistical discrepancy	(-)1,752
Total resources	166,611	Total uses	166,611

Table 2.2 — Russia: production account in 2015 (at current prices in ₽ bn)

Resources		Uses	
Output at basic prices*	141,036	Intermediate consumption	68,671
Taxes on products***	8,739	Gross domestic product at market prices	80,804
Subsidies on products****	(-)299		
Total resources	149,476	Total uses	149,476

*Without indirect taxes on products produced in the country (VAT, sales tax, excise and etc.) but including subsidies on products
**At national prices
***Indirect taxes
****Deducted from the total

Source: Federal State Statistics Service. National accounts (http://www.gks.ru)

Both accounts characterize the production phase, the only difference between them is that the second does not include nay data for foreign trade. The following are examples of how these accounts are used for a country analysis.

- goods and services were sold at market prices of ₽149.5 trn (₽141 trn in basic prices, i.e., only taking direct prices into account, adding ₽8.7 trn of indirect taxes included in the product market price and subtracting ₽0.3 trn of subsidies that reduced the market price of products);
- a portion of the goods and services were sold abroad. About 17% of products produced in the country were exported (23.9 x 100 / ₽141 trn without indirect taxes, which generally not collected on exports, but including subsidies, which are generally assigned to exporters);
- at the same time, a share of goods and services sold in Russia, are imports. Their share accounted for about 12% (17.1 x 100 / (68.7 + 59.1 + 16.8), although for a more precise calculation, indirect taxes should be included;
- GDP at market prices was ₽80.8 trn. This is calculated on the basis of value added and is, therefore, the difference between goods and services produced in the country at market prices (₽149.5 trn) and intermediate consumption during production (₽68.7 trn).

Table 2.3 — Russia: Generation of income account in 2015 (at current prices in ₽ bn)

Resources		Usage	
GDP at market prices	80,804	Compensation of employees including hidden payments for labor and mixed income*	38,132 10,858
		Taxes on production and imports of which: taxes on products other taxes on production**	9,794 8,739 1,055
		Subsidies on production and imports of which: subsidies on products other subsidies on production	(-)580 299 281

		Gross operating surplus and gross mixed income****	33,459
Total resources	80,804	Total uses	80,804

*For unincorporated enterprises article "mixed income" contains element of remuneration for labor that cannot be separated from income of owner or entrepreneur
**Taxes on factor use and payments for licenses and permits (enterprise wealth tax, land tax, enterprise transport tax, license duties and etc.)
***Subsidies on factor use
****Income of producers after deduction of expenses on employee compensation, subsidies adjusted taxes on production and import and also income of unincorporated enterprises (called gross mixed income)

Source: Federal State Statistics Service. National accounts (http://www.gks.ru)

The generation of income account (primary income account) represents a phase of income generation. If it is not possible to ascertain this income, a mixed income category is used. Date from this account can be used, for instance, in the following analysis:

- employee compensation (including hidden and mixed income, which is not always the only income employees receive) represented ₽38.1 trn gross profit in the economy and gross mixed income was ₽33.4 trn (the income of corporation, unincorporated enterprises and non-commercial organizations). The taxes on production and imports, adjusted for subsidies were ₽19.8 trn (this is the basis of government income and, from the point of view of economic theory, can be considered a result of the work of the government units). Therefore, workers produced 47% of the country's GDP (38.1 x 100 / 80.8), entrepreneurs produced 42%, and the government units, 11%.

Table 2.4 — Russia: allocation of primary income account in 2015 (at current prices in ₽ bn)

Resources		Uses	
Gross operating surplus and gross mixed income	33,459	Property income submitted to "the rest of the world"*	3,912
Compensation of employees of which:	37,821		
balance of salary received abroad and paid in Russia to nonresidents	(-)310	Gross national income**	78,649
Taxes on production and imports	9,794		
Subsidies on production and imports	(-)580		
Property income gained from "the rest of the world"*	2,068		
Total resources	82,562	Total uses	82,562

*Income from financial assets, land and other tangible assets received from «the rest of the world" (submitted to "rest of the world")

** Equals to a balance of primary income; differs from GDP by the amount of income balance from property in settlements with the rest of the world and balance of salary received by Russian residents abroad and paid to nonresidents in Russia

Source: Federal State Statistics Service. National accounts (http://www.gks.ru)

The allocation of primary income account characterizes a phase in the primary distribution of income already produced. The following gives an important insight into this account:

- Russia's GNI is lower than its GDP due to a negative balance of income flow from property (mainly direct, portfolio, and other investments) between Russia and the external world to the tune of ₽1.8 trn (₽2.1 trn – ₽3.9 trn). It is also due to the negative balance of salary to the tune of ₽0.3 trn received by Russian residents abroad and that paid to non-residents in Russia. It should be recalled that international capital flows go through the capital transactions account (see below) but capital income transfer passes through the income distribution account (a similar situation occurs with the balance of payments).

Table 2.5 — Russia: secondary distribution of income account in 2015 (at current prices in ₽ bn)

Resources		Uses	
Gross national income	78,649	Current transfers submitted to "the rest of the world"*	955
Current transfers received from "the rest of the world"*	610	Gross disposable income**	78,303
Total resources	79,258	Total uses	79,258

*Mainly contributions to international organizations, grants, money transfers of migrants

**Less amount of gross national income on the amount of current transfers balance received abroad and submitted abroad

Source: Federal State Statistics Service. National accounts (http://www.gks.ru)

The secondary distribution account represents only one aspect of the income transfer phase, namely the balance of current transfers received and submitted abroad on gross national income. Nevertheless, it gives us the amount of the final income, which a country spends on consumption and savings, i.e., gross disposable income.

Table 2.6 — Russia: use of disposable income account in 2015 (at current prices in ₽ bn)

Resources		Uses	
Gross disposable income	78,303	Final consumption expenditure	59,067
		of which:	
		households	43,331
		government	15,403
		non-profit institutions	333
		Gross savings	19,236
Total resources	78,303	Total uses	78,303

Source: Federal State Statistics Service. National accounts (http://www.gks.ru)

The account of the use of disposable income represents the phase of consumption and savings. For example, information from this account can be used for the following analysis:

- Households dominate final consumption, ₽43.3 trn or 55% of gross disposable income (53% of GDP). Government institutions accounted for 20%, a significant proportion of the total. Non-commercial organizations (not-for-profit institutions) comprised less than 1%.
- Of gross disposable income, 25% or ₽19.2 trn was spent on gross saving (a basis for gross accumulation). However, it is more common to compare amounts of gross saving (and gross capital formation) with GDP, and this gives us 24% (in 2015, according to the *World Economic Outlook*, the global average was 26%, and 25% in oil-exporting countries). Moreover, it fluctuates from year to year depending on the amount of net exports. (Russia traditionally has a foreign trade surplus but it depends on the prices of Russia's basis export goods.)

It should be reiterated that savings are a part of disposable income not spent on consumption and services. Gross savings are savings across the whole national economy. The ration of gross savings to GDP is called the gross savings rate (or ratio).

Gross capital formation is achieved, first of all, in the form of investment in the real sector and includes:

- gross fixed capital consumption through the acquisition (deducting disposals) of new capital funds and the modernization of existing funds, expenses on major improvement of existing tangible assets and expenses connected with changes of title to non-productive assets. Gross fixed accumulation usually accounts for more than 90% of the entire gross accumulation;
- change of inventories, mainly supplies of stocks, unfinished production, along with goods and products ready for sale or resale;
- the net acquisition of valuables, made up of the value of the assets acquired with disposal deducted. These include precious metals and stones, antiques, collectables, and other artworks.

In every country, the amount of the country's investment (gross capital formation) may coincide with, exceed, or be less than the amount of its gross savings. In Russia, gross savings traditionally exceed investment.

We must look to economic theory to ascertain the reason for this disparity. According to neo-Keynesian theory, investments are determined by the following equation:

$$I = S - B - D$$

where I is investments, S savings, B a positive current account balance, and D a budget deficit.

The equation proves that the more positive the current account balance, the smaller national investments will be in relation to gross savings. Neo-Keynesian theory argues that, if a country systematically generates more savings than investment opportunities, the savings surplus will leave the country. In the first part of the balance of payments, i.e., the current balance, exports exceed imports (in fact this represents an export of real capital, as commodities are considered to be part of stocks until sold to their end-consumer). In the second part of the balance of payments, i.e., the balance of capital and financial instruments, capital exports exceed imports. A typical situation for Russia is to see a huge flow of income from exports of oil and gas lead to a rapid increase in the gross savings rate, but the gross accumulation rate fail to rise due to difficulties in the investment climate. By contrast, when investments systematically exceed gross savings, the country has a negative balance of payments but a positive balance in capital flows. Moreover, the equation shows that a government deficit induces a government to issue securities in order to cover the deficit, which attract a part of the country's savings, thus preventing them being used for investment.

The following account is a capital account.

Table 2.7 — Russia: capital account in 2015 (at current prices in ₽ bn)

Resources		Uses	
Gross savings	19,236	Gross fixed capital formation**	17,668
Capital transfers received from "the rest of the world"*	17	Change in inventories	(-)906
Capital transfers submitted to "the rest of the world"	(-)34	Acquisition deducting disposal of non-productive non-financial assets	3
		Statistical discrepancy	(-)1,752
Total resources	19,219	Net lending (+), net borrowing (-)	4,207
		Total uses	19,219

*Compensation-free transfer of title to assets including forgiveness of external debt
**Including acquisition deducting disposal of valuables

Source: Federal State Statistics Service. National accounts (http://www.gks.ru)

The capital account represents the last phase of economic circulation, the phase of accumulation (investment). Here, capital inflows and outflows (as with all other forms of capital transfers) are added to gross savings. The country's balance of payments contains more detailed data on international capital flows in this account (see Chapter 13). As a result, it is possible to show that capital outflows from Russia, for example, were much less than inflows. As a result, gross capital formation was ₽16.8 trn (₽17.7 trn of gross fixed capital formation and a decrease in stocks of ₽0.9 trn). This was much less that gross savings (₽19.2 trn) and accounted for 21% of GDP, lower than the world average of 25%, and lower still than the 26% average of oil-exporting countries.

In conclusion, we should add that the SNA uses the accounts mentioned above to produce more detailed accounts and tables.

Input-output balance

The intersectoral balance (input-output balance) shows the relationship between sectors and sub-sectors (the SNA calls them types of economic activity), as well as between institutional sectors in the course of the economic process. The first example in the world of this balance being calculated was in the USSR in the first half of the 1920s, when the country was preparing variants of future five-year plans for the country's economic development. As well as its use in economic planning, it was later also used as a basis for producing Soviet statistics, known as 'the balance of the national economy'. The Russian economist, W. Leontief, who worked on these plans but later emigrated to the USA, developed this theory and popularized this balance, calling it the 'input-output model' (for which he received the Nobel Prize in Economics in 1973). The balance was later integrated into the SNA as the input-output table system, or, more precisely, the tables for goods and services output.

Methods for calculating GDP

The input-output balance data allow for different methods of calculating GDP. We should add that, while a country analysis will often use different methods for calculating GDP, it will not use separate SNA accounts, mainly because GDP calculations are published more frequently in national statistical yearbooks. The different methods used to calculate GDP enable the determination of most of the proportions in the SNA, as well as new ones.

GDP calculated on the summation of gross value added by types of economic activity allows for analysis of the sectoral structure of the economy. However, it should be noted that national statistics often give data on the output of products according to types of economic activity only in basic prices. In order to calculate GDP in market prices, net taxes on products (i.e., taxes less subsidies) are added at the end of the calculation of GDP without dividing these taxes by types of economic activity. To analyze the sectoral structure GDP, we use GDP in basic prices. This is called gross value added according to types of economic activity in basic (but not market) prices.

Table 2.8 — Russia: value added by types of economic activity in 2015 (in current basic prices, as percentage of total)

Types of economic activity	Percentage of total
Agriculture, forestry and hunting	4.4
Fishing	0.3
Mining and quarrying	9.8
Manufacturing	14.1
Electricity, gas and water supply	2.8
Construction	5.9
Wholesale and retail trade; repair of vehicles, motorcycles and personal and household goods	15.8
Hotels and restaurants	0.9
Transport and communications	7.3
Financial intermediation	4.3
Real estate, renting and business activities*	17.3
Public administration and defense, compulsory social security**	8.1
Education	2.6
Health and social work	4.1
Other community, social and personal service activities	1.6
Household activities	0.7

* Including information and computer services, science and scientific services
**Including state (compulsory) pension provision

Source: Federal State Statistics Service. Russia in figures - 2016. M., 2016 (http://www.gks.ru/bgd/regl/b16_12/Main.htm)

Interindustry ratios, more precisely the ratios between different types of economic activity, have already been considered when analyzing the level of economic development in a country to determine the level of correlation between primary, secondary, and tertiary sectors of the economy. It is important, not just to document the structure of the economy by sectors, but also to determine any long-term trends in its development. This poses technical challenges in the case of former Soviet countries because, at the start of the 1990s, their statistics were based on a different system, the balance of national economy (see above). In Russia, the change to the SNA was carried out gradually. As a result, in the 1990s, GDP was calculated on the basis of its division in sectors, but not types of economic activity (as recommended by the SNA). A sector is a combination of companies, grouped according to the industry classification of products being produced. (So, the servicing cost of a boiler owned by a transport company is included in the figures for transport production.) The type of economic activity is a grouping made according to production similarity. (So, the production of a transport company is included in the 'Transport and Communications' category of activity, and the servicing of the boiler is allocated to 'Electricity, Gas and Water Supply'.)

Nonetheless, even when comparing data which are dissimilar in this way, it is possible to identify trends or, as it is more often expressed, shifts in the sectoral structure of the Russian economy. Data from 2002, when Russian statistics calculated GDP according to sectors and types of economic activity are also useful.

Table 2.9 — Russia: value added as per sectors and types of economic activity (in current basic prices, as percentage of total)

Sectors	1990	2002	Types of economic activity	2002	2015
Agriculture and forestry (incl. organizations serving agriculture)	16.6	6.1	Agriculture, forestry and hunting	6.4	4.4
			Fisheries	0.3	0.3
Industry	38.0	27.7	Mining and quarrying	6.8	9.8
Other types of activities on goods manufacturing:-	1.3	0.8	Manufacturing	17.5	14.1
Construction	9.6	7.0	Electricity, gas and water supply	3.7	2.8
Transport and highway system	8.8	7.4	Construction	5.4	5.9
Communication	1.2	1.8	Transport and communications	10.4	7.3
Trade, catering and intermediate products	6.0	22.5	Wholesale and retail trade; repair of vehicles, motorcycles and personal and household goods	23.1	15.8
Information and computer services	0.2	0.2	Hotels and restaurants	0.9	0.9
Real estate operations	-	3.9	Real estate, renting and business activities *	10.7	17.3
General commercial activity on market support	-	4.0			

Geology and exploration survey, geodetic and hydro-meteorological services	-	0.3	Financial intermediation	3.1	4.3
Housing services	2.2	1.4	Health care and social work	3.4	4.1
Public utilities	1.1	1.5	Education	2.9	2.6
Non-productive types of public services	0.6	0.1	Public administration and defense, compulsory social security **	5.1	8.1
Finance, credit, insurance	0.9	3.1	Other community, social and personal service activities***	1.9	1.6
Science and scientific services	2.7	1.1	Financial intermediation services indirectly measured****	- 1.8	-
Health care, physical education and social insurance	2.7	3.1			
Education, culture and art	5.4	4.0			
Public administration (incl. defense)	2.8	5.4			
Public associations	0.4	0.3			
Financial intermediation services indirectly measured****	- 0.5	-1.8			

*Incl. housing and communal services (apart from electricity, gas and water supply), information and computer services, science and scientific services as well
** Including state (compulsory) pension provision
***Incl. culture and art, physical education and sports, public organizations
****Included in production of separate sectors and that is why are marked with a sign "-" on referring them to a separate type of economic activity

Sources: Federal State Statistics Service. National Accounts (for relevant years); Federal State Statistics Service. Russian Statistical Yearbook. Moscow, 2001, p. 282 (in Russian).

Table 2.9 shows that in the Russian economy in the last two decades there has been a shift in the industrialization phase. Agriculture's share of GDP has been decreasing, not just in the 1990s when it was caused by a strong net reduction of agricultural production, but even in the following decade when this production did, in fact, increase. A reduction in the share of GDP produced by industry and construction is a common feature in the post-industrialization phase. But, in Russia, this has not been seen over the last two decades due to the growing importance in the economy of mining. The services industry grew, mainly as a result of an increase in trade, while post-industrial services (except for financial) showed little change, apart from a fall in science and scientific services (see below).

We should add here that, in emerging economies, the sectoral structure needs to be considered alongside the structure of employment. In developed countries, productivity does not differ significantly between sectors. But in less developed countries these differences can be large. For example, if a mining industry is focusing on the volume of its exports, these will be estimated in international prices, which will be much higher than domestic prices in countries with emerging markets. Besides, in these countries, export-oriented and other sectors make extensive use of modern technology. Other sectors, e.g. agriculture and trade, faced with low domestic prices and low take-up of modern technology, become magnets for surplus labor. Thus, in Kazakhstan in 2015, the primary sector accounted for 5% of gross value added; the secondary, 33%; and the tertiary, 62%. But in employment structure, the situation was very different: the primary sector had 18% of all employees; the secondary, 27%; and the tertiary, 55%. Such differences are even more pronounced in less developed countries such as Kyrgyzstan and Tajikistan; and much less pronounced in more developed countries like Belarus, Russia, and Ukraine. So, a comparison of the sectoral structures according to gross value added and employment gives us a better understanding of the situation of the sectoral structure of the economy.

GDP calculated using the income method (GDP per income source) closely matches the generation of income account. See Table 2.10

Analysis of Russian GDP according to income sources shows that a large part of GDP is spent on employee compensation (including for the most well paid). Moreover, a considerable part is paid secretly, mostly to avoid social taxes that would fall to the payroll budget.

GDP calculated using the expenditure approach (GDP according to usage) is shown in Table 2.11.

Table 2.10 — Russia: GDP by income sources in 2015(at current prices in ₽ bn, as percentage of total)

GDP elements	Percentage of total
GDP at market prices	100
of which:	
compensation of employees	45.0
therefrom hidden payments for labor and mixed income	13.1
net taxes on production and imports	11.1
of which:	
net taxes on products	10.1
other net taxes on production	1.0
gross operating surplus and gross mixed income	43.9

Source: Federal State Statistics Service. Russia in figures – 2016. Short statistics digest. Moscow, 2016. p.186.

Table 2.11 Russia: use of GDP in 2015 (at current prices, in ₽ bn, as percentage of total)

GDP elements	Percentage of total
GDP in market prices	100
final consumption	71.7
of which:	
households	52.7
public administration	18.7
among them:	
on individual goods and services	8.0
on collective services	10.7
non-profit institutions serving households	0.3
gross capital formation	20.1
gross fixed capital formation	21.3
changes in inventories	- 1.2
net exports of goods and services	8.2
exports	28.9
imports	20.7

Source: Federal State Statistics Service. Russia in figures - 2015. Short statistics digest. Moscow, 2016. pp.187-188.

Given that, in the short term, GDP is influenced by the use of economic resources and their demand, analysis of GDP statistics can answer the question of what the main forms of demand were in the Russian economy. This form of consumer demand is shown in Table 2.11. This is the demand of households as well as of the public administration, and it is satisfied, to a great extent, by large imports. The other important stimuli are exports and gross capital formation (so-called investment demand).

The non-observed economy and its treatment in the SNA

In calculating GDP, the non-observed economy has been included in the SNA since 2008 (prior to that it was called the 'shadow economy'). This includes economic activity not registered by the authorities. It includes the following:

- The informal economy which operates in the market but does not keep proper accounting records, usually households (part of the production of farm households, small farms, and family businesses working both for themselves as well as the market).
- The production of private households dedicated to their own use (mainly agricultural products and construction using their own resources). It is statistically difficult to separate this from the informal economy so it is often included there.
- The hidden (underground, shadow) economy which produces goods and services allowed by law but hides or minimizes its output for the purposed of evading taxes, social security fees, regulations on the protection of labor, the maintenance of sanitary standards, and the acquisition of licenses. Examples are batches of goods from enterprises operating legally that are not registered; renting or home renovations that are done without proper contracts; tutoring or working in service without a contract.
- Illegal business activity (the illegal economy), which involves the production of goods and services that are strictly forbidden by law such as: the production and sale of drugs; prostitution; smuggling; the production and sale of arms for criminal purposes. This category also includes such illegal redistributive operations as bribery, racketeering, theft, robbery, and fraud.

All elements, except the last one, are included in the SNA and GDP. To ascertain the size of these individual elements, estimates are used based on the following:

- the interindustry balance (e.g. to distinguished the size of hidden payments for labor);
- sampling (e.g. anonymous questioning students and schoolchildren about payments for tutoring);
- similarities (aspects of the hidden economy that are identified in one region can be applied in another with adjustments);
- implicit indicators (e.g. data on household and garden plots along with data on average crop yield allows us to determine approximate amounts of the informal agricultural production);
- expert estimates.

Such methods enable statisticians to increase the calculations of GDP to reflect the size of the non-observed economy. According to data from the first half of the 2000s, in the USA the GDP figure was increased by 1%; in Estonia and Spain by 10–11%; in Italy by 15–17%; and in Uzbekistan by 29–30%. In Russia, in the first half of the 2000s, this figure was around 20%, but on a downward trend. According to the Federal State Statistics Service, in 2013, it decreased to 10.3% of GDP, with 4.5% attributable to the informal economy and 5.8% to the hidden economy.

To make comparisons between countries of the extent of the non-observed economy, in particular the illegal business activity and corruption, three indices calculated by Transparency International are used:

- the corruption perception index (see above);
- the bribery index (the Bribe Payers Index which reflects the tendency of private businesses to give offer bribes in particular countries; and
- the Global Corruption Barometer which reflects shifts in the level of corruption in the majority of countries.

Regional disparities

In all countries of the world, the level of economic development differs from region to region. These differences are most marked in those countries with the largest territory. Thus, in the case of Russia, if we compare regional levels of GDP with the national figure we see that GDP per capita in current basic prices in 2014 was ₽403,000 across the whole country, while in Moscow it was ₽1,053,000; in oil and gas exporting regions it was even higher (₽1,453,000 in Tumen Oblast); while in more backward regions is reached barely a third or a quarter of the national average (₽104,000 in Chechnya).

Table 2.12 — Gross regional product per capita in federal districts of Russia in 2014, ₽ '000s

Central	North West	South	North-Caucasian	Volga	Ural	Siberian	Far Eastern
534.4	427.9	289.3	164.9	308.5	652.9	316.4	518.2

Source:
http://www.gks.ru/wps/wcm/connect/rosstat_main/rosstat/ru/statistics/accounts/#

The main reason for these regional disparities lies in the different levels of highly profitable industries found in each region. The oil and gas exporting regions owe their high GDP to the high returns on oil and gas extraction. Moscow scores well as a result of its highly developed services industries, especially in the financial sector. The backwardness of the Northern Caucasian Federal District can be explained by the predominance of agriculture in the local economy.

Conclusion

1. For the analysis of the ratios that exist within macro economies, the System of National Accounts (SNA) is used in almost all countries. Moreover, the SNA is also used to estimate the potential of a nation's economy in the narrow sense of the volume of goods and services produced in the country (in the broader sense, the potential of a national economy is its economic resources).

2. The balance of input and output between sectors shows the level of cooperation between industries (in the SNA they are referred to as types of economic activity). These data allow GDP to be calculated in different ways: according to types of economic activity, revenues, or usage (consumption, accumulation, net exports of goods and services).

3. When calculating GDP, an amount is included to reflect the non-observed economy (previously known as the 'shadow' economy), which involves economic activity not registered in the normal way by the authorities. All elements of the non-observed economy, apart from illegal activities, are included in the SNA and GDP.

4. In country analysis, we first look at inter-industry ratios as well as the correlation between savings and accumulation which we call the gross savings rate.

5. In analyzing the ratios in an economy, regional differences are very important, as is the correlation of business forms, i.e., ratios between small, medium and large businesses, and government organizations.

Questions

1. Describe the SNA.
2. What do we get from an analysis of the accounts of production of goods and services?
3. What information is provided by accounts of income generation, allocation, and distribution?
4. What is the capital account?
5. Specify the basic elements of the non-observed economy.
6. What are the main proportions or ratios of a national economy?

Sources of additional information

Federal State Statistics Service. National Accounts of Russia. Statistical digest.
Interstate Statistical Committee of the Commonwealth of Independent States. National Accounts of Countries belonging to the Commonwealth of Independent States. Statistical digest.
IMF. World Economic Outlook (www.imf.org)
Transparency International (www.transparency.org)
The World Bank. Indicators (www.worldbank.org)

CHAPTER 3

THE DYNAMICS OF A NATIONAL ECONOMY

Economic Development and Economic Growth

Economic development can be defined as the raising of the level of development in a national economy. This is expressed, first of all, by an increase in the GDP/GNI per capita, progress in the development of the country's industrial structure, and an improvement in the Human Development Index (HDI). In practice, economics often conflates economic development and economic growth. In a majority of cases, an increase in GDP/GNI per capita, an improvement in the industrial structure, and a growth in the HDI occur as a result of economic growth.

But at the same time, we must recognize that economic growth is not always followed by an improvement in these specific indicators. In Russia, for example, since 2000, growth in GDP/GNI per capita has been accompanied by a fall in the sectoral structure (see Chapter 2). In China, the enormous economic growth in recent decades has seen a significant rise in environmental pollution.

So economic development and economic growth are closely linked, but they are not always the same. Moreover, economics recognizes the theory of 'growth without development' which describes economic growth not accompanied by a rise in other indicators, and the term, 'growth quality' which focuses on the efficiency of economic growth and its consequences for the quality of life and living standards in a country.

Measures of Economic Growth

The dynamic of a country's economic growth is measured by its GDP growth rate (i.e. the increment of growth). In order to compare the GDP of different periods, it is necessary to take out the influence of price fluctuations, or, as statisticians prefer to describe it, to calculate the quantity index of the GDP.

Using chain indices, the prices of the previous year are applied to calculate GDP in a given accounting year. For example, using the prices of 2008 (base period), the quantity index of GDP in 2014 was 100.7, by comparison with 2013, and the annual growth rate (the increment of growth) was thus 0.7%. To build a picture of the dynamics over a long period, the indices calculated for each year are chained together with previous years. Using this method, it is also possible to produce data for GDP dynamics over a longer period in constant prices, i.e., using the prices of a single year as a basis for the whole period. Thus, in constant prices of 2008, the quantity index number for GDP in Russia was 105.9 in 2013, i.e., GDP grew by 5.9%. According to this formula, it is possible to calculate the average annual growth rate of Russian GDP from 2009 to 2014 as 1.2%.

Indices for separate components of GDP are also used to convert the index of whole GDP into constant prices. Such indices are called deflators and the index calculated on the base price index for all of the GDP is known as the GDP deflator. This was 107.2 in 2014. This is sometimes confused with the more restrictive consumer prices index which is calculated only for consumer goods and services. This was 111.4 in 2014.

By extrapolation, the dynamics of GDP and its components can be calculated on the basis of quantity indices in each type of economic activity. To do this, we usually take a set of goods particular to one or other type of economic activity.

It should be noted that per capita is the most appropriate way to measure GDP. By contrast, it is comparatively rare to measure GDP dynamics per capita.

As an example, let us consider the economic dynamics of the former Soviet countries in the late twentieth and early twenty-first centuries.

Table 3.1 — Former Soviet countries: GDP growth rate (percentage)

	1992–2000*	2001–2008*	2009–2013*	2014	2015	2016	2017***	2021****
Russia	- 4.0	6.5	3.5	0.7	-2.8	-0.2	1.8	1.5
Belarus	- 1.2	8.2	3.9	1.7	-3.8	-2.6	-1.0	3.1
Moldova	- 9.2**	6.3	5.0	4.8	-0.4	4.3	4.0	3.9
Ukraine	- 8.0	6.9	2.8	-6.6	-9.8	2.3	2.0	4.0
Azerbaijan	- 5.6	17.0	2.8	2.8	0.6	-3.1	-1.0	3.1
Armenia	- 2.9	11.9	4.7	3.6	3.3	0.2	3.5	4.0
Georgia	- 7.9	7.6	5.9	4.6	2.9	2.7	4.0	5.5
Kazakhstan	- 2.7	9.3	6.4	4.3	1.2	1.1	3.3	4.3
Kyrgyzstan	- 3.6	4.7	3.7	4.0	3.5	3.8	3.5	5.4
Tajikistan	- 9.4**	8.8	7.2	6.7	6.0	6.9	4.5	4.0
Turkmenistan	- 2.1**	14.3	11.6	10.3	6.5	6.2	6.5	5.4
Uzbekistan	- 0.1	6.6	8.2	8.1	8.0	7.8	6.0	6.0
Latvia	- 3.7**	7.3	3.8	2.0	2.7	2.0	3.8	3.0
Lithuania	- 2.8**	7.3	3.8	3.0	1.8	2.3	3.5	3.0
Estonia	- 0.1**	6.6	4.7	2.9	1.7	2.1	4.0	3.0

*Annual average rates
**Author's estimate
***IMF estimate
****IMF forecast

Sources: Interstate Statistical Committee of the Commonwealth of Independent States. The Commonwealth of Independent States in 2013. Short digest. Moscow, 2014, p.33; Interstate Statistical Committee of the Commonwealth of Independent States. The Commonwealth of Independent States in 2008. Short digest. Moscow, 2009, p.12; IMF. World Economic Outlook. October 2017, pp. 243 and 246.

Table 3.1 shows a number of things:

- In the 1990s all the former Soviet countries had negative rates of economic growth. This was a consequence of the economic collapse that had begun in the Soviet Union and continued after its collapse in the former Soviet countries until the mid-1990s, or to the end of the 1990s in others. In Russia's case it was almost until the end of 1998.
- In the following decade, the former Soviet countries saw relatively high rates of growth and the majority of them managed to recover to GDP levels they had seen in the Soviet period during the first half of the subsequent decade and exceed them by the time the world economic crisis began in 2008 (Belarus, Azerbaijan, Armenia, Kazakhstan, Turkmenistan, Uzbekistan, and all the Baltic states). However, in 2008, a range of former Soviet countries still had a GDP volume that was lower than it had been in 1990 (Moldova, Ukraine, Georgia, Kyrgyzstan, and Tajikistan).
- The global economic crisis of 2008 again depressed levels of GDP in the majority of the former Soviet countries and the subsequent recession has made it impossible for them to recover their former high levels of growth.

Growth Factors and Macro Models

Economic growth is the result of the use of economic resources (also referred to as growth factors). In the nineteenth and twentieth centuries the majority of economists defined these as labor forces (labor in the language of economic theory), capital (real and financial), natural resources (land), and business resources (business). More recently, a fifth resource, knowledge, has been added to the list. This includes, in particular, the knowledge of technology that has been a major driver of growth in developed countries. These five factors are analyzed in more detail below.

Macroeconomic models of economic growth are created on the basis of these growth factors. The most well known are the neo-classical models of Cobb-Douglas and Solow, and the Keynesian Harrod and Domar models. These models are covered in details elsewhere (e.g. on the Economic Theory course) and so will only be described briefly here.

The Cobb-Douglas model (more precisely, the Cobb-Douglas production function) is the simplest of the economic models and can be applied to micro- and macroeconomic contexts. It is based on the simplest production function, (Y=f (K,L)) and in its most standard form is:

$$Y = A \cdot K^{\alpha} \cdot L^{\beta}, (1)$$

where Y = output (at macroeconomic level, GDP volume); K = capital input (gross fixed capital value); L = labor input (persons-hours worked);α = capital share in aggregate cost of labor employed and capital (this fluctuates from 0 to 1); β = share of labor remuneration in the aggregate cost of labor employed and capital, β=1-α; and A = the coefficient of technological productivity.

The Cobb-Douglas model relies on a range of conditions. One is that capital and labor are interchangeable (i.e. equipment replaces employment and vice versa) and, as a result, the coefficients, α and β, are added to the formula. The other condition states that the coefficient of technological productivity changes only slowly. Over a short-term period, it is taken as a constant and is included empirically. Thus, the Cobb-Douglas model highlights the influence of applied capital and labor forces on economic growth in the short (occasionally medium) term.

The Solow model is also based on the simplest production function (although with the inclusion of combined factor productivity) and, in a simplified form, is a system of equations:

1) $Y = T \cdot f(K, L)$;
2) $Y = C + S$;
3) $S = s \cdot Y$, where $0 < s < 1$; s = const; (2)
4) $S = I$;
5) $I = K' + \mu \cdot K$, where $0 < \mu < 1$, μ=const;
6) $L = g \cdot L'$, g = const,

where T = the combined factor productivity (total factor productivity); C = the volume of final consumption; S = the volume of gross savings; s = the gross savings rate; I = the volume of gross capital formation (investment); K' = net capital gain (without depreciation); μ = the depreciation rate; L' = the addition to the labor force; and g = the utilization rate of the addition to the labor force. We can say that the Solow model shows the extent to which economic growth is dependent on, firstly, combined factor productivity, consumption, additions to the labor force, and investment, the volume of which is defined with the gross savings rate (the higher it is, the larger the volume of GDP/GNI).

In the Domar model GDP/GNI growth is a result of cooperation between investment increment and capital-output ratio (see below):

$\Delta Y = \Delta I / R$, (3)

where ΔY = the national income increment; ΔI = the investment increment; and R = the capital-output ratio (see below).

The Harrod model highlights the extent to which growth rates depend on, not only the capital-output ratio, but also on the gross savings rate (reckoned to be equal to the gross capital formation rate):

$\Delta Yt / \Delta Yt\text{-}1 = \Delta It / \Delta It\text{-}1 = s / R$. (4)

We can thus conclude that the Keynesian models associate economic growth first of all with investment and an efficiency index, such as a return to capital (the capital-output ratio). Neoclassic models, on the other hand, treat economic growth efficiency in a broader way.

Macroeconomic Efficiency and its Indicators

Economic growth is generated by increasing the scale and effectiveness of the utilization of resources. Economic efficiency can be defined as extracting the maximum value from the economic resources available to a country. A narrow definition would be that economic efficiency (or, more precisely, productive efficiency) is a combination of economic resources that minimizes costs while producing a given output.

The first, broader definition aims to determine the potential quantity of output within the defined economic resources, while the second, narrower definition aims to determine how rationally economic resources are used to achieve a given quantity of output. The broad definition is appropriate for analyzing the potential rates of economic growth in a country that has economic resources of a certain quality (e.g. a high proportion of the population employed and with high level of skills). The narrow definition works better when analyzing how rationally the resources of an economy have been used to achieve a given volume of GDP/GNI (in our example, not the whole economically active population, but only the economically engaged population). The narrow definition is used more often.

To measure macroeconomic efficiency, it is better to analyze the T parameter of the Solow model, i.e., total factor productivity. However, in most countries around the world, there are no systematic statistics for the value and dynamics of total factor productivity; there are only estimates. According to these estimates, for the period from 1950 to 2010/13, total factor productivity provided almost two fifths of the world (a half of growth in developed countries, and a quarter in the less developed).[1]

We, therefore, usually apply the most aggregate of the macroeconomic indices, the efficiency of labor productivity, i.e., GDP/GNI volume per employee and, even better, per hours worked. Thus, in 2013 in Ukraine, GNI PPP was US$407,849.7m (according to the World Bank), the annual average people employed was 21.5m. Thus, labor productivity was US$18,895, being 407,949.7m / 21.5m. For comparison, we can note that the figure for Belarus was US$36,666 and, in Russia, US$48,000. However, in Russia there is a high level of non-registered employment due to illegal labor migration, so the real figure for Russia will be more than the official statistics.

The dynamics of labor productivity are also important. In Ukraine, the index of physical GDP volume between 2001 and 2013 was 161%, while the index of the employed was 101.5%. The labor productivity index was thus 158.6% (161 / 101.5). This shows that the labor productivity was increasing with an average annual rate of 3.6%, providing the bulk of the growth in GDP/GNI in Ukraine. The average annual growth of GDP over this period in Ukraine was 5%. There was a similar picture in Russia and Belarus.

Indices of productivity in capital and natural resources are widely used in macroeconomic statistics. These are, above all, indices of real capital available in a country, especially the capital-output ratio as well as indices of the material-output ratio and the energy-output ratio.

The capital-output ratio at a macroeconomic level is defined as the relation of the fixed capital cost to the volume of GDP (the opposite index is called the capital productivity ratio). Thus, in Russia in 2013, gross fixed capital (not including unfinished construction projects) was ₽133,522 trn, the volume of GDP was ₽66,755 trn, and the capital-output ratio was 1.87 (133,522 / 66,190). In other words, to produce every ₽1 of GDP in Russia, ₽1.87 of gross fixed capital was used. The capital-output ratio was 0.5 (66,755 / 133,522). In other words, ₽1 of fixed capital produced ₽0.5 of GDP. However, more often, the other definition of the capital-output ratio

[1] Melyantsev V.A. Long-term tendencies, counter-tendencies and growth factors in developed and developing countries. Moscow, 2015, p. 9 (in Russian).

is used, namely the relation of investment in gross fixed capital to GDP growth (the so-called incremental capital-output ratio), and preferably, this is used over a long period. For instance, in Russia between 2001 and 2013, investment in fixed capital totaled ₽95.3 trn, and GDP grew by ₽59.2 trn. So, the capital-output ratio can be shown as follows: ₽1 of GDP growth, required ₽1.61 of investment in fixed capital (95.3 / 59.2 = 1.61). The opposite index, the capital productivity ratio, over the same period was ₽0.62.

The material-output ratio for the whole economy is hard to calculate due to the extensive classifications of raw and other materials. We, therefore, apply other indices in practice such as the material-output ratio of the consumption of steel, cement, timber etc.

In the case of the energy-output ratio (energy productivity ratio) of the national economy, the calculation is made as a relation of the physical volume of primary energy consumption (in tons of coal, oil, or equivalent) to GDP, preferably per PPP (as the energy productivity ratio is the relation of GDP to the physical volume of energy consumed). Energy consumption is calculated as the consumption per resident or employee in a country. Thus, in Russia in 2013, the energy-output ratio was US$5.17 of GDP per PPP with regard to every kilogram of standard fuel used. Energy consumption was 5.1 tons of standard fuel per resident in 2012 (Iceland, 18.8; USA, 7.0; Canada, 7.3; Finland, 6.2; Belarus, 3.1; Kazakhstan, 4.7; Poland, 2.5; Turkey, 1.6; and Tajikistan, 0.3). It should be noted that energy consumption is affected less by energy consumption productivity than by the presence of high-energy consuming types of economic activity in the country (automobile transport, the electricity and power industries, metal and chemical industries).

The Instability of Economic Growth

Models of economic growth give us a chance to assess the contribution made by different economic resources and the efficiency of their use. But they do not explain the instability of a nation's economic growth. National economic growth varies significantly measured over the short term (by quarters), the medium term (by years), or over the long term (by decades). Moreover, it is obvious that it is severely affected by economic crises, when economists described growth as negative.

A number of factors cause fluctuations over the medium and long term. Firstly, when a less developed country achieves the level of economic development similar to that of developed countries, its growth rate moderates in line with that seen in developed countries. A good example of this is Japan, which achieved a level of development to match the leading economies of Europe and North America in the 1980s and then its growth rate slowed. Secondly, growth in all markets is cyclical, and economic theory tends to pay particular attention to studying the reasons for medium and long-term cycles. Thirdly, an economy is subject to the influence of factors that can cause dramatic increases or decreases in the efficiency of the usage of its economic resources, e.g. volatility in international prices of its export products, fluctuations in international capital flows and in transfers of money from its citizens who are working abroad caused by the ups and downs of the global economy, differences from one year to the next of the success of a country's own economic policies, its defense expenditure, and effects of the weather (good weather can boost agriculture or tourism, while weather or natural disasters can have detrimental effects).

Fluctuating growth rates make it appropriate to estimate growth in retrospect over periods of two or three decades and arrive at hypotheses for the reasons for the fluctuations. Thus, Russia had low growth rates and a tendency to decrease them in the 1980s (an average of 1.6% of GDP).[2] This changed to negative rates in the 1990s (-4% of GDP from 1992 to 2000), and later to higher rates (6.5% from 2001 to 2008), and subsequently back to lower and negative rates. To simplify the analysis, we can suppose that growth rates in the 1980s were influenced by three factors in particular: the weakening impact of the 'catching-up' development (as described above); general decreases in growth rates across the global economy; and ineffective economic policy. The 1990s saw further slowing down in the world economy and still less effective economic policy management. By contrast, in the 2000s, world growth picked up and economic management in Russia improved. From 2008 to 2016, the world economic crisis and the long-term deceleration in growth around the world ("the new normal"), combined with a return to ineffective economic policy (more precisely, a growing incompatibility between the Russian economy and the new global conditions), say the country's economy suffers again.

Dynamic economic analysis also demands consideration of fluctuations in growth patterns over shorter periods as well, also taking into account the

---

[2] Ponomarenko A.N. Retrospective national accounts of Russia: 1961–1990. Moscow, 2002, p. 226 (in Russian).

seasonality of such fluctuations. For example, in Russia, of the four quarters, the first has the fewest working days. This influences the volume output. By contrast, in the fourth quarter, there is a surge of activity caused by pre-New Year retails sales, along with the year-end tax receipts coming in from companies. Since such seasonal fluctuations make it impossible to compare one quarter with another effectively, we compare each quarter with the same period in the previous year.

Macroeconomic Indicators

The Russian Federal State Statistics Service publishes systematic information on economic indicators in the country, covering recent weeks, months, and quarters. This is information on the macroeconomic situation. It is also published by statistics agencies in other countries, with greater or lesser time delays.

The most important statistics are such indicators as GDP dynamics, the unemployment rate, the rate of investment (a key indicator of business sentiment about economic prospects), the volume of production and exports among leading industries, along with indices of demand. In addition, statistics are published on the volume of retail turnover, the purchasing of housing, and manufacturers' stock reserves.

The leading financial indicators include levels of bank credit (averages published daily), inflation rates (used by commerce and consumers alike to predict prices), and the state's budget revenue and expenditure (this has a heavy influence on future state policy).

The main foreign macroeconomic indicators (published by the Bank of Russia) include the current balance of payments, the state of official reserves (a deterioration of which could lead to a devaluation of the national currency), and, of course, exchange rates, published daily.

Conclusion

1. The dynamic of economic growth is measured by GDP growth rates. Economic growth comes as a result of the usage of economic resources (sometimes called growth factors). These are labor resources, natural resources, capital (real and financial), business resources, and knowledge resources.

2. Macroeconomic models of economic growth are created using the statistics of growth factors. The most widely known neoclassical models are Cobb-Douglas and Solow; the most common Keynesian models are Harrod and Domar.

3. Economic growth is produced by increasing and more effective use of resources. Labor productivity is usually used as it is the more aggregate index of macroeconomic efficiency. Indicators on the use of capital and natural resource are widely used. These are, above all, indicators of real capital usage in a country in the form of the capital-output ratio, as well as the material-output and the energy-output ratios.

4. Models of economic growth help to identify the contributions made by different economic resources. But they cannot answer questions about the reasons for fluctuations in the growth of the national economy. This is why economic analysis requires in addition detailed consideration given to the reasons for such fluctuations over short, medium and long term timeframes.

Questions

1. Why did former Soviet countries see a long decline in GDP during the 1990s?

2. Why did this change to active economic growth in the subsequent decade?

3. Why did the economic crisis of 2008–2010 affect the Baltic countries more than those of Central Asia?

4. What contribution do economic growth models make to a country analysis?

5. Specify the most widely-used indices of the economic situation of a country.

Sources of additional information

National economy. Textbook. Ed. by Nureev R.M. Moscow, 2010, Ch.29, 31 (in Russian)

Federal State Statistics Service. Statistical Yearbook of Russia (in Russian).

Interstate Statistical Committee of the Commonwealth of Independent States. Short digest.

IMF. World Economic Outlook (www.imf.org)

IMF. International Financial Statistics (www.imf.org)

The World Bank. World Development Indicators (www.worldbank.org)

The World Bank. Open Data (www.worldbank.org)

CHAPTER 4

INVESTMENT AND FIXED ASSETS

The Investment Process and its Indicators

Savings are a basis for investment, which, in turn, forms the foundation for the production of national wealth and, above all, fixed assets. This process is called capital formation (investment process and investment activity).

It is reasonable to start the analysis of the role of the investment process in a national economy with savings, before moving on to investment, and finishing with capital assets. As we have already looked at savings, let us move on to investment.

Investment

The law, No. 39-FZ, on "Investment activities carried out in the Russian Federation in the form of capital investment," dated February 25, 1999, defines investment as monetary funds, foreign stocks, other property including property rights, other rights with a monetary value invested in objects of entrepreneurial and/or other activities for the purpose of profit and/or achieving other useful affects. Investment activity is defined as investing and carrying out practical deeds for the purpose of profit and/or achieving other useful affects. In practice, this investment involves investment in financial and real capital assets.

Investment in financial assets appears in the Russian statistics as financial investment. A significant part of this investment is transformed into investment in real capital (via the financing of investments) and, therefore, the former cannot be added to the latter.

Investment in real capital (known as gross capital assets, or gross capital stock in the SNA terminology) is referred to as investment in non-financial assets in Russian statistics which pay special attention to investment in fixed (capital) assets. These investments form the basis of gross fixed capital formation (which, as well as investment, includes, on the one hand, depreciation of existing stock and, on the other, the costs of repairing stock). In 2016, investment in fixed capital assets in Russia totaled ₽14,640 bn, while gross fixed capital formation was ₽18,112 bn.

Economists pay particular attention to investment in real capital which is, as a result, often referred to simply as investment. (This often causes confusion, as using the general term 'investment' implies all forms of investment including financial rather than just investment in real capital.)We analyze not only the volume and process but also its composition, looking at different types of investment (housing, buildings and structures, machinery, equipment, vehicles etc.) and then analyzing it according to each type of economic activity, each source of finance, and the equipment-structures ratio (equipment, instruments, and fittings for construction and installation works).

Table 4.1 — Leading post-Soviet economies: dynamics and composition of investment in fixed assets

	Indices of investments in 2015, 2000=100	Structure of investments by source of finance in 2013				
		budgets of different levels	enterprises, organizations and citizens	credits	foreign investors (excl. credits of foreign banks)	other sources
Russia	263	15.4*	49.0*	7.5*	28.1*	
Belarus	364	21.2	46.6	20.6	7.5	4.1
Ukraine	168	4.7	72.0	15.7**	7.6	
Kazakhstan	551	16.8	51.5	11.3	20.4	…
Uzbekistan	501	5.5	55.7	9.4	19.3	10.1

*January-September 2013
**Incl. credits of foreign banks

Source: Interstate Statistical Committee of the Commonwealth of Independent States. Commonwealth of Independent States in 2013. Statistical book. Moscow, 2014. pp.76–77; Interstate Statistical Committee of the Commonwealth of Independent States. Volume Indices of Investment in Fixed Capital (http://www.cisstat.com/eng/frame_macro.htm)

The Investment Climate and its Indicators

The investment climate is a reflection of the conditions for investment. In its strictest sense, it is the climate for the usage of foreign capital, but in a broader sense, it includes national capital as well. Here we use the term in its broader sense.

The investment climate is determined above all by the economic conditions under which an investor operates. But the social, political, and ethical circumstances also have significant importance. The basis for estimating the investment climate is the risk-to-reward ratio which has a mainly predictive character as investments made today are intended to secure profits in the future. Thus, this forward-looking risk-to-reward ratio helps the investor judge the prospects, or attractiveness of investing in a given company, region, or country. If we look only at risks without considering profitability, then our measurement of the investment climate in a country will lead to a one-sided assessment.

The investment climate is estimated from the point of view of two basic groups of economic agents:

- the investors who carry out direct and portfolio investment (shares), and
- the creditors, who conduct portfolio (debt securities) and other investment activity.

For these two categories of investors, there are different methods for assessing the investment climate. The quantitative evaluation of the investment climate is called the rating and it can be expressed in points or degrees. For the first group, the investors, these are called investment ratings. For the creditors, they are called credit ratings.

Ratings are usually calculated and published by specialist companies known as rating agencies. Some work around the world and are called international rating agencies. These are Standard & Poor's, Fitch, and Moody's. They give ratings for large companies and countries (ratings for countries are called sovereign ratings). Calculation methods vary between the agencies, but not significantly. Ratings are defined by letters on a scale: A to C, or A to D. For example, mid-2017, Gazprom was rated by S&P and Fitch to be BB+ and BBB- respectively, matching the sovereign ratings for Russia, also BB+ and BBB-. It should be noted here that a rule stipulated that the credit rating of a company cannot be higher than the sovereign rating of its country. Hence, Gazprom's rating might have been higher, but could not exceed that of Russia. The investment rating of a company is a stock pricing.

Investment ratings are usually calculated for regions as well as countries. For example, the rating agency, "Expert RA" (part of the Russian journal "Expert"), publishes an annual rating of the investment attractiveness of each region in Russia over recent years; it is calculated as a relationship between the integral investment potential of a region and integral investment risk. Thus, in 2015, the greatest investment potential was seen in Moscow (13.9% of all the investment potential of the country), followed by the Moscow region at 5.9% and Saint Petersburg at 4.7%. However, the least risky regions were Krasnodar Territory, Tambov, and Lipetsk. "Expert RA" gave the maximum 1A rating (maximum potential, minimal risk) to four regions: Moscow region, Saint Petersburg, Krasnodar Territory and the Tatarstan Republic. It gave 1B ratings (high potential, medium risk) to Sverdlovsk Region and Krasnoyarsk Territory; 2A (average potential, medium risk) to Chelyabinsk, Rostov, Samara, Irkutsk, Novosibirsk, Kemerovo Regions, Perm Territory, Yugra District, and the Bashkortostan Republic. The remaining Russian regions received lower ratings.

Among sovereign investment ratings, those published by Business Environment Risk Intelligence (BERI) are the most well-known. These are calculated by hundreds of experts, three times a year, for 50 countries. They look both one year and five years ahead and, in some cases, 10 years. Many different calculations are made for each country. These are then grouped into three sub-indices (sub-ratings): operations risk (business transaction risk), political risk, and repatriation of profits and capital by foreign investors. These three are combined to give a total index rating for the country. In 2013, the rating for Russia was 46 points (41 + 39 + 59). Other ratings were: China 57; India 42; Brazil 41; South Africa 41; the USA 58; Germany 68; and Switzerland 75.

Similar methods are used by Political Risk Services Group (PRS Group) in its publications entitled, Political Risk Services (PRS) and International Country Risk Guide (ICRG). The Economist Intelligence Unit (EIU), which is part of the well-known The Economist Group, provides investment ratings in 60 countries. The ratings for foreign direct investment produced by A.T. Kearney, known as the FDI Confidence Index, is also well-known.

We can draw at least two conclusions. Firstly, it should be borne in mind that ratings are produced for different categories of investors and are, therefore, multidirectional. Secondly, ratings cannot cover all aspects of the investment climate that they examine. It is not a matter of one rating agency having disadvantages when compared with another as none of them is able to reflect adequately or precisely the full depth and complexity of a given business activity. Ratings are, thus, useful. But their importance should not be overemphasized.

Fixed Assets and their Conditions

Fixed assets are assets with a lifetime of not less than a year, such as dwellings, buildings and structures, transmission units (electrical power lines), machinery and equipment, fittings and instruments, vehicles, livestock, and perennial plantings. Some intangible assets are also included in this category.

Fixed assets are valued and revalued in local prices. As a result, international comparisons of the absolute and relative dimensions of a fund (per capita or per employee) are seldom published. Analysis focuses mainly on the composition of the capital assets, analyzed by type of economic activity, type of property, renovation, disposal, and depreciation. Let us consider in more detail the analysis of the renovation, disposal, and depreciation or capital assets.

To analyze the renovation of fixed assets, we apply the renovation rate. This is the relationship between capital assets put into operation during a year to their availability at the end of the year. In Russia, the renovation rate was 4.4% in 2016. By comparing this rate with the rate in different years, we can determine whether the renovation rate in a country has accelerated or decelerated. In Russia, this process slowed down markedly in the 1990s and although it subsequently speeded up, it did not return to the level of 1990, 6.3%.

The process of fixed asset renovation runs in parallel with that of disposal. Here we apply a rate for the disposal of fixed assets. This is based on the relationship between fixed assets withdrawn during a year and their availability at the beginning of that year. In Russia, the rate was 2.4% in 1990, 1.3% in 2000, and 0.8% in 2016, a decreasing trend. There are various reasons for disposing of fixed assets. During unfavorable economic conditions, it may fall as the incentive to commission new equipment falls and more emphasis is put on repairing existing equipment.

On the other hand, the slowdown of fixed asset disposal, alongside an acceleration in the acquisition of new assets may point to the return of an old Soviet illness, namely having new fixed assets put into operation alongside old assets that continue to be used. Thus, the average age of equipment does not decrease, as fixed assets do not get any younger!

Indicators of the average age of fixed assets and their depreciation rate help us to understand the process of renewal and disposal of the assets. In addition, it should be borne in mind that, where machinery and equipment, fitting and instruments, and vehicles will inevitably become obsolete with normal use, dwellings, buildings, and structures can remain in normal conditions for centuries with proper maintenance. The age of this latter group, known as active capital assets is of greater importance than that of the former group, known as passive capital assets. In addition, it is important to have up-to-date information on dwellings, buildings, and structures.

National Wealth

The way national wealth is calculated varies from country to country. However, in the majority it includes neither the value of natural assets, nor many intangible assets. For this reason, the statistic is most useful for the analysis of fixed assets. Thus, in Russia, statistics of the national wealth include data on the value of non-financial (₽302 trn in 2014) and financial assets (₽390 trn).

The narrow calculation of the national wealth has encouraged researchers to find new, broader ways of calculating it, to include natural resources and human capital assets. Research along these lines is carried out by the World Bank, but their data are not systematic. Credit Suisse also works in this area, but its approach is debatable.

Conclusion

1. Savings are the basis for investment which is, in turn, the foundation for the production of capital assets and national wealth. This process is called capital formation (investment process and investment activity). Investment in financial capital appears in the Russian statistics as financial investment. A significant part of this investment is transformed into investment in real capital (via the financing of investment) and, therefore, the former cannot be added to the latter.

Investment in real capital is called investment in non-financial assets. Furthermore, investment in fixed assets, which is called capital investment, is highlighted in the statistics. The statistics calculate the ratio of investment to a country's GDP, calling this the correlation of investment rate.

2. Economists pay particular attention to investment in fixed assets. This is often simply called investment. We analyze not only the volume and process but also its composition of this investment, looking at different types of investment analyzed according to each type of economic activity, source of finance, type of capital asset, and the equipment-structure ratio.

3. Fixed assets are assets with a lifetime of not less than a year, such as dwellings, buildings and structures, transmission units (electrical power lines), machinery and equipment, fittings and instruments, vehicles, livestock, and perennial plantings. Some intangible assets are also included. A renewal rate is used to analyze the renovation of fixed assets. The process of fixed asset renovation runs in parallel with that of disposal. Here we apply a rate for the disposal of fixed assets. The depreciation of fixed assets is calculated according to a method that can be presented simply as the accounting of asset consumption per the amortization rate, which reflects the loss of value, rather than physical depreciation.

4. The investment climate is a reflection of the conditions for investment. It is calculated from the perspective of two groups of investors: those who are going to invest in businesses via company foundations, the purchase of an existing company, or by buying shares (investors); and those who are going to buy bonds or extend credit (creditors). The basis for estimating the investment climate is a correlation of the profit and risk or risks (the latter can be numerous). The quantitative evaluation of the investment climate is called the rating and it can be expressed in points or degrees. Ratings are calculated in various ways and are often divided between ratings for investors (investment ratings) and ratings for creditors (credit ratings). However, the majority of ratings only evaluate a risk, rather than a correlation of risk and profit.

Questions

1. What is the difference between investment in capital assets and gross fixed capital formation?
2. Why do economists pay particular attention to investment in capital assets?
3. Which elements of capital assets are most useful for economic analysis, and which indicators are used alongside them?
4. What are the foundations for the analysis of a country's investment climate?

Sources of additional information

Federal State Statistics Service. Russia in figures. (www.gks.ru/bgd/regl/b17_12/Main.htm)
IMF. World Economic Outlook (www.imf.org)
The World Bank. World Development Indicators (www.worldbank.org)

CHAPTER 5

HUMAN CAPITAL

The Economic Potential of a Country and Types of Economic Resources

The economic potential of a country can be defined in a narrow sense as the volume of goods and services produced in the country, or more broadly as the sum of the country's economic resources. The broader definition is more widely used.

Economic resources include:

- labor resources;
- knowledge resources;
- entrepreneurial resources;
- capital resources; and
- natural resources.

Due to their obvious links, the first three of these are often grouped together as 'human capital assets,' although entrepreneurial resources are also frequently considered in the context of business. Research conducted by the OECD in 15 countries (both developed and medium developed), based on the capitalization of their citizens' income, has shown that the stock of human capital far exceeds that of physical assets – by a factor of between 3.5 and 7. In Russia the figure was 5.5. The stock of human capital assets in Russia, in US dollars and at PPP, was equivalent to US$380,000 per capita (for the population aged from 15 to 64). The majority of developed countries had figures between US$400,000 and US$500,000. Poland had a figure of US$230,000 and Romania US$80,000.[3]

---

[3] Kapelyushnikov, R. Cost of human capital assets in Russia. Part II. Voprosy economiki. 2013. No.2. pp. 37–38 (in Russian).

Other economic resources are traditionally divided into real capital (gross fixed capital and inventories) and financial capital (money and securities). When calculating the composition of real capital, gross fixed capital dominates. This is described in more detail in Chapter 4 and the way it functions in each industry is considered in a section of Chapter 7 on the real sector. The financial sector is also examined in Chapter 7.

It should be noted that the importance of natural resources to the national economy decreases as a country develops, though they retain significance. From a methodological point of view, it is preferable to consider them in the context of each separate industry (and each type of economic activity). The most valuable natural resources are minerals. In Russia and in most other former Soviet countries, geological reserves are divided into four categories according to the stage of exploration: category A refers to proven reserves; B to prospected reserves; C1 to sparsely explored reserves; and C2 to prospective reserves. An additional category of expected reserves is often specified. In other countries around the world a different system is used with A referring to proven and measured reserves; B to indicated reserves; and C to inferred reserves.

This chapter focuses on human capital assets and will, therefore, include consideration of resources where appropriate.

Labor Resources

When analyzing a country's labor resources, we look first at its demography. The population size determines the volume of labor resources, and the rate of growth (or shrinkage) of the population indicates the dynamic development of the resource. It should be noted that the rates of growth or shrinkage of a population depend increasingly on rates of migration. For example, Russia and Kazakhstan have both experienced huge influxes of people from neighboring countries, seeking permanent residence, attracted by greater earning potential.

From this we can deduce the quantity of labor resources. This includes the population of working age, as well as pensioners and teenagers who are in employment. Although different countries have their own way of measuring working age, broadly speaking it is the range from 16 to 55–65 for women and to 60–70 for men. We then exclude from the calculation students, invalids, military personnel, those (nearly always women) involved in childcare and housekeeping, and include those pensioners and teenagers in employment. The result we call the economically active population which includes both employed and unemployed people (76.8 mln people in Russia at the end of 2016). Many migrants work illegally without registering as employed, so the real number of people in gainful employment may well be higher than the official statistic. In Russia, 2.3m foreign residents were registered as employed just before the economic crisis of 2008. In practice, many experts believe the real figure could have been as much as four times that.

The correlation between the size of the total population and the economically active population is determined by looking at the composition of the population by age along with the birth rate and the average life expectancy. Tajikistan, for example, has a high birth rate (which results in children and teenagers up to the age of 14% accounting for 35% of the total population) and high mortality (including among those of working age), such that labor resources barely reach 60% of the population. Russia, by contrast, has lower birth rate (and so fewer children and teenagers) and better mortality rate. Here the working-age population is higher, at 70%.

These figures are presented as what we call the dependency ratio. In other words, they describe the burden (i.e. the non-working population) that the working population has to support. To allow for different definitions of working age around the world, this ration is calculated according to the definition which excludes persons up to the age of 14 and over the age of 65 from the definition of the working population. Among the former Soviet countries, the highest dependency ratio is found in Tajikistan at 64%, according to the Human Development Report.

To repeat, the calculation of the economically active population includes both employed and unemployed people. Let us consider the latter. According to the International Labor Organization (ILO), the category of the unemployed includes persons of working age who have no job, are looking for work, and are ready to start work. If students, pensioners or invalids are actively looking for work and are ready to start, they are considered to be unemployed. The registered unemployed include those who have registered with a government employment service. In Russia, there were 3.8m unemployed at the end of 2017, including 0.7m registered. This second figure is significantly lower, reflecting the difficulty of drawing unemployment benefits, and the small amount of the benefit. Although in Russian calculations, both registered and non-registered are taken into account, during the economic crisis, the actual number of unemployed was higher as not all the unregistered and unemployed foreigners left the country.

The unemployment level is calculated from the relationship between the number of unemployed and the economically active population. In Russia, the average annual unemployment rate has decreased to 4% over the last two decades, but increased to 8% during the economic crisis. For this reason, it is preferable to analyze the average time people spend unemployed and break the figures down by profession and by region. Though not easy, it is possible to analyze hidden unemployment. There are expert estimates of this and we can note that it is most common in the trade and agricultural sectors. Moreover, a high proportion of small shops and self-employment in an economy are characteristics not only of underdevelopment in a country but also of hidden unemployment.

When analyzing the employed population, it is important to look at indices that describe, directly or indirectly, the quality of employees. The idea of quality is reflected directly by their levels of education and life expectancy. (In Russia, 78% of employees have higher or secondary vocational qualifications.) In addition, it is reflected indirectly by the type of industry in which people work and by infant mortality rates. (In Tajikistan, 66% of the population is employed in agriculture which is not a technologically advanced industry. In Russia, nine of every thousand babies born die in infancy; in Turkmenistan, the figure is 45.)

When studying the national labor market, as well as the indices mentioned above, we also consider average salaries (preferably with the social taxes paid by the employer), broader employment packages, and systems for redundancy. The last two are included in the World Bank Yearbook and the 'Doing Business' project, which covers most countries.

Knowledge Resources

Knowledge resources can be divided methodologically into scientific, educational and informational.

Scientific resources can be characterized first of all by the scale of research and development (R&D) carried as well as by the scale of innovation apparent in an economy (the introduction of new or improved products and technologies). Volumes of R&D are driven by the amount of expenditure dedicated to it and by the availability of scientists. The scale of innovation is determined mainly by a country's level of technological development and the demand for innovation. In reality, the scale of innovation is more important that the volume of R&D, as it is precisely innovations that improve a country's level of development; innovations can be the result of domestic or foreign R&D, using licenses or patent imports.

Educational resources are measured by the level and quality achieved by the population, and also by the breadth and depth of the country's education system. In former Soviet countries programs for mass literacy were developed many years ago so that their educational resources should by now demonstrate significant levels of achievement at higher and secondary education. According to census date in the CIS countries, Russia and Armenia lead the way for the proportion of people with higher education, while Tajikistan, Turkmenistan, and Uzbekistan have fallen behind. The quality of education around the world is evaluated by the Program for International Student Assessment (PISA) by looking at levels achieved by 15-year-olds in various countries. According to PISA data, Estonia is alone among the former Soviet countries in being included among the leading countries when it comes to the quality of school education. The other Baltic states and Russia are close to the international average, and some Transcaucasian and Central Asian countries that participated in the survey are below the world average.

The breadth and depth of an educational system are hard to evaluate using financial indices as these tend only to reflect government expenditure on education. However, data on the number of schoolchildren and students are widely published. By comparing the number of students with the size of the population, it is possible to gauge access to higher education, the most difficult part of the educational system to measure. Indicators for the numbers in higher education at an appropriate age are generally representative of a country's attainment. They also provide information on the average number of years spent in education by the adult population.

Informational resources are usually measured according to the availability of information resources. These are divided into the traditional (TV, radio, newspapers, stationary telephony) and the new (information and communications technology – ICT). The International Telecommunications Union calculates the ICT Development Index for 155 countries around the world on the basis of 11 indicators including accessibility to ICT, usage of ICT, and the level of the population's knowledge and skills for working with ICT. The developed countries scored highest on the list. Belarus is ranked 38th, Russia 42nd, and Kazakhstan 53rd.

Entrepreneurial Resources

A country's entrepreneurial resources comprise its entrepreneurs, its entrepreneurial infrastructure, and its entrepreneurial culture and ethics.

The number of entrepreneurs, including owners and managers of firms as well as individual entrepreneurs is a very problematic indicator. In less developed countries, the existence of a large number of individual entrepreneurs and family-owned businesses, means that the number of entrepreneurs as a proportion of the adult population is often higher than in more developed countries. Statistics about entrepreneurial education and levels of expertise are patchy and heavily influenced by the business climate in the country. The international project, Global Entrepreneurship Monitor, aims to calculate these indices and publishes the Total Entrepreneurship Activity (TEA) Index. However, not all countries take part. Among the former Soviet countries, only Russia and Latvia do so.

Entrepreneurial infrastructure can be regarded as a market infrastructure in that it is relevant to various aspects of the market: economic policy, commercial banks, commodity and stock markets, etc. It is appropriate to consider the entrepreneurial infrastructure from the perspective of its maturity, and how it influences profitability for a domestic company. The contribution to the profitability of the entrepreneurial infrastructure can be measured by looking at, for example, how the legal climate in the country assists or hinders entrepreneurs. This is shown in the World Bank's annual *Doing Business* report and in the Index of Economic Freedom (see Chapter 6). The maturity of the entrepreneurial infrastructure can be measured against indicators such as the breadth of a country's financial system (see below), or the extent of insurance and auditing within it.

The evaluation of entrepreneurial culture and ethics is also difficult. Indices of corruption can be taken as indirect indicators of entrepreneurial ethics. Entrepreneurial culture develops as a legacy of business training. In Russia, this legacy was destroyed by the Soviet regime. But an extensive system of business training linked to higher education is now being developed.

Conclusion

1. The economic potential of a country can be defined in a narrow sense as the volume of goods and services produced in the country, or more broadly as the sum of the country's economic resources. Economic

resources, being the potential of the national economy, include: labor resources; knowledge resources; entrepreneurial resources; capital resources; and natural resources. Due to their obvious links, the first three of these are often grouped together as 'human capital assets.'

2. Labor resources include the population of working age, as well as pensioners and teenagers who are in employment. We then exclude from the calculation students, invalids, military personnel, those (nearly always women) involved in childcare and housekeeping, and include those pensioners and teenagers in employment. The result we call the economically active population. This includes both employed and unemployed people.

3. Knowledge resources can be divided methodologically into scientific, educational and informational. Scientific resources can be characterized first of all by the scale of R&D carried out (the amount of expenditure dedicated to it and by the availability of scientists) and by the scale of innovation apparent in an economy (the level of technological development and the demand for innovation). Educational resources are measured according to the level and quality of education attained by the population, and by the scope and breadth of the educational system. Informational resources are measured according to the availability of information resources. These are divided into the traditional (TV, radio, newspapers, stationary telephony) and the new (information and communications technology – ICT).

4. A country's entrepreneurial resources comprise its entrepreneurs, its entrepreneurial infrastructure, and its entrepreneurial culture and ethics.

Questions

1. Why does the importance of natural resources decrease?
2. What does a country's human capital consist of?
3. What elements go to make up a country's entrepreneurial resources?
4. What is the structure of a country's knowledge resources?

Sources of additional information

National economy. Textbook edited by Nureev R.M. Moscow, 2010. Ch.3 (in Russian)
OECD Science, Technology and Industry Outlook (www.oecd.or)
UNDP. Human Development Report (www.undp.org)
UNESCO. Global Education Digest (www.unesco.org)
The World Bank. Doing Business (www.worldbank.org)
The World Bank. World Development Indicators (www.worldbank.org)

CHAPTER 6

ECONOMIC POLICY

The Notions of Economic Policy: its Degree, Purposes and Objectives

A government intervenes in its country's economy, regulating and controlling it. Such notions as government intervention, regulation, and control are essentially synonyms. In practice, the term 'economic policy' is the most widely used to refer to the government's strategy towards the economy of the country and the measures it takes. The term 'social and economic policy' is also used to encompass the government's social policy.

It is hard to measure quantitatively the degree of government intervention, though some try. For example, the OECD uses the Indicators of Product Market Regulation (PMR) for its member states. According to these indicators, the degree of regulation in the leading developed economies falls between 1.0 and 1.5 points. In the countries of Central and Easter Europe, it is between 1.3 and 1.7 (Poland 1.7); in Turkey it is 2.5; in the BRICS (Brazil, Russia, India, China, and South Africa) it is between 2.2 and 3.1. Russia scores 2.2.

It is possible to measure indirectly the degree of government intervention in any country by identifying the following:

- the economic basis for the intervention, i.e., the size of the government budget in relation to GDP and the size of the public sector (the share of the value of the nation's wealth owned by the government, firstly in capital funds and/or the public sector's share of GDP production). In the majority of the former Soviet countries, the size of the government budget in relation to GDP ranges from 22% to 36%;
- the scope of the use of administrative and legal instruments in the country (economic instruments are used extensively to an extent in all countries. So, the difference between countries in the extent to

which these instruments are used gives us the degree of government intervention). It should also be noted here that in authoritarian regimes, governments (in the person of state employees) can 'advise' private businesses on their activities in a way that the businesses feel obliged to take the advice. The less the government intervenes, the more the private sector is able to exercise normal rights and freedoms. These rights can be measured on the ranking of the World Bank's 'Doing Business' project (see above), looking specifically at the extent to which the legal framework in a country facilitates or restricts entrepreneurship (in 2017, Russia ranking 40th out of 190, well ahead of the other BRICS countries but behind Armenia, Belarus, Kazakhstan, the Baltic countries, and Poland). The Index of Economic Freedom helps to measure the freedom to conduct business in a country. It is produced by the Heritage Foundation and the Wall Street Journal. In 2017, Russia ranked 114th out of 180, behind the majority of former Soviet countries, Poland, and Turkey.

When considering the purpose and objectives of economic policy, we should mention its theoretical basis. The neoclassical view of economic theory holds that achieving macroeconomic balance should be the ultimate purpose of economic policy and, in order to achieve this, the following objectives should be pursued: natural economic growth (on the basis of a balance between aggregate supply and demand); achieving high employment; ensuring price stability (minimizing inflation); and achieving equilibrium in the balance of payments. These four objectives are hard to achieve simultaneously and are thus called the 'magic quadrangle.'

Keynesian economic theory is more socially oriented. Tinbergen's theory of economic policy holds that a government should do the following in pursuing its economic policy: determine the ultimate purpose (the maximization of public welfare and support for economic and social stability); determine specific objectives to achieve these purposes (e.g. accelerate growth and employment during an upswing, or restore economic growth and employment during a crisis, reduce inflation, enhance export volumes); choose instruments for achieving the objectives; establish mechanisms that enable the instruments to be used to achieve the objectives. It should be added here that for countries with emerging markets, modernization is also one of the ultimate purposes, along with the maximization of public welfare and support for economic and social stability.

Neoclassical synthesis, which united the basic tenets of economic theories, concurs in a practical sense with the Keynesian idea that the main objective of economic policy is the maximization of public welfare and support for economic and social stability. But it also emphasizes that, when defining specific objectives, the objectives of the 'magic quadrangle' should be kept in mind. This theoretical approach to the purposes and objectives of economic policy is widely used. But in developed economics, greater attention is paid to the neoclassical objectives, while emerging markets lean more to the Keynesian approach. However, in times of economic crisis, Keynesian thinking prevails, as occurred during the Great Depression from 1929 to 1933.

It should also be noted that in the theory of economic policy, the 'purpose' refers to overall or ultimate purpose of the policy, while the 'objectives' refer to more intermediate goals. But, in practice, the two terms are often used interchangeably. Finally, there is the term 'economic strategy' which refers to a country's long-term, strategic purpose (two or three purposes). For example, the economic strategy of Russia is aimed at modernizing the country. Economic strategy is closely linked to the term 'structural policy', i.e., a government's decision in terms of the priority guidelines for the country's economic development and the application of the appropriate means for implementing them.

Instruments of Economic Policy

Instruments of economic policy can be divided into two groups: administrative and legal, and economic.

The administrative and legal category is in turn divided in two. On the administrative side, it includes instruments such as permits, injunctions (bids), norms, standards, and other secondary (subordinate) legislation (regulations) issued by executive authority (mainly as government orders) which together form the 'administrative burden', sometimes called the 'administrative barriers' on businesses. The legal side includes instruments such as economic law, the civil code and other laws adopted by legislative bodies which specify the 'rules of the game' in the country's economic life.

Countries with systems of liberal capitalism tend to be characterized by the use of legal instruments (i.e., laws that are directly applicable and need no subordinate legislation), while countries with more government intervention in the capitalist system tend to see more administrative instruments. In the latter case, the active use of administrative instruments is facilitated by the lower level of democracy and the need to administer large amounts of government property (to which the government takes a very 'hands-on' approach).

There is a vast array of economic instruments available to governments, especially fiscal, money and credit, and external instruments. Let us examine these in more detail (they will also feature in the analysis of national economic policies).

The most common fiscal instruments are taxes and government expenditures, with the following specific features worthy of note in the former Soviet countries:

- the importance to government revenue of taxes on the production, processing, and export of fuel and raw materials, taxes on semi-finished articles in countries that export fuel and raw materials (Russia, Kazakhstan, Turkmenistan, Uzbekistan, and Ukraine), and taxes on transit income (in the Baltic states, Belarus, and Georgia);
- the importance of the government's role in final consumption when looking at government expenditure. This reflects not so much expenditure on its bureaucratic apparatus but the role the government plays in running services and maintaining infrastructure, since so much of this belongs to the government. This includes healthcare, education, housing, utilities, transport, and energy networks. In this context, the way the government uses its purchasing power, the way it purchases goods and services, can be one of the most effective instruments for influencing the economy. But it can also be a key source of corruption, by awarding contracts to companies that are controlled by state agents, bribery to secure contracts, and overpricing with surplus profits being skimmed off.

The main money and credit instruments in economic policy are:

- regulation of the money supply (fast growth in the supply can promote economic growth, while restricting it can tackle inflation);
- rules on bank reserves (the more reserves banks are required to keep, the less they are able to provide credit);
- interest rates, which can influence the availability of credit. However, it should be noted that many former Soviet countries have only limited scope to use this instrument. In the USA, for example, all leading banks are included in the Federal Reserve

System so the Federal Reserve's decision on interest rates has to be followed by the majority of the country's banking system. By contrast, in Russia, the Bank of Russia only regulates the key interest rate, i.e., the credit rate that it applies to commercial banks for a week, but not the rates that banks offer their clients. The scope is also limited in former Soviet countries by the relatively small size of stock and government bond markets which results in fewer open market transactions.

The main external economic instruments are:

- the regulation of foreign trade (customs, quotas etc.);
- the regulation of currency, though the ability to intervene is limited by the fact that certain countries with emerging markets have administrative and legal instruments uniting in a system of currency control since many of their currencies are either non-convertible or only partially convertible;
- the regulation of international flows of capital and labor. Various instruments are available, mainly administrative and legal.

The Basic Directions of Economic Policy

Economic policy is implemented in a number of directions: agricultural policy, currency policy, etc. The methodology for determining the separate areas of policy is based on the way in which the national economy is divided into sectors (areas), industries, and inter-industry complexes or networks (see Chapter 7). While the directions of economic and social policy are interconnected, they have specific features.

In any set of economic instruments that a government might use in a market economy, financial instruments always prevail as a modern market economy is increasingly based on the financial sector. Financial policy thus tends to dominate modern economic policy. Financial policy can be divided methodologically into monetary and fiscal areas of policy (which can, in turn, be further subdivided into money, credit, prices, tax, budget, and debt policies). There is also currency policy. Financial policy takes center stage in the economic policy of the former Soviet countries. For this reason, when we analyze these countries, we pay special attention to financial indicators and government control of them (money supply, interest rates, taxes, the size and balance of the budget, and the exchange rate).

Government policy with regard to the real sector is referred to as industrial policy. This involves supporting and promoting the separate industries (types of activity) and inter-industry complexes that are important to the national economy. Many countries have used an active industrial policy to create powerful competitive industries. The motor industry and electronic engineering in postwar Japan are good examples, although the country's attempts to promote an aerospace industry were less successful.

Almost all governments around the world have some level of active industrial policy though many also have passive industrial policies. The most obvious examples of active industrial policy would be agriculture, energy, and transport policy. Government activity in these areas is necessary as, without these sectors, normal economic and social life could not function.

The globalization of the international economy makes it increasingly important for national economies to have an external economic policy. This would cover foreign trade (imports and exports), international capital flows, and labor migration. The smaller an economy is, and the more open it is, the more important it becomes to have an external economic policy.

Finally, there are areas of policy that are not related to any individual sector such as anti-monopoly policy, supported by antitrust law and a law on fair trade. Antimonopoly policy, by preventing monopolistic activities in the market, seeks to create the right circumstances for competitiveness to thrive. However, in many emerging market economies, this area of policy has yet to develop effectively. In Russia, for example, the Federal Antimonopoly Services has yet to act against a single merger.

Economic policy is supplemented by a rich seam of social policy. This includes policies on healthcare, education, population and demographics, housing, and utilities. Of particular importance are policies on incomes and income adjustment, social insurance (including retirement policy), and social security. It should be noted that the distinction between economic and social policy is not black and white. Regional policy, for example, can encompass areas of economic and social policy in seeking to ensure equal levels of development in different regions.

Finally, we should note that the analysis of economic policy, with regard to its separate directions, is traditionally related to the analysis of separate economic sectors (see below).

Economic Programming

In a socialist economy, implementing the state's plans was compulsory. However, in a market economy there are no such obligations, apart from the state budget. Instead, government programs are indicative or recommendatory, rather than directive. We, therefore, apply terms such as 'indicative planning' or 'economic programming' when considering planning in a market economy.

Economic programming or indicative planning is state regulation of the economy on the basis of programs with different orientation and scope. In macroeconomic programs, the purposes and objectives of the state's economic and social policy are set. Terms for their implementation and the amount of financing available are specified. Programs can then be divided into short, medium, or long-term plans. In Russia, an example of a long-term program is the Conception for Long-Term Socio-Economic Development of the Russian Federation up to 2020 (Conception-2020), which was adopted in 2013. There are also number macroeconomic programs which are associated with medium and long-term state programs – either federal special-purpose programs or industrial programs.

Around the world, the efficiency of economic programming is often not high. For example, the Conception-2020 was first adopted in August, 2008, just as the country was being hit by the economic crisis. Within just a few months it already needed re-thinking in terms of the money available for its implementation. Instead, the Forecast of Socio-Economic Development up to 2020 was issued in 2017.

The main reason that many economic programs are not implemented is uncertainty over both the quantitative and qualitative parameters of future development. Moreover, the uncertainty increases the further into the future the forecasting attempts to look. Nevertheless, economic programming – indeed, economics as a whole – cannot avoid forecasting. It is an essential element of the programming.

Economic Forecasting

The main principles of economic forecasting are:

- consistency (ideally driven by the development of a highly detailed national economic model and, in practice, with forecasting of the separate sectors and areas of activity which make up the economy);

- adequacy (based, first of all, on a determining in retrospect the main long-term trends in the national economy and diagnosing any deviations from them); and
- alternativeness (using different scenarios to plan for different outcomes in development);

The following methods are used in forecasting:

- expert estimates (e.g. survey results);
- logical modeling (to forecast qualitative changes in the economy, for example, through comparison with more developed countries);
- mathematical methods (economic and mathematical modeling, as well as the aforementioned models of economic growth);
- normative methods (assessing the achievement of objectives in the economy, e.g., whether per capita GDP has reached the level of other developed countries.

Forecasts differ according to their orientation and scale (regional, industrial, macroeconomic, demographic, social etc.). They are divided into short-term (1–2 years, i.e., short-term forecasts); medium-term (5–7 years); long-term (up to 20 years); and super long-term (over 20 years). A short-term macroeconomic forecast is based on calculations of how components of GDP change according to their usage in: final consumption expenditures; gross capital formation; and net exports of goods and services. Calculating the shares of the components of GDP in a given year and using surveys and statistical data on these components allow us to forecast how they will grow or decrease in the next year and, thus, calculate a forecast for GDP in the coming year. It should be noted that economic factors and total factor productivity change very little over the short term and so are not applied to short-term forecasts. However, medium and long-term forecasts are made on the basis of changes that can occur in factors of economic growth and efficiency. These are calculated by relying on the models of economic growth and methods of forecasting mentioned above.

Ministries of economy and finance, along with central banks, are responsible for the macroeconomic forecasting. Industrial forecasting is the responsibility of the state agencies that regulate industries. In practice, the main sources of forecasts are economic research organizations (an example in Russia would be the Institute of Economic Forecasting of the Russian Academy of Sciences). But one research academic does not develop an entire forecast alone. One individual can, at best, estimate future changes in selected economic indicators (the future exchange rate of the ruble is a popular choice). Instead, a range of forecasts developed by different organizations, agencies, large companies, and banks are drawn on. To illustrate the point, let us consider the sources of the most competent forecasts of social and economic development in Russia.

Among short and medium-term forecasts in Russia are, first of all, the macroeconomic forecasts of the Ministry of Economic Development, the budgetary forecasts produced by the Ministry of Finance, and the aforementioned federal special purpose programs (allocated to the Minister of Economic Development). Forecasts of the world economy, as well as individual countries and regions, issued by the IMF (its World Economic Outlook, issued twice a year, is the most important), the World Bank and the OECD are respected in Russia. Also worthy of note are the consensus macroeconomic forecasts (i.e., based on an average of several forecasts) produced by RosBusinessConsulting and The Economist.

Detailed forecasts published every five to six years by the Institute of World Economy and International Relations of the Russian Academy of Sciences are popular. These cover the world economy and individual countries, including Russia.

Mechanisms of Economic Policy

The mechanisms of economic policy used by a country integrate purposes, objectives, instruments, and the directions of policy. These can be looked at from different perspectives.

From an organizational perspective, they combine the work of various state bodies and agencies, the instruments of economic policy and relevant government programs. For instance, in Russia, the major thrust of economic policy is established by the president and his administration, and then the government (especially the Ministry of Finance and the Ministry of Economic Development) and the Bank of Russia develop the details and implement the policy. The instruments of economic policy are outlined in legislation passed by the Federal Assembly and in accompanying acts issued mainly by the government. Government programs are designed on the basis of the economic purposes (objectives) defined by the president and the prime minister.

Economic policy mechanisms exist to implement current objectives such as tax collection, government expenditures, and regulation of the economy.

They can also be used for prospective objectives, although government programs can be created in this case as well.

The Efficiency of Economic Policy

The efficiency of any country's economic policies can be evaluated using criteria of effectiveness, i.e., the extent to which it achieves its stated purposes and objectives. However, we need to bear in mind that the officially declared purposes of the country may differ from government's real purpose. To be more precise, the declared ultimate purpose (usually the maximization of the public welfare and the support for economic and social stability) is the same in almost all countries around the world and is usually deemed to be the most important. But, in many emerging market economies, we see that, in fact, the government is seeking to increase the personal wealth and power of a small elite. This diverts a country's economic resources from the official purpose and, as a result, the maximization of public welfare and support for economic and social stability are not achieved, while the ruling elite stay in power and line their own pockets. This earns a very low score for effectiveness of economic policy.

This means that economic policy can be more effective in countries where there is less, or no discrepancy between the announced purposes and those actually pursued by the government. In emerging market economies, this can come about in two sets of circumstances. Firstly, where there is a well-developed civil society, a healthy level of democracy, and where the majority of the population is able to realize their goals, and have a measure of control over the government through democratic processes (Central and Eastern European countries, including the Baltics). Secondly, where there is weak civil society and a low level of democracy, but a relatively high culture of moral responsibility in an otherwise authoritarian leadership pursuing common rather than personal goals (Belarus).

Conclusion

1. It is possible to measure indirectly the degree of government intervention in the economy in two ways. The first is to identify an economic basis for measuring the intervention, i.e., the size of the government budget in relation to GDP and the size of the public sector (the share of the value of the nation's wealth owned by the government, firstly in capital funds and /or the public sector's share of

GDP production). The second way is to analyze the scope of the use of administrative and legal instruments in the country (economic instruments are used extensively in all countries. So, the difference between countries in the extent to which these instruments are used gives us the degree of government intervention).

2. Instruments of economic policy can be divided into two groups: administrative and legal, and economic. The legal category includes instruments such as economic law while the administrative category includes statutory acts or documents issued by executive authority which together form the 'administrative burden' on businesses. There is a wide range of economic instruments, such as fiscal, money and credit, and external economic policy.

3. Economic policy is implemented in a number of directions: agricultural policy, currency policy, etc. The methodology for determining the separate areas of policy is based on the way in which the national economy is divided into sectors (areas), industries, and inter-industry complexes or networks.

4. Economic programming or indicative planning is state regulation of the economy on the basis of programs with different orientation and scope. In such programs, the purposes and objectives of the state's economic and social policy are set. Terms for their implementation and the amount of financing available are specified. Programs can be divided into short, medium, or long-term plans. However, around the world, the efficiency of economic programming is often not high. The main reason for this is uncertainty over both the quantitative and qualitative parameters of future development. Moreover, uncertainty increases the further into the future the forecasting attempts to look. Still, economic programming – indeed, economic as a whole – cannot avoid forecasting.

5. The mechanisms of economic policy used by a country integrate purposes, objectives, instruments, and the directions of policy. These can be looked at from different perspectives. From the organizational perspective, they combine the work of various state bodies and agencies, the instruments of economic policy and the relevant government programs. Economic policy exists to implement current objectives such as tax collection, government expenditure, and regulation of the economy. They can also be used for prospective

objectives, although government programs can be created in this case as well.

Questions

1. How does economic theory explain the reasons for government intervention in the economy?
2. How can we evaluate the scope of government intervention in the economy, if only indirectly?
3. What are the specific features of fiscal policy in the former Soviet countries?
4. What are the basic directions of economic policy?
5. Why is Russia's position in Doing Business better than in the Index of Economic Freedom?

Sources of additional information

Applied forecasting of a national economy. Study guide. Ed. by Ivanter V.V. and the others. Moscow, 2007 (in Russian).

World 2035. Global forecast. Ed. by Dynkin A.A. Moscow, 2016 (in Russian).

Ministry of Economic Development of the Russian Federation (www. http://economy.gov.ru/minec/main)

IMF. World Economic Outlook (http://www.imf.org/en/publications/weo)

World Bank. Global Economic Prospects (http://www.worldbank.org/en/publication/global-economic-prospects)

CHAPTER 7

THE SECTORS OF A NATIONAL ECONOMY

For more detailed analysis of a national economy, this study guide divides the economy into the following sectors: the real, the financial, the external, and the social sectors.

Method of Analysis for the Real Sector

Although the System of National Accounts (SNA) is based not on industries but on types of economic activity, when analyzing the real sector, a wider perspective is needed, so we look at groups of separate industries or types of economic activity that we call industrial complexes, such as the agro-industrial complex, or at enlarged industries, such as the consumer goods industry. This approach prevails in Russia partly because the country has, only since 2003, switched – on the recommendation of the SNA – from the All-Union Classifier of Economic Branches (OKONKh) to the All-Russia Classifier of Types of Economic Activity (OKVED) for its statistical accounting. But, more importantly, this industrial approach allows for more effective analysis of the real sector.

In this study guide we will divide the real economy into the following industrial complexes and enlarged industries:

- the agro-industrial complex;
- the fuel and energy complex;
- the metallurgy complex;
- the chemical and forestry complexes combined as one;
- the machine-building (engineering) complex;
- the defense industry complex, sometimes called the military-industrial complex, although the former refers to the defense industry and military research and development, while the latter means the alliance of the armed forces, the state apparatus, and the military industry;
- light industry;
- the construction complex;

- the transport complex;
- communications and data transmission;
- trade and public catering, hotels and household services; and
- recreation complex.

A simpler division of the real sector would be: agriculture; industry (mining and manufacture); construction; transport and communications; and trade. This is used in the case of smaller national economies or where only limited statistics are available.

Agriculture

The agro-industrial complex includes:

- agriculture;
- industries supplying agriculture with material resources (industry producing agricultural machinery, e.g. tractors; industry producing e.g. fertilizers and other chemicals);
- industries processing agricultural products (the food industry) and processing agricultural raw materials for the consumer goods industry, e.g., cotton gin plants;
- infrastructure-related supplies for agriculture, e.g., transportation, the storage and trade in agricultural products etc.

The more developed a country, the smaller the proportion of the agro-industrial complex is taken up by agriculture itself. Generally available statistics on the agro-industrial complex provide detailed information on agriculture itself. However, when using these statistics, errors are often made, for example, when using a single year's statistics as representative. Given the extent to which agriculture is dependent on the weather, it is more appropriate to use average annual figures over three or more years to give an accurate picture.

These concerns also apply to indicators of effectiveness when applied to agriculture in the case of, for example, crop yields or milk yield per cow. Agricultural effectiveness also depends on the level of agricultural technology being used, examples of which include the use of fertilizers and chemicals, or the availability of tractors and other machinery. In the absence of solid data on the effectiveness of the agricultural sector, it is possible to use as a proxy, a comparison between the share of GDP accounted for by agriculture and the percentage of the population working in the sector.

Fuel and Energy

The fuel and energy complex includes both electricity generation and fuel industries such as coal and peat mining, oil, and gas. The definitions used in the SNA are 'mining operations' and 'the production and distribution of electric energy, gas and water', and the fuel and energy complex covers the majority of these types of economic activity.

The study of the fuel and energy complex involves assessing how much of the country's electricity is being produced by the different types of power plants: hydro, thermal, and nuclear. It also assesses the mix of energy resources in the country. In Russia, thermal power stations produced 67% of all electricity; hydroelectric plants, 17%; and nuclear, 16%.

It should also be noted that the per capita production of electricity in a country correlates with that country's level of development. There is a similar, but not exact, correlation between electricity consumption and the level of development.

Table 7.1 — Former Soviet countries: electric energy consumption in 2014 (kWh per capita)

Russia	6,603		Turkmenistan	2,679
Belarus	3,299		Uzbekistan	1,645
Moldova	1,386		Latvia	3,507
Ukraine	3,419		Lithuania	3,821
Azerbaijan	2,204		Estonia	6,732
Armenia	1,966			
Georgia	2,689		*for reference*	
Kazakhstan	5,600		Poland	3.972
Kyrgyzstan	1 941		Turkey	2,855
Tajikistan	1,480		USA	12,987

Source: World Bank Indicators
http://data.worldbank.org/indicator/EG.USE.ELEC.KH.PC

The balance of energy resources plots a table with mining, storage, exports, imports, and consumption of energy resources along one axis, with, along with other, different types of energy resources: natural fuel (oil and gas-condensate, natural gas, coal, and peat), fuel-derived products, combustible secondary energy resources, electric energy, and thermal energy.

A simpler version of this balance would be to divide the primary energy resources produced in a country into different types. In Russia in 2013, out of a total of 1,880 m tons of fuel equivalent, natural gas accounted for 41%; oil and gas-condensate 40%; coal 13%; while peat and timber 0.2%; and nuclear, hydro, wind, and geothermal power together accounted for 6%.

Other complexes

The metallurgy complex includes the ferrous and non-ferrous activities in a country. The chemical complex includes a vast array of subtypes of economic activity, as well as the forest-industry complex. The machine-building complex also encompasses a wide variety of subtypes of activity.

The defense industry complex is not divided into separate types and subtypes of activity. It is thus difficult to separate military goods from civil. As many countries do not have a significant defense complex, it is often omitted from analysis of the real sector. In countries that do have a developed defense complex, the engineering industry is sometimes divided in civil and defense-related branches.

Fabrics play an important part in the light industry in the form of textile manufacturing. Light industry also includes production of clothing, shoes, leather, and leather goods. The term, 'textile manufacturing' sometimes refers to the manufacture of both clothes and fabrics.

The construction complex includes both construction itself (new buildings and renovation) and the construction materials industry. Construction is frequently subdivided into industrial, civil (e.g. office buildings), and housing.

The transport complex is traditionally subdivided into rail, automobile, air, marine, river, and pipelines. When analyzing transport, we use indicators such as shipments (in tons or cubic meters for natural gas), cargo turnover (in ton-kilometers, i.e., tons of cargo shipped multiplied by distance covered), and passenger turnover (number of passenger journeys).

Communications and data transmission include various types of economic activity such as post, telephony, and the internet.

Science and scientific services are included as a subtype of economic activity under the broader heading of 'real estate operations, rent, and the provision of services.'

Trade and public catering, hotel and household services form an interindustry complex that features prominently in developed countries economies. However, in some of the former Soviet countries, it is even more significant. For instance, trade accounts for a larger proportion of Russia's GDP, than it does in the case of the USA. This reflects the fact that thc retail trade (especially individual enterprises) masks a great deal of unemployment. Another reason for the prominence of trade in certain former Soviet countries is that they serve as active transit hubs. Kyrgyzstan, for example, is a major re-exporter of Chinese consumer goods to neighboring countries.

Recreation and entertainment, culture, and sports form a complex which includes tourism alongside a range of other activities.

To sum up, it should be noted that when looking at the real sector, we apply the idea of 'production infrastructure.' This includes power, gas and water supplies, the transport complex, and communications and data transmission.

Analysis of the Financial Sector

When analyzing the financial sector, we look first at the financial capital resources. The most widely used indicator of money supply in statistics is 'M2' or broad money. This, along with GDP, is frequently used to compare different countries. The ration between the two is called the monetization factor. Broadly speaking, the higher the ratio, the more scope a country has to finance economic activity via the banking sector. For example, figures for 2015 show that the monetization factor in Russia was 40%; in Ukraine it was 50%; in Poland and Turkey, around 64%; in the USA 90%; and in China 203%.

Financial capital resources are measured in terms of financial depth. This is calculated as a ratio of total bank assets and outstanding shares and bonds in a country to its GDP. The IMF, in the statistical appendix to its annual Global Financial Stability Report, calculates the financial depth of mostly developed countries. However, anyone with the statistics can calculate it. This notion of financial depth needs to be seen in the context of where a country is in its economic cycle. During an economic upswing, GDP grows, but stock market capitalization can grow even faster. In 2013, the USA's financial depth was 434%; the EU's 548%; Japan's 577%; and that of the Central and East European countries 122%. This indicator is also popular as it enables analysis of the structure of the financial depth, in particular, whether stocks or bank assets predominate.

We then move on to analyze the fiscal system of a country, its fiscal policy as well as its monetary policy and system.

The fiscal system is made up of the tax and budget systems. The tax system is broadly defined as the country's tax authorities, its payment rules for taxes, and the total of imposed compulsory payment in the country in the form of taxes, tariffs, duties, and levies (referred to collectively as 'taxes'). Taxes are divided into:

- method of payment: direct and indirect (in the former Soviet countries, the latter is the most common);
- their nature: proportional, regressive, or progressive (the latter two are rare in the former Soviet countries);
- their revenue objectives: federal, regional, or local (often a tax collected centrally will be split between the three).

By comparing the volume of tax collected with the GDP, we arrive at a figure for the country's tax burden. In the former Soviet countries, this does not stray far from global averages. It is also important to establish where the tax burden falls – onto legal entities or individuals. To calculate the tax burden of legal entities, we compare the tax they pay with their revenues from sales. To calculate the burden on individuals, we compare household incomes with taxes paid, both direct and indirect. For instance, private households in Russia spend about one third of their income on taxes which are mainly indirect in the form of taxes on the purchase of goods and services. Government budget statistics reveal how the tax burden falls for each separate type of tax.

The budgetary system of a country is made up of the total of the central government budget (the federal budget in federal countries), regional budgets (the budgets of parts of the federation in federal countries), local budgets, as well as the budgets of state non-budgetary funds (e.g., in the case of Russia, the Pension Fund, the Social Insurance Fund, and federal and regional compulsory medical insurance funds). The total of the budget of the first three levels is called the consolidated budget. With the state non-budgetary funds added, we refer to it as the general government budget. However, the national statistics in Russia use consolidated budget to mean the general government budget. Reserve funds are an important part of the overall picture. In Russia, the largest are the Reserve Fund and the National Welfare Fund. These are held in reserve to meet future unforeseen expenditures.

When analyzing the budget system, we need to pay particular attention to whether the budget is in balance. A budget deficit leads to public borrowing, increasing government debt. Government debt includes obligations in the country's own currency as well as in foreign exchange. In developed countries, the national currency will be freely convertible, but in emerging markets, the national currency will often have only limited convertibility. Depending on the availability of convertible currency, this may cause government difficulties when it seeks to pay off debt. Such countries, therefore, divide their debt into internal and external, a distinction which is not necessary in developed countries.

The monetary system of a country includes both its money and credit systems. The system of money refers to the way the circulation of money is organized in the country. When analyzing this, we look at the volume, dynamics, and structure of the money supply. We also consider the size of the monetary base. This can be defined in a narrow sense as the total of cash plus the compulsory deposits held in reserve with the central bank; in a broader sense we also add correspondent accounts and the deposits of commercial banks with the central bank. The monetary base is an important indicator, as it correlates closely with the circulation of money in a country.

Research into inflation is equally important. This usually means the consumer price index (CPI) which, as the name suggests, measures consumer prices. The index is calculated either as an annual average or by comparing prices at the end of December with the same point in the previous year. In Russia, this latter method is the most common.

Table 7.2 shows that in Russia and in many other former Soviet countries, inflation is higher than in developed countries. However, the other countries in this group (which includes oil and gas exporters) demonstrate that high inflation is not simply a feature of emerging market economies or of economic backwardness. Rather, it is a consequence of faults in economic policy, or perhaps in the economic models themselves.

Table 7.2 — Former Soviet countries: annual average consumer prices growth rates (percentage)

	2010	2015	2016	2017*	2022*
Russia	6.9	15.5	8.3	5.8	4.6
Belarus	7.7	13.5	11.8	8.0	7.0
Moldova	0.0	9.6	6.4	6.5	5.0
Ukraine	15.9	48.7	13.9	12.8	7.0
Azerbaijan	5.7	4.0	12.4	12.0	6.0
Armenia	7.3	3.7	-1.4	1.9	4.6
Georgia	7.6	4.0	2.1	6.0	3.0
Kazakhstan	7.1	4.0	2.1	6.0	3.0
Kyrgyzstan	6.8	6.7	14.6	7.3	4.0
Tajikistan	6.4	5.8	5.9	8.9	6.0
Turkmenistan	-2.7	7.4	3.6	6.0	3.2
Uzbekistan	12.3	8.5	8.0	13.0	10.0
Latvia	-1.2	0.2	0.1	3.0	3.0
Lithuania	1.2	0.2	0.1	3.0	3.0
Estonia	2.7	-0.7	0.7	3.5	2.5
for reference:					
Poland	2.6	-0.9	-0.6	1.9	2.5
Turkey	8.6	7.7	7.8	10.9	7.5
USA	1.6	0.1	1.3	2.1	2.3

*Estimate
**Forecast

Source: IMF. World Economic Outlook. October 2017, pp.249–250.

The credit system in a country is defined as the summation of all credit relationships (between creditors and borrowers), all forms and methods of extending credit, and credit organizations. Basic credit organizations are commercial banks. So, analysis of the credit system focuses on banks (banking system). Here we look at the credit system's scope, its scale (the size of the banking system as a proportion of GDP), its concentration, and the extent of foreign capital interest. The World Bank publishes statistics on the scale of credit which is calculated as the credit provided by local banks as a ratio of GDP.

Table 7.3 — Former Soviet countries: domestic credit provided by the financial sector in 2016 (percent of GDP)

Russia*	53		Latvia	82
Belarus	47		Lithuania	52
Moldova	32		Estonia	82
Ukraine	79			
Azerbaijan	39			
Armenia	54		*for reference*	
Georgia	66		Poland	
Kazakhstan	45		Turkey	
Tajikistan	25		USA	243

* 2015

Source: World Bank Indicators
http://data.worldbank.org/indicator/FS.AST.DOMS.GD.ZS

Table 7.3 illustrates how the credit systems of Russia and other former Soviet countries do not cope well with their main task of providing loans when compared with the credit systems in other countries of a similar, or even lower, level of development. As a result, many companies in the former Soviet countries have to approach foreign banks for credit (which leads to a growth in foreign debt), or rely on their own resources to fund investment (which limits the scope their own investment have to grow).

The statistics available on the stock markets in former Soviet countries make analysis difficult. Some of this is unavoidable given the small size of the stock markets in these countries. There are a limited number of stocks and small trade volumes.

The Methods of Analysis of the External Sector

There are two possible approaches to analyzing the external economic sector, narrow or broad. The narrow approach would consider the country's balance of payment, its international reserves (gold and foreign currency) and its external debt. It would also take into account the country's currency policy, its participation in international trade and knowledge exchange. It would include international capital and labor flows in and out of the country and its participation in regional integration initiatives along with any other relevant aspects of globalization. The broader approach would do all of this and add in an examination of the real sector's export industries. In this study guide, the narrow approach is used.

Analysis of the external sector of a country's national economy is based primarily on its balance of payments. It should be noted that the first element—the current account balance – includes the balance of trade in goods and services, the balance of income from the remuneration of labor and investments, and the balance of current transfers. The current account balance is so significant for the national economy that it often takes precedence over the wider balance of payments. As Table 7.4 shows, many former Soviet countries have had a tendency to a negative balance of payments over the last decade, with the partial exception of countries that export hydrocarbons. The negative balance is managed with inflows of foreign business capital and further borrowing, pushing up the external debt.

Table 7.4 — Former Soviet countries: current account balances (as percentage of GDP)

	2010	2015	2016	2017*	2022**
Russia	4.4	5.0	2.0	2.8	4.0
Belarus	- 15.0	-3.3	-3.6	-5.3	-2.5
Moldova	- 7.5	-5.0	-3.8	-4.0	-5.4
Ukraine	- 2.2	-0.3	-4.1	-3.3	-3.0
Azerbaijan	28.0	-0.4	-3.6	1.9	5.4
Armenia	-14.2	-2.6	-2.3	-3.6	-5.1
Georgia	-10.2	-12.0	-13.3	-11.9	-9.1
Kazakhstan	0.9	-2.8	-6.4	-5.3	0.5
Kyrgyzstan	- 6.1	-16.0	-9.7	-11.6	-9.7
Tajikistan	- 1.2	-6.0	-3.8	-6.3	-4.3
Turkmenistan	- 10.6	-14.0	-21.0	-15.4	-11.9
Uzbekistan	6.2	0.7	0.7	0.9	-2.0
Latvia	2.3	-0.8	1.5	-0.3	-2.1
Lithuania	- 0.3	-2.3	-0.9	-1.6	-2.6
Estonia	1.8	2.3	1.9	1.8	-2.0
for reference:					
Poland	- 5.5	-0.6	-0.2	-1.0	-2.2
Turkey	- 6.2	-3.7	-3.8	-4.6	-3.8
USA	-2.9	-2.4	-2.4	-2.4	-2.5

*Estimate
**Forecast

Source: IMF. World Economic Outlook. October 2016, pp.245-249.

Information on a country's national debt can be found either in its national statistics or at the World Bank. It is a common mistake to consider only the state's official external debt and ignore private external debt owed by companies and banks. The latter can often be greater than the state's debt (as in Russia) and causes just as many problems for the economy. To give a sense of thc burden of annual external debt payments, the amount needed to be paid is compared with the main source of freely convertible currency, namely the annual receipts from goods and services exports. For instance, in 2016, Russia had to pay US$133bn to service principal and interest on its foreign debts. Receipts from goods and services exports were $332 bn. So we see that servicing the external debt required around 40% of all income from exports. The IMF regards a servicing ratio of 15–25% as a critical threshold.

A country can offer partial security for payments of external debt and cover its current account balance by drawing on official (i.e. government) international reserves of monetary gold and foreign currencies. It is commonly held that a country should hold, as a minimum, international reserves equivalent in value to six months' of its normal imports of goods and services. In order to a ratio between reserves and payments of external debt, the 'Guidotti-Greenspan rule' is applied. This states that a country's official reserves should not fall below the value of its short-term external debt. Both of these benchmarks conform to the 'Reddy criterion' which states that a safe value of official reserves is equivalent to three months' imports plus the annual value of external debt payments. For developed economies, with their freely convertible currencies that can be used to service external obligations, the issue of a safe level of official reserves is not pressing – all the more so if their currency is a reserve currency. This explains their relatively small levels of official reserves.

In countries with emerging markets, international reserves also perform the important function of acting as a supporting base for the national currency. Again, this is not a pressing concern for developed countries, as their highly competitive economies bolster their currencies in international markets. They find ready markets for their high quality goods and services, enabling them to service their external obligations with their national currency. Thus, they do not require large reserves to support their currencies. In the USA and Japan, for example, 90% of the national currency is backed by obligations of the government to the central bank, rather than by foreign currency or gold reserves.

By contrast, countries with emerging markets find it hard to service external obligations with their national currencies. Only 20% of Russia's external debt at the end of 2016 was in its national currency. As a result, the value of the country's official reserves depends not on the national economy but on the world prices of the goods and services that the country exports. So, in order to support a strong exchange rate for the ruble at a time when world prices for Russia's exports are decreasing, huge official reserves are needed and this, in turn, forces the Russian monetary authorities to exceed the international standards of reserve sufficiency during an economic upswing.

Indicators of the size of a country's participation in international trade are based on a comparison of their foreign trade turnover – imports and exports – with its GDP. These indicators are called foreign trade, export and import quotas (not to be confused with a country's share of world trade). However, international trade is based on international prices while GDP/GNI is calculated in internal prices. It is, therefore, appropriate to compare specified foreign trade values with PPP GDP/GNI. So, according to Russia's Federal State Statistics Service, GDP in 2016 was US$3,397 bn. According to the balance of payments statement, in the same year, exports and imports of goods and services reached US$598 bn. In other words, foreign trade turnover was equivalent to 18% of GDP. In addition, exports of goods and services were US$332 bn, equivalent to 10% of GDP and imports stood at US$266 bn, 8% of GDP. This calculation is supported by the data in Table 2.1 (data from the national accounts are more precise, but they are not always available for analysis).

In all other former Soviet countries, these figures are higher, demonstrating that foreign trade quotas are influenced by two factors: the extent to which the national economy is oriented toward the external market (this increases the foreign trade quota), and the size of the economy (this decreases the quota due to the larger size of the internal market.

To assess the quality of a country's participation in international trade, we look at the range (structure) of commodities that it exports. We assume that the higher the share of finished goods (especially high-tech products) is the more progressive the country's exports are. However, it is easy to overemphasize these values, ignoring the fact that more developed economies with rich agricultural and mineral resources will fall behind less developed economies with poor natural resources. Moreover, if we judge the progressiveness of a country's exports according to the proportion of high-tech products in total exports, we should bear in mind that, for example, the USA, at 18%, has a lower score than China, at 27%. But while this reflects the fact that China does indeed export large numbers of high-tech goods, many of these are only assembled in China, using components imported from other countries (including the USA). So, we need to look behind the headline statistics.

The indicators of the liberalization of foreign trade are also important when looking at a national economy. These include the primary level of import tariffs, especially as levied on finished products as these are the products most often subject to protectionism.

Table 7.5 — Simple average tariffs for goods in most favored nation regime in former Soviet countries in 2016(as percentage of price of imported goods)

Russia	7.6
Belarus	7.2
Moldova	5.4
Ukraine	4.5
Azerbaijan	9.0
Armenia	6.2
Georgia	1.5
Kazakhstan	6,9
Kyrgyzstan	6.9
Tajikistan	7.6
Uzbekistan	14,9
for reference	
EU	5.2
Turkey	10.9
USA	3.5

Source: WTO. World Tariff Profiles 2017. Geneva, 2017, pp.8–10.

As Table 7.5 shows, Azerbaijan and Uzbekistan have the highest import tariffs. The Baltic countries, as part of the European Union, have relatively low tariffs. However, the lowest tariffs are in the former Soviet country with the most open economy, Georgia.

Table 7.6 — Balance of international migration over 2008–2012 (thousand people as a whole over 5 years)

Russia	1,118
Belarus	76
Moldova	-10
Ukraine	-200
Azerbaijan	0
Armenia	-30
Georgia	-305
Kazakhstan	160
Kyrgyzstan	-138
Tajikistan	-100
Turkmenistan	-50
Uzbekistan	-66
Latvia	-83
Lithuania	-146
Estonia	-10
for reference:	
Sudan	-589
South Sudan	425
Nigeria	-300
Mexico	-300
Syria	-4,158
Pakistan	-1,082
Bangladesh	-2,526
India	-2,578
Indonesia	-835
Philippines	-650
Myanmar	-474
China	-1,698
Malaysia	782
Singapore	338
USA	4,500
Canada	1,146
Australia	913
EU	2,939
Oman	817
Saudi Arabia	1,590
Lebanon	1,250
Turkey	1,627

Source: The World Bank. Indicators
http://data.worldbank.org/indicator/SM.POP.NETM

Many countries do not have adequate data on flows of international labor. However, using overall migration statistics (i.e., not simply that for labor) and expert analysis, it is possible to make indirect calculations of these figures. One such is published by the World Bank and the International Organization for Migration.

World Bank data on migration may differ from national data from individual countries, but they give us an overall picture of the reality in former Soviet countries. This suggests that Russia has one of the highest rates of inward migration, while the rest of the former Soviet countries are mostly net exporters of migrants. Kazakhstan has emerged as a second attractive destination for migrants as well as Belarus. Comparing these data with expert estimates, we can add that Russia is the main destination for migrants from the Transcaucasus and Central Asia, while migration out of those former Soviet countries in East Europe goes mainly to the EU.

It is logical to examine knowledge exchange as a separate aspect of external economic relations. But, in practice, this is complicated. There are no statistics on citizens of former Soviet countries studying abroad. Likewise, there is scant information on foreign students in the former Soviet countries, with only a few keeping data. According to the data that are available, Russia is naturally the largest destination for foreign students. In the 2016/2017 academic year, 243,000 foreign students enrolled at Russian universities, which included 169,000 on full-time courses. These came mainly from CIS countries.

In the same way, only a few countries publish data on the import and export specifically of technology. In 2016, Russia saw US$1.3 bn of technological exports, and US$2.5 bn of imports.

With such fragmentary statistics on knowledge exchanges, it makes sense to incorporate them into the general analysis on knowledge resources or on science, scientific services, and education.

We judge a country's participation in international capital flows mainly on its balance of payments, adjusting for each country's particular features. The capital account thus reflects external debt relief as well as the import and export of capital assets by migrants. We, therefore, look at it alongside the current account balance. The vast majority of capital flows are reflected in the financial account which divides capital flows into three types: direct investment, portfolio (and financial derivatives), and other (mostly loans and credits).

An important supplement to the financial account is the appendix to the balance of payments. This is called the 'international investment position of a country' and this specifies, not the actual capital flow itself, but its result in the volume of accumulated foreign assets held by the country's residents and that held in the country by non-residents (the latter are referred to as country obligations to foreign residents).

Adding together all types of capital flows only makes sense when analyzing the net inflow/outflow of private capital (the net flow of private capital). The Bank of Russia regularly publishes these statistics by year, quarter, and month enabling analysts to draw key conclusions. In Russia, there is usually a negative balance of private capital flows (outflow exceeds inflow). If this net inflow/outflow is less that the positive current account balance, the country does not need to draw on its international reserves. Indeed, it can even increase its reserves and make early payments on external debts. This strengthens the ruble. If the negative balance of private capital flows is greater than the positive current account balance, international reserves are depleted and the external debt grows, weakening the ruble.

Analysts pay special attention to the flow of inward direct investments, as these tend to be long-term and a rarely repatriated. Rather, their aim is usually to control the enterprise in which they are investing, and this often results in an inflow of knowledge. Owners of direct foreign investments are usually companies and banks referred to as transnational corporations (TNC) or multinational corporations (MNC). They invest overseas either by setting up now companies in target markets or through mergers and acquisitions of domestic companies in the market.

Portfolio investments, either inward or outward, do not play an important role in the former Soviet countries. The capital markets in these countries are limited in size and heavily volatile. Of more significance for these countries is their participation in flows of loan capital, primarily in the form of loans and credits from abroad. We can observe that the capital shortages in the former Soviet countries can be smoothed by inflows of investments other than portfolio investment. When there is a budget deficit or a negative balance of payments, the government will work with the private sector in attracting such investment. In an economic upswing, such an approach has clear benefits, for example, an inflow of loan capital from abroad compensates for weaknesses in the national banking systems. But during an economic downturn, there are negative consequences as it becomes more difficult to service existing credits and loans.

Almost all countries in the world are involved in some or other international association and the context of these memberships need to be taken into account when analyzing a country's economy. There are dozens of such associations around the world. However, most of them achieve only very limited integration among their member countries.

A traditional indicator for showing how important an international association is for its members is to look at an individual member's share of the group's total external trade. However, there are different scenarios. The Baltics, for example, as members of the EU focus their external trade very much on the other members on other EU members. By contrast, the level of trade between members of the CIS is relatively low. In 2015, intra-CIS trade comprised just 16% of the total exports of all CIS countries. The comparable figure for the EU was 69%, for NAFTA 49%, ASEAN 26% and MERCOSUR 15%. The main cause of weakness in an international association is a lack of compatibility between the individual economies. Let us look at this in more detail in the context of international trade.

Developed countries, especially when they are neighbors, tend to have extensive trade links with each other due to their large and competitive exporting industries. The more a developed country exports goods and services the more it needs in turn to import a variety of goods (often finished goods) and services. As a result, the international division of labor in the context of external trade occurs primarily in developed economies, especially neighbors, due to their low transaction costs.

Less developed countries tend to export simpler products, reflecting the lower competitiveness of their industries. While exporting their goods (both finished and simple products) less developed countries prefer to source the products they need, especially finished goods, from the developed countries, where production is more competitive. This complementarity between developed and less developed countries in international trade is matched by their complementarity in the international flow of economic resources. For example, less developed countries can export labor to more developed countries, where they can earn capital and improve their knowledge. For this reason, less developed countries tend to have more links with developed countries than with each other.

Economic integration thus proceeds more slowly among less developed countries. This is seen in the international associations among countries that export raw materials, such as Arab states and those of Latin America.

However, in any association in a region of low or medium development, the presence of a major country with a large market or countries with higher levels of development, makes the integration within the association more profitable for all members. This can be seen in ASEAN, where Singapore and Malaysia are more developed than other members. The same is true for Brazil in MERCOSUR and Russia in the Eurasian Economic Union (EEU).

We can, therefore, conclude that economic integration among less developed countries within international associations tends to proceed more successfully where assisted by the presence of countries, especially if large, that have higher levels of development. If this conclusion is correct, it follows that integration between the former Soviet countries will depend primarily on the progress of Russia's own economic development.

International associations tend to follow a path to integration with certain key stages: free trade zone; customs union; common market for goods, services and labor; and, finally, economic and monetary union. The only example of economic and monetary union in the world is those countries in the European Union that have adopted the euro as their currency. Most other associations are at the first stage, free trade zones. The CIS, ASEAN, MERCOSUR, and NAFTA are all free trade zones.

Within larger international associations, there is scope for subgroups of members to pursue greater levels of integration. A subgroup of EU has adopted the euro as their currency and follows its stricter rules. The Eurasian Economic Union also forms a subgroup within the CIS, comprising Russia, Armenia, Kazakhstan, and Kyrgyzstan.

The Method for Analysis of Social Sectors

The social sector includes a range of industries which together are sometimes called the 'social infrastructure' (education, healthcare, social insurance, housing, and utilities). With the addition of science, informatics, and culture, the sector is referred to as the 'social and cultural sphere.' One can look at all industries listed when analyzing this sector, or adopt a tighter definition focusing on social policy at large.

When analyzing the country's social policy, we should bear in mind that it comprises social insurance policy (the social protection of some members of society), public goods policy, and incomes policy.

However, income statistics pose difficulties for income policy. The SNA certainly contains data on gross disposable incomes (see Table 2.5). Moreover, the integrated table of national accounts (part of the SNA) includes data on the distribution of income after tax across sectors such as 'Private Households', along with data on social benefits and transfers. But these statistics are published with some delay and do not take inflation into account.

As a result, the statistical agencies produce narrow data on incomes promptly. The Federal State Statistics Service produces statistics of incomes per month, the monthly average of nominal gross pay-roll, the amount of pensions paid every month, along with statistics on real disposable income (i.e., after tax and adjusted for inflation). In any event, there are no data on personal incomes in kind (e.g., from household plots), not any on social imputed transfers (e.g. free transport for certain categories of the population). However, the operational rates provide us with a general idea of how incomes are changing among the greater part of the population.

When analyzing incomes, it is important to look at income distributions between different groups within the population, what we call income differentiation. There are two commonly understood methods to measure of income differentiation. The first is to split levels of income according to deciles or quintiles of the population, so layers of 10% (decile) or 20% (quintile). The higher the difference between the amount of income concentrated in the top decile or quintile and the bottom, the greater the income differentiation in the society is. We often speak of how many multiples of e.g. the bottom decile income represents the top decile. This is called the differentiation ratio. The second method is to measure the income inequality by the Gini Index. This is measured either from 0 to 1 or 0 to 100 and reflects the concentration of income. Both indicators are calculated according to income. But they can be calculated according to consumer spending (consumption). In this variant, differentiation tends to be lower.

Table 7.8 — Differentiation of expenditures (income) in former Soviet countries*

	Differentiation ratio (between top and bottom quintiles)	Gini Index
Russia	9.1	0.412
Belarus	3.8	0.265
Moldova	4.6	0.306
Ukraine	3.4	0.248
Azerbaijan	5.1	0.330
Armenia	4.3	0.290
Georgia	8.9	0.414
Kazakhstan	4.0	0.286
Kyrgyzstan	5.4	0.334
Tajikistan	4.7	0.308
Uzbekistan	5.8	0.352
Latvia	6.9	0.360
Lithuania	5.7	0.326
Estonia	5.6	0.327
for reference:		
Poland	5.2	0.328
Turkey	8.0	0.400

*Data are specified over the last available year, ranging from 2003 to 2015

Sources: Russia in figures. Short statistics digest. Moscow, 2016, p.139; UNDP. Human Development Report 2015. N.Y., 2015, p.215–217

When using quintiles to compare countries, the smallest expenditure differentiations among former Soviet countries are seen in Ukraine and Belarus; the largest are in Georgia and Russia. Using the Gini Index gives the same result for the smallest distributions, Ukraine and Belarus, with the largest in Georgia and Russia. We can thus see different economic models in play among the former Soviet countries, with significant differences in these indicators, even between two neighboring countries – Russia and Belarus.

An important aspect of many incomes policies is their focus on alleviating poverty. Different methods are used to try and reduce the numbers of poor people in a country. In order to identify the extent of poverty in a country, various indicators are used. For instance, in Russia, a level of minimum subsistence is identified. This is calculated according to cost of a basket of basic goods required to maintain life and good health (food and non-food along with some minimal services). The cost of the basket is revised every quarter and is differentiated according to ages and different regions. In mid-2017, the cost of the subsistence basket was ₽10,329. Across all of Russia, the percentage of people living on this subsistence level was 13% of the population.

For comparisons between countries, conventional definitions of poverty are used. The World Bank sets the poverty line at US$1.25 PPP per capita a day. It also has a category of US$2 a day and compares the percentage of the population living at these levels in different countries. The Bank also reports data on consumption per capita according to PPP.

Table 7.9 — Former Soviet countries: consumption per capita in 2012–2014 (in dollars PPP in 2011 prices)

Russia	25.1
Belarus	17.2
Moldova	9.6
Ukraine	13.0
Armenia	6.0
Georgia	6.1
Kazakhstan	12.0
Kyrgyzstan	6.0
Latvia	17.9
Lithuania	19.8
Estonia	23.1
for reference:	
Poland	16.3
Turkey	16.3

Source: World Bank. Indicators http://data.worldbank.org/indicator/SI.SPR.PCAP

In many countries, social policy has an important demographic aspect aimed at seeking to limit or maintain the birth rate. No former Soviet country is actively seeking to limit its birth rate. But some countries are seeking to tackle falling birth rates e.g., Russia, Belarus, Ukraine, and the Baltic countries. Social policy also encompasses ecological and cultural aspects.

Of course, to analyze the social sector, we need retrospective indices of human development.

Table 7.10 — Former Soviet countries: Human Development Index

	1990	2008	2015
Russia	0.729	0.770	0.804
Belarus	….	0.764	0.796
Moldova	0.648	0.652	0.699
Ukraine	0.705	0.729	0.743
Azerbaijan	….	0.724	0.759
Armenia	0.632	0.722	0.743
Georgia	…	0.730	0.769
Kazakhstan	0.686	0.744	0.794
Kyrgyzstan	0.607	0.617	0.664
Tajikistan	0.610	0.591	0.627
Turkmenistan	…	….	0.691
Uzbekistan	…	0.643	0.761
Latvia	0.710	0.813	0.830
Lithuania	0.737	0.827	0.848
Estonia	0.730	0.832	0.868
for reference:			
Poland	0.714	0.817	0.865
Turkey	0.576	0.710	0.767
USA	0.860	0.900	0.920

Source: UNDP. Human Development Report 2016. N.Y., 2016, pp.200–203.

As seen in Table 7.10, in a range of former Soviet countries, the level of the Human Development Index is not much higher today than it was in the Soviet era.

Conclusion

1. When analyzing the real sector, a wider perspective is needed looking at groups of separate industries or types of economic activity that we

call industrial complexes (e.g., the agro-industrial complex) or enlarged industries (e.g., the consumer goods industry).

2. When analyzing the financial sector, we look at the fiscal system of a country along with its fiscal policy, its systems of money and credit, and its stock market. This is often combined with analysis of the country's financial resources.

3. Analysis of a country's external sector is based primarily on the country's balance of payments. The first part of a country's current account – current transactions – includes the balance of trade in goods and services, the income balance from the remuneration of labor and investments, along with the balance of current transfers. The current account balance is so important for a national economy that it is sometimes confused with the whole balance of payments. An additional element of the balance of payments, the accounts of capital transactions and financial instruments, reflects a country's participation in international capital flows.

4. The social sector includes a range of industries which together are sometimes called the 'social infrastructure' (education, healthcare, social insurance, housing, and utilities). When considering social policy, we should keep in mind that it can also include incomes policy.

Questions

1. What types of economic activity are included in the agro-industrial complex?

2. Why is inflation in most former Soviet countries higher than international averages?

3. What elements go to make up a country's balance of payments? What does each contain?

4. Why is a positive current account balance usually followed by a negative account balance for capital and financial instruments and vice versa?

Sources of additional information

Russia in figures. Statistical handbook
(http://www.gks.ru/bgd/regl/b17_12/Main.htm)
CIS in Figures (http://www.cisstat.org/eng/index.htm)
IMF. World Economic Outlook (www.imf.org)
IMF. International Financial Statistics (www.imf.org)
UNCTAD. World Investment Report (www.unctad.org)
UNDP. Human Development Report (www.undp.org)
World Bank. World Development Indicators (www.worldbank.org)
WTO. International Trade Statistics (www.wto.org)

UNIT II

THE RUSSIAN ECONOMIC MODEL

CHAPTER 8

THE RUSSIAN ECONOMIC MODEL

The Russian Economic Model

On analyzing the workings of the Russian economy, based on the indicators of the Global Competitiveness Report (see Table 1.1 and comments), we see an economy with a large internal market and a range of strong macroeconomic indicators such as a positive balance of payments and large international reserves. But the Russian economy is also marked by excessive—and not always effective—state participation which dominates the private sector. The latter, in turn, is ill-suited to the current state of the economy as a result of insufficient protection of property rights and a weak banking system. There is also a tendency to monopoly, linked to weak competitiveness.

Evidence for some of these features of the economy can be found in the Index of Economic Freedom in which Russia is ranked 143rd out of 178 countries. The main reasons for this low ranking are the lack of suitable protection for property rights, the high burden of corruption faced by businesses, and restrictions on businesses' freedom to invest and undertake other financial transactions. The state dominates private business and is more favorable to big business, which can be seen in the weak operation of anti-monopoly policies (The Global Competitiveness Report ranks Russia 83rd in this respect.) Government promotion for large companies is a legacy of the Soviet era and the leading (monopolistic) position enjoyed by such companies today is maintained by the close relationship they have with top bureaucrats. The middle and lower levels of the state bureaucracy tend to look after smaller companies. In line with economic theory, the Russian bureaucracy derives a benefit from the political power it is able to exercise over business and society.

It is the state's efforts to control business that explain Russia's weak property rights (in which the country ranks 116th according to the World Economic Forum) and the weakness of the country's institutions. Its position enables the bureaucracy to manipulate businesses, even the larger ones. This has a detrimental impact on entrepreneurship in that businesses, instead of seeking to work and compete in normal market circumstances, have to adapt to and accommodate the wishes of government officials, who can determine the fate of a company. As a result, businesses do not commit to long-term investment in the country, they seek to export capital, they are less adept than they were in the Soviet era at taking advantage of innovations, and they focus on deriving profit from their links with the government (rent-seeking behavior).

Under the watchful eye of the government and in conditions of weak local competition (for which Russia is ranked 72nd in the world), business is inevitably ineffective from a macroeconomic point of view—it is an 'ineffective owner' of its assets.

Dependent on the state in this way, businesses have to buy the right to exist by bribing officials and the rules of the game focus on what is profitable for the bureaucracy. But, of course, for the bureaucrats and the owners of private businesses, this game works very well in that they profit from the monopolization of the most profitable areas of business such as the exploitation of natural resources and access to state funds.

So, the current Russian economic model is characterized by an interweaving of state and business (especially large businesses) with the state as very much the dominant partner. There are many forms of capitalism. Russia's version can be called government capitalism or, more accurately, given the role played by the large business owners or oligarchs, it can be characterized as oligarchic state capitalism. We should note that this state dominance over business owners (achieved by the state's power over property and patronage) has operated in Russia for centuries, being an important feature of 'Oriental Despotism', an economic model seen throughout Asia.[4]

This type of state capitalism aims to use the power of the state to favor the bureaucracy and those companies close to it, rather than focus on the modernization of the country. This profit-seeking coalition only pursues goals of modernization when it can be used to enhance its own control over the economy. This leads to hesitation in implementing economic reform so that policies fall short of genuinely pro-liberal or pro-Keynesian

---

[4] For more detail see: National Economy. Textbook ed. R.M. by Nureev. Moscow, 2010, pp.88–93 (in Russian).

reforms. The status quo is more important for the ruling bureaucracy than serious reforms.

An antidote to this type of economic model would be greater democratization, leading to greater state support for small and medium businesses, a strengthening of property rights, along with a decrease in direct government intervention in the day-to-day management of companies.[5] This would be reinforced by the re-orientation of the banking sector, dominated by public banks, towards more credit for innovative businesses. This would also be supported by the development of an ethical climate for business in the country, which would entail effective control of economic crime, especially corruption, and a greater sense that the government recognized its moral responsibility toward society.

The Russian Social Model

Russia's social model is characterized by heavy stratification between income levels, poverty endured by the majority of the population, and low life expectancy.

Many of those who own assets try to keep them hidden, either because they fear the greed of the state bureaucracy, because they belong to that bureaucracy themselves, or because they are trying to undervalue their assets to avoid taxation. Many are also conscious that the origin of their wealth is of dubious legality. This leads to the extent of private wealth being underestimated in national statistics. Even so, Russia still has one of the greatest disparities of wealth among the former Soviet countries (see Table 8.1).

The significant stratification between levels of society in respect of property results in the level of poverty seen in the 1990s. Even though this fell during the 2000s, this was not matched by any overall economic development of the country (see Chapter 16).

The impact of the economic crisis of the 1990s coupled with an economic model that does not work in the interests of the majority of the population, has led to a low birth rate and a high rate of mortality. This resulted in the size of the population falling, a phenomenon only seen previously during the Civil and Second World Wars and the immediate post-war years. This

---

[5] The destiny of economic programs and reforms in Russia (round-table discussion) // Voprosy Economiki. 2017.N6. pp.5–44 (in Russian).

trend was reversed at the end of the 2000s. In the current circumstances, the increase in the birth rate can be taken as evidence of improvement in Russia's social model.

Table 8.1 — Distribution of income in the Russian population (percentage)

	1991	1995	2000	2005	2010	2016
Income, total	100	100	100	100	100	100
The first quintile* (lowest income)	11.9	6.1	5.9	5.4	5.2	5.3
The second	15.8	10.8	10.4	10.1	9.8	10.0
The third	18.8	15.2	15.1	15.1	14.8	15.0
The fourth	22.8	21.6	21.9	22.7	22.5	22.6
The fifth (highest income)	30.7	46.3	46.7	46.7	47.7	47.1
The Gini Index (as per incomes)	0.260	0.387	0.395	0.409	0.421	0.414

*Distribution of the population income overall total in 20% groups of the population

Sources: Russia in Figures. Short Statistics Digest. Moscow, 2017, p.129; Russian Statistical Yearbook. Statistics Digest. Moscow, 2001, p.187.
http://www.gks.ru/wps/wcm/connect/rosstat_main/rosstat/ru/statistics/population/level/#

The Russian Political Model

The poor level of democracy in Russia (see Table 8.2) reflects more the traditional weaknesses in the very basis of democracy in Russian society than it does the imperfections of the country's institutions. The weakness of civil society, despite the appearance of a functioning democracy, enables the governing elite to pursue their own narrow interests rather than govern in a way that serves the interests of the population as a whole.

In the government's main expression of its long-term strategy—Forecast 2030 of 2013—there is little to suggest any intent toward any political modernization of the country. This confirms the ruling elite's reluctance to share power with business and society at large. This flies in the face of the high and rapidly improving level of education among the population and also with the more open society that is developing under the influence of neighboring Western democracies.

Russia's Ethical Model

The indicators of poor ethical standards in Russia (see Table 8.2) are compounded by the country's position in the world's top 20 for homicides and suicides, and by high rates of alcohol and drug abuse, and rates of mental illness. These are all evidence of the anomie (from the Greek 'anomia', meaning 'out of the norm') in Russia today, i.e., behavior which breaks with social and ethical norms, inspired by a breakdown of the cultural basis of society. When a society is in crisis, those social and ethical norms become less important and anomie rises as a result. This can be seen in greater feelings of hopelessness in life, and widespread feelings that the country's leaders are indifferent to the people's plight. This leads to a decline in social morals and a rise in crime. Anomie can be characterized as an ethical crisis.

Russia has seen rapid changes in public morality and standards. This has been most evident among the political, economic, and cultural elite. It has been due less to the 'depravity' of the elite than to the public's weak control over it. This has led to a significant decline in social and ethical standards in Russia—and they were not that high to begin with. This ethical crisis is probably the country's most serious problem today as it impedes economic, social, and political progress.

However, it should be noted that the country is making some progress in tacking this crisis: in the 2000s the homicide and suicide rates declined. Society looks to the government to set an example in the fight against corruption. So far this has only resulted in anti-corruption legislation, there has been limited progress in seeing arrests and prosecutions rise.

The Business Structure in Russia

Many of the challenges of doing business in Russia results from the way the current economic model operates. The way in which a large number of business owners, both large and medium sized, were created by the privatization process has had two side effects. Firstly, the rapid pace of the privatization process has enabled many unsuitable people to take the reins of businesses. Secondly, the rapid pace of the process, coupled with inadequate legislation, has resulted in many new business owners being in breach of the law, consciously or otherwise. Thus, a significant proportion of Russian business owners are either ill-suited to running a business or are prone to break the law. Moreover, of the 200 richest people in Russia in 2014, 44.5% were not ethnic Russians, even though 81% of the total population are Russian.[6] As a result, a majority of people now want to see a partial or complete renationalization of the country's large companies. The prevalence of this view does little to strengthen property rights in the country.

In addition, the state's dominance over business, coupled with the active participation in business activities by bureaucrats, has the peculiar effect of making Russian entrepreneurs keen to adapt to the ruling authorities. This, in turn, reduces the effectiveness of entrepreneurship in its classic sense.

Taking the World Economic Forum's standard set of 16 problems faced by businesses around the world, their significance for Russian businesses can be represented as follows,

Table 8.2 — Main problems suffered by private business in Russia (the number indicates the percentage of respondents who listed the item as being of "great importance")

Corruption	13.1
Tax rates	13.1
Access to financing	10.2
Inflation	10.1
Tax regulations	9.3
Inadequately educated workforce	7.4
Inefficient government bureaucracy	6.1
Policy instability	5.5
Poor work ethics of the national labor force	5.2
Inadequate supply of infrastructure	3.9
Government instability	3.8
Insufficient capacity to innovate	3.3
Foreign currency regulations	3.2
Restrictive labor regulations	2.4
Crime and theft	2.1
Poor public health	1.4

Source: World Economic Forum. The Global Competitiveness Report 2017–2017. Geneva, 2017, pp.248.

[6] Who is happy in Russia? http://lenta.ru/articles/2014/10/27/reachrthic/ (in Russian)

From Table 8.2 we can conclude that the problems faced by businesses stem from shortcomings in the country's economic model: the inefficiency of the state bureaucracy and economic policy instability, high tax rates, inflation, and access to financing. Ethical shortcomings, especially corruption, are also important factors.

The business structure of a country is greatly influenced by the intensity of local competition. This is improving in Russia, though the country still ranks 72nd in the world for the strength of its domestic competition. The main reasons for Russia's comparatively low level of local competition are:

- the legacy of the Soviet system which placed importance on large and very large companies, creating a tendency to oligopoly and monopoly which in turn depressed competition;
- the almost complete lack of competition to challenge the monopolies in areas such as gas, postal services etc.;
- the current sectoral structure of the Russian economy with a focus on raw materials and industries with low levels of processing. These concentrate production in a few hands and limit market-entry opportunities for newcomers by technological reasons. This structure favors oligopolistic cooperation rather than competition;
- inadequate protection of property rights which discourages new entrants, i.e., it restricts the mobility of capital to go to construction projects for new companies or the purchase of old ones;
- high barriers to entry in the form of burdensome administration which aims to protect existing market participants who enjoy close relationships with local and regional authorities.

Poor competition fuels inflation, the main drivers of which are:

- the exercise of monopoly power in the industries in question (starting with natural monopolies);
- the cartelization of oligopolistic industries. Cartels usually cooperate over price formation, influence peddling, terms of sale, regulation of volumes of production, and coordination over the terms and conditions of distribution. Features of cartelization can be seen in highly concentrated markets such as that in oil products;
- 'tacit collusion' between participants to maintain prices, even in markets with low concentration, e.g., Russian pharmacy chains.

The country's anti-monopoly policies are of low efficiency (ranking 83rd in the world according to the World Economic Forum. As a result, a significant number of monopolies (especially natural monopolies) and oligopolies survive along with their tendency to cartelization and 'tacit collusion' at the consumers' expense.

According to Expert Magazine, which produces an annual ranking, the leading 400 companies (including public sector companies) in 2015 accounted for about 44% of Russia's GDP.

Russian methodology defines a company with 100–250 employees and a turnover of ₽100–400 million as a medium business. The author estimates that these companies, along with larger companies outside that top 400 referred to above, accounted for 35–40% of Russian GDP (including public sector companies).

A majority of large companies and many medium-sized enterprises form part of integrated business groups. These are inter-company arrangements that can be based on either property or non-property relationships. In Russia, there are several hundred such groups, active at both regional and national levels. Some focus on a single industry, others operate in several at the same time.

The operation of these large and medium private businesses in Russia leads to a high concentration of production and property. Unlike in developed countries, many large private companies and business groups as well as many medium companies in Russia are controlled by individuals, sometimes more than one, who have majority share holdings. Thus, the top 22 private business groups were controlled by just 40 people. Such people are often called oligarchs, and Russian state capitalism is characterized as oligarchic.

The high concentration of property in both large and medium companies has a strong influence on their management. The Anglo-Saxon model tends to more disparate ownership and executive control in managers' hands. By contrast, in Russian companies, strategic decisions are taken by a small number of owners. In terms of economic theory, ownership and management are barely separated in Russia. Another feature of Russian businesses is the existence of close though informal links between corporations (especially larger ones) and government bodies.

Small businesses have a low profile in the face of Russia's oligarchic model. Small companies employ 10–15% of the workforce and account for about the same proportion of GDP. During the 2000s, the small business sector benefited from a significant reduction in its tax burden and a simplification of its tax administration. However, it is still hampered by a shortage of available credit, high business administration requirements, and corruption. Small businesses feel this burden more keenly than larger firms.

The public sector in Russia shares some features with other countries, but also has some specific characteristics. Like many countries, it focuses on social issues such as social insurance, healthcare, education, housing, and utilities; science and culture; and on transport, communications, and electricity.

One of the things that set the Russian public sector apart is its strong presence in the mining sector, the processing industries, construction, and banking. In addition, the limits of the sector's role are left somewhat vague because the government has majority, rather than 100% share holdings in certain companies (e.g., Gazprom). In many companies, the government holds a minority share, or a 'golden share' which gives the government a veto in strategic decisions. According to the Federal Antimonopoly Service (FAS), companies with government participation, including a government minority shareholding, produce about 70% of Russian GDP and employ one third of the labor force. These two aspects—the reach of the public sector into areas that are not normal for it, and the vagueness about its limits—come about as a result of the excessive role that the Russian government has sought to play in the country's economy as well as the active use it has made of executive legal instruments for regulation (with the help also of the 'golden shares').

The public sector is built on the public offices (bodies) owned by the state (about 60,000 in the country), state-run (unitary) enterprises (about 9,000), public companies and state corporations with state participation, including those of which the state owns more than 50% of the shares (about 600). These offices, enterprises, companies, and corporations (with a government majority shareholding) account for about 24% of the country's capital assets and about 24% of employment. They provide the bulk of social services, R&D, and transport and communication services. They account for about 14% of the mining sector's output, including about a third of oil production; 13% of the production and distribution of power, gas, and water; and 9% of the output of manufacturing (mostly military).[7] In general, the public sector, with a government majority shareholding, produces about a third of Russia's GDP. The rest is produced by private sector companies, including those with minority government share holdings.

A steady reduction in the extent of public ownership has gone into reverse since the 2000s, as a wave of privatizations has been followed by acquisitions of previously privatized assets by the public sector in an attempt to consolidate public companies and newly emerged state corporations. The assets of the Yukos (a private company privatized some years earlier), for example, were bought by the public company, Surgutneftegas. The process has also led to the creation of new public companies, such as the United Aircraft Building Corporation, the United Shipbuilding Corporation, Rosgeo, and others; or state corporations e.g., Rostech, Rosatom, the Bank for Development and Foreign Economic Affairs (Vnesheconombank, VEB), the Deposit Insurance Agency (DIA), and the Residential Development Agency. Unlike state companies, state corporations are non-commercial organizations and are not, therefore, subject to laws on bankruptcy or procurement. They have free access to the state budget, receive tax concessions and are not required to report on their commercial activities. This is formalized in separate federal laws for every state corporation with huge funds allocated to each in the form of shares, property, and other state assets. There was a wave of state corporations founded in the 2000s to address identified commercial and management problems that were not addressed effectively by the government or the markets. Economic theory and practice in other parts of the world would define these organizations as development institutions (VEB and DIA), quasi-ministries (Rosatom which replaced the former Ministry of Nuclear Energy), or as quasi-holding companies (Rostech which has more than 100 joint stock companies).

It is difficult to assess the efficiency of these state corporations: on the one hand, it is not high in many of them, on the other hand, they have proven themselves to be important in supporting economic modernization and financial stability. The huge concentration of assets in these corporations, along with the lack of effective regulation or a clear determination of their purpose and functions, raises concerns about them. Their activities are subject to less limitation than other state organizations. For this reason,

[7] Slumping Economy of Modern Russia: Tendencies and Perspectives. Ed. by E.T. Gaidar. Moscow, 2010, pp.433–452 (in Russian).

there is an argument that the state corporations should be transformed into public joint-stock companies, which would bring them under normal company law.

Some state corporations, companies, and unitary enterprises enjoy almost complete monopolies over the production of certain goods and services at federal, regional, and municipal levels. In this category we find all hydro and nuclear electric, gas and gas transportation services (Rushydro, Rosatom and Gazprom); those providing services on the electricity grid, oil pipelines and railways (Federal Grid Company, Transneft, and Russian Railways); postal services (Russian Post); and housing and utilities. In Russia, they are regarded as natural monopolies. However, natural monopolies normally have some technological or other justification. But there is none in the case of Gazprom for example. Nevertheless, they come under the Law on Natural Monopolies and the government and the Federal Antimonopoly Service (FAS) regulates the prices and tariffs of their goods and services with annual limits on the amount their prices can rise. But these limits are often higher than the inflation predicted for the year. The government justifies such inflationary practices by a desire to provide profitability to the natural monopolies and by the desire to find an alternative to taxation to secure revenue for the state budget. It also hopes to raise energy efficiency by seeing Russian prices on fuel and energy close to international prices. In the case of housing and utility services, the government hoped these can become self-financing.

Public-private partnerships are increasingly common around the world. These involve cooperation between the government and private business to execute significant projects. Some such partnerships already exist in Russia, primarily as a result of the privatization of companies in which the government does not take a majority shareholding. However, opinion is divided about public-private partnerships in Russia. Their supporters see them as a new wave of privatization in the country which, by virtue of being slow and under government control, will not have the negative impact seen in the accelerated privatizations of the 1990s. Opponents argue that the country lacks the detailed legislation or clear economic policy needed to make them effective.

The Strategic Challenges facing Russia

By identifying the main strategic challenges facing the country, we can define what is needed for the country to achieve successful long-term social and economic development. There are many such challenges:

- Modernization. Russia needs to elevate its economic and social development to the levels seen in advanced countries. In other words, it needs to catch up. This need was first identified over 300 years ago at the end of the 17th century and reasonable progress was made, especially in the hundred years up to 1970, despite wars and the social shocks of the 20th century. Across a range of areas and industries, such as science, education, and defense, a high level of development was reached. There was also noticeable progress in other areas: mining, metallurgy, chemical industries, and social insurance. But in others, Russia lags behind. The reforms that began in the late 1980s as the country was transformed from socialism to capitalism should have given a boost to modernization. Instead, they led to economic disaster in the 1990s which saw GDP fall by 44% and many solid advances that had been made were destroyed. The return to economic growth in the late 1990s helped to mitigate only some of the consequences of the disaster: previous levels of social and economic development were restored, while the situation in other industries and areas of the economy remains critical to this day (e.g., the demographic situation, science, banking sector, and civil engineering). If it is to be successful in catching up with the levels of development seen in developed countries, Russia now needs to modernize its economic model. Formed in the late 1990s and early 2000s, the current model is barely any more efficient than the former socialist model.
- The Eastern and Northern Territories. Russia's population and its economic activity are concentrated in the south and west of the country. By contrast, the centers of mining are found to the east of the Urals and to the north of Saint Petersburg. These vast regions are a source of both strength and weakness to Russia. The source of weakness lies in the fact that, for centuries, the country has had to divert significant funds from the development of traditionally habitable regions to develop the eastern and northern areas. This development has, however, largely ground to a halt as can be seen in the population statistics which show that these areas now account for a falling share of the country's population. As such, these huge and still underdeveloped regions, especially those bordering densely populated and highly developed Asian countries, have become a geopolitical weakness. On the other hand, the enormous natural resources found in these areas are what has made the country a great power and enabled it to overcome the economic disaster of the 1990s. In the future, intense development of these

areas may be an important impetus in the country's economic growth, involving large inflows of both capital and labor, as has been the case since the end of the 19th century.

- Demography. Any solution to the problems mentioned above, has to contend with the country's demographic crisis, brought about by the reduction in the country's population before the start of the current decade. Any hope of fast economic growth, let alone significant economic development of the east and north of the country and Siberia, requires an increasing supply of labor. To address the demographic crisis, the country needs to improve its mortality rates, and encourage a rise in the birth rate. There may also be scope to attract workers from former Soviet countries where there is a surplus of labor. But to attract them, the country will need good economic, social, political, and ethical conditions.
- Economic Reintegration. Russia needs to reintegrate its economy with those of the former Soviet countries. The importance of these countries to the Russian economy is demonstrated by the fact that, in 1990, goods exports from Russia to the former Soviet countries totaled \$145 bn (at 2015 world prices) and \$45 bn in 2015. Without closer integration with these countries, Russia cannot succeed in achieving economic growth, the development of its territory, nor can it address its demographic crisis.
- Democracy. The level of democracy in Russia is low by the standards of modern market economies. It even went into decline in the 2000s, damaging the country's international image. The strong dominance of the authorities over many aspects of business and society, with poor ethical standards, means that the authorities fail to work with the wider interests of the country at heart, but focus instead on personal interests and ideologies. In order to avoid the inevitable public discontent, the government seeks to control the media (especially television where the intellectual level of programming has declined as loyalty to the authorities has gone up), the electoral process (resulting in the remarkable success of 'United Russia'), and the activities of the opposition parties (the LDPR and 'Just Russia' parties). Weak standards of civil society allow the government, working with the oligarchs, to control the country. The solution to the weakness of democratic institutions is to strengthen civil society.
- Ethics. Ethical standards have been traditionally low in Russia. In the 1980s, the problem escalated into a full-blown crisis. The problem permeates all levels of society and acts as a drag on the

country's development, keeping it behind advanced countries, where standards are noticeably higher. Improvement will be a long and complicated process, but it is an issue that Russia cannot avoid.

Conclusion

1. The current Russian economic model is characterized by an interweaving of state and business (especially large businesses or oligarchies), with the government in charge. This type of state capitalism focuses less on using the mechanisms of government to modernize the country as operating in favour of the bureaucracy and those companies close to it.

2. Russia's social model is characterized by heavy stratification between income levels, the poverty endured by the majority of the population, and low life expectancy.

3. The poor level of democracy in Russia reflects more the traditional weaknesses in civil society. Despite the appearance of a functioning democracy, the system operates in favor of the narrow interests of the elite rather than those of the population as a whole.

4. The rapid change seen in public morality and ideas during periods of reform have resulted in a significant decline in social and ethical standards in Russia—and they were not that high to begin with. The country's ethical crisis is the main factor in the deterioration of economic, social, and political life.

5. Many of specificities of the business structure in Russia results from the way the current economic model operates. The rapid pace of privatization enabled many unsuitable people to take the reins of businesses. Certain features of the economic model also affect how people do business in Russia. For example, the state's dominance over the business world and the active role played by bureaucrats in day-to-day management of companies has created a peculiarly Russian business model which is marked by inefficiency.

6. The main problems faced by private businesses in Russia stem from shortcomings in the way the country's economy works: the inefficiency of the state bureaucracy, weak government support for small and medium business, government interference in companies, frequent changes in legislation, taxes and tax regulation, unfair

competition, the pressure of natural monopolies, inflation, and access to finance. There are also weaknesses in ethical standards in the form of corruption, crime, and embezzlement.

7. Russia has a low ranking for competition, although the position is now improving. Poor competition means rising prices. The county's policies to combat monopolies are ineffective, leaving a large number of monopolies (especially natural monopolies) and oligopolies to survive with their natural tendency toward cartelization and 'tacit collusion' at the consumer's expense.

8. Large companies, including those in the public sector, account for 40–45% of Russia's GDP. Medium-sized companies account for 35–40% of GDP. Most large companies and a number of medium ones as well for part of unified business groups. Small companies play only a small role in the economy, producing 10–15% of GDP.

9. The public sector in Russia shares some features with other countries, but also has some specific characteristics. Like many countries, it focuses on social issues such as social insurance, healthcare, education, housing, and utilities; science and culture; and on productive infrastructure in transport, communications, and electricity. The Russian public sector is unique in the strong presence if the mining sector, the processing industries, construction, and banking. In addition, the limits of the sector's role are left somewhat vague in that the government has majority, rather than 100% share holdings in certain companies. In other cases, the government holds a minority share, or a 'golden share' which gives the government a veto in strategic decisions.

10. Russia's strategic challenges are modernization, the development of the eastern and northern territories, the demographic crisis, reintegration with the former Soviet countries, and the poor levels of democracy and ethics.

Questions

1. Did the reforms of the 1990s produce any positive outcomes for Russia?

2. Why do Russian authorities dominate business and society?

3. In China, the authorities dominate business and society even more than in Russia, but China's economic results are better. Why?
4. Do ethics influence the economy? If so, provide evidence.
5. Specify the main barriers to doing business in Russia.
6. Why is competitiveness low in Russia?
7. What characteristics are specific to the Russian public sector?
8. Why is the small business sector underdeveloped in Russia?
9. Suggest additions to the strategic problems faced by Russia listed above.

Additional Sources of Information

The Oxford Handbook of the Russian Economy. Oxford University Press: 2013

Mau V., Russia in an Epoch of Turbulence. Crises and Lessons. Routledge: 2018

Russia in Figures. Short Statistics Digest. Moscow (www.gks.ru).

Economic Intelligence Unit (www.eiu.com)

Heritage Foundation. Index of Economic Freedom (www.heritage.org)

World Bank. World Development Indicators (www.worldbank.org)

World Bank. World Development Report (www.worldbank.org)

World Bank. Doing Business (www.worldbank.org)

World Economic Forum. Global Competitiveness Report (www.weforum.org)

www.gks.ru (the Federal State Statistics Service website)

CHAPTER 9

GROWTH RATES AND ECONOMIC PROPORTIONS

The Industrial Structure of the Economy

Analysis of trends in the shares of various industries in the Russian economy (see Table 2.9) suggests that over the last two decades the picture has, in some ways, been typical of industrial countries transitioning to a post-industrial position: for example, agriculture's share of GDP has fallen. However, Russia has not seen industry's share of GDP fall as might be expected in a post-industrial scenario. This can be explained by the remarkable rise in the mining industry, which has balanced the reduction in manufacturing. The rise in services, also typical of post-industrial economies, has been evident in Russia in trade, while other areas of services (other than financial) have remained largely the same. There has, however, been a sharp drop in the share of science and scientific services.

It should be noted, however, that the increase in trade may be due partly to the way mining (and oil) companies book their sales through affiliated trading companies to reduce their tax liability. Thus, allowing for these peculiarities, and including pipelines and other infrastructure, we can conclude that the sector's share of GDP is about 20%.

In general, it is perhaps wrong to describe the shift in Russia as being industrial to post-industrial. On the one hand, there has been a reduction in agriculture in the 1990s which has still not recovered. The same applies to other branches of industry, even mining and raw materials, fuel and energy. On the other hand, the mining industries have been substituted by traditional rather than obviously post-industrial services. In fact, Russia in an example of deindustrialization followed by a degradation of industry due to a decline in high-technology industries (especially engineering) and their substitution by traditional services, though there has still been fast growth in educations and telecommunications.

In the 2000s, as the country had begun to recover economically, the improvement in the industrial structure was hindered by an occurrence similar to the famous price bubble that affected Holland in the mid-20th century, known in economics as the 'Dutch Disease'. Exports of raw materials, which were rapidly rising in price, led to an increase in revenue flows much of which was spent on consumption and on keeping the exports of raw materials flowing. With the exception of education and telecommunications, little was spent on developing modern forms of economic activity. At the same time, agriculture and manufacturing only partially recovered the falls they had suffered during the crisis of the 1990s.

This has left the country in dire need of modernization in its industrial structure. It needs to end the emphasis on raw materials and seek not only to increase post-industrial production but also to rehabilitate those sectors that have seen a decline, e.g., agriculture and, especially, high-technology industries. In other words, Russia needs a new wave of industrialization, or a so-called neo-industrialization to follow its phase of post-industrialization.

It also needs to tackle its dependence on imports of goods that it is capable of making itself. This dependence has seen the country playing a backward and dependent role in the world economy, rather than that of a leader. This can be seen in the recent economic difficulties that saw the country's GDP fall by 8% in 2009 and still by 3% in 2015. Other BRICS countries have relied on their large internal markets supplied with domestically produced goods. For a large economy, Russia's internal market relies too heavily on imports. Thus, in the retail trade, stocks of imported goods in 1992 were 23%. This role to 54% in 1995, fell to 40% in 2000 but rose again to 45% in 2005 and was still at 44% in 2010. By 2016 it had fallen again to 38%. Russia does not need a significant increase in exports of raw materials as much as the development of the internal market oriented toward domestic production, particularly manufacturing.

Savings and Investment

Unlike during the Soviet period, in Russia today, gross capital formation (investment to gross capital formation and inventories) has declined relatively, falling below the level of gross savings.

Table 9.1 — Gross savings and gross capital formation in Russia, as a percentage of GDP

	1961	1971	1981	1989	1995	2001	2005	2010	2016
Gross savings	19.7	25.0	26.9	30.0	27.9	32.5	31.2	26.4	27.3
Gross capital formation	20.1	23.8	27.3	30.8	25.4	21.9	20.1	22.6	21.6
including gross fixed capital formation	16.0*	20.8*	24.9*	28.7*	21.3**	18.9**	17.7**	21.6**	19.2**

*Investment to fixed capital

**Including increment of valuables

Sources: Ponomarenko A.N. Retrospective national accounts of Russia: 1961–1990. Moscow, 2002, pp.149–150 (in Russian); National accounts of Russia in 2001–2008. Moscow, 2009, pp.21–23; National accounts of Russia in 2006–2013. Moscow, 2014, pp.23–25; Russia in Figures 2017. Moscow, 2017, p.187.

The reduction in the rate of gross capital formation cannot be attributed to a shortage of funds in Russia over the last quarter century. Up to the current decade, the rate of gross savings was high due to increasing demand and rising world prices for the raw materials that Russia was exporting. This also resulted in a systemically positive current account balance which contributes to the calculation of the gross savings. There were three reasons for the reduction in the rate of gross capital formation: the government's diversion of a significant part of the income earned from exports to various reserve funds; the excessive exports of private capital; and the shortage of credit for the bulk of companies.

The first of these reasons comes less from the government's economic modernization policy and more from the constant search of stable rent from abroad for the government and the oligarchs. A substantial part of export returns can be defined as rent as they result largely from the difference between the internal and export prices for Russian raw materials which are abundant. In order to maintain the state reserve funds (which comprised 13% of GDP in 2015), the government used export duties to sterilize substantial part of national income which could be used to modernize the economy.

The second reason reflects a unique characteristic of the Russian economy, namely the dominance of the bureaucracy and the oligarchs, which impedes effective allocation of capital. Some industries, as a result, enjoy excessive profits largely due to their being monopolies, while other have low profiles due to having insufficient fixed capital. Thus, in Russia in 2015, the profitability of goods sold was on average 9.3%; in chemicals it as 33%; mining 26.8%; metallurgy 22.4%; communications 21.4%; and in manufacturing of machinery and equipment 8.2%. This, combined with weak protection for property rights, creates an incentive for the Russian business community to export capital. In 2014, such exports were equivalent to 7% of GDP.

The third reason, shortage of credit, will be studied below.

A question arises: Does modern Russia need the same high rate of gross capital formation as the Soviet Russia of previous decades? The answer is likely to be positive, as countries that are trying to 'catch up' with more developed economies require more investment in capital assets to achieve faster economic growth. Moreover, in Russia, there is not only wear and tear of many fixed capital assets but also acute shortages of investment, especially in infrastructure, agriculture, and housing services (see Chapter

10). The gross capital formation rate should, therefore, be higher than it is at present, 20–23% of GDP. What's more, there is a high gross savings rate for that very purpose.

Regional Disparities

A strategic challenge for Russia is to develop its vast territories that are so far comparatively or completely underdeveloped economically. But this is made difficult by the slow rate of growth in the population. For this reason only the most acute problems are being addressed in these regions.

First, there is a polarization between the regions. Disparities between regions is a feature of larger countries, and Russia has some of the largest such disparities in the world. The differences are more evident when comparing large cities with rural areas, or with factory towns that are dominated by one or two large companies. Moreover, the differences are not reducing.

The regional disparities are the result of different rates of economic development in the regions. Those regions with significant exports, along with the regions around Moscow and Saint Petersburg are the most dynamic. The concentration of the finance sector in the two largest cities along with the wealth of innovation and administrative resources make their economic development sustainable. By contrast, the exporting regions are susceptible to fluctuations in the international prices of their exports. Regions such as the Urals, where there is a balance between exports of raw materials and manufacturing, coastal regions (e.g., Krasnodar), and regions of the interior (e.g., Volga) are less dynamic economically, but their human capital enable them to make a worthwhile contribution to the development and modernization of the economy. The less developed regions (primarily the Caucasus) rely heavily on federal subsidies, financed, of course, by earning from the exporting regions. For the republics of the Caucasus, development will require improvement in their institutions, better education, and an increase in the mobility of the population. These more isolated regions also suffer from poor communications with the rest of Russia, a problem felt most acutely in the Far East.

The government has a regional policy aimed at addressing some of these problems. In Russia today, these are based mainly on budgetary federalism (see Chapter 14) and regional federal target programs. In 2009, the government adopted the Strategy for the Social and Economic

Development of the Far East and Baikal Region. Its plans stretched out to 2025. The Strategy has various federal programs. For example, since 2015, 14 territories in the Far East have been earmarked for rapid development. In these, established companies are exempt from most taxes for their first five years of operation.

In this context, it should be noted that a previous policy of regional development based on special economic zones, a large number of which were created in the 1990s, failed to live up to its high expectations. The idea turned out to be premature and some of the territories chosen were too large. With the exception of Kaliningrad, they had little impact on economic development. A new law in 2005 re-designated these areas as 'Special Economic Zones' (SEZ) with the aim of focusing on smaller areas for development. The new zones received tax, customs, and other benefits. Various SEZs were set up. The law divides them into four categories:

- Innovation: zones focusing on innovative technology. Zones have been established in Moscow (the Zelenograd district), Dubna (in the Moscow region), Saint Petersburg (its two districts), Tomsk, and Tatarstan.
- Industrial: zones created with a focus on creating and developing modern industrial and manufacturing complexes. These have been set up in the Lipetsk Region, Tatarstan (Yelabuga), Tolyatti, in the Sverdlovsk Region ('Titanium Valley').
- Tourist: zones with a tourism and recreation focus. Thirteen have been established in Siberia, the Far East, Kaliningrad, and in the Northern Caucasus.
- Ports: established in Murmansk, Vladivostok and Sovetskaya Gavan in the Far East, and at Ulyanovsk Airport.

The 'Yantar' SEZ still exists, embracing the territory of the Kaliningrad region, and the SEZ under the new legislation has been set up at the 'Skolkovo' innovation center near Moscow.

Rates of Economic Growth and their Sustainability

In the nine years from 1990 to 1998, Russia's GDP fell (the only exception was 1997, when it rose by 0.7%). The overall decrease in GDP over the period was 44%. This compares with a fall of 42% from 1914 to 1922 and 21% from 1941 to 1945.[8]

Economic growth, which picked up again in 1999 has tended to a rate between 5 and 8%. By the start of the economic crisis in 2009, Russia had managed to double the size of its GDP, restoring it to pre-reform levels. Industrial production, however, has only reached 73% of its 1989 level.[9] Growth rates were held back again after 2009, leading to falls in GDP.

Table 9.2 — GDP growth rates in Russia, percentage

1992–2000	-4.0 (yearly average)
2001–2008	6.5 (yearly average)
2009	-7.8
2010	4.5
2011	4.3
2012	3.4
2013	1.3
2014	0.6
2015	-3.8
2016	-0.4
2017	1.6

Sources: Russian Statistical Yearbook for relevant years; http://www.gks.ru/wps/wcm/connect/rosstat_main/rosstat/ru/statistics/accounts/#

The dynamism of the Russian economy in the period after 1998 saw a per capita increase in GDP of 6.8% between 2001 and 2008. This was based on a number of circumstances:

- the heavy devaluation of the ruble during the Asian financial crisis (this hit Russia in mid-1998) gave a boost to economic growth over the following years on the basis of import substitution (see the figures quoted above on the share of retail stocks accounted for by imports);

[8] Sorokin D. Reproduction Vector of Russian Economy: 1999–2007 // Voprosy Economiki. 2008, No.4, p.94 (in Russian).

[9] Dzarasov S. Russian Crisis: Origins and Lessons. // Voprosy Economiki. 2009, No. 5, p.70 (in Russian).

- the significant improvement in the terms of foreign trade from the late 1990s onwards, mainly as a result of higher world market prices for key Russian exports, especially oil;
- greater availability of loan capital from global capital markets in the 2000s, enabling large and medium Russian businesses to plug holes left by shortage of credit, especially long-term, in the domestic market.

However, many of these effects proved to be only temporary. While the impact of a devaluation can last for several years, the benefit in this case for Russia had already evaporated by the beginning of the 2000. The impact of the fluctuation in prices for raw materials and the availability of foreign credit lasted a bit longer, but ran out thereafter.

Russia's economic growth can thus be seen to be unsustainable as it relies too heavily on a combination of factors in global commodity and capital markets. An important reason for this unsustainability is also the low level of gross capital formation, i.e., there is insufficient capital investment to support economic growth. The increased revenue flow in the country, caused by rises in the prices received for its raw material exports, was spent mostly on consumption and the creation of state reserve funds as well as on private capital outflow. A smaller amount was dedicated to investment growth.

Moreover, economic growth in Russia cannot be deemed to be 'qualitative', in that it is based largely on the growth of the raw material industries and it has led to a degradation of the structure of the economy, as described above.

It has, thus, been obvious for a while that the country needs to transit to a model of modernization that involves qualitative and sustainable economic growth. It needs to focus on innovation, human capital and investment as the basis for growth. However, for this to begin, the country's economic model needs to be modernized.

However, the Russian authorities have yet to take any practical steps toward achieving this. The main reason for the low rates of growth in the period following the last stagnation was the fall in 2014 and 2015 of world market prices on oil and other key Russian exports, along with the sharp reduction in capital inflows as a result of Western sanctions. All of this combined to turn low growth rates negative.

The global economy is currently transitioning into a state dubbed the 'new normal (new recession)', characterized by economic growth rates lower than in previous decades. This results in lower growth in global GDP, low prices for raw materials, and less investment by developed countries in economies with natural resources. The Dutch disease that gave Russia dynamic economic growth in the last decade also produced economic stagnation in this decade.

The Dutch disease proved to be a consequence of the inability of the Russian elite to use the high profits earned from exports of raw material to modernize the economy. The rent-seeking behavior of the bureaucracy and the oligarchs frustrated the possible structural modernization which could have supplied both internal and external markets with competitive manufactured goods and services.

We can identify two reasons for this rent-seeking behavior: ineffective democracy and poor ethical standards. The ineffective democracy makes it difficult for the business community and its customers to influence the economic policies put in place and pursued by the elite. The low ethical standards encourage people to focus on their own gain at the expense of the country's long-term interests.

Finally, we can repeat the conclusion drawn in Chapter 8 that, in order to find a way of the situation of low and unsustainable rates of economic growth, a process of active modernization that increases the role and importance of the small and medium business sectors and raises ethical standards across the board is needed. This means wholesale modernization of the country's economic, political, and ethical models.

Conclusion

1. The possible improvement in the industrial structure of the Russian economy is held back by the Dutch disease, a consequence of the increase in capital inflows to the country caused by the rapid increases in world market prices for the raw materials being exported. This revenue was spent mainly on consumption and on state reserves and private capital outflow. Little was spent on the development of a modern economy.
2. The growth in agricultural and industrial production in the 2000s only partially mitigated the falls of the 1990s. The country thus needs to modernize its industrial structure, lessening the domination of raw material exports and increasing post-industrial

production by rehabilitating agriculture and high-technology industries.

3. The increase in the rate of savings, at the expense of any growth in exports of raw materials, enabled the Soviet authorities to decrease the gross capital formation rate. Since the late 1990s, the gross saving rate has increased even more as a result of the growth in international commodity prices. But in Russia today, the rate of gross capital formation has fallen below the rate of the 1980s, resulting in savings exceeding investment. However, a country seeking to catch up with more developed economies needs more investment in capital assets to achieve faster economic growth. Moreover, in Russia there is not only high fixed capital wear and tear but also acute shortages of investment, especially in infrastructure, agriculture and housing services. The gross capital formation rate should, therefore, be higher than it is at present, 20–23% of GDP. What's more, there is a high gross savings rate for that very purpose.
4. The current low rates of economic growth in Russia require a reorganization of its economic model, based on a process of active modernization that increases the role and importance of the small and medium business sectors, an increase in civil activity and a raising of ethical standards across the board.

Questions

1. Explain the difference between the shifts in the Russian economy's industrial structure measured in current prices and the shifts measured in fixed prices.

2. How can the large difference between gross saving and gross capital formation in Russia be explained?

3. Why is economic growth characterized as unsustainable in Russia?

4. Do you agree with the reasons given in this Chapter for the low and unsustainable growth rates in modern Russia?

5. How would you implement economic modernization in Russia?

Sources of Additional Information

The Oxford Handbook of the Russian Economy. Oxford University Press: 2013

Mau V., Russia in an Epoch of Turbulence. Crises and Lessons. Routledge: 2018

Ponomarenko, A.N. Retrospective national accounts of Russia: 1961–1990. Moscow, 2002 (in Russian).

National Accounts of Russia in 2006–2013. Moscow, 2014.

Russian Statistical Yearbook. Statistics Digest. Moscow (www.gks.ru).

Russia in Figures. Short Statistics Digest. Moscow (www.gks.ru).

National Economy of the Russian Soviet Federated Socialist Republic in 1990. Moscow, 1991 (in Russian).

IMF. World Economic Outlook (www.imf.org).

CHAPTER 10

FIXED ASSETS AND INVESTMENTS

Fixed Capital Investments

The positive answer to the question posed in the previous chapter—does Russia need a high gross capital formation rate?—can be justified by analysis of investments in gross fixed capital formation (fixed capital investments). Table 4.1 shows that Russia lags behind other former Soviet countries in terms of these investments. In 2008, fixed capital investment (in comparable prices) was reckoned to be only 64% of its 1989 level.[10] In subsequent years this value has barely changed, it stood at 68% in 2014.

In general, this is a consequence of the country's existing economic model, with its large reserve funds and large capital outflow. In practice it can be seen as a constant shortage of financial resources in a country that exports oil and gas, a shortage felt most keenly in the financial sector, especially the banking system and the stock market.

As can be seen in Table 10.1, a role of bank credit, especially long-term credit, is to finance fixed capital investment, even if they grow but remain insignificant due to their high rates and inaccessibility. The stock market also plays only a small role as it remains underdeveloped. No more than 3–4% of capital investments were financed on the stock market, i.e., only a small portion of the funds under as 'other obtained funds' in the table. The government's role, while not unimportant, is also of less significance in investment finance.

This means that a typical Russian company has to rely largely on its own profits ('own funds' on the table) for its investment finance. They can also use loans from affiliated companies ('borrowed funds of other organizations'). Many Russian companies use this to justify a pursuit of

---

[10]Dzarasov S. Russian Crisis: Origins and Lessons.//Voprosy Economiki. 2009, No. 5, p.70 (in Russian)

profit at any price. However, even under these conditions, large investments are only possible in companies operating in the most profitable industries such as mining, metallurgy, chemicals, communications, wholesale trade, and house construction, though official statistics suggest that these last two areas are less commercially viable.

Table 10.1 — Fixed capital investments by sources of financing (percentage)

	1985	1995	2000*	2005*	2010*	2016
Fixed capital investments, total	100	100	100	100	100	100
own funds	12.0	49.0	47.5	44.5	41.0	51.8
obtained funds	88.0**	51.0	52.5	55.5	59.0	48.2
where:						
bank credits	…	…	2.9	8.1	9.0	10.5
incl. credits of foreign banks	…	…	0.6	1.0	2.3	2.9
borrowed funds of other organizations	…	…	7.2	5.9	6.1	5.4
budget funds	…	21.8	22.0	20.4	19.5	16.0
incl. federal budget	…	….	6.0	7.0	10.0	9.0
resources of non-budgetary funds	…	11.5	4.8	0.5	0.3	0.2
other obtained funds	…	…	15.6	20.6	24.1	17.6

*since 2000 – without small business entities

** government investments

Sources: PonomarenkoA.N. Retrospective National Accounts of Russia: 1961–1990. Moscow, 2002, p.226 (in Russian); Russia in Figures. Short Statistics Digest. Moscow, 2017, p.427.

The other reason for a lack of capital investment is connected to another weakness of the Russian economic model, insufficient protection of property rights. This makes private businesses wary of investment projects with long-term payback terms. Firms will rarely invest in projects of more than five years. When investing in medium-term projects, the focus is always on maximizing profitability.

Let us look at the industrial structure of fixed capital investments and changes that have happened in this area.

Table 10.2 — Fixed capital investment by economic activity (percentage)

	1995	2000	2005	2010	2016	*For reference:* **1985**
Fixed capital investments, total	100	100	100	100	100	100
… by economic activity:						
agriculture, forestry, hunting and fishing	3.9	3.2	4.0	3.4	4.3	Agriculture 14.6
mining and quarrying	14.2	18.1	13.9	13.8	19.4	Industry 37,8 (including mining of energy producing minerals; electricity 15.6, manufacturing of machinery and equipment 9.4)
of which: mining of energy producing minerals	13.0	16.7	12.4	12.7	17.9	
manufacturing	14.8	16.3	16.4	13.2	14.6	
of which: manufacture of chemical products; coke and refined petroleum products; rubber and plastics products	3.2	3.6	3.5	3.7	5.6	
manufacture of basic metals and fabricated metal products	2.6	3.1	3.8	2.3	2.3	
manufacture of machinery and equipment (without the production of weapons and ammunition)	0.7	0.8	0.9	0.7	0.7	
manufacture of electrical, electronic and optical equipment	0.7	0.6	0.5	0.4	0.6	
manufacture of transport equipment	1.6	1.4	0.9	1.1	1.4	
electricity, gas and water supply	7.6	6.0	6.8	9.0	6.4	

construction	4.5	6.4	3.5	3.7	3.0	Construction 3,6
wholesale and retail trade; repair of motor vehicles, motorcycles and personal and household goods	2.0	2.7	3.5	3.7	4.3	
hotels and restaurants	0.8	0.8	0.4	0.5	0.7	
transport and communications of which communications	12.6 1.4	21.2 2.7	24.5 5.4	25.5 2.6	18.6 2.6	Transport and communications 13.6
financial intermediation	2.5	0.8	1.4	1.3	1.6	Housing services 15.4
real estate, renting and business activities of which research and development	25.3 0.4	15.2 0.5	16.8 0.5	17.9 0.8	20.6 1.3	
public administration and defense, compulsory social security	3.2	1.5	1.7	1.4	1.9	Other services 14.9
education	1.8	1.3	1.9	1.8	1.4	
health and social work	2.5	2.6	2.6	2.1	1.2	
other community, social and personal activities	4.3	3.9	2.5	2.7	2.0	

Sources: Russia in Figures. Statistical Handbook. Moscow, 2017, pp. 430–433; National Economy of the Russian Soviet Federated Socialist Republic in 1990. Statistics Digest. Moscow, 1991, pp. 526–527 (in Russian).

A comparison of the structure of capital investment in 1985 and subsequent years shows a reduction in the share accounted for by industry (notably at the expense of the manufacture of machinery and equipment) and, especially, agriculture. The energy sector maintained its share, while transport and communications increased rapidly, mainly due to the construction of new pipelines, along with other services. This development of the structure of fixed capital investments facilitated Russia's deindustrialization and proved detrimental to the structural and physical condition of existing fixed assets.

Fixed Assets

The Russian economy performed poorly during the 1990s due to the low volume of fixed capital investment in almost all industries. Over the subsequent two decades, the situation improved. The rate of renovation of fixed assets picked up, though persistently low levels of investment meant it still fell short of the levels seen in the Soviet era. This low level of investment leaves companies operating with out-of-date equipment, while funds for renovation and maintenance are also cut. This combination of insufficient maintenance and disposal rates results in an increase in the rate of depreciation.

Table 10.3 — Renovation, disposal and depreciation rate of fixed assets, in percentage

	1990	1995	2000	2005	2010	2016
Renovation rate	6.3	1.9	1.8	3.0	3.7	3.7
Disposal rate	2.4	1.9	1.3	1.1	0.8	1.0
Depreciation rate	35.6	39.5	39.3	43.5	47.1	48.7

Sources: Russia in Figures. Statistical Handbook. Moscow, 2017, pp.65–68; National Economy of the Russian Soviet Federated Socialist Republic in 1990. Statistics Digest. Moscow, 1991, pp.314–316 (in Russian)

Across the entire economy, the aggregate indicator of the depreciation rate of fixed assets does not reflect the condition of assets in each area of economic activity. In a range of industries, the depreciation rate has improved in recent years (agriculture and forestry, electricity, gas and water supply), while in others it continues to grow (See Table 10.4).

In addition, we need to take into consideration the fact that the depreciation of fixed assets is something of a statistical notion in that it is determined according to the terms of depreciation and may still apply even if the operational condition of the assets is normal, especially if they have a full care and maintenance regime. Moreover, it is hard to manufacture up-to-date and competitive products on out-of-date machinery. It comes as no surprise that assets that are entirely obsolete (according to the terms of depreciation) are still found operating, most obviously in low-tech industries such as mining and quarrying. The shares of the entire assets in these two sectors that were obsolete were 22.9% and 18.8%, while the level for the whole economy in 2014 was 14.9%.

Table 10.4 — Fixed assets depreciation rate by type of economic activity (percentage)

	2005	2016
Fixed assets, total	43.5	48.7
agriculture and forestry	46.3	42.0
fishing	54.8	51.9
mining and quarrying	54.8	56.1
manufacturing	47.8	49.5
electricity, gas and water	55.6	46.1
construction	42.3	51.8
wholesale and retail trade; repair of motor vehicles, motorcycles and personal and household goods	40.9	40.7
hotels and restaurants	40.1	39.0
transport and communications	51.4	56.9
financial intermediation	37.8	43.1
real estate, renting and business activities	26.7	38.3
public administration and defense, compulsory social security	39.4	48.6
education	37.0	49.4
health and social work	45.2	56.9
other community, social and personal activities	42.9	42.3

Source: Russia in Figures. Statistical Handbook. Moscow, 2017, pp.68–69.

Conclusion

1. In 2014, the level of fixed capital investment was only 68% of its 1989 level.

2. This results from an economic policy which favors financial sustainability over economic growth, through the establishment of various reserves. The other important reason is an investment climate beset by the defects of Russia's social and economic model, in particular its weak banking system, all of which deters entrepreneurs, both foreign and domestic, from investing.

3. The level of fixed assets in Russia saw a weak recovery in the 1990s, due to the low volume of fixed capital investment in almost all industries. Replacement levels picked up in the subsequent years, though continued low disposal rates indicate a lack of new fixed assets.

Questions

1. Why is the level of investment in Russia less than it was a quarter of a century ago?
2. How has the structure of fixed assets in Russia changed over recent decades?
3. Describe briefly the situation with regard to fixed assets in Russia.

Sources of additional information

The Oxford Handbook of the Russian Economy. Oxford University Press: 2013

Mau V., Russia in an Epoch of Turbulence. Crises and Lessons. Routledge: 2018

PonomarenkoA.N. Retrospective National Accounts of Russia: 1961–1990. Moscow, 2002 (in Russian).

National Accounts of Russia in 2006–2015. Moscow, 2014.

Statistical Yearbook of Russia. Statistics Digest. Moscow (in Russian).

Russia in Figures. Statistical Handbook. Moscow.

National Economy of the Russian Soviet Federated Socialist Republic in 1990. Moscow, 1991 (in Russian).

IMF. World Economic Outlook (www.imf.org)

CHAPTER 11

HUMAN CAPITAL

During the 1990s, Russia saw high levels of immigration, but this did not prevent the population declining by up to 1 million people annually. This was due both to a sharp 50% rise in mortality and to a serious decline in the fertility rate which fell by one third in comparison with previous decades.

However, by the end of the 2000s and the beginning of the 2010s, the population was no longer declining. Those two factors, mortality and fertility, both improved, producing a small natural increase in the population, with the exception of 2017 when the mortality rate dropped to 12.4 but the birth rate also dropped to 11.5. A positive balance of migration also played a significant part. The reunification of Russia and Crimea also added 2.3 million to the population. At the end of 2017, the Russian population stood at 146.9 million, though this is still short of the level it reached during the Soviet era (148.5 million in 1990).

Table 11.1 — Demographic Indicators in Russia

	1990	1995	2000	2005	2010	2016
Population size, million people at year end	148.3	148.3	146.3	143.2	142.8	146.8
Natural increase/decline, million people	0.333	-0.840	-0.959	-0.847	-0.240	0.005
Births per 1000 people	13.4	9.3	8.7	10.2	12.5	12.9
Mortality per 1000 people	11.2	15.0	15.3	16.1	14.2	12.9
Positive migration balance, million people	0.164	0.502	0.214	0.157	0.158	0.262

Life expectancy at birth, years	69.2	64.6	65.3	65.3	68.9	72.0
…. men	63.8	58.3	59.0	58.9	63.1	66.6
…. women	74.3	71.7	72.2	72.4	74.9	77.2
Average annual population size, million people of working age	83.9	84.1	88.0	90.3	87.1	85.4*

*2015

Source: Russia in Figures. Statistical handbook. Moscow (for relevant years).

As can be seen from Table 11.1, the high mortality rate is a more significant problem than the low birth rate. The latter is, in fact, almost equal to the 1990 level and still higher than in other European countries. The high mortality rate comes about as a result of a range of harsh conditions faced by the population. According to a survey of the adult population conducted by the Federal State Statistics Service in the summer of 2008, around 72% of respondents said they felt ‘great’ or ‘very great’ anxiety and uncertainty about of their situation (though this is down from 95% in 1998), 45% estimated their level of wealth to be below the poverty line (sufficient resources for only life’s basics), 44% feared losing their jobs, and 27% felt lonely.

Social and economic stress can cause anemia, especially among men aged from 30 to 50 who form for most active part of the economy. Anemia is often the result of people neglecting their own health, leading to a higher risk of mortality from other chronic illnesses among this section of the population. In fact, this age group has an alarming rate of external causes of mortality such as transport injuries etc. which cause about 30% of all deaths. In this age group, 55% of the mortality is accounted for by cardiovascular diseases, the rate of which is between three and four times higher than in other European countries, reflecting the fact that barely 25% of this group are deemed to take good care of their health through diet, avoiding harmful substances, regular medical care.[11] Other common causes of death include: accidental poisoning (often from low-quality alcohol), suicide, murder, and car accidents.

[11] Survey by the Federal State Statistics Service, “Influence of behavioral factors on health status of population” (http://www.gks.ru/free_doc/2008/demo/zdr08.htm) (in Russian).

Migration

The decline in the population has been mitigated by a large influx of immigrants seeking permanent residency. Immigration peaked in 1994, when 1,456,000 people came to Russia. These were mainly ethnic Russians returning to the historical homeland. Although Russia was in a state of crisis at the time, many of the former Soviet countries that they were leaving were faring no better; some had experienced armed conflicts. The flow of immigration gradually decreased after the 1994 peak before picking up again in the 2000s. In 2016 it stood at a little under 600,000. The flow is now largely comprised of non-Russian natives of the former Soviet countries. Coupled with a reduction in emigration (300,000 emigrated from Russia in 2016, compared with 337,000 in 1994), net immigration is now positive in Russia. The government's immigration policy has focused on attracting Russian expatriates and qualified foreigners, including young graduates of Russian universities.

Short-term immigration for work has little impact on the overall population statistics, but it is felt very significantly in the labor market. Russia has become one of the biggest destinations in the world for those seeking temporary work; it welcomes up to 12 million people a year. A formal system to attract foreign workers is in operation. It offers temporary visas to those who have an employer to work for as well as work permits for those temporary migrants with no employer invitation. The migrants have to pay for the visa and permits. However, four-fifths of them are citizens of former Soviet countries, mostly from Central Asia, with which Russia has a regime allowing visa-free travel and they have the right to stay in Russia for 90 days without a visa. Citizens of countries in the Eurasian Economic Union are not restricted by this system and are able to work legally in Russia.

The most popular destination for labor immigrants is the construction industry and trade, which together account for 60% of immigrant workers. These sectors lack low-skilled employees for the low-income jobs. In addition to low skill levels, immigrants struggle to adapt culturally to their new location. However, thanks to a measure of shared cultural heritage between Russia and the former Soviet countries, this problem is not as acute as it is in Western Europe.

Estimates for the number of temporary immigrants that are working illegally vary from one to two million. By hiring illegal workers, employers can avoid expensive paperwork, but this lack of formal records makes it hard to estimate the numbers. Some illegal immigrants settle permanently in Russia.

It is estimated that between 10% and 15% of the economically active population in Russia is made up of immigrants with permanent residency and temporary immigrant workers (including settled illegal immigrants). For the foreseeable future, Russia will continue to attract several hundred thousand people each year for permanent residence and a few million for temporary work.

Internal migration in Russia, that is, people moving within the country, is less significant. However, it is still as important a factor in economic development as immigration since labor mobility—along with knowledge, capital, and entrepreneurship—provides the flow or allocation of economic resources to their most useful purpose. Although the extent of internal migration has more than halved in recent decades (from 4.2m to 1.9m people seeking a new place of residence), it is now increasing again, both for people moving within a single region and those moving to a new region. The North Caucasus, Volga, the Urals, Siberia, and the Far Eastern Federal Districts have a negative balance of internal migration, while the South and the North West, especially the Central Federal Districts around Moscow and Saint Petersburg, have a net positive balance. However, despite internal migration being on the increase again, there are still pockets of high unemployment in some regions and a shortage of labor in others.

The Economically Active Population

Despite the fall in the general population up to the end of the last decade, over the past two decades the population of working age has increased. The decline in the fertility rate meant that the size of the population under working age decreased—by 11.3 million between 1989 and 2014—while the increase in mortality saw the share of the population accounted for by people over working age increased only slowly, by 6.6 million over the same period. So, the number of working-age people increased as did their proportion of the overall population. However, by the end of the first decade of the 21st century, the effect of the low fertility of previous years was starting to be felt and the working-age population has started to decline (from 88.9 million in 2002 to 84.2 million in 2016), a trend that is likely to continue.

The impact of these trends can be seen in the country's economic development. The economically active population grew from 71 million in 1995 to 76 million in 2008. However, since 2009, there has been no significant increase in this section of the population; by 2016 it had risen to just 76.5 million. The resulting shortage of workers, which had been noticeable since the early 21st century, is now becoming one of the main barriers to economic development. Employment growth provides almost one third of the growth in Russia's GDP. There are a number of solutions to this problem:

- Raise the pension age and increase incentives for pensioners to work. However, low life expectancy will limit the effectiveness of this measure.
- Increase internal migration. This may be effective only in the long term in view of significant differences in living standards between the regions.
- More active promotion of immigration. However, labor resources in the former Soviet countries are not endless, and these countries may wish to encourage their own people to stay. Moreover, most of those likely to want to come to Russia, those from the former Soviet countries in central Asia lack qualifications and struggle with cultural adaptation. Russia is unlikely to be able to attract many people from the European Union, and it is difficult to attract people from Asian neighbors that are not former Soviet countries. So while increasing immigration is an obvious solution to the problem, it is likely that it will only be partially effective.
- Increasing productivity so that each worker makes a greater contribution to the country's economic development. This requires economic modernization. This is likely to prove to be the most effective solution to the problem in the future.

A key factor in boosting productivity is education and training, and here the signs are good for Russia. In 2015, about 71% of employees had higher or secondary professional qualifications. This had been rising from 48% in 1992 and 50% in 2000. As well as academic qualifications, experience and training are also important if employees are to improve their productivity, as are their health and ambition. However, a lack of competitive spirit coupled with poor management in the majority of companies means that workers are unable to put their experience and training to its most effective use. The decline in the system of training and other forms of personnel development hinders improvement of skills. On the global index of personnel training, Russia ranks 89th. Poor health is also a factor that impedes the efficiency of workers.

The distribution of employment by sector shows a constant movement of employment to the services sector. This sector already accounts for 73% of overall employment. This shift can be attributed largely to trade and the hospitality sector (hotels and restaurants) which employ 21% of workers, as well as to public administration, defense and social security which accounts for 5.5%. In post-industrial services industries such as transport and communication, medical care, education, research and development, employment has not grown or is, in fact, falling. One exception to this is financial intermediation.

The sectoral distribution also reveals large disparities between the contribution that certain industries make to GDP and their share of employment. Mining and quarrying is a prime example. It accounts for just 1.6% of employment but contributes 9.8% of GDP. For agriculture, forestry, hunting and fishing the balance is the other way: this sector takes up 9.2% of employment but only contributes 4.4 of GDP. The same figures for education are 8.1 and 2.6% and for health and social work, they are 6.6 and 4.1%. At first glance, such disparities suggest very high productivity in the mining sector, with low productivity elsewhere. But care is needed in drawing inferences here. About half of the mining sector's production is calculated at price levels close to those on world markets. The same does not apply to other industries which gives the appearance of much lower output per worker. In the case of agriculture, the low contribution to GDP despite its high share of employment reflects not so much low prices for its goods, but the low level of technology in this industry.

Unemployment

In Russia in recent years, average unemployment, calculated according to the methodology of the International Labor Organization, ranged from 8.3% in 2009 to 5.2% in 2014. At the end of 2017, it was 5.1% or 3.9 million people, including less than 1 million registered with employment bureaux.

It is noteworthy that unemployment did not fall below 5% even during the years of high rates of growth. In fact, it remained consistently high in more backward regions with higher birth rates. In 2016, for example, it was more than 20% in Ingushetia, and over 10% in Dagestan, Kabardino-

Balkaria and Karachay-Cherkessia (republics in the Caucasus), Altai and Tyva (republics in Siberia), as well as in the Zabaykalsky Territory. In times of crisis, those cities which depend on one or two large enterprises also saw high rates. The situation is exacerbated by poor labor mobility. In the Caucasian republics cited above, during the Soviet ear, many workers left these areas to find work elsewhere in agriculture or construction.

The transition from economic growth to the crisis seen in recent years also revealed another key feature of unemployment in Russia, namely that it has low elasticity to economic shocks. During the crisis, growth in unemployment was slowed by major reductions in salaries, the imposition of part-time work, and the withdrawal of paid leave. Difficulties in registering as unemployed or partially employed to receive unemployment benefit (which is equivalent to the minimum living wage) saw many Russian employees forced to accept staying in work despite major pay cuts. This approach suits employers. They are under pressure from the authorities to try and avoid mass lay-offs and keeping staff nominally on the books gives them a pool of labor for expansion in the future. The other side of this coin is that during the economic recovery, the impression is given that unemployment is not falling as fast as one might expect. Instead, there is a marked reduction in part-time work.

The Labor Market

In addition to the prevalence of part-time work, especially during times of economic difficulty, low internal labor mobility, and the large number of job-seeking immigrants, the Russian labor market has a number of specific characteristics.

There is wide disparity in salary levels, both between different industries, and between workers and management. In 2017, the mid-year average annual salary across all industries was ₽ 39,085; in agriculture it was 60% of that size; in education, 77%; in health and social work, 82%; in machinery and equipment manufacturing, 96%; in the metals industry, 12%; in the oil and gas industry, 260% ; and in finance and insurance, 210%. In private limited companies, once bonuses and other benefits are included, the senior management is paid between 200 and 400 times as much as their frontline staff. (In continental Western Europe and Japan, the gap was 10 times; in the USA, about 300 times.) This disparity in private companies has an influence on levels of pay in state-owned corporations, companies and in the upper echelons of the bureaucracy.

Another significant factor in the market is the widespread use of shadow or hidden payments for work and other sources of income. In 2017, the Federal State Statistics Service estimates that compensation of employees and other sources of income not observed by direct statistical methods accounted for 25% of all compensation of employees. This applies equally to legal employees who receive 'under-the-table' payments to supplement their officially declared salary and to illegal or non-registered employees, especially illegal immigrants. Employers go along with this practice out of a desire to avoid compulsory expenditure on social services for their employees. This phenomenon is particularly prevalent in the construction industry and in trade, both sectors being susceptible to fluctuations in consumer demand. It should be noted that Russian official statistics only estimate payments to self-employed workers. In other words, the incomes of freelancers and individual businesses are not covered by direct statistical methods.

The Scale of Research and Development (R&D) Activity

After many years of decline, the number of employees in Russia engaged in R&D has started to increase. In 1992, the number stood at 1,533,000. By 2000 it had fallen to 888,000. By 2010, it was at 737,000; and in 2013, 727,000 (including 369,000 researchers). By 2015, it had increased slightly to 739,000 (including 379,000 researchers). Despite this decline, Russia has maintained a leading place in world in terms of the number of researchers at work. The country has 5–6% of all researchers in the world, behind only the USA, China, and Japan.

The productivity of Russian science has been low, though it is now improving. Only 2.5% of the publications in academic journals indexed by Scopus included Russian research, less than the share of Canada and Australia. The number of patents granted to Russian applicants is now increasing slowly.

This is largely the result of the sharp reduction in the finance available for R&D during the 1990s. Funding began to increase again in the 2000s. In 1990, the USSR spent about 3.5% of its GDP on science (including military research). By contrast, in 1992, the Russian Federation spent 0.7%; in 1995, it spent 0.9%; in 2000; and around 1.1% in this decade. The statistics for the Russian Federation only include expenditure on civil science and so are much lower than the figure for the USSR. However, spending is still way behind other countries that are the leaders in scientific research: the USA spends 2.7% of GDP on R&D; Japan, 3.6%; German, 2.9%; and China, 2.0%.

From this we can see that available labor force in Russian science (reduced but still significant) faces severe cuts in expenditure on science. In 2015, in terms of purchasing power parity, only about 2% of world expenditure on R&D took place in Russia. Russia's expenditure was $40 bn; the UK spent $44 bn; France, $59 bn; South Korea, $72 bn; Germany, $109 bn; Japan, $167 bn; China, $369 bn; and the USA, $457 bn. Russia also faces the problem of low salaries in science; in 2015, the average salary for someone in a scientific field was 123% of the national average earnings. The poor quality of technical equipment is also a problem; in fixed prices, the volume of scientific equipment in 1995 was ₽51,000 per researcher; in 2000 it was ₽31,000; in 2010, ₽45,000; and in 2015, ₽67,000.[12]

The government dominates R&D spending, providing 69.5% of the total in 2015. The decline in spending is, therefore, largely due to the government's cuts in its own science budget. Hopes that the private sector would involve itself actively in this area have not been realized. With little competition in the domestic market and with the monopolies and oligarchs that dominate the market able to find opportunities for profit elsewhere, the private sector in Russia has had little incentive to engage in R&D.

A final reason is that the country's relatively open economy makes it possible for firms to import advance technologies from overseas, rather than try to develop them. Some Russian economists believe that, given the lack of domestic versions of many of the 'breakthrough' technologies used around the world (the hypothesis of the innovation pause related to Kondratiev's 'long waves'), it is more rational to rely on importing technology than to seek to create analogues.[13] This idea is supported by the fact that, in the Soviet era, many of the 'inventions' produced by the country's R&D were little more than copies of something that already existed in the West. In modern Russia, only about 12% of advanced manufacturing is of entirely new technologies created in Russia. As a result, the country has always had a negative trade balance for high-technology goods. In 2015, the value of high-tech exports was $1.7 bn,

---

[12] Indicators of science. Statistics digest. Moscow, 2017 (in Russian) https://www.hse.ru/data/2017/02/07/1167425345/%D0%98%D0%BD%D0%B4%D0%B8%D0%BA%D0%B0%D1%82%D0%BE%D1%80%D1%8B%20%D0%BD%D0%B0%D1%83%D0%BA%D0%B8%202017.pdf

[13] See, for example: Polterovich V. The Hypothesis of Innovation Pause and Modernization Strategy// Voprosy Economiki. 2009, no.6 (in Russian).

compared to $2.2 bn of imports. However, for a large economy like Russia, it is difficult to develop without a powerful domestic scientific sector with a strong focus on R&D, at least in some areas if not in all.

The Innovation Process in Russia

Russia faces difficulties in seeking to stimulate innovation-based development. In 1995, 4.7% of the total output of goods and services were products that had undergone technological changes in the previous three years. In 2010, the figure was 4.8%; in 2015, 8.8%. In 2012, the figure for Poland was 8%; for the USA, 14.3%; and for Germany, 15.5%.

New products can take years to develop and bring to market, so not every company can be expected to launch something new every three years. So the proportion of companies implementing technological innovation differs from the statistics above. In 1995 it was 5.5%; in 2000, 9.3%; and in 2014, 12.2%. This is lower than in countries with similar levels of development. Of course, the Russian statistics are distorted by the large number of fly-by-night companies and the statistics on innovation which we assume to be incomplete.

Nevertheless, even allowing for these issues, the statistics quoted above point to Russian companies failing to invest sufficiently in innovation. There are several reasons for this. Firstly, low competition in the Russian markets provides little incentive for Russian companies to develop new technologies; it is easier simply to import. Secondly, the country's weak financial system fails to provide the investment needed to stimulate R&D activity. Thirdly, the mining and quarrying, and heavy metal industries play a major part in the economy and these are sectors less reliant on innovation and new technology.

As a result, during the economic recovery of the last decade, Russian companies relied less on innovation than on increasing the use of their existing resources, and thus failed to increase production significantly. However, in recent years, the competitive atmosphere has been improving, and companies have exhausted the scope for extracting further benefit from existing resources. This has brought about a slightly greater focus on innovation.

To address this, the government has sought to deploy money from the national budget, creating a system to encourage greater R&D under the patronage of the state. This system is based on the public corporation,

'Rosnano', the public 'Russian Venture Company', and the 'Russian Investment Fund for Information and Communication Technologies (Rosinfocominvest)'. The first of these selects and finances projects for the development of nanotechnologies; the second handles the organization and financing of different venture funds (which, in turn, finance innovation projects on a competitive basis) and the selection of management companies for these funds; and the third provides financial support for companies operating in Information and Communication Technologies (ICT). In addition, there is the Development Bank of Russia, the Fund for the Promotion of the Development of Small Businesses in the Sphere of Science and Technology, and the Russian Technological Development Fund. Finally, the country has set up special economic zones, some of which (the technology innovation zones – see Chapter 9) aim to support the innovation process, and the Skolkovo region near Moscow.

Education

At the start of the current decade, Russia spent 4.7% of GDP on education, including 4.0% from the state budget. However, an estimate for the hidden services might suggest that this overall expenditure was 0.5% higher.

For many years, Russia has scored well in terms of the proportion of the population that has attended secondary school. However, the quality of this education remains a challenge. According to the results of periodic surveys conducted by the Program for International Student Assessment, Russian secondary schoolchildren achieve results below the average of developed countries.

In vocational education, at the secondary but especially at the elementary level, there is an acute shortage of skilled workers. Poor education in this area has resulted in shortages of qualified workers during years of economic growth.

The number of students in higher education has increased. Young people, and their parents, responded to the years of social and economic upheaval by focusing more on education. The numbers entering higher education reached almost three times what it had been in the 1980s. The number of universities doubled, mainly due to an influx of private institutions. As a result, Russia is now among the leading nations in terms of the number of students in post-secondary education and the number of students per 10,000 people in the population.

However, the quality of the higher education on offer is patchy. Only a small number of Russian universities are included in world rankings. Moreover, in the higher education sector, there is a significant amount of 'pseudo education', where deliberately lax standards are allowed to persist. As a result, out of 300,000 graduates with a degree in Economics or Management, estimates as to how many can be considered genuine specialists range from 15,000 to 35,000. Among graduates in law, only about 15% are reckoned to be genuinely skilled.[14] The government is now focusing on attempts to improve the quality of higher education and to increase the research capacity of universities. To do this it is strengthening state support for two groups of universities: federal universities (one in each of seven federal districts) and national research universities of which there are 12. The government is also considering stricter criteria for the certification of universities.

Information Resources

Like other countries with a medium level of development, Russia is not far behind more developed countries in terms of the saturation of traditional information resources such as television, radio, newspapers, land-line telephony. It is also not far behind in terms of Internet resources. In 2015, 73% of Russian households had access to the Internet, which is higher than Poland (68%) and Italy (66%) and not far behind the USA (75%).

Expenditure by Russian companies on ICT is growing relatively fast. The ICT sector itself is also growing. However, its share of GDP and employment—0.7% for each—is lower than in most developed countries.[15]

Conclusion

1. During the 1990s, Russia saw high levels of immigration but this did not prevent a huge decline in the population, due to a sharp increase in mortality and a decline in fertility. However, the trends in both mortality and fertility have improved and, coupled with a large net positive level of immigration, the population is once again increasing.

---

[14] Kuzminov Y., Mau V., and Sinelnikov-Murylev S. The Country where there are very many Bad Universities// Expert. September 28–October 4, 2009, no.37, pp.72 (in Russian).

[15] Indicators of information society. Moscow, 2016, pp. 272–273 (in Russian).

2. In Russia, the mortality rates continue to be high by international standards; the fertility rate, while low, is almost equal to its level in the Soviet era and higher than in most European countries. Harsh conditions which have persisted after the end of the economic crisis of the 1990s partially explain the high mortality rate.

3. The influx of immigrants seeking permanent residence has significantly boosted the size of the population. Temporary immigrants coming for work have a major impact on the labor market, but are less important to the overall size of the population. Russia has become one of the major destinations for temporary migrant labor, welcoming 10–12 million workers a year. Migrants looking for permanent residence, combined with those who are temporary (including illegal immigrants) make up about 10–15% of the workforce. Internal migration within the country is less significant.

4. The absolute number of people of working age grew steadily for many years. However, by the end of the first decade of the 21st century, the effect of the low fertility of previous years was starting to be felt and the working-age population has started to decline, a trend that is likely to continue according to the Federal State Statistics Service. This lack of workers is becoming one of the most important barriers to the country's economic development.

5. Unemployment did not fall below 5% even during the years of high rates of growth (by world standards). This is an indication of its structural nature. It remained consistently high in more backward regions with higher birth rates. In times of crisis, those cities which depend on one or two large enterprises also saw high rates. Another key feature of unemployment in Russia is that it is highly elastic to economic shocks. During crises, growth in unemployment was slowed by major reductions in salaries, the imposition of part-time work, and the withdrawal of paid leave.

6. Though it has reduced in recent decades by cutbacks, the workforce dedicated to science remains large. The government dominates R&D spending and the decline in spending is, therefore, largely due to the government's cuts in its own science budget. Hopes that the private sector would involve itself actively in this area have not been realized.

7. Russia faces difficulties in seeking to stimulate innovation-based development. Firstly, this reflects low competition in the Russian

market which provides little incentive for Russian companies to develop new technologies; it is easier simply to import. Secondly, the country's weak financial system fails to provide the investment needed to stimulate R&D activity. Thirdly, there is insufficient state support of both science and innovation.

8. For many years, Russia has scored well in terms of the proportion of the population that has attended secondary school. However, the quality of this education remains a challenge. In vocational education, at the secondary but especially at the elementary level, there is an acute shortage of skilled workers. Poor education in this area has resulted in shortages of qualified workers during years of economic growth. The number of students in higher education has increased. As a result, Russia is now among the leading nations in terms of the number of students in post-secondary education and the number of students per 10,000 people in the population.

9. Russia is not far behind more developed countries in terms of the saturation of traditional information resources such as television, radio, newspapers, land-line telephony. It is also not far behind in terms of Information and Communications Technologies.

Questions

1. Why did Russian society, and especially its men, suffer from anomie?
2. How well do temporary migrants adapt to Russian society? Think of those where you live.
3. What are the specific features of unemployment in Russia?
4. Explain the large gap between the remuneration of senior managers and frontline staff in Russian companies.
5. Why is the process of innovation slow in Russia?

Sources of additional information

The Oxford Handbook of the Russian Economy. Oxford University Press: 2013

Mau V., Russia in an Epoch of Turbulence. Crises and Lessons. Routledge: 2018

Indicators of Science: 2015. Statistics Digest. Moscow, 2017 (in Russian).
Indicators of Innovation Activity: 2014. Statistics Digest. Moscow, 2016 (in Russian).
Indicators of Information Society: 2015. Statistics Digest. Moscow, 2016 (in Russian).
Russia in Figures. Statistical Handbook. Moscow (for relevant years).
UNDP. Human Development Report. N.Y.

CHAPTER 12

ECONOMIC POLICY

The Evolution of Economic Policy in Russia

Looking back at the history of economic policy of Russia after the demise of the Soviet Union, we can identify three distinct stages:

- the first half of the 1990s;
- the second half of the 1990s and the beginning of the 2000s; and
- the period since.

In the first half of the 1990s, the government undertook a process of systemic reforms while pursuing aims such as the provision of minimal social and economic stability. Under the conditions created by the economic disaster that had started in the USSR in the late 1980s, it was unrealistic to expect too much from government policy in terms of public welfare. The priorities had to be: to ensure the supply of critical imports that were necessary for the country; to secure credit and assistance from abroad as the domestic production of many life-critical goods and services had been declining in the late 1980s and the reserves of currency necessary to buy them were running low; and to tackle the hyperinflation and ensure the minimal required functioning of the financial system, the infrastructure and the social sector.

The systemic reforms had the dual purpose of transforming the economy from a socialist model to a capitalist one. Early steps in this process were the ending of state economic planning, with the cancelation of the five-year and annual plans, the introduction of free pricing, the privatization of state property, and the adoption of legislation aimed at creating a market economy. However, implementation was inconsistent and the country will be living with some of the consequences for decades to come. Many of the systemic reforms were enacted rapidly—in a kind of shock therapy—and were focused on the interests of narrow groups. Mistakes were made. The overly rapid process of privatization led to a radical redistribution of wealth (between 1992 and 1995 the Gini index increased by a half) and the emergence of a large number of inefficient owners who were able to obtain property at nominal prices. The belief was that rapid economic recovery would be achieved by creating in the shortest possible time a layer of new entrepreneurs. At the beginning of 1992, a one-off price deregulation was enacted despite there being shortages of certain goods and services. In a highly monopolized economy, this led inevitably to rapid inflation. Consumer prices jumped by 1,600% in that year and it took many years for inflation to be brought under control. Up to now, in Russia, deflationary policies have been based on curbing monetary growth. But this has ruined many Russian industries by creating shortages of credit for enterprises. At the same time, the fall in income experienced by most of the population saw a drop in demand.

In the late 1990s and early 2000s, as the country recovered from the economic disaster, the government was able to return to all three of its core aims. A greater emphasis was again placed on public welfare (the minimum incomes of both workers and pensioners were raised), levels of economic and social stability were improved significantly (inflation fell sharply, the state budget went from deficit to surplus and external debt began to fall). Economic reforms continued, but shock therapy was a thing of the past.

However, with the Soviet legacy of a highly monopolized economy, the rapid privatization of many enterprises coupled with state support for large businesses (and indifference to small enterprises) led to the formation of a system of oligarchic capitalism. This is characterized by the concentration of the assets of large, and some medium enterprises into the hands of a few individuals or oligarchs. Economic policy began to focus more and more on the narrow interests of these individuals and their business groups. In modern developed countries, by contrast, ownership of the assets of large business groups and their holdings is spread more widely.

In the first half of the 2000s, the government began to tighten its grip over the oligarchs and then to interweave with it. Its influence also stretched down to medium and smaller companies. The result was a missed opportunity to create a democratic version of capitalism as found in developed countries characterized by the dominance of minority owners in medium and especially larger organizations. Instead, a uniquely Russian version of capitalism emerged between the mid-1990s and the early 2000s, which was dominated by the oligarchs operating hand-in-glove with the government. This version of state capitalism determines many of the features of modern economic policy in Russia.

State Intervention in the Economy

State intervention in the economy is more extensive in Russia than in countries of a similar level of development. An important reason for this—though not the principal one—is the size of the state budget and the extent of state property. In relation to GDP, the revenues of the consolidated budget, at 35–40%, are large, but no more so that in countries at a similar level of development. State property ownership is also high at 23–30% of fixed assets (since mid-1990s) but is still far behind the private sector.

The increased level of state intervention in the Russian economy can be explained by another reason, namely the extent to which the machinery of state can work in alliance with the private sector (politically and economically dependent on government not least through government minority shareholdings) under its control to pursue economic policies in its own interests rather than in the interests of the nation as a whole. Economic theory called this 'seizure of power' (also referred to as 'state capture,' 'state seizure,' or 'state capture'). This describes the implementation of economic policy primarily (though not exclusively) in the interests of a narrow group which used the administrative resources for this purpose and profits as a result. In correct terminology, this is called a non-purpose use of institutions, manipulating them to simulate legitimacy despite the fact that they are being subordinated to the interests of a narrow group who are profiting from the arrangement, and that they are being used as a cover for illegal activities and the exploitation of information asymmetries. The impression given to the outside world is of very weak institutions.

Evidence for this idea can be found in the way all three of the main aims of economic policy have been implemented over the last two decades (seen in the context of the theory of economic policy). The growth in prosperity was concentrated on the upper quintile of the population, indeed many in the upper quintile saw their wealth increase even during the years of economic crisis. For many in the country, living standards were not better than they had been under the USSR. The government eventually managed to achieve a measure of social and economic stability but only after a decade of painful systemic reforms. Moreover, success was due more to the huge inflow of petrodollars and the consequent ability to establish huge reserves than to any technical modernization of the economy. Extensive systemic reforms were conducted and Russia laid the foundations of a market economy, but less on the basis of small and medium businesses or the recovery of knowledge-intensive industries, and more on the simpler but high profitable industries which were under the control of the state and the large businesses connected with it.

Statistical evidence for this can be found in the quarterly surveys conducted since 1992 by the Institute of World Economy and International Relations of the Russian Academy of Sciences and published in its 'Russian Economic Barometer Bulletin'. The proportion of CEOs of Russian industrial enterprises that approved of the government's economic policies has never exceeded 22%.

As it is pursuing policies which often do little for the wider interests of the nation, the ruling elite has little interest in transparency. The weak democracy (not far short of authoritarianism) creates uncertainty about the country's economic policy. Uncertainty and poor transparency are thus another important feature of modern economic policy in Russia. As a result, a high proportion of Russian entrepreneurs claim not to understand the government's economic policy. According to the Russian Economic Barometer Bulletin, the proportion of directors of industrial enterprises who understood economic policy has never been more that 53%, and of those who approve of it, never more than 47%.

At the same time, there are signs that the state–oligarchic nature of the economy is weakening. This can be seen in attempts to promote knowledge-intensive industries through government-financed systems of innovation, reduced taxation on small businesses since 2000, raising pensions to be in line with the living minimum wage, and the strengthening of economic programming and forecasting.

However, real economic progress will require solutions to two key problems: corruption and the poor level of protection of property rights. Only with real progress on these two the economy will have any chance of developing along with lines of other countries that practice a form of state capitalism, such as Japan, South Korea and others. Chances of oligarchic or democratic capitalism are lower as the level of maturity in Russian civil society is too high to be compatible with an oligarchic capitalism, but it is not high enough for democratic capitalism.

Instruments of Economic Policy

Almost all of the classical instruments of economic policy can be seen at work in Russia. However, there are aspects of how instruments are selected and used that are unique to Russia and which reflect the state–oligarchic nature of Russian economic policy.

This is marked by a preference for administrative (permits, prohibitions, norms, standards, and other acts of documentation from executive departments) over legal (laws adopted by the Federal Assembly). This phenomenon can be explained by the fact that while legal instruments determine the long-term and quite liberal 'rules of the game', the administrative instruments allow the state machinery to control Russian businesses according to rules that are changed frequently and involve extensive corruption. Legal instruments give the Russian economy a liberal face, while the administrative instruments produce its bureaucratic, 'seamy' side, characterized by a high 'administrative burden' for local businesses, often referred to in Russia as 'administrative barriers.' Let us turn our attention to the shortage of legal bills with a focus on the protection of properly rights and serious prosecution of corruption.

The Russian government makes active use of various economic instruments such as fiscal, monetary and external in its management of the economy. The scale of the use of such instruments in Russia is indicative of a market economy. But the way they are deployed reflects the state-oligarchic nature of the economy specific to Russia, with its tendency to stagnation rather than modernization. Thus, fiscal policy, for example, aims not to encourage economic growth, but rather to improve state reserves. On the one hand, this provides protection from fluctuations in world prices of the commodities that the country exports and which might threaten the part of the economy based on raw materials. On the other hand, it is a way of 'sterilizing' excessive money supply in the economy and thus depressing growth. It is also noteworthy that the state exercises only weak control over the monetary and credit sectors, which are precisely the favored areas of activity for the oligarchs and rich state officials. In the area of external economic policy, there is no active use of economic instruments to support the export of finished goods. However, in the early 2000s restrictions on the export of capital were lifted. This can be described as a pro-oligarch move.

Corruption plays a significant role in the functioning of economic policy. Government procurement is a prime example. It accounts for more than 10% of GDP. Estimates suggest that collusion between government officials and businessmen leads to the diversion of between 15 and 20% of the total volume of government purchasing each year. The need to pay bribes to officials pushes procurement costs up.

The Principal Directions of Economic Policy

As in most countries, Russian economic policy is dominated by financial policy considerations, that is, the government's regulation of the fiscal, monetary, and currency operations. External economic and social policies are also active areas for the government. Less attention tends to be paid to industrial and regional policies, and the least attention of all is paid to anti-monopoly policy.

The lack of attention paid by the government to industrial policy reflects the fact that some of the industries in the real sector are relatively well managed by private businesses e.g., the metals industry, parts of the chemical industry, the cellulose and paper industry, and the food industry. More active economic policy would be needed in the engineering and consumer goods industries. These have declined significantly in recent years, but could be restored to an acceptable level of competitiveness in the long term. In fact, the government's main focus for economic policy falls on certain key industries such as the agro-industrial complex, the defense industry, and communications and transport (especially the pipe-lines essential to exports). There is also a level of focus on commercially valuable sectors that are highly competitive and partly state-owned such as mining and quarrying.

By the same token, the lack of focus on anti-monopoly policy reflects the fact that any active pursuit of its aims would run counter to the interests of the oligarchic state capitalism. There are, however, signs that this is changing. In 2009, a law 'On Trade' was adopted that limited the monopoly of the distributive networks. In 2010, legislation 'On Medical Circulation' was introduced that limited monopolistic pricing in the pharmaceutical industry.

The recent economic crisis and subsequent recession demonstrated clearly the vulnerability of the economy created by over-reliance on raw materials. The need for modernization across society, including among the ruling elite was obvious. During the crisis of 2008–2009, the government had been forced to take active industrial measures to save some leading enterprises in various sectors. We can thus expect to see a more active industrial policy in the coming years. After all, without an active industrial policy, the government will struggle to achieve the ultimate aim of its economic policy, namely the modernization of the country. Without modern industry, especially manufacturing, this will prove impossible[16].

Economic Programming and Forecasting

In the first half of the 1990s, economic programming and forecasting in Russia were general short-term in nature. However, a more medium- and long-term approach has started to develop since. Today, a variety of programs and forecasts are available over different time horizons.

Short- and medium-term forecasting is based mainly on annual resources such as the presidential address to the Federal Assembly, the president's budget message, and on the document prepared by the Bank of Russia, 'The Main Directions of State Monetary and Credit Policy.' These are used to develop the annual projects in the federal budget. Since the second half of the 2000s they have been prepared with three-year horizons, the first year in detail, the subsequent two years in summary. In turn, the federal budget is used to develop the consolidated budget, which includes income and expenditures of both federal and regional governments, as well as non-budgetary funds such as pensions, medical care, and social security funds.

Medium-term forecasting is based on government programs and federal target programs. There are dozens of these, consisting of the following sections: a description of the problems that the program is intended to solve; an outline of the aims and objectives of the target program, specifying the stages of implementation and their duration, along with indicators of success; details of the program's activities; the source of the funding for the program; the implementation mechanisms for the program, including details of the management and how state clients will interact; and an estimate of the social, economic, and environmental impact of the program. In the federal budget, the majority of expenditure is earmarked for the implementation of such programs. It should be noted that all such programs and projects rely on state procurement which is one of the most corrupt instruments of economic policy (see above).

The 'Forecast of the Social and Economic Development of the Russian Federation for the Period up to 2030,' along with long-term sectoral programs such as the 'Energy Strategy of Russia for the Period up to

---

[16] Titov B., A. Shirov. Strategy of Growth of Russia //Voprosy Economiki. 2017.N12. pp.24–39.

2035,' dominate long-term programming. These works describe the targets to be achieved. But they are only forecasts, they do not impose obligations. Thus, the forecast published in 2013 contains three alternative scenarios: conservative, moderately optimistic, and forced. In the first scenario, average annual growth rates between 2013 and 2030 will be 2.5%; according to the second, 3.5%; and the third, 5.3%.

The Mechanisms of Economic Policy and its Efficiency

In Russia, the president and his administration determine the main direction of economic policy. The government, especially the Ministries of Finance and Economic Development, works with the Bank of Russia to develop and implement the policy. From an organizational point of view, this is a two-tier system used in many other countries with a similar political order.

How effective are Russia's economic policy mechanisms? When it comes to dealing with current issues such as the collection of taxes, managing government expenditure, or day-to-day economic life, the systems works comparatively well. It even copes sufficiently with extraordinary circumstances like economic crises. However, it is less effective when it comes to long-term challenges (see Chapter 8) such as the modernization of the economy, the development of the eastern and northern territories, and the demographic problem facing the country. There has been some success in dealing with the issue of economic reintegration with the former Soviet countries. Finally, there has been no progress on improving the levels of democracy and ethical standards.

This all goes to suggest that the country does not only need to address the individual elements of economic policy, but look more at the management of economic policy in the round. In other words, the country needs to replace its model of oligarchic state capitalism with a state capitalism. Moreover, there is evidence that such an approach would have the support of the majority of the country's people and its business community.

We should note finally that Russian economic policy is often analyzed in a certain way, with an emphasis on the direction of economic theory being followed by the leadership in managing the economy: neoliberal, neoclassical, or neo-keynesian. This analysis will be used in the following chapters. Here we make the following two observations: firstly, current economic policy is always a mixture of these approaches, with, however, one of them predominating (currently neoliberal thinking prevails in

Russian economic policy, though this has not always been the case); and secondly, when examining economic policy in a context of oligarchic state capitalism, it is more important to look at what the state's priorities are and which layers and groups in society are more affected by the policy.

Conclusion

1. Russia had the opportunity to create a democratic capitalism in the early 1990s. But in the middle of that decade and the early 2000s, a system of oligarchic capitalism emerged which then evolved into a system of oligarchic state capitalism as the government became more involved in managing businesses, especially larger ones. This oligarchic state capitalism determines the key features of modern Russian economic policy.

2. Russian economic policy is dominated by financial policy considerations, that is, the government's regulation of the fiscal, monetary, and currency operations. External economic and social policies are also active areas. Less attention tends to be paid to industrial and regional policies, and the least attention of all is paid to anti-monopoly policy.

3. In the first half of the 1990s, economic programming and forecasting in Russia were general short-term in nature. However, a more medium- and long-term approach has started to develop since. Today, a variety of programs and forecasts are available over different time horizons.

4. In Russia, the President and his administration determine the main direction of economic policy. The government, especially the Ministries of Finance and Economic Development, works with the Bank of Russia to develop and implement the policy. From an organizational point of view, this is a two-tier system.

Questions

1. Why did Russian economic policy evolve as it did?

2. What is characteristic of the way the Russian government intervenes in the economy?

3. What are the main directions and priorities of economic policy in Russia, and why does the government set its priorities?

4. Describe the main aspects of programming and forecasting in Russia.

5. Do you agree with the assessment of the efficiency of the mechanism of economic policy management in Russia as described above?

Sources of additional information

The Oxford Handbook of the Russian Economy. Oxford University Press: 2013

Mau V. Russia in an Epoch of Turbulence. Crises and Lessons. Routledge: 2018

The forecast of the long-term social and economic development of the Russian Federation for the period until 2030 (www.economy.gov.ru).

CHAPTER 13

THE REAL SECTOR

The Real Sector in Russia

As in most countries, the real sector forms the basis of the national economy in Russia. The sector employs nine tenths of the population and produces about the same proportion of GDP.

Inevitably, in a large economy, the Russian real sector includes a wide range of industries. It is, however, dominated by mining and quarrying, along with raw material and semi-manufactured goods such as metals and fertilizers. On the one hand, this is a natural consequence of the country's extensive natural resources, especially minerals, which gives Russia a competitive advantage. But, on the other hand, it is the result of the deindustrialization of Russia. During the Soviet period, when some industries declined, the other, more advanced industries grew to take their place. More recently, however, developed industries have reduced and not been replaced. Less complex industries proved better able to withstand the crisis of the 1990s and we left well placed to take advantage of the return to growth in the early 2000s, thanks to high global demand for their products. Other parts of Russia's real sector suffered due to their lack of competitiveness (the defense industry was one of the exceptions). Many industries in the real sector still have levels of output that are below where they were before recent reforms, especially engineering.

As a result, the real sector can be divided into two parts:

- Export-oriented industries focused on foreign markets, such as mining and quarrying, metals, and a large part of the chemistry, timber, and defense industries. This also includes the service elements of these industries, such as pipelines and sea transport. This part of the real sector employs only about 5% of the country's workers but brings in half of its foreign earnings. It thus is the main contributor to the state budget and creates a significant part of domestic demand.

- Industries focused on the domestic market. This part of the real sector accounts for about 70% of employment but is noticeably less profitable due to its low levels of competitiveness. Exceptions to this are trade and construction which meet the demands of workers in the first sector. But, in general, incomes in this half of the real sector are low, which feeds through into low demand among the bulk of the population and companies in Russia.

This situation is typical for the Dutch disease, with significant redistribution of incomes and economic resources toward the export-oriented raw materials industries and their service branches. This leads to domestic products being replaced by imports. This phenomenon does not affect all countries with large reserves of raw materials (e.g., USA, Canada, Australia, and Norway). In other countries, with poor standards of governance and weak institutions, the economic elite are seduced by the huge profits to be had from exporting raw materials and acquiesce in postponing modernization and industrial development to maintain the status quo; in Nigeria and Saudi Arabia, for example, large exports of oil led to slower economic growth and the so-called 'resource curse.'

Active support for manufacturing industries, especially knowledge-intensive industries, is the best way to cure the Dutch disease. In previous decades the Russian government paid little attention to industrial policy. Only more recently it has started to prioritize it in the context of economic modernization. So, the Forecast-2030 highlights those high-tech industries in which Russia has, or claims to have, significant competitive advantage: aircraft and shipbuilding, rocket and aerospace industries, nuclear power generation, radio electronics, ICT, medical technologies, energy efficiency, and energy saving.

The Agro-Industrial Complex

Russia has the third largest area of arable land in the world and a significant non-urban population. Agriculture is thus an important industry. But it is not without its problems, caused largely by the state's dominance over the private sector and, related to this, by the weakness in property rights for farmers, a characteristic of Russia old and modern. A feudal system of serfdom existed from the 17th to the mid-19th century. This was developed and maintained by the ruling elite as it served their interests. It was abolished in 1861 with a system of large redemption payments which left little land for farmers. Later, in the Soviet era, prosperous farmers were liquidated and corralled into collective farms (kolhhozes) and state farms (sovkhoves). With this legacy, the role of private ownership in the sector has remained weak, and the sector as a whole has failed to prosper or develop markets effectively.

The agrarian reform of the sector, which began in the 1990s, mainly involved ending the state's monopoly of land ownership and the conversion of the collective and state farms into limited liability companies, partnerships, or cooperatives with the members being given conditional shares in the property of the enterprises, which gave them the right to withdraw from the enterprise to farm privately while retaining their shares. However, the withdrawal process was complicated and the numbers wanting to withdraw were low as a result. Moreover, government support for farmers was weak (especially for those not in the regional elites). The number of private farms thus remains low (268,000 in 2013). These farms have, however, strengthened their role in the market and increased their share of the country's overall agricultural production, from 2% in 1995 and 3% in 2000 to 12.5% in 2016. The extent of private farming is in fact larger than the statistics suggest as they fail to include people who only farm part time and have other business activities.

The former state and collective farms—the kolkhozes and sovkhozes—are still the major producers of agricultural output, accounting for 15–20% of the total (author's estimate). Members of companies, partnerships and cooperatives retain an interest in their continued existence as they are a source of significant income. Moreover, the former state and collective farms provide their members with agro-technical assistance such as tractors, feed, and fertilizers for their personal subsidiary plots.

Individual households with small plots (either rural inhabitants or summer residents) are an important part of agricultural production in Russia. In 1990 they accounted for 26% of total production. This rose to 54% in 2000 but has since declined gradually and stood at 35% in 2016. They are the source of most of the country's potatoes, fruits and vegetables, and a significant proportion of meat, milk, and eggs.

Other agricultural enterprises consist mainly of private agricultural companies and holdings (combining production, processing, and often trading in agricultural products). Many of these companies bought out the shares of the former state and collective farms and recruited their workforce from them. Such companies account for 30–35% of the country's production. As former state and collective farms, they specialize in the production of grain, sugar beet, meat, milk, and eggs. Together with farming households, they are the most dynamic sector of Russian agriculture.

During the agrarian reforms of the early 1990s, 70% of agricultural lands were privatized and passed over to agricultural organizations, farmers, and individuals. But initially, the intensity of land use declined. Between 1989 and 2015, the area under crops halved (mainly as a result of poor quality land being taken out of use), the livestock population decreased by over 60%. However, during the first decade of the 21st century, these statistics have started to rise. This partly reflects a growth in productivity: between 1986 and 1990, the grain yield was 1,590 kg per hectare, between 2011 and 2016 this rose to 2,320 kg per hectare; the milk yield increased from 2.7 tons of milk per cow in 1988 to 5.9 tons in 2016; there were similar increases in the production of pork and beef from cattle. Overall, some types of agricultural production fell drastically during the 1990s (milk, potatoes, wool and flax-fiber, sunflower seeds) and other types increased (vegetables, fruits, sugar beet). Production began to recover after 2000. The grain harvest (weight after processing) averaged 104 million tons between 1996 and 2000. This fell to 65 million tons between 1996 and 2000, but has recovered to 98 million tons between 2011 and 2016. In 1989, meat production (slaughter weight basis) was 10.1 million tons. It fell to 4.4 million tons in 2000 and has climbed again, reaching 9.9 million tons in 2016. Pork and poultry were the main drivers in the increase in meat production thanks to low prices for domestic grain and the shorter time it takes to see pay-back from investment by comparison with other forms of meat production. Beef production, for example, can require seven years for a return on investment. The beef sector in Russia also faces competition from cheaper imports and has to struggle with a lack of succulent fodder.

However, at a time when the consumption of basic foodstuffs has returned to, or exceeded, the levels seen in the Soviet era, the shortages of some staples are worse than at the end of the 1980s. So, Russia has had to increase its imports of milk and dairy products due to the fall in the dairy herd. Certain popular tropical and sub-tropical foods have always been imported and this had continued. A large proportion of the country's grain production has traditionally gone to feed cattle. The fall in the size of the cattle herd has meant that, despite a fall in the production of grains, the country has been able to continue exporting them, often in exchange for beef and milk. The low cost of grain production in Russia compared with international standards has driven this increase in exports. Russia has become the third largest exporter of grains in the world, ranking with Australia and Canada, and behind the USA and the EU. However, according to an article, “Food commodities and agricultural raw materials (except textiles)”, the country has a substantial deficit in this trade. In 2000, imports exceeded exports by $6 bn, and in 2014, by $21 bn. Later this deficit started decreasing (by about $7 bn in 2016–2017) mainly due to Russian counter sanctions against Western sanctions and the substitution policy of Russian agro-business.

However, the country’s failure to meet all its own needs despite its vast agricultural resources can be explained by the failure of the agrarian reforms to encourage ‘kolkhozniks’ to continue as farmers. Other factors were also in play, such as: the lack of machinery, fertilizers, and skilled personnel; price disparities; and insufficient government support. The price disparity—prices for products not keeping pace with input costs—which reduced the profitability of the sector came about as a result of the government’s weakness in tackling monopolies in the production of agricultural goods and services. At the same time, large distributive networks were able to keep the wholesale prices paid to farmers low (often little more than the cost of production) while adding on high margins in the distribution process.

It is well known that agriculture contributed to industrialization in the 1930s, 1940s, and 1950s. But in the final years of the Soviet era, it swallowed up huge subsidies from the government. Even during the crisis of 1990, 27% of all capital investment went on developing the agricultural sector.[17] Subsequently, this share decreased sharply to about a quarter of its peak.

The agricultural sector is thus large and continues to grow. But significant expansion with government support is unlikely. The state-owned company, Rosagroleasing, exists to assist farmers with purchases of agricultural machinery and breeding stock. It also intervenes in the grain market, purchasing grain to maintain profitable domestic prices. In order to support domestic producers, there are quota systems for the import of various foodstuffs, such as meat. Imports above the quotas attract higher duties. Agricultural enterprises have also had their debts restructured and, in addition, they can qualify for various grants and forms of compensation from the state budget (mainly to subsidize interest payments on credit

[17] National Economy of the Russian Soviet Federated Socialist Republic in 1990. Statistics Digest. Moscow, 1991, p. 399 (in Russian).

obtained from the state bank Rosselkhozbank and from Rosagroleasing). Support from the state budget forms part of the government's 2013–2020 program for agricultural development and regulation of the markets in agricultural products, raw materials, and foodstuffs. Embargos, introduced in 2014, on food imports from countries that had imposed economic sanctions on Russia have also given impetus to the agricultural sector.

Around the end of the last decade and the start of the current decade, the total state support for agricultural producers amounted to about 15% of the cost of all agricultural production. This was about the same level as in Canada; it was higher than in Australia, Brazil, and China; but less that in the USA, the EU, and Japan. However, most of the subsidies were allocated to a relatively small group of a few hundred of the largest agricultural organizations. In other words, state support tends to go to large and already profitable organizations (companies and holdings). This is to be expected in a system of oligarchic state capitalism.

Faced with an absence of government orders, weak demand from the private sector, the uncompetitive nature of its products, the production of tractors and other forms of agricultural engineering saw its output collapse by around 90%. In 1986, 264,000 tractors were produced. In 2000 this had fallen to 19,000 and fell further to less than 8,000 units in 2017. For combine harvesters, the figures for the same three years were 112,000 units, 5,000 and 6,000 units. There have been imports of both tractors and harvesters, but not in sufficient numbers to arrest an overall decline in the numbers operating in the country. The number of tractors per thousand hectares of crops fell by two thirds and the number of fertilizers by a half. The amount of fertilizer used per hectare of crops fell from 88 kg in 1990 to 17 kg in 1995. It has since risen and stood at 49 kg in 2016.

Developments in the manufacture of mineral fertilizers have been less dramatic. This has been focused largely on exports, with 90% of total production exported. Production itself totaled 19 million tons in 1988 and 22.5 million tons in 2017.

Under these general conditions, the food industry and the domestic trade in food products has relied heavily on imported raw materials and finished products. In doing so, domestic demand has continued to be met. Another concern is the high proportion of faulty or sub-standard products being produced and sold.

On the whole, the country's agricultural policy seeks to ensure that:

- domestic demand is met from domestic production;
- the living standards of the rural population are raised and the gap between urban and rural communities is reduced;
- the competitiveness of the country's agriculture is improved;
- imports of animal products are substituted;
- export potential is maximized (especially in plant products).

A key part of the plan it to increase meat and grain production.

The Fuel and Energy Complex

The fuel and energy complex is backbone of Russia's economy. Russia produces about 10% of the world's primary energy, half of which is exported and half is used domestically.

Table 13.1 — The Energy Balance in Russia by Consumption of Tons of Fuel Oil Equivalent (percentage)

	2008	2012
Natural gas	53.1	51.6
Oil and gas condensate	18.9	15.5
Coal and other solid fuel	17.7	17.4
Non-fuel sources (hydro power, nuclear power, and unconventional energy)	10.4	12.5

Source: Ministry of Energy of the Russian Federation. Energy Strategy of Russia for the period until 2030. Project, attachment no. 4 (in Russian).

As can be seen from Table 13.1, Russia's economy is characterized by a dependence on gas, which is due less to its abundance (there are even higher reserves of coal) than to the low price of gas in the domestic market by comparison with other fuels. In terms of fuel oil equivalence, gas is just 60% of the price of coal. It is also seen as having less environmental impact. Many of the country's thermal power stations have been converted away from coal to gas. Gas now account for 70% of the country's power production.

Russia's oil production peaked at 569 million tons in 1988/1989 (at the time, this was 17% of world production). By the second half of the 1990s, this had fallen to 310–307 million tons. By 2016–2017, production had recovered to 546–549 million tons (about 12% of world production and 6% of global reserves). Russia's oil is mostly produced by large state-owned and private companies. These companies also process the oil and are thus referred to as 'vertically integrated' oil companies. Independent companies play a small part, producing about 3% of the country's total oil output (the equivalent figure in the USA is 46%). About half of Russia's oil production is exported, mainly to Europe, supplying about 30% of the continent's oil needs. However, the introduction of new fields in the east of the country and the construction of the Eastern Siberia–Pacific Ocean pipeline has opened up scope for greater access to the markets of Asia, especially China. Russia's energy strategy foresees only slow growth in oil production, with increases in both exports and domestic consumption. This is partly due to the introduction of new fields failing to keep pace with the depletion of old reserves. The government's withdrawal from active geological exploration led to a sharp overall reduction in the level of exploration. In 1990, deep exploration drilling (for oil and gas) totaled 5.3 million meters. But in subsequent years this fell to a level of between 1.1 and 1.7 million meters. The government is planning to use the state-owned holding, Rosgeology, to control exploration.

The oil processing industry is mainly focused on the needs of the domestic market, but still exports considerable amounts of product with low level of processing, e.g., black fuel oil. There is a shortage of capacity in the processing plants built during the Soviet era. They amount to just 7% of world capacity and now need only expansion and modernization. In particular, increasing numbers of passenger cars in the country have seen demand for gasoline increase significantly, while the number of freight vehicles has declined, and reduced demand for diesel oil accordingly. About half of oil production is exported. But, as noted above, this is mostly oil with a low level of processing. The government's 'Energy Strategy of Russia up to 2035' envisages growing this export business to balance the lack of growth expected in exports of crude oil. Russia, like most other countries, is not expected to increase the production of shale oil (although it has some of the richest deposits in the world) because of the high cost of production. It is focusing instead on exploiting hydrocarbons on the Arctic Shelf in future.

The gas industry is dominated by the state-owned company Gazprom, though a number of smaller private companies, notably Novatek, operate. Some oil companies also produce gas. Russia has some of the largest reserves of natural gas in the world (17% of global reserves). Production has been maintained at high levels for some time. In 1990, the country produced 641 billion cubic meters, and in 2017, 691 billion cubic meters. Russia exports about a third of its gas production. Only about 7% of these exports are liquid gas. However, the global demand for liquid gas has risen significantly in recent years and this has affected overall demand for Gazprom's natural gas. It has suffered in particular in Europe which takes about a quarter of Russia's gas exports. This casts some doubt over the government's target, contained in the Energy Strategy up to 2035, to increase gas exports by 150%. However, while exports to Europe decline, new markets in the Asia-Pacific region may bring the target within reach.

Russia's coal industry reached its peak in 1988 with production at 425 million tons. This declined significantly during the 1990s but recovered to 410 million tons in 2017, largely thanks to demand for exports which account for about a third of all production. Russia boasts about 18% of world coal reserves (enough for another 500 years). This gives the country huge potential in energy, great scope for export earnings, and the ability to provide abundant coking coal to its own metals industry (which takes about a quarter of all coal production). The 10 leading companies in the sector produce 77% of the country's total coal production.

In 1990, the Russian electrical power industry produced 1,082 billion kWh; in 1995, 860 bn; and in 2017, 1091 bn. Over the last three decades, the country's power generation capacity has barely increased. With deindustrialization, the capacity left by the Soviet era was sufficient for the country's needs. However, the infrastructure is ageing and is in need of replaced. Nuclear power accounts for 19% of the power generated; hydroelectric power, 17%; and thermal generation, 64%. A small proportion of power generated is exported to neighboring countries, about 20–30 bn kWh a year, although the Energy Strategy predicts that this could increase by 200–300%.

An initial stage of reform of the power generation industry ended in 2008, having lasted several years. It had focused on privatization and demonopolization. Out of the former natural monopoly (RAO United Energy System of Russia), six wholesale and 11 territorial generating companies were founded. These now own nearly all thermal power plants in the country. Some large hydropower plants were incorporated into the state company, RusHydro. The maintenance of electricity transmission lines is handled by the state-owned Federal Grid Company of the Unified Energy System and RAO Energy System of the East. The distribution of electricity is managed by the state-owned companies System Operator of the United Power System and Russia Grids. The export and import of electricity is managed by the state-owned company Inter RAO.

The creation of an open wholesale electricity market is close to completion. It is currently controlled by the company Trading System Administrator of the Wholesale Electricity Market, which is a subsidiary of the non-commercial partnership, Market Council, which, in turn, consists of all the players on the wholesale market. All generating companies (except Wholesale Generation Company–1 and RusHydro) are under the control of nine private companies. In the course of the privatization of the generating capacity of the former RAO United Energy System of Russia, the new owners signed agreements with the government to cover the supply of capacity (i.e., obligations to build new power stations and energy units at existing plants in return for guaranteed high tariffs). Signed in 2006, this formed part of the framework of an overall plan for the power industry that would run until 2020. It obliges the companies to make large investments in the sector.

Russia's nuclear power industry operates as part of the nuclear power generation power complex, rather than as part of the electric-power industry. It accounts for 7% of world generation of nuclear power; around 16% of global construction of nuclear plants; and 17% of world production of nuclear fuel. Russia ranks third in the world for uranium reserves. All of this managed by the state corporation Rosatom, which has ambitious plans to expand the capacity of nuclear power plants both in Russia and abroad.

The Metal, Chemical, and Timber Complexes

After the fuel and energy complex, the metal, chemical, and timber complexes make a significant contribution to the exports of the real sector. Domestic demand has reduced since the Soviet era, leading to a fall in production, but this has been mitigated by growing exports, in a way similar to that of the manufacture of fertilizers mentioned above.

The metals industry produces about 5% of Russia's GDP and provides about 10% of the country's exports. In 1988, the sector produced 94 million tons of steel. This collapsed by 50% in the 1990s, but in the following decade saw a recovery to 70 million tons (2017), leaving it behind only China, Japan, the USA, and India in terms of production. In world exports, Russia now ranks fourth. However, when it comes to the production of special steels and alloys, especially those intended for engineering, production volumes are much lower as equipment is often old and in a poor state of repair. In the case of the non-ferrous metal aluminum, Russia's production total of 4 million tons is second only to

China, largely as a result of the low price for electricity which is an important factor in the production of aluminum. Russia is the largest exporter of aluminum. Thanks to its large geological reserves, Russia is the world's largest producer of nickel at 0.3 million tons. The country has the third largest deposits of gold in the world and ranks third for gold extraction. In 2017 it extracted more than 300 tons (70% more than in the Soviet era). However, despite its large gold deposits, Russia has been slow to develop new sources to replace depleted areas due to a shortage of funds and relevant technologies.

During the decade of the 2000s, the country's strong export performance enabled the metals industry to re-equip its facilities with modern equipment (mostly imported). The government's Strategy for the Development of the Metal Industry up to 2020, which was written in 2009, expects the production of all metals to increase, funded largely by the metallurgical companies themselves who have plentiful resources and some experience of purchasing the relevant assets abroad.

The chemical and petrochemical complex encompasses a wide range of industries, in particular, mineral fertilizers, chemical crop protection products, synthetic resins and plastics, synthetic rubber, tires, rubber technical goods, artificial and synthetic fibers and filaments, paints and varnishes, and synthetic detergents. These are all manufactured in Russia and account for about 2% of GDP, and 6–7% of exports. A problem that survives from the Soviet era is that in the domestic chemistry industry, the primary processing of natural resources is of a reasonable standard. However, secondary processing tends to be of a lower standard, while later processing stages are of a lower standard still. As a result, Russia ranks only 20th in the world for chemical production, even though it has a strong export performance, mainly of simple products such as mineral fertilizers, synthetic rubber, synthetic resins and plastics. It has to import the more expensive complex chemical products. The country's exports have helped fund and support domestic production of chemicals. In some cases, e.g., tires, growing domestic demand has led to growing production. However, in other cases, e.g., chemical fibers and filaments, varnishes and paints, and chemical crop protection products, there has been a fall in demand or a demand for improvements in quality that producers have been unable to meet. This, coupled with foreign competition, has seen production in some areas fall. For example, in recent years, paint producers report operating at 37–43% capacity.

The chemical and petrochemical complex has strong links to the pharmaceutical industry. This industry has been in severe decline since the Soviet era, due to its continued failure to satisfy the country's demands for modern pharmaceutical products. As a result, in the domestic market, Russian products account for 62% of sales by quantity, but this equates to just 25% by value. The government's Development Strategy for the Pharmaceutical Industry up to 2020 (Pharma 2020) hopes to see the industry's share of the domestic market grow to 50% by value. This is to be achieved by modernizing the industry, using both domestic and foreign technologies, and relying on significant state support. The strategy even envisages a sharp increase in Russia's currently small pharmaceutical exports. Preliminary data suggests that the strategy is having some effect, although those industries seeking to produce products domestically to replace imports are still importing many of their basic ingredients.

The timber complex (forestry, wood processing, and the pulp and paper industries) provides 2.5–4% of Russia's exports. The timber industry's production volume has been gradually increasing. In the current decade, about 120 billion cubic meters of dense timber have been harvested (not including illegal deforestation). It is unlikely that this figure will ever match the levels of the Soviet era when 250–280 billion cubic meters were harvested each year. This reflects lower demand due to a general transition away from timber to other materials for construction, as well as more rational use of timber. About 40% of the country's timber and lumber production is exported. Despite the long-term trend away from timber in construction, there has been a short-term increase in demand which has helped the industry grow. However, the poor quality of its products (e.g., domestic furniture) means it is unable to grow its exports. The pulp and paper industry concentrated on exports for many years (exporting half its production) and benefited from major involvement by foreign capital. But it has still faced difficulties and does not even figure in the list of the world's top ten producers. This reflects the fact that the country's pulp and paper plants, of which there are 165, do not produce sufficient volumes of high-added-value products such as coated paper or high-quality cardboard. The timber complex faces various problems, many as a result of the country's lack of roads which restricts access to raw timber. It also struggles to secure credit.

The Engineering Complex

The engineering complex is the bedrock of Russia's manufacturing industry. It employs more than 3 million people, about a third of all manufacturing employment. Its traditional focus on the needs of the domestic market has led to difficulties in recent years as the machine-building industry has seen demand fall from all sectors of the real economy. The 1990s saw a catastrophic fall in production due to a number of factors: a reduction in government support; a fall in government orders; a sharp decline in domestic demand; and competition from foreign suppliers. The industry was unable to boost exports to take up the slack (as the country had been able to do with raw materials) because most domestically produced engineering goods were not competitive in world markets. (Two exceptions to this were military equipment and nuclear power plants.)

During the 2000s, domestic demand for engineering products returned to growth, but, given the low quality of many domestically produced products, as much as 50% of this increased demand was met with imports. The state of Russian engineering has a huge influence on the competitiveness of the Russian economy. But industrial policy focuses largely on those industries that are actively involved in defense, such as aircraft engineering, shipbuilding, the rocket and space industry, nuclear power, and the radio and electronics industry.

Transport engineering has fared better than the rest of the engineering complex. This is mainly car manufacturing. The production of trucks fell sharply, from 0.7 million in 1985, to 0.2 million in recent years. By contrast, production of buses has exceeded previous levels. The production of passenger cars has increased from 1.2 million a year in the 1980s to 1.1–2.0 million more recently (in 2017, 1.4 million). However, as much as a third of this production involves 'screw-driver assembly' of foreign cars using imported components. The production of rolling stock for rail transport (not including freight cars and high-speed equipment) has exceeded the levels achieved in the Soviet era. Production of aircraft, however, has been hit by the liberalization of the market which has allowed more competitive foreign aircraft. Russian airlines have bought or leased their aircraft from foreign manufacturers, benefiting from higher technical standards and characteristics, especially for long-range aircraft. During the Soviet era, about 80 long-range aircraft were produced each year. In 2009 this was just 14. This has recovered slightly to 37 in 2014, but the fleets of Russian airlines are about 80% foreign aircraft. In recent years, expenditure on the development of the national civil air technology has increased significantly with the hope of achieving an upswing in exports. Civil shipbuilding is relatively small, as it was in the Soviet era. Foreign-built ships account for about 90% of the Russian fleet.

Before the fall of the USSR, the country's power engineering industry met domestic needs in full and also exported equipment. However, following a collapse in investment in new equipment during the 1990s and an end to government support for exports, the power engineering industry now lags a long way behind foreign counterparts both in levels of technology and prices—though, hydro-power equipment has fared better. The country's share of world markets in power equipment fell from 10% in the Soviet era to just 2% now. Even in the domestic market, though still dominant, it is declining, apart from nuclear plants. A recent process of modernization of electric-power generation facilities has given Russian engineers an opportunity to catch up. But this will require greater access to modern technology.

The machine-tool industry is unlikely to return to its previous level of production. Although the level of technology prevalent in the Soviet era was not high, there was significant production of metal-cutting and pressing machines: 90,000 and 31,000 units respectively in 1987. This sector declined for many years, with the fall being stopped only at the end of the first decade of the 21st century. In 2017, 7,000 units each of metal-cutting and pressing machines were produced. Russia's share of the world market for machine tools now stands at just 0.3%. The country is awash with worn-out and obsolete machinery. The number of operational metal-cutting machines is reckoned to have declined from 2.5 to 1.5 million units. With the machine-tool industry fast losing competitiveness in terms of both technical standards and price, domestic consumers have increasingly looked to imports which now account for 90% of the market (even domestically produced equipment can contain as much as 70% imported components). Full modernization of the Russian economy will not be achieved unless this industry can be revived since full access to technology in world markets is often restricted by governments' security concerns over access to military technology. Chinese manufacturers have overcome this problem by purchasing European machine-tool companies in Europe. The Russian government has sought to address this issue by investing public funds in this sector under the auspices of the federal special purpose program.

A similar situation pertains in the production of metallurgical equipment: up to 85% of such equipment is imported. The production of mining equipment (for both coal and ore mining) fares better, with Russian producers taking 70% of the market, ahead of the 60% achieved by producers of equipment for the production of oil. Domestic production of the highways engineering sector has remained stable and is now growing, thanks largely to its being competitive on price. But while the production of this sector is growing, it is also facing growing imports.

Domestic production of some consumer appliances and equipment (e.g., watches, radios, cameras) has almost disappeared. In the case of some products (e.g., vacuum cleaners, microwave ovens, televisions), domestic production survived by relying on imported components, but still lagged far behind imports. In other areas (washing machines, refrigerators, freezers), foreign investment has enabled domestically produced goods to hold their own against imports.

The Defense Complex

During the Soviet era, the defense complex accounted for more than 60% of the engineering complex (not including the nuclear industry which manufactures arms under the auspices of the nuclear power generation complex). Today, this has fallen to about a third[18] and the number of people employed by the sector has also fallen dramatically.

The defense complex is largely based around large holdings, e.g., Rostech; corporations, e.g., the United Shipbuilding Corporation, the United Aircraft Corporation, Almaz-Antey, and others; and unifying companies which are fully or partly state-owned. These organizations are engaged in both military and civil production. The military side is on behalf of the Ministry of Defense and other defense and law-enforcement agencies. The civil side accounts for 40% of total production.

Between 1992 and 1998, government orders for defense equipment decreased dramatically, by over 90% (at fixed prices). This was in addition to decreased government investment in the fixed assets of the defense complex. Since the late 1990s, defense production has recovered, thanks largely to increasing exports. In 2016, exports amounted to $15 bn, with aircraft and anti-aircraft and naval equipment in the forefront, most of it

[18] National economy. Textbook ed. by Nureev R.M. Moscow, 2010, pp. 213–219 (in Russian).

destined for China, India and the Middle East. According to estimates from the Stockholm International Pease Research Institute (SIPRI), Russia's share of the global arms market reached one quarter, second only to the USA at one third 31%.

In recent years, increasing arms procurement by the Russian army has been a more important factor than exports in the expansion of the defense complex. Government orders for arms and military equipment are at the heart of the government's Armaments 2020 Priority Procurement Program, the main aim of which is to increase the share of the armed forces' arms and equipment that can be described as modern to 70%. Under the program, the government plans to allocate about ₽19 trn to equip the army with modern armaments, and nearly ₽4 trn to re-equip the companies producing the armaments. Changes to this program and the emergence of various other problems led to its replacement with a revised program covering the period 2016–2025.

The Consumer Goods Industry

The Russian consumer goods industry is heavily dependent on the business environment which, in turn, is influenced by world markets. On the one hand, this industry faces stiff competition from Asian manufacturers (some of whose products are imported illegally). Between 80 and 90% of the textile, clothing, and footwear market is imports. On the other hand, the Russian consumer goods industry relies heavily on foreign raw material, components, and equipment.

Domestic production of clothing reduced by 60 % for suits and jackets, and by 90% for coats, dresses, and shirts. Some products, especially in the middle price range, have bucked this trend. At the same time, a sharp fall in the production of fabrics has been reversed, partially thanks to greater production of synthetic fabrics made from cheap domestic raw materials, though production levels are still short of those achieved during the Soviet era: between 5 and 6 billion square meters, compared with between 8.4 and 8.7 billion square meters previously. Shoe production also collapsed completely, but has now recovered to between 100 and 120 million pairs of shoes a year, still less than in the Soviet era (385 million pairs of shoes in 1990).

The Construction Industry

The construction industry includes both industrial and domestic construction as well as the production of construction materials. The de-industrialization process that Russia experienced led to a sharp decline in industrial construction which affected all areas of activity: construction-and-assembly, extensions, repair, reconstruction, modernization of non-residential properties, and engineering construction. Demand for housing picked up in the 2000s, leading to some recovery in housing construction (see Chapter 12) which is higher than before the collapse of the USSR. As a result, the number of people employed in the sector fell from 7 million people to between 5.5 and 6 million people.

Less industrial construction meant less production of basic construction materials. This was only reversed after 2000: in 1985 cement production totaled 84.5 million tons. This fell to 32 million tons in 2000 and then recovered to 55–62 million tons in 2015–2017.

The Transport Industry

During the 1990s the freight being moved fell sharply before recovering after 2000 when it exceeded the levels of the Soviet era. The freight turnover in cargo movements are dominated by transport in pipelines which accounts for 50% and rail transport which accounts for 43%. The weakest link in Russia's transport system is the low level both of the development in its transport network and of much of the technology in use. This is estimated to reduce GDP by over 3% a year. It also results in a sharp fall in the population's mobility.

Rail transport is dominated by the state-owned company Russian Railways, which, together with its subsidiaries (who do not have to follow government-set tariffs), handles more than half of all rail freight. The rest is handled by private companies. The Strategy for the Development of Rail Transport in the Russian Federation up to 2030, which was adopted by the government in 2007, envisages a 60% increase in rail cargo turnover. This will be facilitated by the construction of 16 and 21 thou km of new lines and by a growth in passenger numbers thanks to the construction of high-speed networks.

Road transport takes only a small share of freight turnover, but predominates in freight shipment (two thirds) due to the domination of shipments of goods over short distances. This reflects the fact that the proportion of the Russian paved road network is relatively small, barely a third of what is needed, and technically obsolete. Improvement and extension of the network has only been happening very slowly. Between 2010 and 2015, the length of federal highways (which account for 3% of all roads but carry 60% of commercial and passenger turnover) increased from 50,000 km to 52,000 km. In that period, the Federal Road Agency (Rosavtodor) built 1,400 km of federal highways at a cost of ₽1.5 trn, i.e., ₽1 bn per kilometer (significantly more expensive that in e.g., Germany or the USA). In total, there are 1.5 million km of roads in Russia, while in the USA there are 6.4 million km, and in China, more than 4 million.

Water transport (by sea or internal waterways) no longer plays a significant role in domestic cargo transport. The volume of goods being transported this way has fallen dramatically as a result of increasing costs and the deteriorating state of the fleet, the port facilities, and the navigable waterways. In addition, Russia lost the majority of its ports on the Baltic and Black Seas, and saw a drastic reduction in the delivery of goods to the northern territories due to the curtailing of development plans for that region at the end of the 20th century. However, marine transport continues to play an appreciable role in external trade, carrying the bulk of the country's external trade (67% of exports and 9% of imports). Although Russia has a sea-faring cargo fleet of 18 million tons deadweight, 67% of the tonnage is operated under foreign flags for tax avoidance purposes. Only 5% of Russia's external trade is transported under a Russian flag.

Pipeline transport is the fastest development segment of the transportation sector. The network of main oil and gas pipelines continues to grow thanks to intensive construction of new export lines.

The ratio of private vehicles per head of population has grown significantly. As a result, volumes of passengers using public transport have declined from 49 million people in 1990 to 20 million in recent years. Air transport is not included in these figures; following a major decline in passenger numbers during the 1990s, the use of air transport grew steadily. There were 91 million air passengers in 1990; 23 million in 2000; and 94 million in 2015.

Communications

The communications industry has seen apparently contradictory patterns of activity in recent years. On the one hand, up to the beginning of this decade, Russia has struggled to maintain the 24 satellites needed to support the Global Navigation Satellite System (GLONASS, equivalent to the USA's GPS), while, on the other hand, the country has launched a vast number of foreign satellites on commercial terms.

Russia's domestic postal service, 'Russian Post', has declined to a parlous state, largely as a result of a major collapse in newspaper subscriptions and a significant fall in the sending of parcels.

By contrast, since the collapse of the Soviet Union, the number of telephones on the network has almost doubled. The number of mobile telephones is almost double the size of the population. 75% of households have access to the Internet.

Trade and Consumer Services

Activities involving the trade and repair of vehicles, household goods, and personal items employ more than 18% of the population and account for about the same proportion of GDP. The large number of people attributed to this sector partly reflects the fact that in the conditions of high unemployment that have plagued Russia and neighboring countries this kind of activity acts as a kind of 'buffer' absorbing surplus labor at low wages.

This sector's high contribution to GDP is a reflection of the market nature of the Russian economy. Russian manufacturers often complain about the number of agents involved in the sale of their products. There is an argument that this comes about as a result of the power of bureaucracy, with affiliated entrepreneurs organizing chains of agents that a producer cannot bypass. Another reason may be the separation of the manufacturer from the companies that do the selling (for tax purposes). This is common, for example, in the oil and gas sector with much of the activity listed as trade in official statistics.

Russian trade also exhibits an important macroeconomic feature, namely a high proportion of imported goods in the retail mix, 38% by turnover. In a large economy, with a relatively open market and large exports, this can be seen as evidence of how domestic goods are not competitive in global markets. It also demonstrates how export earnings are being spent on consumption rather than investment.

Conclusion

1. The real sector forms the basis of the national economy in Russia and has a major influence on its development. Inevitably, in a large economy, the Russian real sector includes a wide range of industries. It is, however, dominated by mining and quarrying, as well as the production of basic materials. The real sector can be divided into two parts: those industries (fuel and energy, metals, much of the chemical industry, timber, and defense) that have a major focus on foreign markets, and their service branches (pipelines and sea transport); and those industries with a domestic focus.

2. Most agricultural land has been privatized and passed to agricultural organizations, farmers, and individuals. However, land is not used effectively. During the 1990s, agricultural output for most products fell dramatically, recovering steadily after 2000.

3. The fuel and energy industry is the backbone of the Russian economy. The country produces about 10% of the world's primary energy, with half going to export and half used at home. This sector includes the developed fuel industry and the powerful electricity-generation industry which includes nuclear power.

4. The metals, chemicals, and timber industries make a significant contribution to export earnings. They all produce less than in the Soviet era due to reduced domestic demand. However, they have compensated this by increasing exports.

5. With one or two exceptions, the engineering industry has struggled more than any other part of the real sector. Demand for engineering products has grown since 2000 but this had largely been met with imports, reflecting the low levels of technology deployed in Russian civil engineering.

6. Production of military goods in Russia stands at about a third of the level achieved in the Soviet era. The number of people employed in the industry has fallen by 80% in this period. The industry is made up of holdings, corporations, and unifying companies, either partly or fully state-owned. The industry has civil as well as defense-related production.

7. The Russian consumer goods industry is heavily dependent on the business environment which, in turn, is influenced by world markets.

On the one hand, this industry faces stiff competition from Asian manufacturers. Between 80 and 90% of the textile, clothing, and footwear market is imports. On the other hand, the Russian consumer goods industry relies heavily on foreign raw material, components, and equipment.

8. The de-industrialization process that Russia experienced led to a sharp decline in industrial construction. Demand for housing picked up in the 2000s, leading to significant recovery in housing construction.

9. Freight shipment is dominated by transport in pipelines which accounts for 50% and rail transport which accounts for 43%. The weakest link in Russia's transport system is the low level both of the development in its transport network and of much of the technology in use. This is estimated to reduce GDP by over 3% a year. It also results in a sharp fall in the population's mobility. Pipe-line transport continues to develop.

10. The communications sector displays conflicting trends: postal services are in decline, while telephony and the use of the Internet are growing.

Questions

1. Does the fact that Russia exports grain indicate that the domestic agricultural sector is in good health?

2. How did the fuel and energy sectors become the backbone of the Russian economy?

3. Which branches of engineering are the most successful in Russia today and why?

4. Describe the current state of the Russian consumer goods industry?

5. Looking at figures for freight turnover, why has road transportation decreased rapidly in Russia?

6. Why does Russia's postal service fail to function effectively?

Sources of Additional Information

The Oxford Handbook of the Russian Economy. Oxford University Press: 2013

Mau V. Russia in an Epoch of Turbulence. Crises and Lessons. Routledge: 2018

Russia in figures. Statistical handbook. Moscow

CHAPTER 14

THE FINANCIAL SECTOR

The Russian government has always attached importance to the financial sector, believing it to be a leading sector of the economy[19]. The Ministry of Finance has enjoyed a corresponding profile as the leading ministry. This approach has achieved a measure of financial stability. The large government deficit, a feature of the 1990s, was turned into a surplus and international and other reserves grew.

Although the financial crisis of 2008 saw government finances fall back into deficit and reserves decline, the country's economic position remains far better than it was in the 1990s. The country does still, however, face two serious challenges: high inflation (except for the two last years); and a weak banking sector which provides less credit in relation to GDP than banking sectors in other countries at similar levels of development (see Table 7.3).

The Budgetary System and Policy

In Russia, the state budget is managed on a number of different levels:

- Local budgets—the budgets of local government bodies and municipal entities. These budgets are funded primarily from local taxation and transfers from regional budgets. They are generally used to meet the needs of local infrastructure and social services;
- Regional budgets—the budgets of the regional entities that make up the Russian Federation. These are funded by regional taxes, as well as by a portion of federal taxes allocated automatically to the regions and other payments from the federal budget. As well as infrastructure and social services, they are used to support the development of regional aspects of the financial sector. Russian statistics often consider local and regional budgets together as

---

[19] Kudrin A., Knobel A. Budgetary policy as a source of economic growth //Voprosy Economiki. 2017. N10. pp.5–26.

'consolidated' budgets of regions of the Russian Federation (the word 'consolidated' is often omitted). They are also sometimes referred to as the territorial budgets. In recent years these budgets have been equivalent to between 12 and 14% of GDP;

- The federal budget—the budget of the national government. In addition to expenditures on social services, infrastructure, regional support, and the financial sector, this budget funds expenditure on international security, defense, security and law enforcement, and public debt management. In recent years, the federal budget has been equivalent to between 19 and 22% of GDP;
- The budgets of state-run non-budgetary funds—these are the Pension Fund of the Russian Federation, the Social Insurance Fund of the Russian Federation, and Federal and Territorial Compulsory Medical Insurance Funds. These are separate from other budgets as they are funded largely from hypothecated taxation. Expenditures from these budgets is equivalent to between 4 and 5% of GDP.

In the Russian Federation's Budget Code, the combination of budgets at all levels is referred to as the budgetary system. In Russian statistics, they are defined as the 'consolidated budget of the Russian Federation and the budgets of the state non-budgetary funds' or simply 'the consolidated budget'. However, in international statistics it is described as the 'budget of the general government' since state non-budget funds are not usually included in the statistics of the consolidated budget. In the current decade, the revenues in this budget have been equivalent to between 31 and 38% of GDP, while expenditure has been between 32 and 41%. This is close to the average for OECD member countries.

The federal and other budgets are planned and enacted every three years ('three-year rolling budget'). This includes a detailed budget for the coming year and indicative budgets for the following two years, based on forecasts of likely social and economic development. In the case of the federal budget, these forecasts are worked out by the Ministry of Economic Development. This three-year budget, with its two constituent parts, forms an important element in the medium-term planning of the country's economic policy.

Budgetary Structure

The structure of Russia's consolidated budget indicates the country's high dependency on external economic revenues, particularly those earned from oil and gas.

Table 14.1 — The Structure of Russia's Consolidated Budget (billions of rubles)

	2005	2008	2009	2016
Revenues	**8,580**	**16,004**	**13,421**	**28,186**
percentage in total revenues	100	100	100	100
of which:				
profit (income) tax of organizations	15.5	15.7	9.4	9.8
income tax of individuals	8.2	10.4	12.4	10.7
value added tax	17.2	13.3	15.3	16.2
excise taxes	3.0	2.2	2.6	4.6
revenues from international economic activity	19.6	22.4	20.0	9.2
Expenditures	**6,821**	**13,992**	**15,847**	**31,324**
percentage in total expenditures	100	100	100	100
of which:				
objectives affecting the state as a whole, law enforcement and state security	19.6	17.0	16.0	12.3
national defense	8.5	7.5	7.5	12.1
national economy	11.2	16.1	17.6	12.4
education	11.8	11.9	11.2	...
social-cultural arrangements	41.6	39.1	41.2	57.2

Source: Federal State Statistics Service of Russia (www.gks.ru)

As in most other countries, over 90% of the revenues in the Russian budget come from taxation. But a characteristic of the Russian budget is that a large proportion of these taxes are raised from the external sector of the economy. These do not come solely from duties on exports and imports (see the article, "Revenues from International Economic Activity"). It should be noted here that enterprises involved in exports provide two-thirds of the profit tax of the organizations (corporate tax). Moreover, about half of the money raised from VAT, is levied on imported goods. From this we can conclude that tax revenues from the external sector accounted for between 30 and 40% of the consolidated budget. At the heart of these revenues are the various payments made by companies in the oil and gas sector, particularly for the use of natural resources in addition to the export duties on gas, oil, and related by-products. Revenues from oil and gas, along with other revenues from the external sector go into the federal budget.

As in most countries, Russia's budgetary expenditures are devoted mainly to the social arena. In Russia, they are often referred to as 'social and cultural' spending. It is worth noting that, by comparison with the middle of the previous decade, the amount of the state budget dedicated to the national economy has increased. Indeed, it increased even before the last world economic crisis.

The Taxation System and Tax Policy

Taxation performs a social function in smoothing inequalities in earnings, a guiding function by promoting economic development and mitigating cyclical changes, and a fiscal function in financing government expenditures.

The main feature of the Russian taxation system is its inadequate performance in pursuit of its social goals. Two factors support this contention: the flat tax applied to personal income, and the low levels of personal property tax collected. The current rate of personal income tax in Russia is a flat 13%. Very few countries have a similar system; those that have are most in Central and Eastern Europe. Most countries, by contrast, seek to use their tax systems to achieve a measure of equality or income distribution and so adopt progressive systems of personal taxation. In the USA, for example, the top rate of personal taxation is 37%, in France it is 45%, in Japan 50% and in Brazil 27.5%. However, in Russia, the ruling elite see it as being very much in their interests to maintain the current system and the government has thus made clear that the flat rate system will not be changed and any increase in its level will only come in the longer term. The property tax (of particular importance for more affluent tax payers) which is the bedrock of local government budgets around the world, contributes only 11% of the revenues of regional budgets in Russia (1.5% of the total consolidated budget).

The Russian taxation system also has a poor record in terms of its regulatory function though. In 2009, the level of corporation tax was lowered from 24% to 20%. Russia maintains a system of small investment tax credits and tax credits for research and development activities and innovation. In 2019, the rate of VAT was increased to 20% (from 18%).

According to the annual report, 'Paying Taxes,' produced by PWC, taxes (excluding tax credits) in relation to total revenue in the middle of the current decade were 49% in Russia, while in Brazil, India, and China, they were between 61 and 69%; in the EU, 41%; and in the USA, 44%.

The Relationships between Local, Regional, and Federal Budgets

As a country with a federal structure and a system of budgetary federalism, the relationships between the budgets of different levels of government are important in Russia. The system of budgetary federalism is based on the division of responsibilities and the designation of authority between the budgets, and the extent to which each level has autonomy. For example, defense expenditure falls exclusively to the federal budget. However, this budgetary federalism is rarely achieved in full. On the one hand, some responsibilities have to be divided between the budgets (education, culture, medical care, and social security) and, on the other hand, taxation cannot provide all the revenue necessary for most of the local and regional budgets or for the state non-budgetary funds. To address this, the higher-level budgets have to subsidize the others with various inter-governmental transfers, 'splitting' their revenue to provide part of the revenue for the lower-level budgets.

Under the Russian budgetary system, the bulk of revenues (around 50% in 2016) flow into the federal budget which then transfers a significant portion of its revenue to the territorial budgets and to the state non-budgetary funds in the form of transfers (between 2 and 3% of GDP). These transfers can be equated to the inter-governmental transfers in other large federal countries.

Balancing the Budgets

After the huge budget deficits of the 1990s (10.5% of GDP in 1994), Russia began to reduce the consolidated budget and moved into large surpluses after 2000 (8.1% of GDP in 2005, 4.8% in 2008). This surplus came about largely as a result of international economic activity, especially the export of hydrocarbons. The surplus was used to replenish the reserve funds.

However, falls in international prices for some of Russia's basic export commodities saw the surplus turn into a deficit. This was initially relatively high, standing at 7% of GDP in 2009. A small surplus was achieved in 2011–2012. Between 2013 and 2016, the budget was again in deficit at 1.1–3.5%. However, in 2017, the rise of oil and gas prices gave the consolidated budget the chance to achieve a small surplus.

Public Debt

During the 1990s, government debt rose considerably to 20% of GDP. After 2000, this was reduced to a situation in which internal and external public debt were each equivalent to about 4% of GDP. The internal debt is mostly in the form of various issues of federal loan bonds, circulating in the Russian market. The external debt is various issues of euro loan bonds.

The economic crisis of 2008 and the subsequent stagnation, combined with a decline in earnings from hydrocarbon exports affected the position of Russian public debt: in 2017, internal government debt was equivalent to 15% of GDP, while external government debt was about 4.5%. Nevertheless, Russian debt levels remain considerably lower than in most leading world economies: In 2017, China's public debt was equivalent to 49% of its GDP, in the USA the figure was 108% and, in Japan, 251%. For Russia, therefore, the cost of servicing this debt is comparatively low: between 2015 and 2017, about 1% of all expenditures from the consolidated budget.

Sovereign Funds

In 2008 Russia has established two sovereign funds: the Reserve Fund and the National Wealth Fund. The Reserve Fund was set up to address shortfalls in the federal budget, while the National Wealth Fund was set up mainly to support the country's pension system, though 10% of its resources are dedicated to financing profitable national infrastructure projects. These funds were financed at the expense of the oil and gas revenues of federal budget and consist of foreign assets.

The value of the Reserve Fund has fluctuated greatly. It has been as high as 12.5% of GDP to a low of 1.1% by the end of 2017. The National Wealth Fund stood at $ 65bn (4% of GDP) at the start of 2018. As noted above, the National Wealth Fund is intended mostly to support the Russian pension system. However, since 2009, some of the fund's reserves were used to plug holes left by the financial crisis. In recent years, it has returned to its original secondary purpose of infrastructure financing. As a result of growing non-pension expenditures of the National Wealth Fund and the growing weakness of the Reserve Fund, the latter was closed at the beginning of 2018.

The existence of these funds is controversial in Russia. Some believe that the resources should be used in government support for the real sector and, thereby, to increase the competitiveness of the Russian economy and improve its diversification, to cure it of the Dutch disease, and, more generally, to support modernization.

However, the government line has been that these reserves are necessary, on the one hand, to protect those areas of the budget that are heavily dependent on oil and gas revenues and to protect the Russian pension system, while, on the other hand, to 'sterilize' part of the money stock in reserve to act as a break on inflation (see below). The Ministry of Finance does not consider it appropriate to use reserves to support the modernization of the economy. This is an important feature of the country's fiscal policy.

Let us turn to the monetary system. Key features of Russia's monetary system have been high inflation up to the latest two years, low monetization of the economy, a strong dependence on the money stock from the flow of foreign exchange, and a notable dollarization of the entire economy.

Inflation and Monetization

High inflation has been a feature of the Russian economy since the beginning of the 1990s. It was caused by the chaos and huge deficits experience in the final years of the Soviet economy as it had tried and failed to conduct market-based reforms. In 1992, the economy suffered a one-off peak in inflation caused by the shock transition to free-market prices. It subsequently had some success in managing inflation, except for 1998 which saw a spike as a result of the fourfold devaluation of the ruble, and 2014–2015 again due to a twofold devaluation. Nonetheless, it remains high by international standards, standing at 5.5% in 2016 but lower, 2.5%, in 2017.

Table 14.2 — Consumer Price Indices in Russia (December to December – percent)

1990	1991	1992	1993	1994	1995	1996	1997	1998	1999	2000	2001	2002		
5	161	2509	840	220	130	22	11	84	37	20	19	15		
2003	**2004**	**2005**	**2006**	**2007**	**2008**	**2009**	**2010**	**2011**	**2012**	**2013**	**2014**	**2015**	**2016**	**2017**
12	12	11	9	12	13	9	9	6	7	7	11	13	5	2

Sources:
Russia in Figures (for relevant years); National Economy of the Russian Soviet Federative Socialist Republic in 1990. Statistics digest. Moscow, 1991, p.177 (in Russian).

Monetary inflation, i.e., inflation due to the growth of the money stock, is important in Russia, but it is not the main cause of inflation. In 1992, the government pursued an anti-inflationary policy to address that it had itself caused by the shock transition to free-market prices, it limited the growth of the money stock which saw the monetization ratio (the ratio of broad money, M2, to GDP) decrease from 60% in 1991 to a record low of 10–12% between 1993 and 1996. However, putting the economy on this 'starvation diet' for so long proved counterproductive because the inevitably huge reduction in GDP meant that the monetization ratio gradually recovered due to growth in the money stock exceeding economic growth. The growth in the money stock was driven by the inflow of export revenues as a result of rising world prices for Russia's fuel and other material exports. The bulk of earnings from exports are converted into rubles, thus causing the ruble money supply to grow. The government's attempts to de-dollarize the economy which encouraged residents to convert foreign currency into rubles contributed to the effect. Over the course of a decade and a half, the monetization ratio was restored, reaching a level of 59–64% in 2015–2017, which is in line with other countries at a similar level of development (Poland, Turkey etc.) but lower than in the whole group of middle income countries (130%). The growth in the money stock also makes a small contribution to inflation; in 2007, it was estimated that this monetary factor was responsible for roughly a fifth of the total rate of inflation.[20]

When considering the non-monetary factors of inflation, we should note that the above-mentioned deflationary policy, which led to the collapse of many industries due to the reduction in consumer demand and of the supply of money by banks, caused demand-side inflation. As a result, when economy recovery began in earnest in 1998, many sectors of the economy were unable to respond adequately to the rapid growth in consumer demand, for example. Fueled by revenues from oil and gas, demand for housing, services, and consumer goods began to outstrip supply, creating an imbalance. This factor may be the main reason for Russian inflation being higher than in the other BRICS countries in recent years.

Another non-monetary factor contributing to overall inflation has been supply-side (cost-push) inflation. This is largely generated by the intense

[20] Porshakov A., Ponomarenko A. Problems of identification and modelling of interrelation of monetary factor and inflation in Russian economy. Voprosy economiki. 2008, no.7, p.76 (in Russian).

monopolization of the internal market and made worse by the insufficient level of innovation that is a characteristic of the Russian economy (since new technologies usually lead to lower prices for goods). For example, the costs of rent as well as utilities like gas and electricity, which are a substantial part of any business's costs, traditionally grew faster than consumer inflation. As a result, there was inflation despite there being a reduction in GDP output and a reduction in the volume of the money stock. The scarcity and rising cost of credit also led some firms to use profits to finance investments, which encouraged them to raise prices.

The attempt by the Bank of Russia in 2016 and 2017 to decrease inflation by monetary instruments was comparatively successful (see Table 14.2). But the leading instrument—high credit rates—resulted in negative and low rates in the real sector and the whole Russian economy during 2016 and 2017.

Monetary Policy

In line with liberalism, and especially the school of monetarism, Russian monetary policy is targeted heavily at curbing inflation.

To do this, the Russian financial authorities make most use of those deflationary instruments that have an impact on monetary inflation but remain neutral to non-monetary inflation (or, even, stimulate it). In this way, the Ministry of Finance restricts growth in the stock of money, even though it can tend to grow of its own accord due to the inflow of export earnings (see below). What the Ministry is, in fact, doing is 'sterilizing' that part of the money stock that has already been issued by the Reserve and National Wealth Funds since the resources of these funds are held in foreign stocks and in foreign banks, rather than in Russian banks or stocks. An exception to this has occurred more recently with the Reserve Fund has been used to finance the national deficit, and the National Wealth Fund has been used to finance infrastructure spending. Even so, statistics show that there is no significant correlation between movement in the stock of money and the consumer price index.

In recent years, the Ministry of Finance and the Bank of Russia have adopted a policy of inflation targeting; they now focus monetary policy on the achievement of a target level of inflation, which they have set at 4% as a long-term objective. Management of other macroeconomic indicators such as exchange-rate stability and economic growth are subordinated to the achievement of this target. Initial attempts at pursuing an inflation target in 2014 and 2015 were frustrated by the devaluation of the ruble. Inflation reached 11.4 and 12.9% respectively. But the authorities have remained determined and by the end of 2016 had got inflation down to 5.4% and to 2.5% by the end of 2017.

Another important feature of the monetary policy in Russia is that the money supply is based largely on earnings from exports and foreign investments, rather than on internal sources. As part of its targeting of inflation, the Ministry of Finance limits issuance of the national currency and government bonds. But there is no limit on the inflow of earnings from exports or foreign investment. As a result, the money stock consists mostly of rubles that have been exchanged for export revenues or earnings from those foreign investments. The volume of the money supply in Russia thus depends primarily on ups and downs in the formation of the stock of money from external sources, rather than on the state of the Russian economy. This is important because the volume of this supply is out with the control of the Russian monetary authorities. In the Soviet era, the stock of money was largely based on internal sources (as is the case today in the USA, EU, and Japan). By contrast, in modern Russia, it is formed by the uncontrolled inflow of foreign currency. We can, therefore, state that the money supply in Russia correlates primarily with the volume of international reserves as foreign currency entering the country is mostly exchanged for rubles issued by the Bank of Russia to purchase the currency and that the Bank of Russia receives foreign currency in return for its international reserves (gold and foreign currency). International reserves account for about two-thirds of the money supply in Russia. From this, it can be seen that the monetary system in Russia is not independent in the way one would expect for such a large economy.

This is borne out by another important feature of the Russian monetary system, its high levels of dollarization. The 1990s saw significant dollarization of the Russian economy caused by high inflation and the instability of the ruble. Dollarization fell after 2000 but peaked again during the crises of 2008–2009 and 2015–2016. Foreign currency deposits are in the region of $150 bn. Some dozens of billion dollars are in the hands of individuals, held in cash and in corporate transaction accounts. In 2015, this represented about 25% of the total money stock (including resources held in foreign currency). As well as dollars, there are significant holdings of euros.

The Credit System

The credit system remains one of the weak links in the Russian economy. At the beginning of 2017, there were 575 banks and 48 non-banking credit organizations operating in the country, including 92 banks and non-bank credits organizations with predominantly foreign ownership. A majority of these were small banks focused on the settlements and payments and credit for small businesses.

There has been a trend towards consolidation in the banking sector for some years. In the middle of the 1990s, for example, there were nearly 3,000 banks in the country. Nowadays, the five largest banks hold 53% of the country's bank assets. Five of these are wholly or partially state-owned: Sberbank, VTB, Gazprombank, VTB 24, and Otkrytie. Many smaller banks have joined banking groups headed by one of the larger players. However, this process only goes so far towards tackling one of the main weaknesses in the Russian banking system, i.e., the insufficient monetization that prevents even the largest banks from having large assets. It is also worth mentioning in this context the level of poverty in the country, as this puts a break on banks growing their deposits. Only about 35% of the population have bank deposits.

As a result, Russian bank assets in 2016 were equivalent to 93% of GDP, compared to an average of 110% in countries of a similar level of development. The amount of credits and loans outstanding was equivalent to 56% of GDP in 2015, much lower than in other BRICS countries, and they are mainly short-term. As a result, the share of bank credits in investments does not exceed 8–9% (see Table 10.1).

With such a weak national banking system, companies have to seek credit abroad, especially if they want long-term loans. But, since 2014, Western financial sanctions have closed off this route to credit.

Credit Policy

As well as the five leading banks listed above, may other Russian banks, are wholly or partially owned by federal or regional authorities, or state-owned companies. Such state or quasi-state banks account for about 70% of the country's bank assets. This could enable the government to pursue an active credit policy. But the government instead focuses on its financial rather than any macroeconomic goals. Moreover, federal and regional officials are able to influence the state and quasi-state banks to focus on their business interests.

Russia's Central Bank does not have a role in relation to economic growth in the way that the Federal Reserve in the USA or the Bank of Japan do. Instead, its purpose is solely on money and credit, as well as on the reduction of inflation in particular, which makes its role more similar to that of the European Central Bank. Russian economists are critical of the way the central bank's role is confined to economic stability rather than growth. Many believe that the federal law, 'On the Central Bank of the Russian Federation (the Bank of Russia)' should include some consideration of economic growth and of the need to increase investment and employment as key roles for the bank. They also argue that the bank should also be required to transfer money to help refinance the commercial banks for the collateral on their existing credit requirements and government bonds.[21]

The Stock Market

As part of the monetary system, the primary function of the capital or stock market is to finance and regulate the economy, to redistribute of capital, and to determine the market price of certain companies. However, the Russian stock market is poor at performing these functions.

The market's poor performance in supplying finance to business can be seen in the fact that, in 2014, of the total amount invested in basic stocks, the share obtained through the issuance of corporate bonds or capital stock was just 1%. This reflects not just the low monetization of the Russian economy as a whole, but also the lack of interest among Russian oligarchs in large stock issues on the open market as this would entail surrendering some control over their companies.

The stock market also struggles to fulfill its role to regulate the national economy as so few Russian companies are listed on it. Moreover, it is estimated that less than 30% of all stocks are in free circulation. In addition, the Russian stock market is heavily dependent on foreign investors. It is estimated that during the years of growth, half of all purchases of stocks on the Russian stock market were made by non-residents. When we add sales overseas in the form of depositary receipts

[21] For example: Glaziev S. Mistakes that worse than crime. Expert. October 27–November 2. 2014, no. 44, pp. 52–55 (in Russian).

for Russian stock and Eurobonds, the share is two-thirds. This means that the Russian stock market has only a weak connection with what is actually happening in the country's economy. It is rather more influenced by events in the West. However, it should be noted that a significant proportion of the non-residents who purchase Russian stocks are, in fact, Russian citizens who are keeping their assets overseas, mainly in offshore jurisdictions. Despite their formal status as an indicator of what is happening in the Russian economy, the stock indices have only a weak connection with it.

The Russian stock market's purported role in redistributing capital between companies is severely hampered by the small number of companies listed on the market. The leading companies on the market, the 'blue chips' are the main mining companies and banks. Their shares are traded actively as they are seen as viable investment by Western investors. Trades in seven oil and gas companies account for about half of the total turnover of the country's main market, the Moscow Stock Market.

The stock market is, however, more successful in its function of determining the market prices of certain companies. But even here, economists point to a weakness in that the general lack of money stock in the country deprives the market of liquidity and many stocks are reckoned to be undervalued as a result. This was true even during times of economic growth. In Russia there are two principal stock indices: the Moscow Exchange (MOEX) and the Russian Trading System (RTS). MOEX quotes prices in rubles, RTS in dollars. At the start of 2018, the MOEX Russia Index was not substantially higher, at 2,300 points, than it had been in the autumn of 2008, 1,400 points. The RTS Index was, in fact, lower over the same period: 1,200 points compared to 2,500.

Overall then, the Russian stock market, on the one hand, lists the stocks of large companies of which it has considerable volume. But on the other hand, it fails in some of its basic functions. We can thus conclude that the market is mostly speculative. This conclusion is supported by the heavy volatility of both MOEX and RTS indices. From 2004 to 2007, they increased fourfold, before falling by 66% in 2008. This level of volatility was far higher than in other large countries. The Russian indices are still at comparatively low levels.

The speculative nature of the Russian stock market could be reduced if more government stocks were listed. But this does not happen, for two key reasons. Firstly, the small amount of national internal debt means that the issuance of such stocks would not attract sufficient interest. Secondly, government stocks serve as quasi-money in the market and would be included in the M2 calculation of money supply. As such, they would impinge on the goal pursued by the Ministry of Finance and the central bank to limit the growth of the stock of money and the 'sterilization' referred to above.

Conclusion

1. The Russian financial sector is more stable than was the case in the 1990s. However, Russian finance is still affected by two problems: inflation and a weak banking sector which provides less credit as a proportion of GDP than the banking sectors in most countries at a similar level of development.

2. In the Russian budgetary system, most budget revenues start in the federal budget and are then transferred to the territorial budgets and to the state non-budgetary funds. These transfers are equivalent to 2–3% of GDP. These intergovernmental transfers are comparable with similar arrangements in other large federal countries.

3. Monetary inflation, i.e., inflation due to the growth of the money stock, is important in Russia, but it is not the main cause of inflation. Non-monetary demand inflation was created by the deflationary policy that led to the collapse of many industries. As a result, when economic recovery began in earnest in 1998, many sectors of the economy were unable to respond adequately to the growth in consumer demand. The main cause of Russian inflation has been the other non-monetary factor, supply-side (cost-push) inflation. This is largely generated by the intense monopolization of the internal market and made worse by the low level of innovation that is a characteristic of the Russian economy (new technologies make goods cheaper).

4. In line with liberalism, and especially the school of monetarism, Russian monetary policy is targeted heavily at curbing inflation. To do this, the authorities use those deflationary instruments that have an impact on monetary inflation but remain neutral to non-monetary inflation.

5. Another important feature of the monetary policy in Russia is that the money supply is based largely on earnings from exports and foreign investments, mostly credit but not from internal sources. The volume

of the money supply in Russia thus depends primarily on ups and downs in the formation of the stock of money from external sources, i.e., on the state of the world economy, and it is key to recognize that this supply is not under the control of the Russian monetary authorities.

6. Another important feature of the Russian monetary system is its high levels of dollarization. The 1990s saw significant dollarization of the Russian economy caused by high inflation and the instability of the ruble. Dollarization fell after 2000 but peaked again during the crises of 2008–2009 and 2015–2016.

7. There has been a trend towards consolidation in the banking sector, but this only goes so far towards tackling one of the main weaknesses of the Russian banking system, i.e., the insufficient monetization that prevents even the largest banks from acquiring large holding of financial assets. The level of poverty in the country is also a factor as it puts a break on banks growing their deposits. Only about 35% of the population have bank deposits.

8. State or quasi-state banks account for about 70% of the country's bank assets. This could enable the government to pursue an active credit policy. But the government instead focuses on its financial rather than any macroeconomic goals. Moreover, federal and regional officials are able to influence the state and quasi-state banks to focus on their business interests.

9. Russia's Central Bank does not have a role in relation to economic growth in the way that the Federal Reserve in the USA or the Bank of Japan do. Instead, its purpose is solely on money and credit, as well as on the reduction of inflation in particular, which makes its role similar to that of the European Central Bank.

10. The Russian stock market, on the one hand, lists the stocks of large companies of which it has considerable volume. But on the other hand, it fails in some of its basic functions. We can thus conclude that the Russian market is mostly speculative. This conclusion is supported by the high levels of volatility on Russian stock indices.

Questions

1. What is the importance of oil and gas revenues for the Russian economy?
2. What is the purpose of the National Wealth funds?
3. Why is a flat tax applied to personal income in Russia and other CIS and CEE countries?
4. If inflation in Russia is non-monetary in nature, why it is combatted primarily by monetary policy instruments?
5. Why does the Russian economy have a low level of monetization?
6. Why is the Russian stock market speculative in nature?

Sources of Additional Information

The Oxford Handbook of the Russian Economy. Oxford University Press: 2013.

Mau V. Russia in an Epoch of Turbulence. Crises and Lessons. Routledge: 2018.

Russia in Figures. Short Statistics Digest.

http//www.minfin.ru (website of the Ministry of Finance)

http//www.cbr.ru (website of Central Bank of the Russian Federation)

CHAPTER 15

THE EXTERNAL SECTOR

Russia's current model for participation in the world economy is based primarily on its exports of fuel and energy, capital turnover, labor immigration, and technology imports.

Russia in World Trade

Russia's share of world trade is not great; its share is about the same as its share of world GDP. However, the country is among the world leaders in terms of its exports of certain commodities: energy resources, metals, diamonds, timber, synthetic rubber, fertilizers, and grain. In the case of high-tech exports, Russia's participation in world markets is mostly related to military equipment. In the world rankings, Russia's imports show a similar pattern of large quantities of a limited number of goods: beef, sugar, fruit and vegetables, pharmaceuticals, textiles, and cars.

In 2016, Russia's export quota—the value of exports of goods and services expressed as a proportion of GDP—was 26%. The same figure for other major economies was: Brazil, 12.5%; USA, 12%; Japan, 16%; India, 19%; and China, 20%. Thus, Russia has not quantitative problem when it comes to participating in world trade.

However, Russia's relatively high export quota is made up of a small group of industries, whose goods and services produce only small added value (with the exception of military equipment). The country's participation is thus not as effective as it might be; it is held back by the unsophisticated make-up of its exports. For example, the share of global exports taken by Russian civil engineering products is barely 0.4%.

Table 15.1 — Structure by Commodity of Russian Merchandise Exports according to Customs Statistics (US$ bn)

	Exports			Imports		
	1995	**2008**	**2016**	**1995**	**2008**	**2016**
Total	78.2	468.1	285.5	46.7	266.9	182.2
including:						
foodstuffs and agricultural raw materials (excl. textile)	1.4	9.4	17.1	13.2	35.2	24.9
mineral products	33.3	326.0	168.9	3.0	8.3	3.2
chemical products, rubber	7.8	30.3	20.8	5.1	35.1	33.8
leather raw materials, fur and related articles	0.3	0.4	0.3	0.2	1.0	0.8
wood, pulp-and- paper products	4.4	11.6	9.8	1.1	6.5	3.4
textiles, textile articles, and footwear	1.1	0.9	0.9	2.6	11.6	11.0
metals, precious stones and articles thereof	20.9	62.2	38.0	3.9	19.3	11.8
machinery, equipment, and transport means	8.0	23.0	24.3	15.7	141.0	86.3
others	1.0	4.5	5.5	1.9	9.1	7.1

Source: Russia in Figures. Short statistics digest (for relevant years).

Table 15.1 shows the extent to which minerals (mainly fuel and energy) are accounting for 60% of the total in 2016. Chemicals (mainly fertilizers), metals, agriculture (mainly grain), and engineering goods (mainly armaments) make up a further 34%. So, despite the recent growth in these last two groups, Russian exports today continue the Soviet pattern of relying heavily on minerals.

The break-down of Russian exports by commodity also demonstrates the country's poor competitiveness and the extent to which production of many products is insufficient even for the domestic market. Russia, despite its enormous agricultural potential, continues to be one of the world's largest importers of agricultural products. Moreover, despite the growth in exports of agricultural raw materials, this negative balance continues to be large, though it is falling. Import of machinery, equipment, and transport means are rising rapidly. Around 20% of this category is accounted for passenger cars and their spare parts, and about 10% by household appliances and consumer goods, from TVs to cellular phones and laptops. This gives Russian imports a strong consumer bias: consumer goods represent 38–40% of the total, while in most developed countries, this would range from 20–30% and much lower still in certain key markets, e.g., India and China, 4%; South Korea, 9%; and Brazil, 10%.[22] The remaining 60% of imports to Russia are accounted for by investment and intermediate goods. In fact, Russia can be said to consume the essential part of its imports, rather than using them to improve the country's fixed assets. The country has developed a very specific pattern for its trading activities: a large part of the economy is dedicated to digging up raw materials for export and, rather than being invested sensibly, the earnings are spent on imported consumer goods.

The Geography of Russia's Overseas Trade

Geography poses another problem for Russia's overseas trade. In post-Soviet times, it has had to reorient itself about from the former Soviet countries to Europe. In the current decade, it has to change again to focus on China.

Table 15.2 shows the collapse that occurred in trade between Russia and the other former Soviet countries. Within the Soviet Union, around 60% of the imports and exports into and out of the Russian Soviet Federative Socialist Republic were in trade with other republics of the USSR. In the 1990s, trade with these republics fell by around 90%. It recovered somewhat after 2000 but still remains a quarter of what it was in the Soviet era. The reason for this was that Russian manufactured goods lost their competitive edge in the former Soviet countries. These countries were becoming more open and their economic and political ties with Russia were weakening. They were increasingly able to look elsewhere for their goods.

The collapse of Russia's relationships with the former Soviet countries was one of the main contributors to the length and severity of the economic crisis in the 1990s. Russian industry, which had exported 18% of its output, two-thirds of that to the former Soviet countries, was particularly badly hit. Its main exports had been engineering products, oil

---

[22] Spartak A.N. Strategy of Russia in the Age of Globalization. Digest "Russian economy: ways for competitive growth" ed. by KholopovA.V. Moscow, 2009, p.80 (in Russian).

and gas, and products derived from them. The Russian oil and gas industry managed to mitigate the effects of the crisis by finding new markets beyond the CIS, but the Russian engineering industry was hampered by its lack of competitiveness. As it struggled, the former Soviet countries continued to take 40% of the engineering sector's exports and remain promising markets.

Table 15.2 — Geography of Russian external trade (US$ bn)

	Exports			Imports		
	1990	**2008**	**2016**	**1990**	**2008**	**2016**
Total	227*	468.1	285.5	179*	266.9	182.2
including:						
CIS countries	145*	69.9	37.4	96*	36.6	19.3
among them:						
Ukraine	...	23.6	6.3	...	16.2	4.0
Belarus	...	23.6	14.1	...	10.6	9.4
Kazakhstan	...	13.4	9.4	...	6.4	3.6
other countries	92*	398.2	248.1	83*	230.3	162.9
among them:						
EU countries	....	301.0	130.5	...	115.0	69.9
USA	...	13.5	9.4	...	13.8	10.9
Japan	...	10.4	9.4	...	18.6	6.7
China	...	21.2	28.0	...	34.7	38.1
Turkey	...	27.7	13.1	...	6.1	2.1
India	...	5.2	5.3	...	1.7	2.4
Brazil	...	2.0	1.8	...	4.7	2.5

*Statistics for 1990 of the inter-republic trade within the USSR, calculated in the world market prices, in dollars.

Sources: Statistics of the Federal State Statistics Service and the World Bank.

The backbone of Russia's post-Soviet trade has been its trade with Belarus, Ukraine, and Kazakhstan. This accounts for a third of the turnover of merchandise traded. The trade and other economic relations between these countries will be foundation of greater integration between the former Soviet countries.

In addition to the lack of trade with former Soviet countries beyond these three markets mentioned above, the country's eurocentrism poses another geographical problem for Russia. Europe currently accounts for about half of Russia's external trade. While Europe is very large, it is not the most dynamic market in the world and Russia has sought in recent years to strengthen its ties with Asia, and China in particular.

Trade in Services

Russia's external trade in services is relatively minor. Moreover, unlike for its trade in commodities, it runs a deficit. In 2016, the country exported $50 bn worth of services and imported $74 bn.

Transport, tourism and business services make up the bulk of Russia's services trade. The large deficit is mainly due to the large discrepancy between the number of tourists visiting Russia and the number of Russians traveling abroad. Transport services enjoy a surplus, especially rail cargo and pipelines. Russia thus attaches importance to the various transport corridors that pass through its territory.

Russia in International Capital Movement

Despite the shortage of capital in the country, Russia still manages to export significant amounts of it, sometimes coming second only to China among developing countries. Its exports outstrip its imports in this area. Even in 2015–2017, when foreign investment into Russia and Russian investment overseas began to decline as a result of Western economic sanctions, the net inflows/outflows of private capital remained negative. In 2016-2017, outflows exceeded inflows by $20–31bn. It had been $134 bn in 2008, and $152 bn in 2014.

Geography is again a problem. In the case of direct investment, according to data published by the Bank of Russia, offshore territories figure predominantly as destinations for Russia's exports and as sources of imports. Countries like the United Kingdom and the Netherlands which have close ties to their offshore jurisdictions also figure in the list for other forms of capital movements. Outflows of illegal capital are also a significant factor though diminishing. They tend to prefer offshore jurisdictions and appear in accounts as 'net errors and omissions' or 'fictitious transactions.' In 2016, this amounted to $18 bn in the form of revenues that were not returned to the country nor resulted in any goods or services being received in line with contracts. In some cases, money was transferred under fictitious stock transactions.

We can thus conclude that most of the capital exported from Russia goes to offshore jurisdictions, or 'offshore-related' countries, and in a way designed to avoid tax and protect the anonymity of those involved. We can further see that Russian assets that go abroad return in a variety of ways. We can also observe that Russian assets held abroad do, in fact, return to Russia in a variety of ways, but mainly in the form of direct investment, loans, and credits from these offshore jurisdictions and 'offshore-related' countries. More than two-thirds of capital flowing into the country came from these locations. So while Russia is active in movements of international capital, it cannot be said that this demonstrates the maturity of Russian business or any attractiveness of Russia as an investment destination. Rather, it simply demonstrates the extent of the links between Russia and the offshore centers. The main reason for the preponderance of this kind of capital flow is the weakness in the protection of property rights in Russia, and the ample opportunities for tax evasion. These factors encourage Russian owners of capital to export and register their assets offshore (and they choose precisely those offshore centers that offer comparative anonymity and low taxation) before returning the assets to Russia.

This export of capital from Russia is also increasing as a result of the increasingly international nature of Russian oil and gas, metals, and telecommunications companies, many of which have direct investments in dozens of countries. There is also interest among foreign investors in Russia as a destination for investment. However, the key motive for the export of Russian capital remains what is known in economic theory as 'capital flight,' even though, in Russia's case, most of the capital returns to the country in the guise of foreign investment.

In the Soviet era, the government exported large volumes of capital. This is less the case today: $1–2 bn a year, mostly in the form of government trade credits, various kinds of aid, and an accumulation of public debt from other former Soviet countries. During the decade following 2000, the Russian government took very few loans from other governments or international organizations, the exception being some small loans from international organizations for technical support (i.e., services from specialists).

Russia's International Investment Position

As a result of large scale capital outflows, the overseas assets of Russian residents exceed the assets of non-residents in Russia, these are listed in official statistics as liabilities to non-residents. So-called public reserve assets (foreign reserves) are listed in the balance of payments as investment in external assets since they are primarily invested in foreign stocks and currency.

Table 15.3 — International investment position of Russia at the end of the year, billion dollars

	Assets			Liabilities		
	2000	**2007**	**2017 (end Sept.)**	**2000**	**2007**	**2017 (end Sept.)**
Directs investments	20.1	370.2	455.4	32.2	491.2	499.7
Portfolio investments and derivatives	1.3	28.4	89.5	32,1	363,9	231.6
Other investments incl. loans and credits foreign currency in cash and deposits	199.4 22.1 62.4	222.0 93.7 67.2	353.1 169.1 148.9	119,9 98.3 6,1	389,5 341.6 42,6	320.4 205.2 97.2
Reserve assets	28.0	478.8	424.8			
Total	248.8	1099.3	1322.7	184.2	1244.7	1051.8

Source: http://www.cbr.ru/stattistics/credit_statistics

Table 15.3 shows the extent to which Russian residents have accumulated direct investment overseas (mainly in offshore companies), substantial portfolio investments, as well as other larger investments, mainly in the form of loans and credits to their own companies abroad. There are also substantial holdings of foreign currency held in cash deposits in both Russian and foreign banks.

Russian liabilities held by non-residents are mostly in the form of direct and portfolio investments, along with loans and credits. According to the (incomplete) data of the Federal State Statistics Service on the sectoral structure of foreign investments in Russia, the majority of these investments are invested in the mining industry (17%) and manufacturing (38%). In manufacturing, they are invested in the production of machinery, equipment and means of transport (just 4% despite significant investment in automobile assembly plants) but more in the food industry, 4%; and the chemical complex, 20%. The other favorite industries for foreign direct investors were trade and repair, 18%; financial and real estate activities, rent and the provision of services, 14%; and transport, 6%. This range of foreign investment does not provide a sound basis for modernizing the economy. The loans and credits received from non-residents were taken largely by Russian banks and non-financial companies. In other words, foreign loan capital (even though it originated in Russia) plays a role that had been traditionally done, and done badly, by Russian banks. However, from 2014 onwards, Western economic sanctions against Russia resulted in a dramatic slowdown in capital inflows.

External Debt

The Russian Federation inherited the Soviet Union's roughly $100 bn of external public debt, mostly accumulated in the last few years before its collapse. During the 1990s Russia's external debt increased rapidly, reaching $188 bn by 1998, to finance deficits in the state budget. After 2000, external public debt fell ($146 bn in 2001) as the country began an active program of paying off the debt and not taking out new borrowings. However, the private sector's external debt grew rapidly to fill the shortfall left by the national banking sector's lack of resources to meet the demands of a growing economy. This meant that, despite the falls in public debt, the overall amount of the country's external debt increased rapidly, reaching $729 bn in 2013. But thereafter, under Western economic sanctions and the resulting fall in capital inflows, combined with the repayment of many older loans and movements in the exchange rate, Russian debt again fell sharply.

Table 15.4 — External debt of Russia at the end of the year (US$ bn)

	1995	2000	2008	2017 (end Sept.)
Total	132.7	160.0	479.4	536.7
including in rubles	…	…	83.3	137.3
External debt of public sector incl.	…	…	161.3	266.6
public corporations	125.1	128.6	32.3	54.3
incl. general government banks	…..	…..	61.7	91.5
other sectors	…	….	67.4	120.9
External debt of private sector	…	…	318.1	270.0
incl. banks	….	…	104.6	38.3
other sectors	…	…	213.5	231.8
External debt sustainability ratios, percentage:	38*	60*	29	36
-external debt to GDP (indicative thresholds recommended by IMF, 30–50)	…	…	92	138
-external debt to exports of goods and services (indicative thresholds recommended by IMF, 100–200)	…	…	29	40
-external debt service to exports of goods and services (indicative thresholds recommended by IMF, 15–25)				

**Author's calculations

Source: http://www.cbr.ru/statistics/credit_statistics

Table 15.4 illustrates the role of state and quasi-state banks and companies in the generation of external debt. Instead of seeking to strengthen the national banking system by expanding the assets of the state and quasi-state banks by, for example, refinancing from the central bank (Bank of Russia) or issuing government bonds on their assets, the government has been content to allow them to borrow money abroad. The state and quasi-state non-financial companies have been significant users of foreign loans, with companies in the private sector following their lead.

This large external debt inevitably requires significant debt-servicing payments. In the case of many companies and debtor banks, this involves a transfer of money from the national coffers to those overseas, most to Western banks. This debt servicing swallows up a large proportion of the foreign currency coming into the country, equivalent to between a quarter and a third of revenues earned from the export of goods and services.

Foreign Public Debt Owed to Russia

Russia inherited a large stock of outstanding foreign public debt owed to the USSR. At the end of 1991, this stood at $143 bn at the official exchange rate at the time ($1/₽0.6).[23] However, this debt had a number of features that made its servicing difficult:

- The terms for servicing the debt were inadequately documented. Loans were often in the forms of goods and documented in rubles. But there was often no clear guidance on whether repayments were to be made - in goods or currency, if in currency whether it should be dollars or rubles, and what exchange rate was to be used. This situation had arisen because much of the debt was in the form intergovernmental loans with the political objective of supporting a friendly government;
- Much of the Soviet debt was with countries in poor financial situations who struggled to make the payments or meet the deadlines;
- An estimated 80% of the debt was loans provided by the USSR to other countries for the purpose of purchasing Soviet armaments. Some countries cited this fact as a reason not to repay the loans, as the Paris Club of creditor nations—of which, Russia became a member in 1997—does not cover war debts.

In this situation, Russia sought to develop additional documentation for the public debt, for example, to establish a $1/₽1 exchange rate. It also sought to restructure it, for example, by prolonging the terms of servicing. But the bulk of the debt was written off. By the end of 1999, the country's debt had been reduced to $109 bn, and by the end of 2016, to $35 bn. Russia wrote off over $100 bn of debt, more than any other country (calculated in relation to its own GDP). This came about largely as a result of the earlier policy of providing intergovernmental loans, and partly because the Russian government did not pursue debtors actively.

---

[23] Heifets B.A. External debt-based assets of Russia. Moscow, 2001, pp.34–35 (in Russian).

Russia's Role in International Labor Migration and the Exchange of Knowledge

The huge influx of immigrants to Russia has benefited the country by supplying a ready source of workers for industries suffering labor shortages. The economic activity generated by these workers, and the taxes they have paid, have boosted Russia's economy. However, this is limited by the fact that these workers, who are mostly temporary migrants, send some of their earnings home. The Bank of Russia estimated that in 2014 the value of private transfers abroad was $27 bn, which included $14 bn listed as 'Payments for Labor.' This, of course, is balanced by the money being returned to Russia by Russian citizens working overseas.

Russia's activities in the international exchange of knowledge can only be partly reflected in official statistics since, as in the case for all countries, much of this exchange is done gratis, for example, across the Internet. In 2017, Russia received $1.3 bn from the sale of technologies and spent $2.5 bn on technology itself. There was significant trade in computer and information services: Russia had exports of $3.9 bn and imports of $5.4 bn in 2016. Russian exports of educations services are estimated to be about $1 bn a year.

The Balance of Payments

The balance of payments can be expressed as the balance of economic activity between residents and non-residents of the country.

Table 15.5 Russian balance of payments (neutral presentation) (US$ bn)

	1995	2000	2005	2007	2013	2016
CURRENT ACCOUNT	8.0	46.8	84.6	77.0	34.8	25.5
Goods and services	11.3	53.5	104.6	111.3	123.7	66.4
Exports	93.5	114.6	268.8	393.8	593.6	332.4
Imports	- 82.2	-61.1	- 164.2	- 282.5	- 469,7	266.0
Primary income (compensation of employees, investment income, rent)	-3.4	-6.8	-18.9	-30.7	-79.6	-34.6
Receivable	4.3	4.7	17.5	47.4	42.2	40.5
Payable	-7.7	-11.5	-36.2	-78.1	- 121.8	75.1

Secondary income (current transfers)	0.1	0.1	-1.0	-3.5	-9.3	-6.3
Receivable	0.8	0.8	4.5	8.4	17.3	8.6
Payable	-0.7	-0.7	5.5	-11.9	-26.6	14.3
CAPITAL ACCOUNT	-0.3	10.9	-12.8	-10.2	-0.4	-0.8
Capital transfers*	-0.3	10.9	-12.8	-10.2	-0.2	-0.8
Receivable	3.1	11.8	0.7	1.4	0.4	1.0
Payable	-3.4	-0.9	-13.4	-11.6	-0.6	1.8
Gross acquisition/disposals of non-produced nonfinancial assets**	…	…	…	…	-0.1	24.8
FINANCIAL ACCOUNT (INCLUDING RESERVE ASSETS)	1.0	-48.6	-63.9	-53.0	-24.1	20.2
Direct investment	1.6	-0.5	0.1	9.2	-17.3	-10.2
net acquisition of financial assets	-0.4	-3.2	-12.8	-45.9	-86.5	22.3
net incurrence of financial liabilities	2.0	2.7	12.9	55.1	69.2	32.5
Portfolio investment and financial derivatives	-2.4	-10.3	-11.6	7.2	-11.3	-1.9
net acquisition of financial assets	-1.7	-0.4	-9.8	-7.2	-3.3	-12.5
net incurrence of financial liabilities	-0.7	-9.9	-1.8	14.4	-8.1	-10.6
Other investment	11.2	-21.8	9.0	79.5	-17.6	24.1
net acquisition of financial assets	5.2	-17.6	-33.3	-59.8	-80.8	-2.3
net incurrence of financial liabilities	6.0	-4.2	-42.3	139.3	63.3	-26.4
Reserve assets***	-9.3	-16.0	-61.4	-148.9	22.1	8.2
NET ERRORS AND OMISSIONS	8.8	9.1	7.9	13.8	-10.3	-4.6
OVERALL BALANCE	0	0	0	0	0	0

*Basically exports/imports of property by migrants and remission of government debts

** Purchasing/sale of patient, trademarks etc.

*** "+" means decrease, "-" means increase of reserve assets

Source: Bank of Russia statistics for relevant years; http://www.cbr.ru/statistics/credit_statistics

Table 15.5 illustrates the following characteristics in Russia's balance of payments:

- The current balance of payments (the current account) has traditionally been positive. This is explained by exports being larger than imports. This partly reflects low domestic demand for investment goods (a consequence of low investment in the national economy) and the fact that local demand there is largely met by imports.
- The capital account is often negative due to large debt write-off to other countries.
- The financial account is, in fact, negative as a result of the outflow of private capital being larger than the inflow. Another factor is the growth of reserve assets which is shown as capital outflow in the balance of payments.

International Reserves

The official reserves of the USSR were almost used up in the early 1990s before Russia took over what was left. However, thanks to rises in world market prices for the commodities that Russia was exporting and increases in the inflows of foreign capital, they soon began to recover rapidly. By the summer of 2008, they had reached a record level at $597 bn. Despite a large fall in reserves in 2014–2015, Russia continues to have one of the largest reserves in the world.

Table 15.6 — International reserves of Russia (at the end of years) (US$ bn)

1992	**1995**	**2000**	**2005**	**2007**	**2008**	**2009**	
4.5	17.2	28.0	182.2	478.8	426.3	439.5	
2010	**2011**	**2012**	**2013**	**2014**	**2015**	**2016**	**2017**
479.4	498.6	537.6	509.6	385.5	368.4	377.7	432.7

Source: http://www.cbr.ru/statistics/credit_statistics

At the end of 2016, Russia's international reserves were equivalent to $377.7 bn (the six-month imports of goods and services were about $116 bn). This exceeded the reserves criterion in terms of imports according to the Greenspan-Guidotti rule (see Chapter 7): Russia's entire short-term debt, public and private, amounted to $48 bn. In relation to the Reddy criterion, in 2016, the three-month imports of goods and services stood at less than $58 bn and payments on external debt for the year were about $132 bn.

According to the Bank of Russia, official reserves consist of foreign stocks and currency (82%), and monetary gold (18%). The substantial part of these reserves takes the form of the National Wealth Fund managed by the Ministry of Finance as a sovereign fund. This does not go against IMF rules.

Currency Policy

Let us consider first exchange rate policy as an aspect of currency policy. Due to the ups and downs in the Russian economy during the 1990s, the ruble fell in value, suffering several sharp falls in relation to the dollar. In the past the Bank of Russia's main policy objective in relations to exchange rates was to smooth the movements of the ruble. As a result, even the devaluation of the ruble at the end of 2008 and beginning of 2009 was achieved gradually, over several months. However, more recently, the Bank has moved to inflation targeting. This includes a policy of not interfering in exchange rates. This leaves the ruble free to rise in value if world market prices for the commodities that Russia exports rise and the country amasses large reserves. However, if these indicators fall, the ruble will fall with them, as happened in 2014–2015.

According to some liberal economists in Russia, if the ruble is low, exports will grow and imports fall, the latter reducing competition of locally produced goods. A low ruble is also attractive to foreign investors seeking to purchase assets in Russia.

Russian economists of the Keynesian school prefer a higher ruble. In their view, Russian exports are affected more by world market prices than the exchange rate. In the case of imports, they believe a strong ruble would encourage the import of investment goods. A strong ruble also helps with the servicing of external debt, as rubles are changed into dollars to pay creditors. Finally, the Keynesians believe that a strong ruble would act as a symbol of economic stability and attract foreign investors.

During the same period, there was an increasingly liberal currency policy. At the moment, the ruble is fully convertible, both for current and capital transactions. However, as in many developing countries, some restrictions and controls are maintained such as, for example, the requirement for exporters to repatriate their overseas earnings, though there is no obligation that these be converted into rubles. The maintenance of controls on exchange, couple with some continued instability in the ruble, limits the currency's ability to develop as an international currency.

Russia as a Regional Financial Center

The Russian government has sought to promote Russia (in fact, mainly Moscow) as an international, or at least regional, financial center. This could be supported by making the ruble into a regional reserve currency and the establishment of a ruble zone in which participating countries would use the ruble in their international dealings and hold it in their international reserves. To be an international financial center, Moscow would need to develop the necessary infrastructure.

The idea of making the ruble a regional currency has in its favor the fact that the ruble is freely convertible and that the country has a sufficiently large GDP. However, there are other factors that militate against the idea. The ruble's exchange rate, despite a period of stability after 2000, has suffered fluctuations and devaluations in 2008–2009 and 2014–2015. High inflation has seen the internal purchasing power of the ruble has fallen more than for most other leading currencies. Finally, the Russian capital markets, their range maturity, and openness, remain underdeveloped. This is especially true of the bond market, where non-residents are unable to purchase products to hold as part of international reserves.

While the ruble is certainly tradable outside Russia, demand for it is lower than for other currencies and it has yet to achieve the status of a world reserve currency. This puts it on a par with the currencies of e.g., Canada, Australia, New Zealand, Sweden, Denmark, Norway, South Korea, Singapore, and Hong Kong. This situation results largely from the fact that Russian exports, which are mainly paid for in foreign currency, are mainly raw materials of commodities for prices of which are traditionally set by the leading exchange markets around the world in dollars. To develop beyond this situation, Russia would need to develop its own network of national commodity exchange markets to trade in the raw materials. Economists estimate that it would be possible to conduct all of the trade with CIS countries and up to one third of trade with non-CIS countries in rubles.[24]The situation with bonds is better developed. Ruble-denominated Eurobonds are seen as viable investments and are sought after by domestic and foreign investors alike. It is worth noting that some countries, e.g.,

---

[24] Moiseev S. Ruble as a Reserve Currency. Economic Matters. 2008, no.9, pp.16.

Belarus and China, have begun to hold part of their international reserves in rubles.

The transformation of the ruble into a regional currency brings with it both benefits and costs. The benefits would include cost savings when converting the ruble into foreign currency, a reduction of exchange risks, an increase in total turnover with the creation of a ruble zone, a growth in foreign investment with more active purchasing of ruble stock by foreign investors who will also open ruble deposits, an improvement of the stability of the Russian economy and its resilience to external shocks, a financing of the theoretic balance of payments deficit, revenue generation from seigniorage, and a more independent foreign policy. The costs would include the need to maintain a stable exchange rate (particularly to rule out devaluation as an instrument of economic policy), less control over the money supply (which will increase with the inflow of foreign currency to purchase rubles), the possible upward pressure on the exchange rate due to external demand for the currency, and the elimination of exchange restrictions and controls. These costs can outweigh the benefits if a currency is traded more overseas than domestically. The ruble, however, should be safe from this fate for the foreseeable future.

As well as making the ruble a regional currency, a further step necessary to develop Moscow as a regional financial center is the development of appropriate infrastructure. This does not involve just the obvious financial infrastructure—the presence of a significant international banks, large exchange markets, strong insurance companies, and leading consultancies—it also requires the development of an environment conducive to professional financial business—low taxes, high quality accommodation, good communications, general safety, and a convenient visa regime. Moscow's development is still lagging behind in all these areas. It has many obstacles to overcome to catch other centers such as Singapore or Dubai and the most acute of them is the growing number of Western financial sanctions since 2014.

Russia's Role in International Economic Integration

One of the main strategic concerns facing Russia is its economic reintegration with the other former Soviet countries in the CIS. The country is seeking to strengthen its economic relations with the leading economies of the CIS. Belarus, Kazakhstan, and Ukraine are major trading partners for Russia. For them, Russia is their largest trading partner. They are also important destinations for Russia investment. In the case of

Belarus and Kazakhstan, the integration has become more formal. By contrast, Ukraine has been developing closer links with the EU, including the signing of an association agreement, which holds it back from closer ties with the countries of the CIS.

The CIS includes the Eurasian Economic Union (EEU) of Russia, Belarus, Kazakhstan, Armenia, and Kyrgyzstan. There is also a deeper integration between Russia and Belarus. The EEU has created a customs union, although each country retains the right to set its own duties of hydrocarbons exports to third countries. The customs union has elements of a common market, such as allowing the free movement of labor and capital. The members plan to remove the remaining trade restrictions by 2025, and to create a unified financial regulator. This would be a major step towards the creation of a complete common market within the EEU.

Conclusion

1. Russia participates actively in world trade. However, it is held back by the obsolete structure of its foreign trade, especially its exports. In addition, it has only limited trade with other former Soviet countries.

2. Despite a shortage of capital in the country, Russia exports large amounts—more than it imports. A further problem lies in the fact that most capital flows to and from offshore jurisdictions and countries closely related to offshore centers.

3. During the 1990s, Russia's public external debt rose rapidly as a result of the deficit in the state budget. After 2000, government debt decreased significantly, as old debt was paid off and the government limited the amount of new borrowing. However, the debt of public and private companies rose rapidly due to the domestic banking industry's shortage of assets which persisted despite economic growth. From 2014 onwards, the overall external debt position began to shrink as a result of less foreign loans flowing into the country.

4. Russia became a world leader in writing off the debts of foreign countries (in terms of the amount of write-offs expressed as a percentage of GDP). This came about partly as many of the loans Russia inherited from the Soviet Union had poorly documented repayment terms and partly due to the Russian government's decision not to pursue certain loans actively in the hope of economic or political concession from the debtor countries.

5. Russia's balance of payment has the following characteristics:
   - The current balance of payments (the current account) has traditionally been positive. This is explained by exports being larger than imports. This partly reflects low domestic demand for investment goods (a consequence of low investment in the national economy) and the fact that demand there is largely met by imports.
   - The capital account is often negative due to large debt remission payments to other countries.
   - The financial account is usually negative as a result of the outflow of private capital being larger than the inflow. Another factor is the growth of reserve assets which is shown as capital outflow in the balance of payments.

6. The Bank of Russia's main policy objective in relations to exchange rates was to smooth the movements of the ruble. However, more recently, the Bank has moved to inflation targeting. This includes a policy of not interfering in exchange rates. The Russian government has sought to promote Russia (in fact, mainly Moscow) as an international, or at least regional, financial center. This could be supported by making the ruble into a regional reserve currency and the establishment of a ruble zone in which participating countries would use the ruble in their international dealings and hold it in their international reserves.

7. One of the main strategic concerns facing Russia is its economic reintegration with the other former Soviet countries in the CIS. First of all, the country is seeking to strengthen its economic relations with the member countries of the Eurasian Economic Union (EEU—Russia, Belarus, Kazakhstan, Armenia and Kyrgyzstan).

Questions

1. Why do Russian exports consist mainly of oil, gas, and other raw materials?

2. Why does Russia have only limited trade with other CIS countries?

3. Why have Russian capital outflows and inflows gravitated toward offshore centers and the countries closely related to them?

4. How has Russia's external position changed in recent years?

5. What are Moscow's prospects of achieving the status of a regional financial center?

6. Why is Russia focusing its integration efforts mainly on the EEU?

Sources of additional information

The Oxford Handbook of the Russian Economy. Oxford University Press: 2013.

Mau V. Russia in an Epoch of Turbulence. Crises and Lessons. Routledge: 2018.

The Russian Direct Economy and Foreign Direct Investment. Routledge: 2015.

Russia in figures. Short Statistics Digest.

Statistics of the Central Bank of the Russian Federation (http://www.cbr.ru/statistics)

IMF. World Economic Outlook (www.imf.org)

IMF. International Financial Statistics (www.imf.org)

World Bank. World Development Report (www.worldbank.org)

CHAPTER 16

THE SOCIAL SECTOR

Following the economic recovery and the restoration of GDP to pre-reform levels, Russia has managed by the end of the first decade of the 21st century to restore real household disposable income to a level last seen in the Soviet era and then to increase further. However, other indicators present a mixed picture in the social sector, exacerbated by unsuccessful policy.

Poverty

Russian statistics define as poor (low income) those people whose income is below the national poverty line (minimal cost of living). To calculate it, a basket of consumer goods is used which includes a basic set of food items, non-food goods and services necessary of the preservation and support of life and health. Compulsory payments and fees are also taken into account. The figure is calculated every quarter with separate figures worked out for an able-bodied person, a pensioner, and a child and separate calculations made in each of the constituent parts of the Russian Federation based on current prices in each region. In the last quarter of 2017, the monthly average cost of living was 10,328 (₽11,160 for an able-bodied person, ₽8,496 for a pensioner, and ₽10,181 for a child). There were regional fluctuations depending on the prices for goods and services. The highest cost of living was in the north, in Kamchatka Territory, where it worked out at ₽19,220.

On the basis of this approach, the percentage of the population classified as low-income in recent years has ranged from 21–34% between 1992 and 2000 to 11–13% between 2011 and 2014 and 13–14% in from 2015 to 2017, reflecting movements in GDP. There is another way of defining poverty, that is people with less than 50% of median income. In Russia, by this definition, there are 22% of people living in poverty.

Low incomes and salaries are a significant contribution to poverty. In 2017, the average monthly salary in Russia was ₽39,085, equivalent to less than $700. This explains why two thirds of the people defined as poor in Russia are, in fact, in work but poorly paid. Such people are mainly in the agricultural sector, the consumer goods industry, education, medical care, culture, and sports. Many families with children, especially in small towns and rural areas fall into this category.

This situation of the 'working poor' reflects Russia's oligarchic state capitalism, a system in which income distribution is highly unequal. According to calculations done by the team headed by Thomas Piketty, author of the famous book "Capital in the Twenty-First Century", in Russia, 20–40% of national income between 2005 and 2015 is in the hands of dollar billionaires, compared to 5–15% in the USA, Germany, and France.[25]

Inequality

In 2016, the top quintile of the population took 47% of all income. According to the Federal State Statistics Service, the income of the top decile was 16 times that of the lowest decile. However, this statistic has fallen slightly from 16.7 times in 2007. The Gini index has also fallen from 0.421 in 2010 to 0.413–0.414 in 2015–2016.

Taken together, these two suggest a reduction, however slight, in income inequality. But the inequality remains huge. It is higher than in most over former Soviet countries and higher than in countries of a similar level of development (see Table 7.8). Russian society has traditionally had a strong focus on justice and the sense of injustice at this 'unjust inequality' is spreading. This is fueled in part by the notion that firstly, most Russian oligarchs acquired their income through the process of accelerated privatizations, rather than as the fruit of their own entrepreneurial skills or hard work, and secondly, that the bureaucratic elite have acquired great wealth by abusing their positions for their own benefit.

---

[25] Ph. Novokmet, Th. Piketty, and G. Zucman. From Soviets to Oligarchs: Inequality and Property in Russia, 1905–2016//NBER Working Paper 23712. August 2017. P.14.

The social survey suggests that the best way to overcome inequality is through social mobility which can be achieved through a focus on education and on the establishment of social relations.[26]

Social Insurance and Social Security

Besides income policy, another important trend in social policy is the development of social security and social insurance for the population. These are aimed at the vulnerable in society: pensioners, the disabled, children from vulnerable families, orphans, and single mothers. These social payments account for a significant portion of the consolidated budget (around 12% of GDP). Two-thirds of these payments are pensions, the rest are made mainly in the form of subsidies, for temporary disability, family and maternal allowances, unemployment benefit, and scholarships. In total, these social payments make up around 19% of all income in Russia, targeted at the most vulnerable in society. We can observe that the system of oligarchic state capitalism targets these efforts at the lower-income section of society in the hope of maintaining political stability in the country.

The Pension System

The Russian pensions system has been undergoing reform, with only varying levels of success. In the Soviet era, pensions were paid directly from the budget, i.e., the system was distributional (defined benefit) and worked effectively given the proportionately large number of workers compared to pensioners. But by 1990, there were 33.8 million pensioners, 23% of the population and by 2016 this had risen to 44.2 million, 30% of the population. In other words, the ration of workers to pensioners has gone from 4:1 in 1970 to 1.6:1 in 2016. This is expected to rise still further as life expectancy continues to improve. The ability to pay decent pensions is, therefore, a growing concern for Russia. To achieve this, and in line with many countries with ageing populations, a defined contribution pension system has been introduced.

In 1990, in the Russian Soviet Federative Socialist Republic, a non-budget Pension fund was founded to finance the payment of pensions. In subsequent reforms, a two-tier pension system was developed, involving

[26] Avramova E., Maleva T. On the Reasons for the Spread of Social and Economic Inequality: What Shows the Resource-based View.Voprosyeconomiki. 2014, no.7, pp.150–52 (in Russian).

basic universal pension, supplemented by an insurance element for those in employment. For those born in or after 1967, the insurance element of the pension in accumulating, and the individual can choose for it to be held on account in a non-state pension funds or at the public Bank for Foreign Economic Activity. Government and employers both contribute to both elements of the pensions. In addition, individuals are able to supplement their pensions with additional voluntary saving and insurance schemes. Large companies also provide occupational pension schemes for their employees. Nowadays the overwhelming majority of pensions is formed by compulsory social insurance on employers (they pay into non-budgetary funds the equivalent of 30% of their employees' wages of which 70% goes to the Pension fund) and subventions from the federal budget.

However, during the transition from a defined benefit to a defined contribution system, the so-called 'effect of double burden'' arises. This refers to the situation in which those financing the pensions will have to pay the contributions of those in work, but also pay the pensions of those already retired who did not accumulate their own savings in the past. This situation is expected to last for 50 years, peaking in 2024. As a result, the Pension Fund of the Russian Federation runs a permanent deficit which, in 2015, was equivalent to 0.9% of GDP.

One potential solution to this would be to raise the pension age according to the Pension reform started in 2019. Until that period Russia has had one of the lowest pension ages in the world: 55 for women and 60 for men. Although mortality rates among the working population are comparatively high, once Russians reach retirement age their life expectancy is almost on a par with pensioners in the West: 15 years for men and 25 years for women. Due to the Reform, the pension age will rise gradually in 2019-2028 to 60 for women and 65 for men. Today, about a third of pensioners continue to work beyond pension age, so earning a salary as well as their pension. For them, a rise in the pension age would mean a fall in their household disposable income.

How generous are Russian pensions? While the absolute amount is important, what matters more is how a pension relates to the individual's cost of living, and the 'replacement rate' i.e., the ration of the pension to an average salary. In terms of the pension's ratio to the cost of living, in recent years this has been 1.6–1.7:1. The replacement rate has been 34–36%, i.e., the average pension is a little more than a third of an average salary. Between 1986 and 1990, before the collapse of the Soviet Union, it stood at 36–39%. From this we can conclude that pension reform has at least lifted the system out of the crisis of the 1990s when an average pension dropped to just 70% of the average cost of living. However, the system still falls short of the recommendation of the International Labor Organization that the replacement rate should not fall below 40%.

Health Care

In terms of numbers of doctors, nursing staff, and hospital beds per population, Russia far outstrips most developed countries. But at the same time, Russians seem to suffer illness more than citizens of developed countries. The number of people, per thousand, being diagnosed with an illness for the first time increased from 615 in 1992 to 768 in 2008 and 778 in 2015. Mortality rates still exceed those of the Soviet era: 12.5 in 2017 compared to 11.0 in 1990. The reason for this lies less in anomie, which has clearly weakened in Russian society, but in the fact that, on the one hand, the population is ageing and, on the other, the public health care system has improved little since the Soviet era despite increased spending.

This is confirmed by the statistics of costs in fixed prices. These fell during the 1990s, recovered after 2000 and have continued to rise. Health costs are now estimated to be around 7% of GDP which corresponds to other countries at a similar level of development. Expenditure is split roughly evenly between public and private services, though other estimates suggest the proportion spent on the public side are much higher, even as much as four times the private expenditure. Moreover, in recent years, medical institutions have increased their levels of medical equipment and supplies.

The emergence of a private medical sector alongside the public has not yet produced substantial improvement in the efficiency of medical care. The vast majority of medical treatment is still provided by public health care institutions on the basis of compulsory medical insurance, contributions to which are paid by employers for their workers and by the government for pensioners, students and those under age. However, patients also find themselves having to pay for some services in the form of tariffs, which medical institutions and their employees see as additional to basic medical services. This system, with its combination of sources of income, reduces any motivation that public institutions might have to improve their services or invest in better equipment. Nevertheless, there are some signs of improvements in efficiency taking place: mortality rates are falling and levels of bed occupancy and turnover in hospitals are improving.

The Culture, Recreation, and Tourism Sectors

The number of newspapers and magazines per thousand people has been growing. But for books, the opposite is true: 8,839 books were published per thousand people in 1992, but just 3,138 in 2016. The number of publicly accessible libraries has also gone down. The number of visits to theaters has been recovering after a decline, while the number of visits to museums and cinemas has been recovering even more strongly. This is accompanied by an increase in the number of Russian films being released. These now make up 19% of all film distribution.

The number of visits to resort centers and recreational institutions is also recovering but still lags behind the numbers seen in the Soviet era: 13.3 million visits in 1992 compared with 10 million a year more recently. The number of people actively pursuing a sport is growing, with the number of gyms and swimming pools open significantly higher than it was in the Soviet era. The number of Russian tourists traveling overseas has grown enormously, from 1.6 million in 1993 to 32 million in 2016.

Housing Stock and Utilities

For many years after the collapse of the Soviet Union, the rate of housing construction was lower than it had been before 1990. But this has now recovered and overtaken the rates seen in the Soviet era. Between 79 and 85 million square meters of housing were built annually between 2014 and 2017, compared to 73 million in 1987. The housing stock has grown throughout and in 2016 stood at 3.7 bn square meters. With the population decreasing, this has meant that the amount of housing available per head of population has grown, from 16 square meters two decades ago to 25 square meters in 2016. The vast majority of urban housing was sold off by the authorities and is now in private hands. In rural districts and villages, housing has traditionally been privately owned.

At the end of the last decade, 17% of all housing under construction was for social housing, mainly for the poor. The government either builds such housing itself or purchases it, some through the 'a share of the city' scheme which involves off-setting the value of the land. But most house building is done by the private sector.

House construction continues to be very expensive. In Russia, the average market price of a square meter of primary housing is 1.6 times an average monthly salary. This is largely the result of the artificial monopolization of housing construction (building licenses are awarded to the companies affiliated with local authorities as well as the high cost of those elements of the construction process that are overseen by local officials such as land valuations, design work, approvals, and permission. In 2010, in Moscow, the cost of building a square meter of housing was only 21% of its eventual market value. Administrative costs (leases, encumbrances, design approvals, and connections to utilities) brought this up to 40–50%. The rest was left to the builders many of who enjoy close relationships with the local authorities.[27]

The housing market operates on a system of mortgages. But loans are often expensive. As a result, only 27% of families can afford to buy a house with a mortgage, supplemented by savings, though this is three times as many as was the case in 2004.[28]

In the previous decade, the Federal Housing Construction Promotion Fund was founded. Federal lands were transferred to it to be used for housing. This was intended to increase the stock of land available for housing and so lower its price. To support the mortgage system, the State Agency for Residential Mortgages was founded. This redeems mortgage loans from small commercial banks in exchange for its own bonds, guaranteed by the government. The Bank for Foreign Economic Activity redeems mortgage-backed bonds from large banks and also credits the Agency. In 2015, the Fund and the Agency were merged to form the Agency for Residential Development.

When local authorities sold off (privatized) their stock of housing, they became less interested in its condition. This reflected their lack of resources, as in many areas the money they had received in rent did not cover the cost of maintenance. This has thus become a large area of concern by the government who now subsidize housing maintenance and utilities. Since the bulk of these costs fall on local authorities, most of whom are short of money, they resort to the 'economy' of repairing existing houses, rather than building new ones. As a result, the proportion of the housing stock that is of poor condition or substandard rose from 1.3% in 1990 to 3.2% in 2008. To address this problem, the Housing and Utility Reform Foundation, founded in 2007 in the form of a state-owned

[27] Rostroy unmasked a cost account. Commersant. 10 April, 2008, pp.13 (in Russian).

[28] Kosareva N., Polidi T., Puzanov A., Yasin E. How to "humanize" square meters. Expert. 6–12 April, 2015, no. 15 (in Russian).

corporation, began to move people out of substandard housing and into new, low-cost accommodation and undertake major repairs, paid for from the federal budget. As a result, the percentage of substandard housing fell to 2.4% in 2016.

A further problem is the lack of housing infrastructure. In rural areas and villages, a significant proportion of houses lack basic amenities: 20% of houses do not have running water or sewerage and 32% do not have baths or showers, though these statistics have been steadily improving.

The need to create competition in the provision of housing services has been partly addressed. People are able to participate in electing management companies for their dwelling (although many do so reluctantly) and the local authorities are very keen to put themselves forward to be elected. In this process, the costs of housing and utilities are often overstated.

Conclusion

1. Following the economic recovery and the restoration of GDP to pre-reform levels, Russia has managed to restore and increase real household disposable income to a level last seen in the Soviet era. However, other indicators in the social sector present a mixed picture.

2. Russian statistics define as poor (low income) those people whose income is below the poverty line. This covered 13-14% of the population between 2015 and 2017. Most poor people in Russia are, in fact, working but on very low salaries.

3. In 2016, the top quintile of the population took 47% of all income. Russian society has traditionally had a strong focus on justice and the sense of injustice at this ‘unjust inequality’ is spreading. This is fueled in part by the notion that firstly, most Russian oligarchs acquired their income through the process of accelerated privatizations, rather than as the fruit of their own entrepreneurial skills or hard work, and secondly, that the bureaucratic elite have acquired great wealth by abusing their positions for their own benefit

4. The Russian pension system has been undergoing reform, with only varying levels of success. Reforms have led to the creation of a two-tier pension system was developed, involving a basic universal pension, supplemented by an insurance element for those in

employment. This is funded by both government and employers. New reform in 2019-2028 is aimed at raising the pension age.

5. In terms of numbers of doctors, nursing staff, and hospital beds per population, Russia far outstrips most developed countries. At the same time the health care system has seen improvements in its effectiveness.

6. Over the last two decades there has been a marked increase in the amount of housing available per head of population, from 16 to 25 square meters. However, new houses and mortgages continue to be very expensive. Substandard housing is also a problem.

Questions

1. Try to enumerate and describe the major groups of poor people in Russia.

2. Why is income inequality so high in Russia?

3. What will be the different component parts of your pension?

Sources of Additional Information

The Oxford Handbook of the Russian Economy. Oxford University Press: 2013.

Mau V. Russia in an Epoch of Turbulence. Crises and Lessons. Routledge: 2018.

Russia in Figures. Short Statistics Digest. http://www.economy.gov.ru (website of the Ministry of Economic Development).

UNIT III

THE ECONOMIC MODELS OF BELARUS, MOLDOVA AND UKRAINE

CHAPTER 17

SIMILARITIES AND DIFFERENCES IN THE ECONOMIES OF BELARUS, MOLDOVA, AND UKRAINE

Belarus, Moldova, and Ukraine make up the East European sub-region of the CIS. Their economic potential differs significantly, as reflected in their populations: of a total of 56 million, Ukraine's population is 42.5 million (excluding the Autonomous Republic of Crimea and the city of Sevastopol), Belarus's 9.5 million, and Moldova's 4 million. They are linked by geography, common borders, a shared history and culture, as well as similar social and economic problems.

Similarities and Differences between Economic Models

This sub-region's economy is in transition. The transition to a market economy in the 1990s had largely the same social and economic impact on all three countries, leaving them all in crisis, with GDP falling, inflation and unemployment increasing, and living standards dramatically declining.

Toward the end of the 1990s, the three countries' economic and social paths began to diverge. Belarus chose the path of a socially oriented market economy with the focus on state regulation and the preservation of a large public sector, Moldova and Ukraine chose liberal economic models.

The countries' national economic models were formed against a backdrop of a severe political turmoil. In Moldova, in 1990, this escalated into an armed conflict and the division of the country into two. In Ukraine, divisions between political forces and among the population slowed down the country's development for many years. In the middle of the 2010s, this led to partial disintegration. In Belarus, the power struggle led to the formation of a closed political regime which put a drag on the market reforms.

The Potential, Size and Dynamics of Economic Development

In 2017, the sub-region's GDP by PPP was about US$562 bn. Belarus accounted for US$176 bn of this, Ukraine US$366 bn, and Moldova only US$20 bn. In terms of the per capita GNI by PPP, there were significant differences between the countries: in Belarus it was US$16.600, in Ukraine US$8.700 and in Moldova US$5.700.

Belarus reached the low point in its transition from a planned to a market economy in 1996. Moldova and Ukraine reached the same point in 1999. In the subsequent years, all three countries experienced fast economic growth, helped by high global prices for goods that they exported, inflows of investment to the privatization programs of state assets, and, in the case of Ukraine and Belarus, economic subsidies from Russia. However, the world financial crisis of 2008 and the subsequent recession saw their growth rates slow, a situation that was compounded by international political events surrounding Ukraine.

Economic growth was accompanied by significant changes in the sectoral structure of GDP. Simple services predominated, while high-technology products decreased markedly. This simplification of the sectoral structure took place in a context of a depreciation of fixed assets, inherited from the planned economies of the Soviet era.

Investment growth in the sub-region which lasted from 2000 to 2008 was in the form of gross capital formation. During this period, indices of investment in fixed capital increased by 340% in Belarus and Ukraine and by 240% in Moldova. However, at the beginning of the current decade there was a trend toward a reduction in the rate of gross capital formation which, in turn, has had a negative impact on the investment process. This is especially true in Ukraine where there has been a decline in manufacturing output due to underinvestment in the economy since 2012.

Table 17.1 — GDP growth rates year-on-year

	Year									
	2000–2008 average	2009	2010	2011	2012	2013	2014	2015	2016	2017*
Belarus	8.0	0.1	7.7	5.5	1.7	1.6	1.7	-3.8	-2.6	0.7
Moldova	5.9	-6.0	7.1	6.8	-0.7	9.4	4.8	-0.4	4.3	4.0
Ukraine	7.0	-15.1	0.3	5.5	0.2	0.6	-6.4	-9.8	2.0	3.2

* Estimates

Source: Commonwealth of Independent States in 2015: Digest of Preliminary Statistical Results. Moscow, 2017; IMF World Economic Outlook, October 2017

Table 17.2 — Gross capital formation in the GDP of Belarus, Moldova, and Ukraine (percentage of GDP)

	2005	2010	2012	2014	2016
Belarus	27.9	32.6	35.1	34.8	25.3
Moldova	30.8	32.7	23.6	24.4	23.8
Ukraine	22.6	24.8	19.6	13.4	21.5

*Estimate

Source: Interstate Statistical Committee of the Commonwealth of Independent States http://www.cisstat.com; World Bank data http://data.worldbank.org/indicator/NE.GDI.TOTL.ZS?view=chart

Similarities and Differences in Economic Policy

The economies of the three countries in the East European sub-region of the CIS are market-based. Belarus retains the most active (even if redundant) role of the state, while Moldova and Ukraine are characterized by much less government intervention in the economy. However, even in these two countries, levels of intervention vary greatly depending on which political forces are in power.

All three countries have placed importance on integration into economic associations. But they have adopted different approaches. Moldova and Ukraine have set the long-term objective of joining the European Union. Both singed an association agreement in 2014. By contrast, Belarus has sought active integration with Russia and other former Soviet countries. It is a member of the Eurasian Economic Union.

Structural features of the respective economies have largely determined the different approaches to integration in the three countries. Belarus has sought to develop its engineering sector and has thus focused on exporting its products mostly to Russia. At the same time, the country has a developed chemical and petrochemical industry that relies on Russian oil and gas, and in turn exports value-added final products. Moldova is less well developed and agriculture and the food industry play a more important part in the economy. Active economic development thus requires inflows of external capital. Hence the primary focus is on the European Union with its large capital resources. For Ukraine, the choice to favor integration with the European Union was driven largely by political, rather than economic considerations. However, the majority of Ukraine's high-value-added exports have traditionally gone to the CIS, and economists agree that even preferential access to the EU will not compensate Ukraine if it loses access to the CIS.

Social and Economic Problems

In all three countries, the years of economic transformation saw significant declines in population: by 13% in Ukraine (not including the Crimea), 7% in Belarus, and 8% in Moldova (including Transniestria). Low birth rates and high rates of mortality contributed to this, but these were compounded by high levels of emigration. Every year, hundreds of thousands of Ukrainians and Moldovans seek temporary work in neighboring countries. The money such people remit back to their home countries has a positive effect (the same is true to a lesser extent in Belarus) but it cannot hide the problem these three countries have in seeking to provide their own people with gainful employment at decent salaries.

All three countries can boast high levels of educational attainment, and these continue to rise. Thus all three have seen rapid increases in the numbers of students in higher education as well as specialist secondary schools, but at the same time, the number of scientific organizations, and the number of people employed in the fields of science and innovation, have decreased markedly. Expenditure on Research and Development (R&D) was 0.7% of GDP in Belarus and Ukraine, and 0.5% in Moldova. As in Russia, the private makes only a paltry investment in R&D, leaving the job to the state.

All three countries lack their own oil and gas resources and are thus economically dependent on exporters of hydrocarbons and find themselves at the mercy of fluctuations in market prices. However, these countries have significant mineral resources of their own. Ukraine boasts major deposits of iron and manganese ores, coal, and the world's largest reserves of black soil. Belarus's main resources are potash and rock salt that are practically inexhaustible. Moldova is less well off in this regard, its main resource being black soil.

These East European countries of the CIS have transport networks that carry important international transport corridors. However, high wear and tear on the systems means they are no longer fit for the requirements of the various economies. Lack of investment is the main cause.

All three countries have suffered from inflation which, in turn, has devalued financial assets and restrained investment activity.

Table 17.3 — Growth in Consumer Prices (percent)

	2007	2008	2009	2010	2011	2012	2013	2014	2015	2016	2017*
Belarus	8.4	14.8	12.9	7.7	53.2	59.2	18.3	18.1	13.5	11.8	8.0
Moldova	12.4	12.7	0	7.4	7.6	4.6	4.6	5.1	9.6	6.4	6.5
Ukraine	12.8	25.2	15.9	9.4	8	0.6	-0.3	12.1	48.7	13.9	12.8

* Estimate

Sources: Interstate Statistical Committee of the Commonwealth of Independent States http://www.cisstat.com.
IMF. The World Economic Outlook. October 2017.p.177.

The three countries in the sub-region are still characterized by low levels of monetization (the ration of M2 to GDP). Between 2000 and 2013, the monetization factor increased significantly (52% in Moldova and Ukraine and 38% in Belarus). However, the current level still falls short of what is needed for rapid development of the banking systems and, with them, greater availability of credit.

External Problems Faced by the Countries of the Sub-Region

The balances of payments in the countries of the sub-region have negative balances in their current accounts, compensated by positive balances in the financial account.

Inflows of foreign investments have both standard and distinct features. In Belarus, for example, direct investments make up the lion's share of investment, while Moldova mostly attracts loans, borrowings, and trade credits. All three countries attract only small quantities of portfolio investment due to the lack of development in their stock markets.

In general, the countries of the East European sub-region have little to interest foreign investors. As of 2015, the accumulated foreign direct investment in Belarus was US$18 bn, in Moldova US$3.5 bn, and in Ukraine US$61.8 bn. One of the factors that discourage foreign investment is the poor standard of their economic institutions, which can be seen in their high levels of corruption and difficult business conditions.

Table 17.4 — Positions of Countries of the East European Sub-Region of the CIS in International Quality Ratings of Economic Institutions

	Belarus	Moldova	Ukraine
Index of Economic Freedom, 2016	157	117	162
Doing Business, 2016	44	52	82
World Competitiveness Index, 2015–2016*	–	84	79
Corruption Perception Index, 2015	107	103	130

* Belarus is not included in the World Competitiveness Index.

Sources: The Heritage Foundation. 2016 Index of Economic Freedom; Doing Business 2016.
World Economic Forum. The Global Competitiveness Report 2015–2016.
Transparency International. The 2015 Corruption Perceptions Index.

These countries' external debt tends to increase due to the activities of the private sector. As in Russia, this comes about as a result of their own shortage of domestic finance, which forces business to look to foreign creditors.

The economy in all three countries is oriented toward exports, while the balance of foreign trade is negative. The main exports are: from Belarus, oil and oil products, and engineering products; from Ukraine, agriculture products, metallurgy, and chemicals; from Moldova, textiles and wine.

Conclusion

1. The East European sub-region of the CIS countries is heterogeneous in terms of its social and economic development. The countries share geographical proximity, common borders, a shared history and culture, and similar economic and social conditions. What distinguishes them from each other are their geopolitical interests and the ways in which they have sought to tackle their political polarization and the politicization of their external economic relations.

2. The economy of the sub-region is characterized by high exposure to world prices for energy resources and other raw materials, as well as the poor state of many of their fixed assets.

3. All countries in the sub-region relay heavily on external trade and earnings from exports, although they all run negative balances in external trade.

4. All the countries in the sub-region face demographic problems as a result of natural decline coupled with labor migration.

5. The sub-region's monetary and credit systems suffer from low levels of capitalization in banks and the resulting low level of monetization in the economy.

Questions

1. What level of social and economic development is seen in the countries of the East European sub-region of the CIS?

2. Describe the similarities and differences in potential, markets and main features of the economies of the countries of the sub-region.

3. Describe the demographic situation in the sub-region.

4. How important is the role of Russia in the social and economic development of the three countries of the sub-region?

5. What are the main external problems faced by the countries of the sub-region?

Sources of Additional Information

Post-Soviet Area in Globalizing World. Problems of Modernization/ Publishing. Ed. by L.Z. Zevin. Saint-Petersburg. 2008 (in Russian).
Commonwealth of Independent States in 2015: Digest of Preliminary Statistical Results. Moscow. 2017.
Finances. Investment and Prices of the Commonwealth of Independent States 2011–2015. Statistical Abstract. Moscow. 2016.
Foreign Trade of Countries of the Commonwealth of Independent States 2015. Moscow. 2016.
National Accounts of Countries of the Commonwealth of Independent States 2009–2013: Statistics Digest. Moscow. 2014.
Macroeconomics and Finances of the CIS Countries and Particular Countries of the World 2010–2014: Short Statistics Digest. Moscow. 2015.
Social Indicators of the CIS Countries and Particular Countries of the World 2010–2013: Short Statistics Digest. Moscow. 2014.
IMF. World Economic Outlook (http://www.imf.org).
The World Bank. World Development Report (http://www.worldbank.org).
UNCTAD. World Investment Report (http://www.unctad.org).
National Statistical Committee of the Republic of Belarus (http://www.belstat.gov.by).
State Statistics Service of Ukraine (http://www.ukrstat.gov.ua/).
National Bureau of Statistics of the Republic of Moldova (http://www.statistica.md).

CHAPTER 18

BELARUS

The Economic Model

Government participation in economic and social life is a cornerstone of Belarus's economy. The main principles of the set-up are outlined in the National Strategy for Sustainable Social and Economic Development until 2030. Belarus is characterized by the following:

- The government maintains a leading role in the economy, allowing gradual development of the private sector.
- The government pursues an active social policy, seeking to ensure political stability, social equity, public order, and large state investment in health care, education, and targeted social assistance along with opportunities citizens to achieve professional and cultural progress.
- The multi-vector natures of the country's external economic policy, but with the focus being on integration with the other countries of the Eurasian Economic Union. The aim is to ensure sustainable development.

This model is combined with political authoritarianism, dominance by the public sector, a paucity of privately owned industrial companies, and a weakness of competition in the economy. However, despite much inconsistency in the country's economic and social development, it can claim to have achieved a generally positive economic performance in recent years. During the second half of the 1990s, the foundations of a positive macroeconomic position were laid, the labor market was improved, and levels of social security were raised. As a result, Belarus weathered the storm of the economic crisis in 2008–2010, in social and economic terms, better than many of its neighbors.

The country's goal is to match levels of development seen in Europe's leading economies. Currently, the country enjoys a level of economic and social development on a par with Russia, but still lagging behind the Baltic countries.

The small business sector constitutes an important part of the Belarusian economy. The sector's share of the economy has been gradually increasing. In 2014, it accounted for 15% of GDP. In terms of industrial production, the sector accounted for 9% of total volume; 26% of the retail turnover of trade organizations; 32.5 and 28% respectively of exports and imports of goods. The small business sector encompasses many activities including trade, auto repairs, household goods and personal items, industry, real estate and others. Belarus has sound infrastructure for small businesses and a network of support, including 92 business support centers and 16 small business incubators. This support for small businesses has pushed Belarus up the ranking in the 'Doing Business' survey from 115th in 2008 to 44th in 2016, the highest position among the three countries in the sub-region.

Its ratio of trade volume to GDP puts Belarus in the top ten countries in Europe. But the country has only partial involvement in international capital movements, with only a small inflow of foreign investment. It should be added that Belarus's economic success is largely due to the privileged position it enjoys in its close economic ties with Russia.

Economic Performance

Between 1990 and 1995, Belarus experienced negative growth. The country returned to growth in 1996 and by 2003 (earlier than other CIS countries) had exceeded its pre-reform GDP. In the 2000s, Belarus saw stable and high rates of economic growth, averaging 8.2% between 2001 and 2008, though this slowed very sharply after the crisis in 2009.

The national Strategy for Sustainable Social and Economic Development until 2030 was approved in 2015 and envisages that GDP will grow by 150–200% during the period and that GDP per capita will reach US$30–39 thousand (compared with US$17 thousand in 2015). However, current economic performance suggests that these targets are unlikely to be met.

The services sector dominates GDP. During the 1990s, the proportion of GDP attributable to the services sector rose from 28.5% to 55%, but has since stopped increasing. In 2014, agriculture, forestry, hunting, and fishing accounted for 7.3% and industry and construction for 37%.

Table 18.1 — GDP growth in Belarus (percent)

Yearly average for 1993–1995	-10.1
Yearly average for 1996–1999	6.5
Yearly average for 2000–2008	8.0
2009	0.1
2010	7.7
2011	5.5
2012	1.7
2013	1.6
2014	1.7
2015	-3.8
2016	-2.6
2017*	0.7

* Estimates

Source: Commonwealth of Independent States in 2015: Digest of Preliminary Statistical Results. Moscow, 2017; IMF World Economic Outlook, October 2017

GDP growth in Belarus has been achieved by a rapid increase in investment. The share of gross formation in GDP is between 30 and 38%. There has been a considerable volume of very active investment. Industry has taken 36% of investment over the period, agriculture 14%, transport and communications 10% and housing construction 23%. A significant proportion of investment into fixed assets comes from companies' own resources (38%) and the public budget (21%). However, economic growth in the country has to rely on outdated technology which has a negative impact on company competitiveness and financial standing. It also affects the attractiveness of the country as an investment destination.

The economy has also suffered setbacks, mainly in the industrial sector. The share of GDP taken by raw materials increased sharply, especially the fuel and energy sectors which uses mainly Russian raw materials (in some years this exceeded 25% of GDP). The share attributable to engineering, metals, and consumer goods decreased. Raw materials thus now play a more important role in the Belarusian economy and this can be seen in the structural changes in exports. In 2000, 34.3% of the country's exports were machinery, equipment and vehicles, while mineral products (mainly oil and fertilizers) accounted for just 10.7%. But the corresponding figures for 2014 were 19.1 and 33%.

It is important to note that Belarus enjoys free access to the Russian market and this gives the country a distinct advantage over many of Russia's other neighbors. The improvement in Belarus's economic and social environment since 1996 has thus been largely due to Russia taking over Belarusian debt to the tune of US$1 bn. Russian subsidies to Belarus are estimated to be around US$1.5–2 bn, made up of supplies of energy resources at prices significantly lower than those payable by other CIS countries, financing of joint programs, orders for defense equipment, and the provision of long-term currency and trade credits, some of which are not refundable. A further US$50 bn was gained by Russia not charging the normal customs duties on supplies of oil until 2007. Belarus was able to process the cheap Russian oil in its oil-processing plants and export higher value products. In 2014, Russia placed an embargo on food imports from the European Union and many Belarusian companies took the opportunity to increase the food exports to Russia, helped by the absence of customs controls.

World markets also helped, especially in the period leading up to the crisis of 2008–2009. For example, the price of potash, one of Belarus's main exports, grew fivefold from the late 1990s. By refocusing itself as a conduit for flows of commodities, the country has benefited from Russia bypassing Ukraine and Baltic countries.

However, many of the factors that have helped the Belarusian economy grow are external, e.g., cheap Russian raw materials and energy resources, cheap Russian credit, the technology base inherited from the Soviet era. However, many of these are no longer available to the same extent. Other factors have held back economic development, such as the poor state of repair of many fixed assets, the unprofitability of most industries, the unstable financial position faced by many companies, a chronic problem of unpaid salaries, and limited market outlets.

Economic Policy

Belarus embarked on its chosen economic model in 1994. This was to involve a socially oriented market economy with the emphasis on government regulation and a large government sector. Along with the transition to a market economy, the government retained the tools of economic planning, including at the macroeconomic level, as well as a state industrial policy.

The country has adopted a particular approach to privatization, taking into account the views of the personnel in enterprises that are to be privatized, ensuring social protections are in place and safeguarding national security. In this way, Belarus rejected the voucher privatization as adopted in Russia. It also eliminated investment funds founded before 1994. The main targets for privatization were catering and shopping facilities, consumer services enterprises, construction companies, and agricultural processors. Over 60% of enterprises privatized were in the services sector where state ownership had dominated.

The privatization program was pursued actively between 1994 and 1999, when more than 2,700 enterprises passed into private hands. The rate of sell-offs declined dramatically with just 16 companies being sold off in 2006, 13 in 2007, and 113 in 2008. Belarus has the highest rate of state ownership in Europe. The country's leadership has made a conscious choice not to privatize large-scale operations. This reflects a belief that efficiency should not be the only consideration in economic activity as private companies do not always operate in the public interest. Privatizations are now rare and only at a high price and with guarantees over how the privatized company will operate. A plan to speed up the process of denationalization and sell off 244 companies between 2011 and 2013 was adopted but soon shelved.

State control extends to the private sector, in the form of price controls, various exemptions, and the provision of employment. Between 1997 and 2008, the government held a 'golden' share in privatized enterprises giving it a further measure of control. In addition, complicated bankruptcy procedures acted as a disincentive to operators hoping to enter the private sector and the government retained the right to renationalize previously privatized companies.

Thus public ownership and tough state regulation remain the dominant features of the Belarusian economy with all large enterprises either in public hands or with a government controlling share. The government determines which industries and enterprises will receive state support. These include agriculture, housing and capital construction, transport engineering, and the largest industry associations.

Human Capital

The population of Belarus in 2015 was 9.5 million, down from 10 million in 2000. The current demographic outlook is characterized by a low birth and relatively high mortality rates (especially among men of working age) which are compounded by emigration. This has led not just to a declining population, but to a deterioration in the age pattern and an ageing population. In the late 2000s, the rate of population decline slowed as the birth rate among the population born in the mid and late 1980s was high. Once this generation has passed, the country expects a return to population decline.

Despite this, the percentage of the total population that is of working age remains relatively high at 64%, preserving a high level of employment. In 2017, the number of registered unemployed stood at 34,200, just 0.8% of the economically active population, one of the lowest rates in Europe. However, the capacity to create new jobs is expected to decline in the future.

Private companies account for 56% of employment, though this includes companies with some state participation in their authorized capital. Wholly owned state companies account for 41%, with the remaining 3% being those working for enterprises in foreign ownership.

Between 2000 and 2010, there was a significant increase in the proportion of companies actively involved in innovation. In 2014, it stood at 20.9% and the share of innovative products in the country's total exports was 13.9%. Both indices double their equivalents in Russia. However, the World Bank estimates that only 2.6% of Belarus's exports were products of high technology. The scientific and technology sector lags behind most developed countries and is failing to close the gap.

There are 500 scientific organizations, universities, and large productions plants involved in research and development. Together they employ 29 thousand people, including 18 thousand researchers. During the years of market reform, the volume of research activity more than halved, with only a small proportion of the country's activity in this area being on a par with foreign competitors. The impact of research on GDP has reduced significantly. Over recent years, expenditure on R&D has been 0.7% of GDP which does not augur well for the development of advanced technologies. There is a serious need for both technological and structural modernization of production. According to data from the Comprehensive

Program for Scientific and Technical Progress in the Republic of Belarus, 48% of the technologies being used between 2001 and 2020 existed before 1985.

One of the country's strategic goals between now and 2030 is to raise expenditure on R&D to 2.5% of GDP, accompanied by an effort to attract investment into R&D activity from venture capital funds and businesses, and an improvement in the effectiveness of academic science by integrating it more closely into the real sector of the economy.

The agro-industrial complex in Belarus includes dairy, beef, and pig breeding, and flax and potato cultivation. There are also important areas of arable land given over to grain and sugar beets. Less than 10% of all people employed in the economy work in agriculture.

Belarus's 'On the Land' code provides the right to private ownership but limits the size of permitted holdings. The bulk of agricultural land is still owned by the state. Kolkhozes, sovkhozes, and farms do not enjoy property rights over their land. Instead they have an absolute right of use, established by law. The potential of the country's land and other resources is reckoned to be high; Belarus has 0.92 hectares of farmland and 0.56 hectares of arable per capita, figures which are as much as double the comparable figures in Western European countries. The country also has significant forestry resources: forests cover 39% of the country, and the stock of timber is 130 cubic meters per capita, again more than double the European average.

Between 2000 and 2008, agricultural output increased by 50%. However, following the economic crisis this growth slowed down so that between 2010 and 2013, the gain in output of crop production (in value terms) was just 12.1% and animal production went up by 11.7%. Agriculture in Belarus is noted for being productive. Between 2000 and 2014, the yield of crops and legumes increased from 19.4 hundred kilograms per hectare to 36.6 hundred; potatoes from 134 to 204 hundred kilograms per hectare; and vegetables from 134 to 242.

Agricultural companies take the leading role in the country's production, accounting for 95% of corps, 92% of milk, 89% of cattle and poultry, 80% of potatoes, 78% of fruits and berries, 70% of eggs, and 68% of vegetables. By contrast, the share produced by farm businesses is insignificant.

Heavy depreciation of fixed assets is the main challenge faced by the agricultural sector as well as inefficiencies in the labor market. Outdated equipment causes high costs and low quality products, as well as a loss of competitiveness in world markets. Because of low demand and a lack of agricultural raw materials, the country's processing companies run at 40–60% capacity. The most critical situation concerns supply of labor. Agriculture has an image problem and is failing to attract workers as more young people leave the land and head to the cities. Between 2009 and 2013, the number of unprofitable agricultural organizations increased threefold, farms by 50%. Some economists argue that letting unprofitable enterprises go to the wall would be good for the general health of the sector, but the government is keen to avoid this, mainly for social reasons.

Belarus has only limited energy resources. It produces an annual output of 1.7 million tons of oil and 0.2 bn cubic meters of gas. Even with the peat and brown coal that it has available, it is a long way short of meeting its own demands for energy. The country has to import more than 90% of its energy needs, mostly from Russia. The mainstay of the country's energy complex is the electrical power industry. In 2012, Belarus consumed about 38.4 bn kWh of electricity. Its own productions totaled 30.8 bn kWh, almost all of which was produced in thermal power plants. In future the country will have access to nuclear power, with the building of a nuclear station able to produce 2,300 MW, the first block of which is scheduled to be completed in 2018. This is expected to reduce the cost of electricity by 20% and lead to a drastic fall in the consumption of natural gas.

Belarus's most valuable mineral resources are its potash and rock salt, with proven reserves amounting to 6.9 bn tons and 22 bn tons respectively (i.e., practically inexhaustible). Between 29 and 32 million tons of pot ash is extracted each year, along with less than 1 million tons of rock salt. The country's chemical industry, therefore, focuses on the production of potash, nitrogen and phosphate fertilizers that are in demand on foreign markets. In the wider chemical industry, in 2013, nearly 5.6 million tires and 216,000 tons of chemical fibers were produced, the bulk of which is exported. Belarus has some of the largest exports of mineral fertilizers and tires in Europe.

In addition, the country has a strong petroleum processing industry which is able to meet domestic demand and export large volumes. There are also many furniture factories, exporting a part of their production.

The engineering complex is one of the country's leading industries. The country produces trucks and trailers, super-heavy dump trucks for the mining industry, metal-cutting equipment, tractors, bulldozers, agricultural equipment, motorcycles, TV sets, household refrigerators and other items. Between 2000 and 2013, production of tractors and busses increased by 260%, refrigerators and freezers by 150%, and washing machines by 370%.

Table 18.2 — Structure of manufacturing industry (percentage of total)

Coke and oil products, nuclear materials production	18.7
Chemical products	13.1
Wood, pulp-and-paper products and publishing activity	4.0
Rubber and plastic products	3.6
Other non-metallic mineral products	5.0
Textile and textile articles, leather articles and footwear	4.0
Metals and finished metal products	6.9
Production of machinery and equipment	7.4
Production of electrical, electronic and optical equipment	3.9
Production of transport vehicles and equipment	3.4
Food (including beverages) and tobacco production	27.3
Other manufacturing	2.7

Source: Belarus in figures. Statistics digest. Minsk. 2016 (in Russian).

Belarus has a well-developed building industry, which before the crisis of 2014 accounted for about 10% of GDP. In 2014, domestic dwellings with a total floor space of 5.5 million square meters were completed, 70% more than in 2000. The industry that produces construction materials is able to export as well as satisfying internal demand. However, the industry suffers from high levels of depreciation on its fixed assets, and hefty production costs, all of which impinge on its competitiveness.

The transport sector benefits from well-developed infrastructure which has supported steady growth in cargo transportation since 2000. However, there has been a slow-down in investment such that the infrastructure would now prove unable to support any further accelerated development. Fixed assets are ageing. In the case of rail vehicles, both diesel and electric, they are in need of replacement.

Freight in the country is dominated by rail. Road transport benefits from a good and rapidly expanding road network with around 100 thousand kilometers, 87 thousand of which are paved. There is also an extensive network of pipelines, with around 3 thousand kilometers of pipelines, 750 km being for oil and 8 thousand for gas (including branch lines to cities and other locations).

Belarus stands at a major transport crossroads, with the main rail and road links between Russia and Europe passing through it. Its ability to offer good transit infrastructure is vital to its economy.

The country also has modern digital infrastructure for telecommunications. It is the leader among CIS countries for the number of telephones per head, the level of Internet penetration (97% of companies use the Internet), and mobile communications where the number of subscribers exceeds the population.

The Financial Sector

The country's consolidated budget is formed mainly from VAT (30% of the total), corporation tax (11%), tax revenues from foreign economic activity (12%) and excise duties (9%). Revenues from other taxes are insignificant. A further 13% of the budget comes from non-tax revenues, such as income from the use of government-owned property, fines, and other deductions.

The majority of expenditure from the consolidated budget goes on social spending. Between 2005 and 2014, social spending steadily increased reaching as much as 42% in some years. Expenditure on other states activities also increased from 3% to 24% during the same period. However, the share of expenditure on the national economy for items such as investment in manufacturing, agriculture and roads, has been gradually decreasing from 20% to 17%.

Between 2000 and 2008, the consolidated budget revenues of Belarus increased dramatically from 35% of GDP to 52%. Expenditure also increased significantly from 35% of GDP to 46%. However, the economic crisis forced the authorities into a rethink their budgetary policy. Government investments were reduced dramatically as well as, to a lesser extent, subsidies to companies. At the end of 2014, budget revenues were equivalent to 27.2% of GDP and expenditure, 27.1%.

The country's banking system is overseen by the National Bank of Belarus. There are 28 commercial banks, including more than 20 with some level of foreign investment. Six banks have Russian capital. Due to under-capitalization, most Belarusian banks are unable to undertake large or long-term investment in the national economy. Even so, during the decade that began in 2000, there was an increase in credit provided to companies, organizations, and individuals which, in some years, amounted to as much as 32% of GDP. However, this was followed by a negative trend in the area of long-term credit, where the share of long-term credit fell from 25% of GDP to 14.6% between 2008 and 2014.

Government intervention in the banking system bolsters public confidence. A presidential decree (No. 22 of November 4. 2009), "On guarantees of the safety of monetary assets of individuals deposited in accounts and (or) stocks in bank (deposits)" provides a guarantee for all public deposits in the country's banks. Moreover, as in Russia, interests on monetary assets in bank deposits are not taxed.

The major challenge for the economy is inflation, which is higher than in most other former Soviet countries. In 2011/2012, the consumer price inflation exceeded 50%. In accordance with the government's national strategy for the period up to 2030, monetary policy aims to create a sustainable monetary basis for the country's development. It also aims to target inflation.

The External Sector

Belarus's balance of payments on its current account was positive in 2005, but has been negative since, mainly due to the country's traditional trade deficit. This is partly balanced by a surplus in services. Primary incomes (salaries and investments) along with secondary incomes (cross-border flows and transfers) which include payments to Russia within the framework of having import duties distributed are also in negative balance.

The balance of the country's financial account has traditionally been positive, thanks not so much to inflows of foreign direct investments, credits or loans, but by the fact that the outflow of capital from Belarus has been small.

Table 18.3 — Belarus: Balance of Payments for 2010–2016 (US$ bn)

	2010	2011	2012	2013	2014	2015	2016
Current account	***-8,280.1***	***-5,052.5***	***-1,862.2***	***-7,567.3***	***-5,094.0***	***-1 831,0***	***-1 675,9***
Goods and services	-7,500.1	-1,208.9	2,834.0	-2,340.9	-399.5	100,7	-77,5
Primary incomes	-1,096.6	-1,361.4	-1,473.2	-2,684.8	-2,398.9	-2 465,8	-2 206,6
Secondary incomes	316.6	-2,482.2	-3,223.0	-2,541.6	-2,295.6	534,1	608,2
Capital account	***0.0***	***4.1***	***3.7***	***10.3***	*7.7*	***4,6***	***6,5***
Financial account	***7,575.0***	***4,014.0***	***961.2***	***8,492.3***	***5,699.2***	***1 322,2***	***746,3***
Direct investments	1,342.8	3,876.9	1,308.1	1,983.9	1,799.1	1 545,7	1 124,0
Portfolio investments	1,185.6	854.1	-191.0	-59.1	-8.6	-952,1	646,1
Derivative financial instruments	0.0	-594.6	51.2	0.8	-29.6	-24,7	-2,3
Other investments	4,238.1	2,668.2	-126.1	5,709.3	2,528.0	133,2	-538,9
Official reserves	808.5	-2,790.6	-81.0	857.4	1,410.3	620,1	-482,6
Net errors and omissions	***705.1***	***1 034.4***	***897.3***	***-935.3***	***-612.9***	***504,2***	***923,1***
Overall balance	0	0	0	0	0	0	0

Source: The National Bank of the Republic of Belarus

During the first decade of the 21st century, Belarus's external trade saw positive trends, mainly thanks to prices. Between 2001 and 2012, the volume of external trade increased by 580%, but then started to fall after 2013, as the prices of Belarusian exports started to fall. The external trade balance for goods remains negative, mainly due to large energy imports.

Belarus's economy is oriented toward exports. The value of goods exported is equivalent to around 50% of GDP. The country's main exports consist of oil products; mineral fertilizers; refrigerators, freezers, and refrigeration equipment; tractors; trucks; and food products. Belarus's main market is Russia which takes 45% of all its exports. The European Union (mainly the Netherlands, Lithuania, Latvia, Germany, and the United Kingdom) takes about 30% of the country's commodities and about half of its services. Russia takes only a quarter of Belarus's service exports.

Table 18.4 — The Commodity Structure of Belarus's External Trade (2014)

	Exports		Imports	
	$ bn	% of total	$ bn	% of total
Total	36,080	100	40 502	100
Live animals and products of animal origin	3,377	9.36	893	2.2
Products of vegetable origin	590	1.64	1,603	3.0
Fats and oils of animal and vegetable origin	146	0.4	174	0.4
Food preparations, alcoholic and nonalcoholic beverages, tobacco	1,415	3.92	2,117	5.2
Mineral products	12,327	34.17	12,146	30.0
Chemical products	4,265	11.8	3,178	7.8
Plastics and products made therefrom, rubber and rubber goods	1,562	4.33	2,312	5.7
Leather raw materials, leather, furs and products made therefrom	81	0.2	159	0.4
Timber and its products (excluding furniture)	794	2.2	219	0.5
Wood, pulp-and-paper products	223	0.6	668	1.6
Textile and textile articles	1,313	3.6	1,091	2.7
Footwear, head wear, umbrellas and similar products	214	0.6	386	0.9

Products made from stone, gypsum, concrete, ceramics and glass	662	1.8	540	1.3
Nonprecious metals and products made therefrom	2,362	6.6	3,704	9.1
Machinery and equipment, electric machinery, audio electronics	2,562	7.1	6,701	16.6
Vehicles, their parts and supplies	2,549	7.1	2,851	7.0
Optical, photographic, and cinematographic, medical and surgical devices and equipment, watches, musical instruments, their parts and supplies	366	1.0	705	1.7
Other manufactured goods	674	1.9	586	1.5

Source: External trade of the Republic of Belarus. Statistical yearbook. Minsk, 2015.

Belarus's imports include a significant proportion of oil, natural gas, electricity, ferrous metals, synthetic rubber, internal combustion engines, machinery and vehicles for harvesting and threshing of crops, cars, machinery for automatic data processing, and vegetable oils. Between 2000 and 2013, imports of oil doubled, natural gas rose by 20%, ferrous metals by 50%, synthetic rubber by 250%, internal combustion engines by 400%, cars by 350%, and machinery for data processing by 190%. The main sources for imports were Russia (43%), Germany (7%), China (6.5%), and Ukraine (4.8%).

From 2000 to 2010, foreign direct investment increased annually. In 2005, the country attracted US$0.3 bn, and in 2013, US$2.3 bn. Cumulative investment stood at US$18 bn at the end of 2015.

Russia led the way, accounting for 57% of investment into Belarus, with Cyprus, Austria, the Netherlands, Germany, and the United Kingdom also involved. Russian investment was targeted on pipelines, manufacturing, and retail. Wary of Russian business gaining too strong a foothold in the country, the Belarusian government pursues an undisclosed policy of protectionism when it comes to investments, seeking to keep Russian companies out of certain strategic industries. (This is despite the free flow of capital required within the Eurasian Economic Union).

To attract foreign investment, Belarus has set up six free economic zones which offer preferential tax and customs regimes. Revenue and value-added taxes for residents of such zones are half what they are in the country as a whole. For five years after the creation of such a zone, the residents are exempt from taxation on revenues deriving from their own production.

During the decade of the 2000s, the National Bank of Belarus made it a priority to achieve the convertibility of the Belarusian ruble and supported its purchase to this end. The growth of revenues from exports and of international reserves helped to stabilize the exchange rate of the Belarusian ruble to the dollar and the Russian ruble, and it thus avoided excessive volatility in the run-up to the economic crisis.

However, in 2011, faced with an increased deficit in the balance of trade and a fall in gold and currency reserves, the central bank had to end the support of the Belarusian ruble, which lost two-thirds of its value in a year. In subsequent years, the authorities devalued the currency a number of times to try and promote exports.

Belarus's external debt, both private and governmental, is growing rapidly. At the beginning of 2018, it totaled US$39.6 bn, equivalent to 73% of GDP. Governmental debt alone was US$16.7 bn, equivalent to 30.7% of GDP.

Belarus's economy is based largely on a single economic complex; it survives on Russian energy resources. The country earns significant revenues from the transit of Russia's energy resources, and from the subsequent re-export of Russian oil. In turn, Russia relies on Belarus as the main transit corridor for delivering its goods to and from Europe.

Belarus and Russia cooperate closely in high-technology engineering; about 8 thousand Russian companies have Belarusian partners and there is cooperation over the development of research establishments in both countries focusing on innovation and new technologies. Some estimates suggest that 65% of the high-technology goods produced in Belarus are the product of cooperation initiatives with Russia. In turn, Russia is the main importer of Belarusian engineering products. There are also well-developed mechanisms of cooperation in the fields of defense, border and military technology, involving 280 companies and organizations from the two countries.

Belarus participates in several joint integration projects with Russia, including the Eurasian Economic Union. However, economic relations between the two countries are not without their difficulties, especially in the areas of trade and over the rate of integration processes which have slowed since the end of the Soviet Union. Russia's own economic difficulties have pushed the Belarusian leadership to consider closer ties with the EU which is seen as a profitable market for Belarusian goods as well as a source of investment and the modern technologies that the country needs for its own development.

The Social Sector

Belarus's approach to social development has enabled it to achieve a measure of social stability and a higher index of human development than any other former Soviet country (apart from the Baltic states). From 2004 until 2014, the average monthly salary increased from US$133 to US$621. However, salaries given in dollars are liable to fluctuations given the instability of the Belarusian ruble and the resulting movements in the exchange rate. Pensions in the country (US$160 per month in 2017) are slightly lower than in other developed CIS countries such as Russia and Kazakhstan. Income inequality in Belarus is the lowest it has been since the Soviet era, with the latest estimate of the Gini index being only 0.265.

Formal secondary and higher professional education have developed at an impressive pace. With 395 students per 10 thousand population, Belarus outstrips many developed European countries. The majority of students (90%) study at state universities. Private higher education is still underdeveloped. But the state sector is quickly becoming commercialized with an increasing number of students paying fees to study.

The timescale for achieving the level of quality in the educational system that will be needed to meet the needs of a post-industrial society will stretch until 2030. Belarus attaches particular importance to having educated and highly qualified people available. This will give the country a competitive advantage and propel it into the new global knowledge economy. However, the country's education system still faces a number of problems which it is hoping to tackle in the coming years through increasing computerization in educational establishments, implementing the use of information technologies in teaching and learning processes, and improving educational facilities.

Positive trends can also be seen in the development of the country's medical services. According to the World Health Organization, Belarus is ahead of all other CIS countries, including Russia, when it comes to the availability and quality of medical care. However, the population is still beset by high morbidity and mortality rates in relation to the main categories of disease such as cardiovascular and oncological conditions. Like Russia, it also has a high injury rate. Rates of certain diseases such as drug addiction and HIV have been increasing among the population. Funding has been inadequate and resources have been depleted as a result, leading to a preference for simple medical equipment and procedures. The high cost of drugs affects the supply of drugs to the public.

Between 2000 and 2014, the supply of new housing increased from 354 to 583 square meters per thousand people. In terms of new housing supply per capita, Belarus ranks alongside most developed countries.

Conclusion

1. Government participation in economic and social life is a cornerstone of Belarus's economy. This is combined with political authoritarianism, dominance by the public sector, a paucity of privately owned industrial companies, and a weakness of competition in the economy. However, despite much inconsistency in the country's economic and social development, it can claim to have achieved a generally positive economic performance in recent years. Even during the second half of the 1990s, the foundations of a positive macroeconomic position were laid, investment activity grew, the labor market improved, and level of social security were raised. As a result, Belarus weathered the storm of the economic crisis in 2008–2010, with growth rates outstripping many of its neighbors.

2. The country's goal is to match levels of development seen in Europe's leading economies. Currently, the country enjoys a level of economic and social development on a par with Russia, but still lagging behind the Baltic countries. Its ratio of trade volume to GDP puts Belarus in the top ten countries in Europe. But the country has only a small inflow of foreign investment. Belarus's economic success is largely due to the privileged position it enjoys in its economic ties with Russia.

3. The economy has suffered setbacks, mainly in the industrial sector. The share of GDP taken by raw materials increased sharply, especially the fuel and energy sectors which use mainly Russian raw materials. The share attributable to engineering and metals decreased. In engineering, the share of knowledge-intensive and technologically advances sectors decreased. As a result, the share of the economy taken by raw materials has increased, which can be seen in the changes in the structure of the country's exports.

4. Public ownership and tough state regulation are the dominant features of the Belarusian economy, with all large enterprises either in public hands or with a government controlling share. The government determines which industries and enterprises will receive state support. These include agriculture, housing and capital construction, transport engineering, and the largest industry associations.

5. Belarus has only limited energy resources. The main minerals resources it has are potash and rock salt.

6. A mainstay of the country's industry is the chemical-timber forest and machine-building sector. The former is based on Belarusian salts and Russian oil, while the latter is based on its high quality labor force. Both sectors have a high focus on exports.

7. Between 2000 and 2008, the consolidated budget revenues and expenditures in relation to GDP increased dramatically. However, this was followed by sharp decline as a result of the worsening position with regard to foreign business activity. At the same time, the government has maintained high levels of social expenditure.

8. The Belarusian economy is export-oriented, based on oil and its by-products, mineral fertilizers, and engineering products. During the first decade of the 21st century, Belarus's external trade saw positive trends, mainly thanks to prices. However, the external balance of trade for goods remains negative.

9. Belarus's approach to social development has enabled it to achieve a measure of social stability, a high index of human development, and fast growth of salaries and pensions (especially between 2000 and 2008). Income inequality is the lowest it has been since the Soviet era.

Questions

1. What is the role of the government in the economy of Belarus?

2. What natural resources does Belarus possess?

3. Describe the demographic situation in Belarus.

4. What are the main sources providing investment in the Belarusian economy?

5. Describe the main elements making up the country's balance of payments.

6. What are the main features and the structure of the country's external trade activity?

7. What are the main indicators that help define the development of the social sphere and the country's living standards?

Sources of additional information

Post-Soviet Area in a Globalizing World. Problems of Modernization. Ed. by L.Z. Zevin. Saint-Petersburg, 2008 (in Russian).
National Strategy of Sustainable Social and Economic Development of the Republic of Belarus until 2030. Minsk, 2015 (in Russian).
The Commonwealth of Independent States in 2015: statistical yearbook. Moscow, 2016.
Finance, investments, and prices of countries of the Commonwealth of Independent States 2009–2014: statistics digest. Moscow, 2015.
External trade of countries of the Commonwealth of Independent States 2013: statistics digest. Moscow, 2014.
Social indicators of the CIS countries and particular countries of the world 2010–2013: short statistics digest. Moscow, 2014.
Belarus in figures, 2015: statistics digest. Minsk, 2015.
Statistical yearbook of the Republic of Belarus. Minsk, 2014(in Russian). Belarus and Russia – 2014 (http://www.gks.ru/bgd/regl/b14_37/Main.htm).
National Statistical Committee of the Republic of Belarus (http://www.belstat.gov.by).
Council of Ministers of the Republic of Belarus (http://www.government.by).
National Bank of the Republic of Belarus (http://www.nbrb.by). Interstate Statistical Committee of the Commonwealth of Independent States (http://www.cisstat.org).
Union State (http://www.soyuz.by).
Ministry of finance of the Republic of Belarus (http://www.minfin.gov.by).
Agriculture of the Republic of Belarus. Statistics digest. Minsk, 2015.
External trade of the Republic of Belarus. Statistical Yearbook. Minsk, 2015.

CHAPTER 19

MOLDOVA

The Economic Model

Moldova was one of the more under-developed of the Soviet republics and remains so today. It is Europe's poorest country. It is poor in natural resources, especially energy resources, and has little apparent industrial, scientific or technical potential. It does, however, have worthwhile agricultural resources.

Moldova's situation is made worse by its having no access to a sea port. Nor can it benefit from being a transit country, like Belarus. Worse still is its division into two halves: in the early 1990s, the 'National Front of Moldova' adopted an aggressive position leading to a military conflict and, ultimately, to the division of the country with the creation of Transniestria (the self-proclaimed Moldovan Transniestrian Republic).

The country is characterized by the number of small and medium enterprises who provide work for 57% of the people of working age.

The National Economy

The economic recession associated with the transition to a market economy was deeper in Moldova and lasted longer than in Ukraine or Belarus. The bottom of the recession was reached in 1999, when GDP stood at just 34% of its 1990 level.[29]Between 2000 and 2008, the Moldovan economy recovered with an annual GDP growth rate of 5.9%. However, the country's economic development is beset by instability and is vulnerable to changes in the external business environment and the state of the agricultural markets.

---

[29] Hereafter, the indices are provided excluding the data of the self-appointed Moldovan Transdniestrian Republic, and which are not specified in the official statistics of the republic of Moldova.

Between 2000 and 2014, real GDP doubled, and although this was still short of its 1990 level, it represented a period of relative macroeconomic stability: inflation fell from 44% in 1999 to 2.4% in 2016; the exchange rate of the Moldovan leu remained relatively stable, with only a moderate devaluation between 2009 and 2014; the reserves of the Bank of Moldova increased significantly. Government debt fell from 83% of GDP in 2000 to 19% in 2008. Since then, however, it has started to increase again and, in 2017, stood at 41.3% of GDP.

These positive economic results were achieved with tax reform, along with tight monetary and fiscal policies. In addition, the money sent home by Moldovan migrants abroad: between 2000 and 2013, these increased from US$52 million to US$1.6 bn, equivalent to 25% of GDP.

Table 19.1 — Changes to Moldova's GDP (%)

1993–1999, yearly average	-6.8
2000–2008, yearly average	5.9
2009	-6
2010	7.1
2011	6.8
2012	-0.7
2013	9.4
2014	4.8
2015	-0.4
2016	4.3
2017*	4.0

* Estimates

Source: Commonwealth of Independent States in 2015: Digest of Preliminary Statistical Results. Moscow, 2017; IMF World Economic Outlook, October 2017

Services dominate the Moldovan GDP, accounting for 64.3% of the total in 2014. Industry and construction make up just 20%, although this has been increasing slightly in recent years. At 15.7%, the share taken by agriculture, forestry, and fishing is one of the largest in Europe. The sector also accounts for 30% of all employees. The leading industry is manufacturing, in particular, food, beverages, and tobacco. These use mainly locally produced raw materials and make up 41.6% of all manufacturing.

During the period of economic growth, Moldova saw investment in fixed assets increase and, with it, the rate of gross capital formation. This peaked at 34% in 2008 and has since declined gradually, standing at around 23.8% in 2016. Investment in fixed assets is dominated by company assets, 56.9% of the total, following by the budget at 11.4% of the total, and foreign investments which make up 7.5%.

Human Capital

Moldova faces demographic challenges: the mortality rate exceeds the birth rate and, as a result, the population has been declining since 1999, and this is exacerbated by a negative net migration balance. In 2015, the population stood at 3,554,000, 2.5% less than in 2000. In the Moldovan Transniestrian Republic, the situation is even worse, with the population falling by 20% over the same period. Mass emigration has been the major cause.

The size of the economically active population decreased from 1,655,000 to 1,236,999 since the turn of the century. The number of people employed fell from 1,515,000 to 1,173,000. At the end of 2013 29% of all employment was in the primary sector, 15% in the secondary sector and 56% in the tertiary. Average life expectancy is on a par with Russia at about 68 years for men and 76 years for women.

Research and Development (R&D) is insignificant in the Moldovan economy, with barely 5,000 people actively involved. Expenditure on R&D is equivalent to just 0.5% of GDP.

Moldova's population is relatively well educated. 46% of all people in employment have higher or secondary professional qualifications. From the 2000/2001 academic year to 2008/2009, the number of university students increased from 79 thousand to 115 thousand; those enrolled in secondary technical school went up from 20 thousand to 33 thousand. But this trend has since gone into reverse, as a result of the demographic challenges described above.

The Real Sector

Moldova's main natural resource is its soil, in fact, various kinds of black soils. Coupled with its warm climate, it thus enjoys very favorable agricultural conditions. Between 2006 and 2013, despite the financial crisis of 2009 and a drought in 2012, agricultural output grew by 44%.

Around the middle of the decade of the 2000s, over half (52%) of agricultural output was produced by individual households. This had fallen to 43% by 2014. The percentage produced by agricultural companies, on the other hand, grew from 28% to 44%. Under current legislation, foreign citizens have the right to rent farm land for up to 30 years, and this is an opportunity that investors from across the European Union have taken advantage of.

Looking at overall agricultural output, the share accounted for by sunflower, feeding crops, and grain (30%) has been increasing, while that taken up by potatoes, vegetables, melons, and livestock products has been decreasing. In the 2000s, the proportion accounted for by grapes declined and has now stabilized at around 8–10%. The agricultural sector has refocused its production on those products that can be produced most competitively under the conditions particular to Moldova.

The wine industry also plays an important part. However, although the wine producers focus heavily on exports, they face stiff competition on price in world markets. The relatively low quality of their wines is also a hindrance to export success. The government has sought to assist the industry by lobbying the EU for larger quotas for Moldovan wines.

The fuel and energy complex involves only the electric-power industry, the main feature of which is the Moldovan state power station in Transiestria. Domestic electricity production (around 0.9 billion kWh) supplies only 25% of domestic consumption. The country thus has to import electricity from neighboring countries. All energy resources are also imported, mostly from Russia and Romania, the latter following the opening of the Iasi–Ungeny pipeline.

The engineering sector produces agricultural machinery, machine tools, household appliances, electrical machinery, equipment and facilities for radio, television and communications, medical devices, and optical instruments. Some enterprises of the former Soviet defense complex still operate in Transniestria.

A relatively well-developed textile industry has survived from the Soviet era and is thriving. A significant proportion of its output—fabric, clothing, and carpet—is exported.

The construction industry focuses mainly on house building. Between 2000 and 2013, the supply of new housing increased from 59 to 145 square meters per thousand population, most of which was constructed by the people themselves. Around 70% of new building is in the capital, Chisinau. Outside the capital, construction is very slow.

Between 2001 and 2008, the volume of cargo transport (of all kinds) increased by 140%. Rail transport increased by 130%, road haulage by 140% and river transportation by 650%. However, it fell sharply in 2009 as a result of the financial crisis and has not yet recovered to its pre-2009 levels. Road haulage is the main form of transport used for cargo, handling 84% of the total. This reflects the small size of the country and the high density of the road network.

As in other CIS countries, telephone ownership has increased in Moldova from 0.5 million in 2000 to 1.2 million in 2014. This increase has been seen especially in rural areas. In 2011, the number of mobile phone subscriptions exceeded the total population.

The Financial Sector

In 2015, the revenues of the consolidated budget were equivalent to 36% of GDP, while expenditures were 40%. In 2000, these figures had been 26 and 27% respectively. Budget revenues are raised mainly from VAT, 45%; contributions to the state social insurance scheme, 21%; and income tax, 11.5%. The proportion of the budget raised from mainstream taxes has changed little over the last decade. The consolidated budget usually runs at a deficit, that exceeds the threshold of 3% of GDP.

Government expenditure is dominated by outgoings on social and cultural activities (67%). These include education, healthcare, social security, culture, art, and sport. Expenditures on the economy are 15%, while 7% goes on defense and public order, and 5% on general government services.

The Moldovan banking system has two levels: The National Bank of Moldova, and 14 commercial banks, most of which have foreign investors: four are 100% owned by foreign interests. As of 2014, 76% of the authorized capital of Moldovan banks was foreign investment. The banks are relatively small: only six of them have capital in excess of US$8 million. A banking scandal in 2015, involving three leading Moldovan banks connected to political elites, has damaged the banking sector.

Between 2000 and 2013, the National Bank of Moldova increased the broad money supply significantly, fromL5.6 bn to L14.1 bn. In this way, it was able to increase the amount of bank credit available. In 2008, such credits were equivalent to 37% of GDP, or 42% if long-term credits are included. This monetary growth led to high inflation; between 2003 and 2008, it averaged 12–13% a year. To control this inflation, the central bank switched to a tough monetary policy, including rises in interest rates and increases to the reserve requirements on banks. This succeeded in taming inflation which, in the years following 2010, was among the lowest in the CIS.

The External Sector

Moldova's external policies are increasingly focused on the EU. In 2014, the country signed an association agreement with the EU which, among other things, paves the way for a free-trade agreement and aligns the country's regulatory framework into line with that of the EU. At the same time, however, Moldova has sought to maintain its traditional links with Russia, Ukraine, and other CIS countries. These still account for about one third of the country's external trade.

Moldova's external turnover is approximately equivalent to its GDP, which is a result from the country's high level of openness to the world economy. However, the problem of negative external balances remains: in 2016, exports of goods worth US$1.4 bn, while imports totaled US$2.0 bn.

Table 19.2 — Commodity structure of Moldovan external trade for 2014

	Exports		Imports	
	US$ bn	% of total	US$ bn	% of total
Total	2340	100	5317	100
Live animals and products of animal origin	60	2.6	159	3.0
Products of vegetable origin	550	23.5	195	3.7

Fats and oils of animal and vegetable origin	78	3.3	26	0.5
Food preparations, alcoholic and nonalcoholic beverages, tobacco	378	16.1	340	6.4
Mineral products	28	1.2	1154	21.7
Chemical products	168	7.2	624	11.7
Plastics and products made therefrom, rubber and rubber goods	46	2.0	328	6.2
Leather raw materials, leather, furs and products made therefrom	35	1.5	43	0.8
Timber and its products (excluding furniture)	8	0.3	102	1.9
Wood, pulp-and-paper products	20	0.9	121	2.3
Textile and textile articles	330	14.1	357	6.7
Footwear, head wear, umbrellas and similar products	34	1.5	30	0.6
Products made from stone, gypsum, concrete, ceramics and glass	59	2.5	134	2.5
Pearl, precious and semi-precious stones, precious metals, imitation jewelry, coins	0	0	9	0.2
Nonprecious metals and products made therefrom	55	2.4	346	6.5
Machinery and equipment, electric machinery, audio electronics	309	13.2	801	15.1
Vehicles, their parts and supplies	28	1.2	330	6.2
Optical, photographic, and cinematographic, medical and surgical devices and equipment, watches, musical instruments, their parts and supplies	36	1.5	96	1.8
Various manufactured goods	117	5.0	122	2.3

Source: Statistical Yearbook of the Republic of Moldova. Chisinau, 2015.

The most important among Moldova's exports are its agricultural products, wine in particular, food preparations, and textiles. As of 2016, the EU was the main market for Moldovan products, which took 65%, with Romania, Italy, Germany, and the United Kingdom being the main targets. The countries of the CIS took 20%. The Moldovan Transniestrian Republic also focused on the EU, which took 46% of its exports, with only 14% going to Russia (and this figure is decreasing rapidly). The self-proclaimed republic's main exports are ferrous metals and electricity.

In 2006 and 2007, a Russian ban on imports of Moldovan wine and agricultural products had a major impact on the Moldovan economy, resulting in a slowdown of GDP growth. The same happened in 2014 when Moldova signed its association agreement with the EU; in order to prevent the re-export of European goods, Russia introduced customs duties on goods coming from Moldova and placed restrictions in imports of meat and fresh fruits.

In terms of imports, Moldova buys mineral products (especially fuel), engineering goods, chemical products, and consumer goods. The bulk of imports, 45%, come from EU countries, mainly Poland, Italy, and Germany. Imports from Russia account for 30% of the total and supply most of the country's energy needs.

Foreign direct investments in Moldova amounted to US$3.5 bn in 2015, equivalent to about 50% of GDP. Just over half of this, 53%, came from the EU; 12% from CIS countries; and 36% from elsewhere. Of the investments from the EU, 25% came from the Netherlands and Cyprus, countries with preferential tax regimes often used as investment locations by companies from CIS countries. The main targets for foreign capital are the financial sector (28% of the total), the manufacturing industry (23%), and the distributive industries (17%).

The economy of Moldova inspires only limited interest among foreign investors. There is a level of mistrust based on political and economic instability, the underdevelopment of market infrastructure, high administrative barriers, the high level of government intervention in the economy, the size of the informal economy, and the absence of a stock market.

The country's balance of payments is negative. Although Moldova receives substantial money transferred home by labor migrants, these do not match the size of the negative trade balance in goods and services.

Table 19.3 — Moldova's balance of payments: 2000–2015 (US$ bn)

	2010	2011	2012	2013	2014	2015
Current account	***-437.4***	***-773.4***	***-538.2***	***-398.6***	***-451.1***	***-414.84***
Goods and services	- 2,242.9	- 2,839.0	- 2,915.0	- 2,966.9	- 2943.5	-1,956.9
Primary income	504.7	571.5	814.2	860.7	795.7	457.89
Secondary income	1,300.8	1,493.1	1,562.6	1,707.5	1,696.7	1,084.26
Capital account	***-28.4***	***-29.5***	***-36.7***	***-35.5***	***-62.4***	***22.88***
Financial account	***402.1***	***726.3***	***489.6***	***365.8***	***581.3***	***443.72***
Direct investment	204.4	267.6	175.3	207.4	166.2	227.94
Portfolio investment	1.0	0	21.3	9.8	13.2	2.27
Derivative financial instruments	-0.6	0.2	-0.2	0.1	0.6	0.70
Other investment	491.7	736.6	790.9	430.5	-137.2	-93.68
Official reserves	-294.4	-278.1	-497.6	-282.0	538.4	306.49
Net errors and omissions	***63.6***	***76.6***	***85.2***	***68.3***	***-67.8***	***-51.76***
Overall balance	***0***	***0***	***0***	***0***	***0***	***0***

Source: The National Bank of Moldova

Moldova covers its external trade deficit with external borrowing. Between 2000 and 2014, the country's external debt increased from US$1.7 bn to US$6.5 bn, and in 2015, it exceeded the volume of GDP. It has accumulated mainly from private sector debt. However, the government's external debt has also been increasing, from US$0.8 bn to 1.5 bn over the same period.

The Social Sector

Moldova can be said to suffer from a social crisis. In 2015, the average monthly nominal wage was just US$230 before tax. This is one of the lowest in the CIS in terms of the purchasing power of the national currency. The best salaries, often double the national average, are to be found in industries such as finance, insurance, transport, and communications. The agricultural sector has the lowest rates of pay.

Moldova is introducing market mechanisms into the area of medical care. Between 2000 and 2013, the number of hospitals fell from 132 to 86, reducing the number of equipped beds available by 25%. The number of doctors also fell but is now stable at 36.4 per 10 thousand population.

Between 2000 and 2013, the amount of housing stock rose slightly from 76 to 81 million square meters. This represents an average of 23 square meters per capita. Nearly 50% of dwellings are without running water and sewerage, 60% are without central heating, while 66% do not have hot water. Over the last 15 years, all these indicators have been gradually improving.

Conclusion

1. Moldova was one of the more under-developed of the Soviet republics and remains so today. It has little industrial, scientific, or technical potential. It is poor in natural resources. It does, however, have worthwhile agricultural resources. Its situation is made worse by having no access to a sea port, nor is it a transit country. Finally, it is divided into two distinct parts.

2. The country is predominantly agricultural, though the agricultural sector relies heavily on outdated equipment which adversely affects the country's ability to benefit fully from its efforts to modernize. The need for economic development has to compete with political power struggles for the attention of the country's rulers.

3. Between 2001 and 2014, the agricultural sector grew, albeit unevenly. Agriculture is based largely on personal family plots, but agricultural companies have been growing in importance. A greater emphasis has been placed on products, principally corn, that are in demand in overseas markets. The food industry is relatively well developed. The specialty is wine.

4. In the years after 2000, the National Bank of Moldova increased the broad money supply and the volume of bank credit went up significantly. However, the growth in the money supply led to high inflation, to tackle which, the National Bank adopted tough monetary policies.

5. Moldova's external policies are increasingly focused on the EU, signing an association agreement in 2014. At the same time, however, Moldova has sought to maintain its traditional links with Russia, the major supplier of its energy resources and a key export market.

6. Moldova can be said to suffer from a social crisis. Average earnings remain the lowest among the CIS. However, certain social indicators, such as income and the state of housing, are gradually improving.

Questions

1. Describe Moldova's natural resources.

2. Describe the main features of Moldova's demographic situation.

3. What are the main features of Moldova's external trade?

4. What are the main features of the country's balance of payments?

5. How is Moldova developing its economic relations with the EU, and with Russia?

6. What are the core indicators that reveal living standards in Moldova?

Sources of additional information

Post-Soviet area in globalizing world. Problems of modernization. Ed. by L.Z. Zevin. Saint-Petersburg, 2008 (in Russian).

The Commonwealth of Independent States in 2015: Statistical Yearbook. Moscow, 2016.

Finance, investments, and prices of countries of the Commonwealth of Independent States 2009–2013: Statistics Digest. Moscow, 2014.

External trade of countries of the Commonwealth of Independent States 2013: statistics digest. Moscow, 2014.

Social indicators of the CIS countries and particular countries of the world 2010–2013: Short Statistics Digest. Moscow, 2014.

Statistical Yearbook of the Republic of Moldova. Chisinau, 2015.

Moldova in figures, 2015: statistics digest. Chisinau, 2016
Interstate Statistical Committee of the Commonwealth of Independent States (http://www.cisstat.org).
National Bureau of Statistics of the Republic of Moldova (http://www.statistica.md).
National Bank of Moldova (http://www.nbm.md).
Ministry of finance of Republic of Moldova (http://www.mf.gov.md).

CHAPTER 20

UKRAINE

The Economic Model

At the time it achieved independence, Ukraine was one of the most developed of the former Soviet countries. It had large industrial, scientific, and technical resources, well developed agriculture and transport, high levels of educational achievement, a skilled labor force, and significant natural resources. Moreover, Ukraine sits on important transit routes needed by other countries, for example, access to sea ports. It is major conduit for Russian gas being exported to the EU.

For the initial stage of transitioning to a market economy, Ukraine chose 'shock therapy' in economic policy. However, subsequently, rivalries between different political groups emerged, sparking a struggle over the redistribution of property, and this led to slower and inconsistent implementation of economic reforms. The reform process, in fact, dragged on for years and was accompanied by falling living standards and growing social and economic inequality. This has led in recent years to a major crisis and the partial disintegration of the country. In 2014, Ukraine's GDP was just 62% of the level it enjoyed in 1990. It has still not reached its pre-reform level.

Like in Russia, monopolization is a feature of Ukraine's economy, with many large companies controlled by a small number of individuals or oligarchs. But unlike Russia, where a certain distance is maintained between the large businesses and the government, in Ukraine the oligarchs play an active role in politics, holding important public positions and using the parliament (Verkhovna Rada) to promote their interests. The Donetsk and Dnipro 'clans' enjoy considerable political and economic power, and the rivalry between them was one of the main factors that led to the civil war that began in 2014 in the eastern part of the country.

Conditions for small businesses are worse in Ukraine than in Russia. The Doing Business Report ranks Ukraine last in terms of the availability of credit, the complexity of tax procedures, obtaining building permits, and rights of access to foreign markets. This demonstrates the weakness of the country's monetary system, the dominance of the government over the economy, and the monopolistic nature of the most profitable businesses. Small businesses accounted for just 7% of GDP in 2013. This figure is likely to have fallen even further in recent years since many small businesses were located in Crimea which is now part of Russia.

The public sector maintains an active role in the Ukrainian economy, in particular in the infrastructure and defense sectors. The size of the defense sector has been increasing significantly; military expenditure rose by 23% in 2014.

Ukraine's Economy

Between 1992 and 2000, Ukraine's economy recorded negative growth, with an annual average of -8%. Over the period, the size of the country's GDP fell by over 60%, a much larger fall that in most other former Soviet countries. Over this period, the country increased its focus on raw materials. At the same time, the ferrous metal sector became the major export earner. Steel and rolled metal products make up more than 40% of the country's exports.

During the 1990s, the conditions Ukraine faced in the aftermath of independence and the economic policies implemented during the transitional period can be said to have been the main causes of the steep fall in the country's GDP. Much of Ukrainian industry was uncompetitive and remains unprofitable today. Moreover, the defense industry accounted for a third of industrial output, but it has lost a large part of its main source of income, orders from the government. Much of what the government did during the transition to a market economy turned out to be irrational, in particular: subsidies given to unprofitable companies; limited budgetary discipline; the slow pace of privatization; the failure of privatization in the agricultural sector; and the introduction of trade restrictions. The country also faced the problem of seeing the world prices for its main exports fall during the 1990s.

The nadir of the crisis was reached in 1999, after which the country experienced a decade of growth. Between 2000 and 2008, the economy grew by an average of 7% a year. But there was a measure of volatility; the 7% average masks the fact that the growth in individual years ranged from 2.2% to 11.8%. External economic factors played a major part in the country's economic growth, for example, the devaluation of the Ukrainian currency, the hryvnia (₴), in 2004 gave a boost to the development of the country's industry. World prices for Ukrainian exports (especially metals) recovered and coincided with economic growth in Russia where demand for Ukrainian products is high. Increased revenues from the transit of Russian gas also made a significant contribution to the economic recovery, along with Russia's long-term subsidization of the economy in the form of preferential prices for energy resources.

Ukraine's GDP fell by 15.1% as a result of the crisis of 2008–2009, more than in the other countries of the sub-region. Industrial production fell by 21%. This had an inevitably severe impact on government finances. There was a mild recovering in 2011, but the country then entered a period of stagnation, exacerbated by the crisis that began in 2014. This entailed both a political destabilization and a sharp deterioration in relations with Russia, a key economic partner.

Table 20.1 — Annual change in Ukrainian GDP (%)

Yearly average: 1993–1999	-9.3
Yearly average: 2000–2008	7.0
2009	-15.1
2010	0.3
2011	5.5
2012	0.2
2013	0.0
2014	-6.4
2015	-9.8
2016	2.0
2017*	3.2

* Estimates

Source: Commonwealth of Independent States in 2015: Digest of Preliminary Statistical Results. Moscow, 2017; IMF World Economic Outlook, October 2017

The services sector dominates the calculation of GDP as it accounts for 59% of the total. Industry and construction account for 29%, and agriculture, forestry, and fishing account for about 12%. The definition of industry includes production of food, beverages, and tobacco which account for 20%; metal production, 18%; engineering, 10%; the chemical industry, 7%; and minerals (mostly mining of coal and metallic ores), 13%. The food industry's share of the total is growing rapidly. By contrast, that of the metal industry is falling.

The extent to which Ukraine lags behind other countries in terms of technology grew during the years of reform. The country has to rely on outdated fixed assets, dating from the Soviet era. High-technology industries (the aircraft industry; shipbuilding; the production of turbines, electronic devices, etc.) contribute just 4% of industrial output.

The economy of Ukraine relies heavily on resources. The share of intermediate use in the volume of industrial production has reached as high as 73%. In developed countries, it rarely exceeds 45%. At the same time, the economy consumes a lot of power and so is at the mercy of high world energy prices. Since 2010, rises in energy prices, especially those coming from Russia, have significantly dented Ukraine's competitiveness.

Even at its peak of 28% (in relation to GDP) in 2008, Ukraine's rate of gross capital formation was insufficient for the normal development of the economy. But it has fallen to just 15% in 2015. The financing of fixed capital investment relies mainly on companies' own funds. Against the backdrop of the crises that the country has faced, own funds are being used more and more. They made up 57% of the total in 2008, this rose to 71% by 2014. By contrast, the share accounted for by credit from Ukrainian banks or other loans is very low at 9%—a similar situation to that of Russia. Breaking the figures down by sector, we see that industry takes 32%, communications 18%, construction 16%, and agriculture 9%.

The investment climate in Ukraine is far from favorable. The main factors behind this judgment are the political instability and the perception of an inefficient government, affected in particular by corruption at most levels of government, as well as the political influence wielded by the industrial 'clans'. The latest Doing Business report ranked Ukraine 83rd out of 181 countries for its conditions for doing business. This puts it significantly behind other countries of the east European sub-region of the CIS.

Economic Policy

Throughout two decades of economic, social, and political transformation, Ukraine has been unable to find a path to sustainable economic and social development or to political stability. The latest report of the World

Economic Forum placed the country 76th out of 144 surveyed. However, it scored better for its infrastructure, placing 68th and higher education, placing 40th. Nonetheless, it 'failed' on such indicators as the institutional environment (130th), macroeconomic stability (105th), the efficiency of the commodity markets (112th), and the maturity of the financial markets (107th). In these aspects, the judgment of Ukraine matches that of Russia. But Russia scores far better on the index of macroeconomic stability. Ukraine's poor ranking here reflects the instability of its political situation and its heavy dependence on energy imports.

Since 2005, Ukraine's market reforms have been carried out in an atmosphere of permanent political crisis. Decisions on economic policy were often heavily influenced by events. On the verge of a default in 2008, the country applied to the IMF for a loan. This was granted but with conditions attached to require economic restructuring and tighter budgetary controls. In 2013, Ukraine again had to seek external help, this time from Russia who provided a line of credit. In 2014, Ukraine once again secured an aid package from the IMF worth US$15 bn.

The only idea on which the entire political elite in the country (even those keen on close ties with Russia) could more or less agree was the focus on integration with the EU, subject to a thorough assessment of its likely economic impact. The signing of the association agreement with the EU in 2014 and the subsequent political confrontation with Russia led to the loss of traditionally important markets for Ukraine and an inevitable deterioration in the make-up of its exports in the form of an increasing emphasis on products with low added value.

Human Capital

Since the beginning of 1993, Ukraine's population has declined from 52 to 42 million people. This was mainly due to a natural decline of 0.67% a year, caused mainly by the mortality rate exceeding the birth rate, combined with emigration up to 2004. Since 2005, the country has seen positive net migration but at a rate that is insignificant to the overall population statistics. The transfer of Crimea, with its population of 2.3 million, is an important factor in the decline.

In line with the fall in overall population, over the last two decades, the economically active population has decreased, standing at 17 million in 2017, compared to 22.8 in 2000. This includes 20.4 million in employment and 1.6 million who are unemployed. This gives an unemployment rate of

7.2% which is lower than in most European countries. However, the employment situation has worsened rapidly since 2014.

Ukraine's workforce can boast a high level of education and qualifications, and can produce high-tech products for both domestic and external markets.

Ukraine inherited a substantial scientific infrastructure from the Soviet era but has failed to make the most of it. It spends a meagre 0.7% of GDP on research and development. The number of researchers in the country declined from 121 to 70 thousand between 2000 and 2013.

The fall in scientifically based production leaves Ukrainian industry unable to satisfy internal demand. Innovative activity on the part of Ukrainian companies remains low, and the infrastructure needed to support innovation is under-developed. What infrastructure there is—in the form of technology parks and towns, and venture funds—is not up to the task of kick-starting innovative development. As a result, the share of industrial output taken by innovative companies is just 16.8% and the innovative products make up just 3.8% of all output.

Between the academic years 2000/2001 and 2008/2009, the number of university students increased from 1.4 to 2.4 million but has since declined in line with the fall in the overall population. As of 2014, there were 325 universities in Ukraine, 225 of which are public institutions. In addition, there are 478 secondary technical colleges attended by 300,000 students. However, demand for this type of education has fallen rapidly and many of these colleges have closed or merged with others. Ukraine scores well in global rankings for the provision of age-appropriate secondary and tertiary professional education.

The Real Sector

Ukraine has very good farmland. The black soil of which there are 16 million hectares is particularly sought after. It only represents about 6% of the country's total of land being used for agriculture, but it includes more than half of the arable land and it accounts for about 80% of all agricultural production. However, fresh water is in short supply, so Ukraine has a system of seven large reservoirs and 1,103 smaller ones. Even so, consumption of fresh water per person in Ukraine is significantly higher than in EU countries.

Almost half (49%) of all agricultural output is produced by individual households, but this share is declining in the face of the growth of agricultural companies and larger farms. Farms in Ukraine are, on average, 108 hectares.

The main crops are grains (50% of the total), sugar beet, sunflower, flax, potatoes, tobacco, and feeding crops. Production of grain exceeds the country's own needs so a significant proportion of the production is exported. In the agricultural year 2013/2014, Ukraine exported 9.4 million tons of wheat, 20.1 million tons of corn, and 2.5 million tons of barley. This represented a 42% increase on the previous year, though it should be noted that exports vary greatly from year to year.

By contrast, production of meat and milk is not enough to meet domestic demand, due in part to the low profitability of livestock in the country. Despite this, production of meat between 2005 and 2013 increased by 240%, enabling the country to substantially reduce its imports.

Ukraine has a diverse food sector. Between 2000 and 2013, manufacture of sausages increased by 68%, vegetable oil by 460%, while production of sugar fell by 28% and butter by 30%. Ukraine also has extensive production of agricultural machinery and tractors, though this has been declining gradually since 2010.

Ukraine is the leading country in Europe (not including Russia) for both the quantity and quality of its mineral resources. With just 0.4% of the world's landmass and 0.7% of global population, Ukraine provides 5% of world production of minerals. According to estimates from the Council for the Study of Production Forces at the Ukrainian National Academy of Sciences, the market value of confirmed mineral reserves is US$7.5 trn. The country has within its territory, 8% of global iron ore reserves, 44% of the manganese ore, and about 20% of titanic ores.

There are more than 33 bn tons of proven coal reserves, nearly 4% of the global total. However, Ukraine has only limited resources of other fuels and energy sources, especially oil and natural gas. It also has only scant reserves of non-ferrous metal ores such as bauxite, copper, lead, and zinc. The same is true of certain chemical raw materials, in particular those needed for the manufacture of fertilizers such as apatite, phosphates, and potash salts. The country is thus a large-scale exporter of iron ore, manganese concentrates, and ferroalloys and an importer of oil and natural gas.

Despite its large coal reserves (in the Donbass region), mining activity in the country is declining. Between 2000 and 2016, the amount of coal mined fell from 81 to 30 million tons. The country's oil and gas reserves remain small, despite increasing efforts to exploit them. Between 2000 and 2013, Ukraine extracted an annual average of between 2 and 4 million tons of oil, and over the same period, extraction of natural gas increased from 18 to 20–21 billion cubic meters. Generation of electricity increased from 171 to 199 billion kWh, but then declined to 164 billion in 2016.

The energy resources that are imported, mainly from Russia, represent about 30% of the country's total imports. For electricity generation, there is an even split with 47% being produced in thermal power plants and 43% in nuclear plants. The rest is made up by hydroelectricity. Ukraine hopes to achieve energy independence from Russia through the development of shale reserves. However, progress toward this goal is being hampered by a lack of investment, high costs, and the location of the deposits in politically unstable regions in the east of the country.

Ferrous metals are Ukraine's leading industry. There are more than 300 enterprises involved in the mining and processing of ores, the production of metals, pipes, metal products, ferroalloys, refractory materials, and secondary processing of ferrous metals. The metallurgical complex, which includes the mining of raw materials for the metallurgy industry, employs half a million people, produces about a quarter of the country's GDP, and makes 28% of the country's export earnings. Ukraine exports about half of its mined iron ore, found steel and other rolled products. Even so, its metal products struggle to be competitive in world markets since, following the collapse of the USSR, the country failed to carry out the fundamental reconstruction of the industry that was needed. The non-ferrous metals industry is less well developed. It produces aluminum, titanium, magnesium, mercury, and zinc.

The chemical and timber industry is mostly engaged in the manufacture of fertilizers, the production of sulfuric acids, soda, plastics, chemical fibers, and technical rubber products. Between 2000 and 2013, manufacture of mineral fertilizers went up from 2.3 to 2.9 million tons. But this sector faces still serious problems due to a lack of raw materials and poor sales.

Engineering remains an important part of the Ukrainian economy despite its contribution to GDP falling significantly. The sector's main activity is the production of machinery and equipment for the mining and metallurgy industries, the power generation industry, as well as the electrical engineering and machine tool industries. The country also has a high-technology sector that is able to produce competitive products. This sector includes nuclear power engineering, rocket production, aviation, naval shipbuilding and others. However, many of these have seen a decline in their activities since 2014 when trade and cooperation with Russia became more difficult. Between 2000 and 2008, there was a significant increase in the manufacture of automobiles, from 17 to 402 thousand. But in recent years this has been falling gradually. In 2015, manufacture was suspended altogether due to the crisis in the country.

The consumer goods industry, which had been one of the country's most well developed in the early 1990s, is now facing serious difficulties, mainly as a result of foreign competition.

Between 2005 and 2013, the construction of new housing supply increased by 140% and the housing available per capita went up from 21 to 24 square meters. Like many other former Soviet countries, Ukraine has seen a boom in housing construction though the levels are still below what they were in the Soviet era.

Rail transport carries over half (56%) of cargo in the country. Pipelines carry 28% and road haulage 16%. For passenger transport, 50% go by road. There is an extensive rail network with 35.9 km of rail per thousand square kilometers of territory serving almost the entire country, even the Carpathian mountains. In 2010, work began on high-speed railway communication (the main driver being the Ukraine's hosting of the European Football Championship in 2012) and now Kiev, Kharkov, and Odessa are connected by high-speed links. The extent of the road network has changed little in recent years and stands at 169,600 kilometers or 365 km per thousand square kilometers of territory. Pipelines form a major part of the transport infrastructure, the length of all pipelines (oil, oil products, and gas) reached 46,600 km in 2014.

Ukraine's role as a transit country, especially for Russian pipelines taking gas to Western Europe, is a major contributor to the economy. The pipeline capacity in the country exceeds 140 billion cubic meters a year. The country's seaports (Odessa, Nikolayev, Kherson, Illichevsk) were used by Russian ships regularly up until the middle of the 2010s. However, Russia is seeking to diversify the transport of its energy resources and so the share of the trade passing through Ukraine is reducing steadily.

At the end of 2013, there were 56 fixed telephone lines for every 100 households. As in other CIS countries, mobile telephony has been developing rapidly. The number of subscriptions to mobile networks is around 60 million, significantly more than the population. The level of Internet penetration among the adult population has been growing consistently, reaching 50% in 2013. This is still less than in Russia.

The Financial Sector

In 2013, the revenues of the consolidated budget were equivalent to 30.2% of GDP, while expenditures were 34.5%. The corresponding figures for 2000 were 28.9 and 28.3%. These revenues come mainly from VAT (29%), personal income tax (16%), corporation tax (12%), and excise duties (8%). Non-tax revenues make up 19% of the total, coming mainly from government property and the business activities of publicly-owned companies.

In 2013, the main areas of expenditure from the consolidated budget were social (29%), education (21%), medical care, and expenditures by public and administrative authorities (12%). Expenditure on economic activity was relatively low, not exceeding 10%. Expenditure on the military and law enforcement has been increasing in recent years.

The consolidated budget runs with a large deficit. Between 2009 and 2014, the average size of the deficit was 4.7%. However, this has been falling since then. To finance the deficit, the government has sought foreign loans on several occasions, leading to a major increase in government debt.

The banking system has two levels: the National Bank of Ukraine, and the commercial banks, the number of which has been consistently decreasing. In 2010, there were 197 commercial banks. By the middle of 2015, only 130 remained. Of the commercial banks, 45 have received foreign capital investment (a relatively low number among countries of the sub-region), 19 of them are wholly owned by foreign investors.

Table 20.2 — Consumer price inflation in Ukraine (%)

2005	2006	2007	2008	2009	2010	2011	2012	2013	2014	2015	2016	2017*
13.5	9.1	12.9	25.2	15.9	9.4	8.0	0.6	-0.3	12.1	28.7	13.9	12.8

* Estimates

Sources: Interstate Statistical Committee of the Commonwealth of Independent States http://www.cisstat.com.
IMF. The World Economic Outlook. October 2017.p.177.

The External Sector

Between 1991 and 2002, Ukraine imposed restrictions on imports of foreign goods in an attempt to protect domestic producers. These measures have been relaxed in more recent years, signaling a more liberal approach. The country has sought to emphasize its role as an export-oriented economy, based principally on the export of ferrous metals, metal ores, and, more recently, grain. Revenues from the transit of Russian goods increased for a number of years.

Since the 'Orange Revolution' in 2004, Ukraine's foreign policy has focused on its attempts to achieve rapid development of its relations with the EU, initially with the 'European Neighborhood Policy' and, from 2014 onwards, on the basis of the association agreement signed with the EU. However, this policy has not produced a significant opening up of EU markets to Ukrainian goods. There have only been limited successes, such as the increase in the quote for Ukrainian steel entering the EU market, and the maintenance of the quota-free regime for Ukrainian textiles. There was no perceptible increase in investment from the EU, except in the purchase of metallurgical enterprises. To attract more European capital, Ukraine will seek to improve the conditions for doing business in the country and promote the harmonization of standards with the EU. Some measures toward this have already been taken, but the process will take a long time.

Geography, history, and culture all pull Ukraine in the direction of Russia, and Russia remains one of the country's main economic partners despite the 43% fall in bilateral trade in 2014. This was exacerbated in 2016 with the ban on free trade between the two countries.

External trade is important to the Ukrainian economy. The country's external turnover has, in some years, reached the equivalent of 85% of GDP, indicating a high degree of openness to the outside world. However, the country runs a negative balance for trade in goods equivalent to 5.8% of GDP. This is financed mainly by external borrowing. In 2014, Ukraine's trade with the EU amounted to 35.5% of its total external trade, while the CIS (in fact, mainly Russia) accounted for 29%. Germany, Italy, and Poland were the main markets within the EU for Ukrainian goods.

Breaking down Ukrainian exports by product, metals and metal products (mainly steel, rolled products and pipes) made up 28% of all exports; vegetable products made up 16%; minerals, 11%; and engineering goods,

10%. The proportion of the total taken by metals is declining gradually due to falling demand in overseas markets and also as a result of the political instability in the east of the country where the largest metallurgical plants are located. As a proportion of all exports, the part taken by vegetables is increasing. The main imports are minerals (fuel, oil, and gas) which account for about 30% of the total, and engineering goods which account for 16%.

Table 20.3 — Individual commodities in Ukraine's external: 2014

	Exports		Imports	
	$ bn	% of total	$ bn	% of total
Total	**53,902**	**100.0**	**54,429**	**100.0**
Live animals and products of animal origin	1,014	1.9	1,124	2.1
Products of vegetable origin	8,736	16.2	2,032	3.7
Fats and oils of animal and vegetable origin	3,822	7.1	302	0.6
Food preparations, alcoholic and nonalcoholic beverages, tobacco	3,096	5.7	2,602	4.8
Minerals	6,104	11.3	16,095	29.6
Chemical products	3,054	5.7	6,782	12.5
Polymer materials, plastics and products made therefrom	586	1.1	3,638	6.7
Unprocessed furs, and weeded out leather	157	0.3	223	0.4
Timber and its products	1,263	2.3	295	0.5
Wood, pulp- and-paper products	986	1,8	1,290	2.4
Textile and textile articles	786	1.5	1,883	3.5
Footwear, head wear, umbrellas	203	0.4	431	0.8
Products made from stone, gypsum, concrete	479	0.9	801	1.5
Natural or cultural pearls, precious and semi-precious stones	161	0.3	297	0.5
Nonprecious metals and products made therefrom	15,229	28.3	3,324	6.1
Machinery and equipment; electric machinery	5,657	10.5	8,721	16.0

Vehicle for land transport, flying vehicles, watercrafts	1,472	2.7	2,648	4.9
Optical and photographic devices and equipment	232	0.4	673	1.2
Various manufactured goods	736	1.4	902	1.7
Artwork	0.2	0	9	0.0
Goods purchased in ports	10	0	248	0.5

Source: State Statistics Service of Ukraine

In recent years about 60% of the trade flowing to Ukraine from Russia has been made up of energy resources. In turn, Russia is a key market for Ukrainian exports of ferrous metals and engineering products. Ukraine exports a more diversified range of products to Russia which includes a larger share of high-value-added goods.

In the early 2000s, foreign direct investment into the Ukrainian economy amounted to about 20% of the country's cumulative stock of investment in fixed assets. In 2015, the accumulated foreign direct investment in Ukraine totaled US$62 bn. However, against the backdrop of the on-going crisis, inflows of foreign direct investment have dried up, mainly as a result of the devaluation of the hryvnia and the repatriation of assets by some Russian companies.

Foreign direct investment in Ukraine has focused heavily on oil refineries, metallurgy, and the food industry. Most of this investment came from the EU (a total of US$44 bn of which US$19 bn came from Cyprus) and Russia. Ukraine's overseas direct investment amounted to US$10 bn, mostly in Cyprus and other similar jurisdictions with favorable tax regimes. Most of the outgoing investment goes to Cyprus and then returns to Ukraine as a foreign investment into the country. It can thus be inferred that Ukraine's role in international capital movements is insignificant.

Between 2006 and 2014, Ukraine had a deficit in its current account balance of payments, mainly due to the deficit in foreign trade. In 2013, it reached US$16.5 bn and the National Bank used a mixture of gold and currency reserves, along with loans, to cover it. In 2014, the deficit was reduced to US$5.3 bn, thanks largely to a sharp reduction in imports.

Table 20.4 — Ukraine's balance of payments, 2000–2016 (US$ bn)

Articles	2010	2011	2012	2013	2014	2015	2016
Current account	***-3,016***	***-10,233***	***-14,335***	***-16,518***	***-5,332***	***-189***	***-3,450***
Goods and services	-3,982	-10,145	-14,346	-15,634	-5,342	-1,704	-5,470
Primary incomes	-2,009	-3,796	-2,965	-3,033	-1,531	-1,113	-931
Secondary incomes	2,975	3,708	2,976	2,149	1,541	2,628	2,951
Capital account	***188***	***101***	***40***	***-60***	***400***	***456***	***92***
Financial account	***7,859***	***7,677***	***10,120***	***18,601***	***-8,375***	***582***	***4,704***
Direct investment	5,759	7,015	7,195	4,079	299	3,012	3,268
Portfolio investment	4,342	1,569	4,689	8,787	-2,700	367	293
Other investment	-3,593	-1,878	-3,157	6,375	-6,522	-2,653	1,660
Net errors and omissions	1 351	971	1 393	-640	548	-144	-517
Reserves and connected articles (reserved assets and credit of International Monetary Fund)	***-5,031***	***2,455***	***4,175***	***-2,023***	***13,307***	***-849***	***-1,346***
Overall balance	***0***	***0***	***0***	***0***	***0***	***0***	***0***

Source: The National Bank of Ukraine

In the balance of payments, there is a large positive balance in current transfers, lists as 'secondary transfers', which is made up of money transferred home by millions of Ukrainians working overseas. In the capital transactions and financial accounts, the large overseas borrowings are particularly important (especially in 2014), more so than the relatively small movements of direct and portfolio investments.

Between 2004 and 2014, Ukraine's external debt increased from US$30.6 bn to US$142 bn. Before the crisis, most of the increases in government debt were due to the private sector (as in Russia), but since 2009, government borrowings have increased rapidly. In 2009, government debt was equivalent to only about 20% of GDP, by 2014, it had climbed to 71% and looks set to continue increasing. By contrast, private sector debt has begun to go down.

The Social Sector

Ukraine continues to face many severe social difficulties. Despite the growth of incomes in money terms during the 2000s, the living standards of most of the population are worse than in the Soviet era. In 2013, the average monthly nominal wage was US$400 a month, but with the devaluation of the hryvnia, this fell to as low as US$150 in 2016.

The country has been reforming health care and transitioning to a system based on compulsory medical insurance. Between 2000 and 2013, the number of doctors decreased, but has remained steady since. From 2005 to 2012, life expectancy went up from 74 years to 76 for women, and from 62 to 66 for men.

Between 2000 and 2013, housing stock increased from 1,105 billion square meters to 1,097 billion. This represents an increase of 20.7 square meters per capita to 23.8 square meters. More than 90% of the housing stock is more than 20 years old. The pace of construction of new housing has slowed.

Conclusion

1. As it began its process of reform after independence, Ukraine was one of the most developed of the former Soviet countries. Initially, the country chose 'shock therapy' in economic policy. However, subsequently, rivalries between different political groups emerged, sparking a struggle over the redistribution of property and this led to

slower and inconsistent implementation of economic reforms. The reform process, in fact, dragged on for years and was accompanied by falling living standards and growing social and economic inequality. This has led in recent years to a major crisis and the partial disintegration of the country.

2. The investment climate in Ukraine is far from favorable, the main factors being political instability and the inefficient government affected in particular by corruption at most levels and the political influence of the industrial 'clans'.

3. Ukraine's workforce can boast a high level of education and qualifications, and can produce high-tech products for both domestic and external markets. Ukraine inherited a substantial scientific infrastructure from the Soviet era but has failed to make the most of it.

4. Ukraine's mineral resources are of good quality and quantity. Its main resources are iron, manganese, titanic ores, and coal. However, it has only scant resources of oil, natural gas, and nonferrous metal ores and so has to import these.

5. Ferrous metals are Ukraine's leading industry. There are more than 300 enterprises involved in the mining and processing of ores, the production of metals, pipes, metal products, ferroalloys, refractory materials, and secondary processing of ferrous metals. The metallurgical complex provides a significant proportion of the country's export earnings.

6. During the 1990s, Ukraine's monetary and credit systems were beset by the instability of the hryvnia, high inflation, a low monetization factor, and a lack of back credit. After a devaluation of the hryvnia in 2004 and the stabilization of its exchange rate, the National Bank quickly expanded the stock of money and increased the level of monetization. This helped increase the availability of bank credit. The country's banking system was badly affected by the world financial crisis in 2008 and 2009. By the middle of the 2010s, it was on the brink of collapse.

7. Between 1991 and 2002, Ukraine imposed restrictions on imports of foreign goods in an attempt to protect domestic producers. These measures have been relaxed in more recent years, signaling a more liberal approach. The country has sought to emphasize its role in an export-oriented economy, based principally on the export of ferrous metals, metal ores, and, more recently, grain. Since the 'Orange

Revolution' in 2004, Ukraine's foreign policy has focused on its attempts to achieve rapid development of its relations with the EU, boosted in 2014 by the signing of the association agreement. This strategy has caused strains in the country's traditional economic relationship with Russia which, nonetheless, remains the main foreign trading partner.

8. Ukraine continues to face many severe social difficulties. Despite the growth of incomes during the 2000s, the living standards of most of the population are worse than in the Soviet era.

Questions

1. Describe Ukraine's demographics.
2. Describe Ukraine's natural resources.
3. What are the main sources of fixed asset investment in Ukraine?
4. Which commodities, and in what proportions, make up Ukraine's external trade?
5. Describe the main features of Ukraine's balance of payments.
6. What are the main social indicators that help quantify living standards and other aspects of life in Ukraine?
7. Describe Ukraine's relationship with Russia.

Sources of additional information

Post-Soviet Area in a Globalizing World. Problems of Modernization. Ed.by L.Z. Zevin. Saint-Petersburg, 2008 (in Russian).

Vinokurov E., Kulik S., Spartak A, Urgens I. Deadlock of the Integration Struggle in Europe. Moscow, 2014 (in Russian).

The Commonwealth of Independent States in 2015: Statistical Yearbook. Moscow, 2016.

Finance, Investments, and Prices of Countries of the Commonwealth of Independent States 2009–2013: statistics digest. Moscow, 2014.

The External Trade of Countries of the Commonwealth of Independent States 2013: Statistics Digest. Moscow, 2014.

Social Indicators of the CIS Countries and Particular Countries of the World 2010–2013: Short Statistics Digest. Moscow, 2014.

Ukraine in Figures 2013: Statistical Publication. Kyiv, 2014.
Statistical Yearbook of Ukraine for 2013. Kyiv, 2014.
Interstate Statistical Committee of the Commonwealth of Independent States (http://www.cisstat.org).
State Statistics Service of Ukraine (http://www.ukrstat.gov.ua).
Ministry of Finance of Ukraine (http://www.minfin.gov.ua).
Ministry of economic development and trade of Ukraine (http://www.me.gov.ua).
National Bank of Ukraine (http://www.bank.gov.ua).

UNIT IV

THE TRANSCAUCASIAN ECONOMIC MODELS

CHAPTER 21

SIMILARITIES AND DIFFERENCES IN THE ECONOMIES OF TRANSCAUCASIAN COUNTRIES

The Transcaucasian region is a heterogeneous economic and geopolitical area in which the various countries have aspects in common, as well as other features to differentiate them. Proximity and a common history unite them. However, geostrategic factors, which drive ethnic and political conflicts, separate them, as does the way in which their external economic relations have been politicized.

All Transcaucasian countries are densely populated. In 2012, Azerbaijan was the most densely populated with 112 people per square kilometer; in Armenia the figure was 104 people; and in Georgia, 79. In a fluctuating history, the collapse of the Ottoman Empire, the inclusion of the Transcaucasian region in the Russian Empire and later the Soviet Union, have all brought about migration between the countries of the region, resulting in the creation of large ethnic enclaves in different countries. This was one of the main triggers for political and military conflict around the time of the collapse of the Soviet Union. Armenia and Azerbaijan have yet to resolve the conflict in Nagorno-Karabakh whose population insists that the region is part of Armenia. South Ossetia and Abkhazia have seceded from Georgia. These conflicts usually end up in military action and often involve resettlement of populations which has a negative impact on the region's economy and prevents integration.

The prevalence of conflicts in the region and the military spending involved have placed a severe strain on the local economies. This has been exacerbated by the increase in emigration from the region, mainly to Russia. This emigration peaked in the 1990s, with the numbers reaching the millions. Subsequently, with the conflicts abating somewhat, the emigration decreased and net migration across the entire region fell below 600,000 people. Nonetheless, this was enough for the population of countries in the region to decline by an annual average of 0.4% in Armenia, 1.0% in Georgia, and 0.9% in Azerbaijan.

The subtropical climate and soils, especially in Georgia and Azerbaijan are favorable for agriculture, with the more mountainous regions suitable for cattle. Easy access to the sea, especially the Caspian Sea near Azerbaijan with its large fish stocks, has helped the development of a fishing industry.

Broadly speaking, the Transcaucasian region has a sufficiently wide range of natural resources to support the development of industry. These include oil and gas in Azerbaijan, non-ferrous metals in Armenia, and manganese and iron ores in Georgia. However, the resources necessary for modern development are unevenly distributed across the region. Only Azerbaijan has both oil and gas. Armenia is in the weakest position, and has no link to the sea.

Similarities and Differences in the Economic Models of the Countries of Transcaucasia and their Participation in the World Economy

The biggest influence on the economic development of the countries of Transcaucasia has been their shared history as part, first of the Russian Empire, and then within the Soviet Union. Their demography and natural environments have also played a part. Before the collapse of the Soviet Union, Transcaucasia was a diverse region with both industry and agriculture. Industries included oil extraction and processing, metallurgy, chemical, and consumer goods.

The economic systems of the Transcaucasian republics were heavily integrated into the Soviet Union's single economy which saw any development of regional or independent economic activity as counter to its interests as the unified state. The overarching aim in the economic development of the Transcaucasian republics was stronger links with Russia, rather than with each other. The role of Azerbaijan as a supplier of oil to Transcaucasia was kept to a minimum; from 1973 onwards, all the region's needs were met by imports of Iranian gas via a pipeline which passed through Azerbaijan en route to Armenia and Georgia. The region's economies, being integrated into the Soviet system, were characterized by the monopolization of production and its concentration in large enterprises, diminishing any role for small-scale production.

For this reason, the break-up of commercial arrangements in the Soviet Union brought to a standstill many enterprises in Transcaucasia that had a union-wide perspective on their production and consumers. However, the

Soviet legacy was not all bad, it did leave the regional economies with a relatively well qualified labor force and well-developed social services. This continued to have an impact after the end of the Soviet era as the countries sought to embark on a path of development with the Soviet industrial infrastructure as their starting point.

The creation of new market structures and new models for economic development after the collapse of the Soviet Union was slow and painful. Market reforms were pursued in more or less the same way as in other former Soviet countries with emerging economies. State regulation of prices was virtually abolished and government-owned enterprises were privatized. Foreign capital and direct investment began to enter the markets. The structure of agricultural landholding and land use were radically changed.

The region's political authoritarianism has had a major impact on the way the economic models function, but less so than in Central Asia. It is perhaps most obvious in Azerbaijan, South Ossetia and Abkhazia. Georgia and Armenia have adopted more liberal models. This is evident from the 'Doing Business' survey which ranks countries according to the favorability of their business climate. In 2016, Georgia was ranked 16th in the world, with Armenia 38th and Azerbaijan 65th.

Similarities and Differences

In the years immediately following independence, the economic capacity of the countries in Transcaucasia fell dramatically. In 1995, the GDP of Azerbaijan fell to just 42% of its 1991 level, Georgia's to 36%, and Armenia's to 58%. Thereafter the economies recovered: in 2004, Armenia reached the level of GDP it had seen in 1990. Georgia's recovery was initially very slow. Azerbaijan began its recovery later than Georgia but did so at a faster pace. From 2000 until the global financial crisis, the countries of the region managed relatively high levels of growth: more than 10% in Georgia and over 25% in Azerbaijan. After 2008, Armenia and Azerbaijan saw their rates of growth halve, while Georgia suffered an 80% fall in its growth rate. Armenia suffered the most from the crisis, only returning to positive growth in 2010.

Table 21 — Some macroeconomic indices of the Transcaucasian countries in 2016

	Azerbaijan	Armenia	Georgia
Population, million people	9.8	2.9	3.7
GDP, US$ bn	37.9	10.6	14.4
GDP PPP per capita, US$	16,130	9,020	9,510
GDP, annual growth, %	-3.1	0.2	2.8

Source: World Bank Country Profile, World Development Indicators. October 2017.

In 2016, the region's GDP totaled US$62.5 bn. Azerbaijan accounted for 60% of this, Georgia, 23%, and Armenia, 17%. (In 2015, the region's GDP had totaled US$77.5 bn, with Azerbaijan accounting for 68% of this, Georgia 19%, and Armenia 13%).

All three countries saw significant decreases in the share of GDP taken by their primary sectors: during the 2000s, Azerbaijan's fell from 17% to 6%, Georgia's from 22% to 9%, and Armenia's from 26% to 18%. This had knock-on effects on the industrial structure in the region.

In the first half of the 1990s, inflation was high. But tough measures, including a contraction of the internal markets, helped bring it under control in all three countries. This held until 2016 when Azerbaijan saw its inflation rate rise again to 14.6%, while Georgia's remained low at 4.2% and Armenia's likewise, at 0.5%.

Azerbaijan has a low rate of external debt; in 2016, it was equivalent to just 40% of GDP, while in Armenia the figure was 92% and in Georgia, 118%.

Similarities and Differences in Economic Policy

The countries of the region have followed similar paths of economic policy in the creation of competitive environments. This has included a process of privatization aimed at improving the efficiency of public and management institutions. In all countries, the objectives of economic policy were to diversify production and improve the countries' integration with the wider world economy. All countries, therefore, sought to improve the climate for investment and business, and to create a proper modern legal framework to facilitate business activities.

Where there are differences in economic policy, these reflect differences in the structural differences between the economies, as well as differences in the external economic policy and orientation. Thus, in the case of Azerbaijan, the country's oil and gas reserves slowed down the privatization process but an acceleration of the process of encouraging foreign and domestic capital to work together on joint activities. In comparison to the other countries of the region, Azerbaijan pursued a more gradual reform process, with foreign capital encouraged to participate in the consumer goods industry, general trading activities, and relations with Turkey.

Despite the formal Soviet system of managing agriculture in kolkhozes, more traditional approaches survived in Transcaucasia, enabling the rapid setting up of farming households to form a significant part of the sector. This process was most marked in Armenia. In Azerbaijan and Georgia, vineyards and tea plantations are an important part of the sector and these had been run as sovkhozes and kolkhozes. As a result, the development of farming households was slower. In Azerbaijan, the process of land privatization is largely complete. The process was accelerated after the passage of land reform legislation in 1996 which has meant that all agricultural production is now done by private enterprises. However, the rapid pace of the process and the resultant lack of proper preparation meant that much of the privatization was mechanical in nature, with little regard for local conditions.

Regardless of their foreign policy stances, all countries in the region—including Abkhazia and South Ossetia—focused their economic policy on attracting foreign investment from Russia, Turkey, and the West. In 2015, US$5.6 bn of investment flowed into the region. Azerbaijan took 72% of this and Georgia 34%. Foreign capital played a particularly important role in industries focused on exports. At the same time, Georgia became an important transit conduit for Azerbaijani oil and gas.

In more recent years, the countries in the region have sought to develop technology parts and other industrial areas. In Azerbaijan, for example, the Balakhninshy Industrial Park and the Sumgayit Chemical and Industrial Park have been established. Since 2014, Georgia has also commissioned a park focused on high technology and innovation, while in Armenia, the first technology park was opened as early as 2001, with American money.

The Heritage Foundation publishes an annual Index of Economic Freedom. In 2018, Georgia, ranking 16th in the world, was the highest placed country among those of Transcaucasia. It was included in the group of countries judged to have predominantly free economies. Armenia was ranked 44th and featured in the group of countries with moderately free economies. Azerbaijan was in the same group, ranked 67th overall.

Economic Problems Affecting the Whole Region

The lack of close cooperation between the Transcaucasian states during the Soviet era, continued after the collapse of the Soviet Union and was, in fact, exacerbated by political and ethnic divisions. All countries in the region have seen their economic development held back by the effects of war, the damage to transport routes, and the presence of large movements of refugees.

Region-wide integrated transport and energy systems would enhance the attractiveness of the region and offer a boost to economic development. All countries in the region face the same challenges of dismantling both the surviving state monopolies and the commercial monopolies that resulted from initial attempts to privatize government enterprises which lacked any policy designed to encourage competition and create a new class of small and medium-sized business owners.

The Regional Economy: Cooperation and Contradictions

Despite all countries in the region following a similar policy focused on encouraging exports, there is only very limited cooperation within the region. There is little complementarity between the economies, and one of the most important trading relationships, that of oil and gas deliveries from Azerbaijan to Georgia, has been adversely affected by falls in world energy prices. There are scant reliable statistics on trade within the region. However, some estimates suggest that intra-regional trade is only about 5–6% of the region's total external trade. But even this exceeds the level seen in the final days of the Soviet Union, when it did not exceed 4%. Intra-regional trade reaches its peak in 1997, when exports accounted for 15% of the total and imports, 8%.

As noted, political and ethnic conflicts have put significant barriers in the way of developing economic cooperation within the region. Despite a ceasefire in 1994, the conflict between Armenia and Azerbaijan over Nagorno-Karabakh has meant a continuing break in economic relations between the two countries. Officially, there is no trade between the two, though black-market activities do take place. The conflicts in Abkhazia and South Ossetia significantly reduced the region's transport infrastructure. The corridors between Turkey and Armenia have been blocked since 1993. Because of its poor relations with Azerbaijan, Armenia uses Georgia and its transport routes to access foreign market. It has also begun to make use of new routes through Iran (both rail and gas pipelines). However, US sanctions on Iran limit the extent to which this is a viable alternative route. The differences in approach to their external economic relations have also slowed the development of regional integration. This is unlikely to change in the short term, as the ethnic and political problems remain unresolved and economic differences between the countries persist.

Common Problems in Relation to External Economic Policies

Russian exports to Transcaucasia include electricity, oil products, metals, transport, and heavy machinery, in return for traditional goods and food products. But the countries of Transcaucasia are now increasingly looking beyond their traditional likes with Russia and the other former Soviet countries, and focusing instead on seeking to develop closer links with the West.

There continues to be a significant black market, not just between the countries of the region, with further afield as well. At the same time, the unstable economic climate creates major flows of migration, much of it illegal, mostly to Russia.

The region faces the challenge that all countries have increased their military capabilities, in response to the continued existence of unresolved conflicts between the neighbors. Government budgets have had to meeting growing demands for rearmament and for commissioning military services from overseas. NATO has been the main supplier to Georgia and Azerbaijan, while Russia has fulfilled the same role for Armenia, Abkhazia, and North Ossetia. The regional countries have identified stronger external economic relations as a solution to problems caused by greater militarization.

The activities of foreign capital in the region impact not just the domestic economies, but also on the volume and structure of the countries' external relationships. In 2015, the volume of accumulated foreign direct investment in the Transcaucasian countries was US$39 bn. This fell in 2016 to US$20 bn of which Azerbaijan took 88%, Georgia 9% and

Armenia 3%. Foreign capital was primarily focused on export-oriented industries.

In 2016, the index of openness of the countries of the region (that is, the ratio of external trade to GDP) stood at 59% for Azerbaijan, 65% for Georgia, and 48% for Armenia. These figures illustrate how these countries see external trade as a means to achieving economic growth. Between 2000 and 2012, the GDP of the region as a whole increased by 970%, while foreign trade turnover went up by 1,140%. Until the middle of the 2000s, the region as a whole had a negative trade balance. But thanks largely to the growth of Azerbaijan's exports of energy resources—their exports exceeded imports by a factor of three—the balance became positive in 2013.

Azerbaijan boasts the largest share of the region's external trade. Moreover, it rose from 58% in 2007 to 75% in 2013 before falling back to 55% in 2016. When just looking at exports, its share has been even higher: 79% in 2007, 89% in 2013, and 70% in 2016. In 2007, Armenia had a trade deficit of 45.8%, and Georgia had a deficit of 61.6%. By 2013, these had decreased to 35.3% and 45.9% respectively. In 2016 Armenia's deficit had decreased to 29%, but Georgia's has risen to 55%. Georgia and Armenia have managed to increase their exports by developing their processing industries. In the case of Azerbaijan, the increase is the result of greater sales of crude oil and gas, which are, of course, highly vulnerable to fluctuations in world prices. In their external relations, the countries of the region focus on developed nations, with Russia, Turkey, and Iran also growing in importance. Turkey is a significant importer of gas from Azerbaijan, while Iran exports gas to Armenia. Georgia and Armenia are members of the World Trade Organization. Azerbaijan is preparing to join. Azerbaijan is a member of the regional Organization for Economic Cooperation, Armenia is a member of the Eurasian Economic Union.

Problems with Transportation of Caspian Oil

Problems relating to the transportation of Caspian oil have become an important factor driving regional cooperation and a joint approach to external economic relations. For a long time, exports of Azerbaijani oil have been transported along the Russian Baku–Novorossiisk pipeline and the Baku–Supsa pipeline in Georgia. In 2005, the Baku–Tbilisi–Ceyhan pipeline through Turkey came into operation. This established the cooperation between Azerbaijan and Georgia, the latter and the transit country. In 2006, the Baku–Tbilisi–Erzurum (BTE) pipeline came on stream, passing through Georgia. There is also a long-term plan to supply Azerbaijani gas to Europe along the Trans-Anatolian pipeline through Turkey.

However, the various delivery routes for Caspian oil have also become a factor slowing down regional integration because of the competition between the states of the region and their different political climates. Transportation of Kazakhstani oil through the Baku–Tbilisi–Ceyhan pipeline began in 2008. The USA and the EU were behind the construction of the pipelines through Georgia. Their motivation was a hope to isolate Russia from the Caspian energy sector as much as possible. This made it more difficult for Russian business to participate in the region's economic development. Armenia, which shares a border with Iran, completed the construction of an oil pipeline from Iran with Russian help in 2008. The gas it receives is destined for its internal market. Building pipelines to connect Central Asia to world markets through the TANAP and TAP (Trans-Adriatic Project) can play an important part in regional integration. By having energy resources transported over their territory, the countries of Transcaucasia plan to increase their commercial attractiveness.

The Region's Economic Relations with Russia

There have been a number of factors that might have lessened Russia's role with the countries of Transcaucasia: the decline in economic relations after the 1990s; the difficulties in the political relationships between Russia and Georgia; and the efforts by the USA and EU to limit Russia's competitive advantage in energy markets, particularly in relation to the transportation of Caspian oil. But, despite all this, Russia remains the main external economic partner of the region. It dominates trade with Armenia, accounting for 20% of the country's imports and exports. It also accounts for 14% of Azerbaijan's imports. In the case of Georgia, Russia accounts for 7% of imports and 6% of its exports. Russia also continues to be the main destination for labor migrants from the Transcaucasian countries and, thus, the main source of money transferred home by migrants. In the case of Abkhazia and South Ossetia, Russia has a virtual monopoly over their external relationships.

Region-wide Social Issues

The most pressing issue to face the countries of Transcaucasia is that of unemployment. This has been exacerbated by the fact that the economies of the region have barely risen above the levels of economic development achieved during the Soviet era. The problems are further compounded by structural and institutional weaknesses. In 2016, Armenia's official unemployment rate was 19%; Georgia's was 12%; and in Azerbaijan, the figure was 6%. However, according to unofficial data, the actual rate in all three countries around the middle of the 2000s was between 20% and 28% of the working-age population. This contributes to the problem of migration which remains unresolved.

The common factor in the countries of the region is poverty. The level of GDI on PPP per capita seen in the sub-region corresponds to that of other middle-income countries. In Georgia, 31% of the population live below the national income poverty line. In Armenia, the figure is 26%, and in Azerbaijan, 24%. The level of material inequality is high (see Table 7.8), especially in Georgia where the issue has led to social unrest and repeated changes of leadership.

Corruption is a problem throughout the region, endangering both economic and political stability. In 2017, the Corruption Perceptions Index placed Georgia in 42nd position, Armenia 107th, and Azerbaijan 122nd. Georgia's better showing in the table can be attributed to better law enforcement.

Conclusion

1. The Transcaucasian countries weathered the economic crisis of the 1990s and achieved fast growth during the 2000s and early 2010s.The countries of the region have achieved a level of development on a par with other middle-income countries. The region has yet to form a coherent single economic entity. In some ways, the countries are even further apart economically today than they were in the Soviet era. This results from political rather than economic factors.

2. The countries of the region have followed similar paths of economic policy in the creation of competitive environments. This has included a process of privatization aimed at improving the efficiency of public and management institutions. In all countries, the objectives of economic policy were to diversify production and improve the

countries' integration with the wider world economy. This is most pressing for Armenia, Georgia, Abkhazia, and South Ossetia as they do not have energy resources—the most in-demand commodity on world markets.

3. The most pressing issue to face the countries of Transcaucasia is that of unemployment, caused by structural and institutional weaknesses in their economies. Tackling inflation is also a priority.

4. The economies of the region are open and place importance on their external economic relationships as a means to achieve economic development. Azerbaijan has the largest share of the region's economic activity. Its exports alone give the region a positive trade balance.

Questions

1. How do the differences in reserves of natural resources in different geographical locations affect the economy of the countries of the Transcaucasian region?

2. How can we evaluate the participation by the countries of the Transcaucasian region in the exploitation of the Caspian and Iranian energy resources?

3. What factors prevent greater regional integration among the countries of Transcaucasia?

4. What is the economic impact of migration on the countries of the region and on Russia?

5. Which of the Transcaucasian countries is most attractive to foreign (including Russian) investment and why?

6. Using macroeconomic indices, compare the levels of economic development of the countries of Transcaucasia with Russia, other former Soviet countries, and other neighboring states.

Sources of Additional Information

Vardomsky L.B., Pylin A.G. and Sokolova T.V. Countries of Southern Caucasus. Moscow, 2014 (in Russian)

Sudin A.V. The oil and gas sector of the economy of independent Azerbaijan: results for 20 years. IVRAN. Moscow, 2012 (in Russian)

www.ca-c.org (Caucasian Institute of Strategic Research).
www.eurasianet.org
www.cisstat.com (Interstate Statistical Committee of the Commonwealth of Independent States).

CHAPTER 22

ABKHAZIA

Abkhazia is a small country. Its territory comprises less than 9,000 square kilometers and its population in 2016 was 243,600. Of this population over half are ethnic Abkhazian, while there are 45,000 Georgians, 42,000 Armenians, and over 22,000 Russians. The 1989 census recorded 527,000 people. But after the military conflict with Georgia, the population declined sharply, as a result of both emigration and the relocation of the Georgian population.

In 1921, Abkhazia was given the status of a Soviet Socialist Republic. Although this changed several times, it remained an equal partner of the Transcaucasian Federation. Only in 1936 it was formally incorporated into the Georgian Soviet Socialist Republic. It has, de facto, been an independent state since 1993 when it became the Republic of Abkhazia (Apsny). It adopted a new constitution in 1994. This declared the country independent in international law. It was recognized by Russia in August 2008.

The Abkhazian Economy

Agriculture and food processing dominated the Abkhazian economy during the Soviet era. In addition, there was an energy sector, a consumer goods industry, engineering, and the production of construction materials. The Leisure industry was also important. It was one of the major tourist destinations during the Soviet era and, as such, suffered significantly from the collapse of the Soviet Union. Military conflict with Georgia in 1992 and 1993 aggravated the situation. In addition to around 3,000 casualties, the damage was estimated at between US$11 and 13 bn. The towns of Sukhum, Ochamchira, and Tkvarcheli were badly damaged, along with many smaller villages. A large amount of technical equipment and transport vehicles were taken by Georgia.

As a result of the war, most commercial activity came to a standstill. Transport connections with Russia were closed, putting a brake on economic development. Traditional external economic relations were cut off, in particular, the country had no access to sources of external financing. From 2008 onwards, with the help of Russian investment, economic development was able to restart. But it was only temporary; Russia's own economic crisis, coupled with falling oil prices and sanctions against Russia in response to its actions in Ukraine, had a knock-on effect on the economy of Abkhazia.

Abkhazia has yet to establish a proper macroeconomic accounting system. In 2015, the volume of GDP amounted to ₽28.6 bn (GDP in 2011 was estimated at US$710 million). Agriculture makes up 6.5% of GDP, while industry—including energy and construction—make up 35%. The services sector represents more than 60% of GDP, of which trade is more than 25% and tourism more than 10%. Services generate a third of the country's budget revenues. According to Abkhazian estimates, the hidden economy or black market is equivalent to more than half of GDP.

Economic Policy

Transition to a market economy is the guiding principle of Abkhazia's social and economic development and was at the heart of the government's strategy outlined in the State Program for the Social and Economic Development of the Republic of Abkhazia 2000–2010. In 2014, an updated strategy was developed with plans running until 2025. Although there is a law on privatization, the country has privatized very little, the emphasis being on selling off government-owned land as the land prices in resort areas tends to be very high. Under a law on leasing, a large amount of land in Sukhum, Gagra, and Pitsunda with extensive resort facilities was leased. Private enterprise in Abkhazia was held back by the lack of transport connections with Russia. Although links have now been reestablished, Abkhazia now faces stiff competition from the well-developed agricultural sector in the south of Russia.

The Real Sector

In the Soviet era, the main crops grown in Abkhazia and supplied to the rest of the Soviet Union were citrus fruits, along with tea, tobacco, and nuts. In addition, the cultivation of vines, vegetables, and corn has been developed. Extensive pasture enabled high-yield animal breeding. The food-processing industry had accounted for half of all industrial production during the Soviet era.

In the years since the collapse of the Soviet Union, citrus and tea production was almost completely wiped out, largely as a result of the loss of agricultural equipment. There are a total of 397,262 ha of agricultural land. However, about 60% of it has not yet been cultivated. Today, almost all cultivated land is given over to corn, with some small corps of tobacco. Since the Soviet era, the number of livestock—cattle, goats, and sheep—has declined. The availability of agricultural machinery and tractors has declined and more than 90% of machines in operation are beyond their normal expected lifespan.

Tea and citrus crops had been cultivated mostly by individuals and families. Following its collapse, production of these crops began to recover around the time of the Winter Olympics in Sochi in 2014. Production of wine, cognac, liqueurs, and mineral water has also started to increase again. In 2013 and 2014, around 1,000 hectares were given over to grapes, citrus fruits, pineapples, guava, persimmon, and other fruits. Abkhazia has around 70 agricultural companies, 47 of which are state-owned with the other 23 being private. Of the companies, 90% specialize in crop production (28 companies focus on citrus, 9 on other fruits, and 26 on vegetables). The national budget gives substantial assistance to the agricultural sector. Russia also helps with an investment program of assistance to Abkhazia's social and economic development. In fact, under this scheme, Russia provides eight times as much assistance to the agricultural sector as the Abkhazian budget. Nonetheless, the industry remains unprofitable.

The food industry accounts for more than 40% of industrial enterprises in Abkhazia. There is also fishing and related production of fish oil and fish meal. There is significant investment going into the development of trout farms. Forestry is also an important sector thanks to the variety of woods that grow in the country. A ban on deforestation came into force in 1978, but this was ended at the time of the war with Georgia. High-value wood is exported, with furniture factories in Russia and Turkey being the main customers.

In terms of natural resources, the most beneficial for the development of industry are the country's reserves of coal, dolomite, granite, marble, tuff, barite, and lead. In the 'Shelf' Black Sea area, there are small oil and gas fields. Abkhazia also has mineral and thermal water resources. Its mountain rivers also have the potential for the development of hydro-electric power.

However, the deposits of oil and gas are not currently being exploited. Coal production remains in the doldrums. Hydro-electricity is thus the basis of the country's energy sector. A thermal power plant in Tkvarcheli is out of commission. A hydro-power plant in Sukhum and other smaller plants have been damaged and are also not operational. The main supplier of electricity is the Inguri hydro-electric power plant with four stations. The dam supplying the hydro-electric facilities lies within Georgia. The power plant and the four stations are in Abkhazia, on the River Eristskali and in the Gali reservoir into which water flows through a tunnel. Electricity generation has reached 3.2–3.5 bn kWh, depending on the water level in rivers. Half of the power generated by Inguri is delivered to Georgia. In 2019, the plant will be shut down for three months to repair the tunnels. Electricity will be supplied by Russia.

The recovery of the industrial base that began after 2008 has proceeded slowly. The bulk of the country's manufacturing (44%) is located in Sukhum. There are metal-working enterprises which use ferrous and non-ferrous scrap metals, producers of construction materials such as concrete and paving slabs, clothing and furniture manufacturers, and a publishing and printing industry.

The Winter Olympics in Sochi gave a boost to the production of construction materials in Abkhazia. In recent years the investment climate has improved as industrial facilities destroyed in the war have been reconstructed, while new enterprises are set up. This is likely to lead to a growth in industrial production.

In recent years, construction of housing and urban infrastructure has been increased rapidly, most of all in Sukhum itself. In 2014, about 65% of all construction was in Sukhum. The main resort centers, Gagra and Pitsunda, are also seeing an increase in construction, as is the region near the border with Russia. In 2014, construction accounted for 35% of GDP. The vast majority of companies active in the construction sector are privately owned. However, the absence of a law on land privatization often slows development down.

Abkhazia has significant potential in the area of tourism and existing resorts and recreational facilities. In 2013, there were 89 health resorts and facilities with the capacity to cater for 15,000 people. This includes 22 recreation centers, six sanatoriums, eight holiday centers, eight recreation camps, and 45 hotels. In 2013, according to official data, 133,000 people spent time in a health resort of facility. The total number of trips made exceeded one million.

The automobile provides the main form of transport in Abkhazia. There is a main highway along the coast, the Military Sukhumi road, that connects Sukhumi to the Kodori Gorge, an area of strategic importance. The country has 474 km of highways and 1,831 km of local roads. The entire road network is in need of modernization. Many roads and bridges were destroyed in the war. Car imports have increased several times over in recent years. Gasoline is imported from Russia, Turkey, and Romania.

The country has 239 km of railway. The main track follows the coast, connecting Sochi with Sukhumi and Samtredia. There is a branch from Ochamchira to Tkvarcheli for the export of coal. Since 1992, Abkhazia has been closed as a transit country. Before the war, all rail tracks were electric. But now electrification is confined to the section from Psou to Sukhumi. Part of the rail network has been dismantled. In 2004, Russia restored the direct link between Moscow and Sukhumi, and in 2008, the section from Sukhumi to Ochamchira was restored, also with Russian help. The locomotive and rolling stock is old and needs replacing. All railways are publicly owned. In 2009, they were transferred temporarily to Russian control.

Abkhazia is located on the Black Sea and sea transport plays an important role in the country's transport mix. The main port is Sukhumi, and there are three further ports at Ochamchira (home also to a Russian military base), Gagra, and New Athos. The latter two handle smaller vessels. The ports are government-owned and, currently, all shipping traffic is carried about by a publicly owned company.

Before 2009, there was no air transport. However, the country has two airports: Sukhum, designed for passengers and cargo aircraft up to 200 tons; and Gudauta (which is primarily issued for naval aviation) and other aircraft.

The government also dominates the telecommunications industry. However, the private sector is gradually gaining a toehold in cellular communications.

The Financial Sector

Abkhazia uses the Russian ruble. The country's revenues come from the collection of taxes. The tax structure is broadly similar to that of Russia, but with lower rates. Thus, income tax is set at 10%, VAT at 10%, and Corporation Tax at 18%. In addition to these there are payments to non-budgetary funds, such as land tax, taxes on the use of natural resources, property taxes, and various excise duties.

More than 30% of all budgetary expenditures are dedicated to investment, giving the government a continuing and important role in the investment process. Up to one-third of all expenditures are defense-related or dedicated to the maintenance of public order.

The government has created an environment what is now favorable to foreign capital. It also has a preferential customs regime. Enterprises with foreign investment are exempt from taxation as long as any profit is reinvested in one of a list of designated activities: production, processing and storage (in the case of agricultural firms), the production of technical equipment for the disabled, or the development of alternative energy sources (including small hydro plants). There is a scheme of preferential customs rates on the import of manufacturing equipment. Agricultural producers pay only the land tax.

The country's banking system is overseen by the National Bank of the Republic of Abkhazia. There are 14 commercial banks. Turkish and Russian capital are both significant in the sector. The largest bank is the Savings Bank of Abkhazia, the assets of which total more than 46% of the country's total bank assets. Since 2004, Abkhazian banks have been able to open correspondence accounts in Russian banks.

External Economic Relations

In 2013, Abkhazia's external trade amounted to ₽18 bn, but with a negative trade balance as exports were just one-sixth the value of imports. The country's main trading partners are: for exports, Russia (80%) and Turkey (17%); for imports, Russia (60% including food, alcohol and tobacco products, manufactured goods, fertilizers, medicines), Turkey (18% including industrial goods, tobacco products etc.), and Romania (20% including gasoline and diesel fuel).

In 2013, of all exports, industrial production (e.g. wood veneer, coal, scrap of ferrous metals, gravel and crushed stone) amounted to 20%. The remaining 80% was agricultural products such as citrus and other fruits and hazelnuts. Export earnings also include the money earned from the sale of licenses to Turkish vessels to fish in Abkhazian waters.

Russia's decision to recognize Abkhazia gave the country an ideal opportunity to activate its external economic profile. Most of the ruling elite believe that integration with Russia should be the priority for the country's economic strategy. Economically, the country has always relied on Russia. During the Soviet era, it had close links with the Kuban region. Russia's recognition of Abkhazia has strengthened ties still further.

Russia's interests in the relationship lie in Abkhazia's agricultural products and also in its traditional role as a tourist destination for Russians. Abkhazian wine and cognac make up 64% of Russia's imports from the country. A further 26% are citrus fruits, mineral water. Russia delivers flour, sugar, fuel, machinery and equipment to Abkhazia.

Moreover, under the Association Agreement signed in 2008, Russia maintains military bases in Gudauta and Ochamchire, giving a further boost to economic relations. After 2009, a number of agreements were signed under which Russia offers financial support to pay public sector salaries, child allowances, pensions, scholarships, medical care, and the maintenance of other public institutions. In November 2014, the two countries signed an agreement on partnership and integration. This came into force in March 2015 and saw Russia's assistance to Abkhazia significantly increased. The previously agreed level of support for 2015 was ₽5 bn, this was increased by a further ₽4 bn. Russia also became fully involved in the reconstruction of Abkhazia's rail system. Finally, an agreement was signed between the Abkhazian Ministry of Economic Affairs and the Russian company Rosneft, under which Russia became involved in the development of the Abkhazia's oil and gas fields.

Social Issues

The Abkhazian population has seen a great deal of social strain in recent years. The transition to a market economy and the emergence of 'new Abkhazians', coupled with the continued unresolved status of the country on the world stage, causes problems which are only made worse by the level of poverty. The granting of Russian citizenship has given a significant part of the population access to a Russian pension which has helped to maintain living standards. More than 25% of the population are in receipt of some form of pension or allowance. Despite healthy growth in recent years, the average salary remains low. The country hopes that the financial support from Russia will see salaries and pensions rise to match the levels seen in Russia's southern districts.

Questions

1. What are the main obstacles to Abkhazia's economic development?
2. Which sectors of industry hold out the most promise in terms of Abkhazia's economic development?
3. How can Abkhazia's external economic relations be characterized?

Sources of additional information

Republic of Abkhazia: Main Trends of Economic Development. 2005–2009. Abkhazian branch of the fund of Eurasian research. Sukhum, 2009 (in Russian).

Review of the Economy of the Republic of Abkhazia for 2013. (www.ved.gov.ru)

www.nb-ra.org. (website of the National Bank of Abkhazia).

www.abkhaziagov.org (official website of the president of Abkhazia)

CHAPTER 23

AZERBAIJAN

Azerbaijan's Economic Model

Azerbaijan's economic model is the product of the country's history as well as other natural factors. Prior to its integration into the Russian Empire, Azerbaijan was part of a large Islamic empire, which has left its mark on the people's ways of thinking and on their attitude to the role of government as a direct participant in economic life. The Soviet era also saw a strong role for the government in managing the economy. This heritage has provided a counterweight to the development of more European business patterns since the fall of the Soviet Union, with the penetration of foreign capital, particularly into the oil industry, being a major factor.

Since the 1990s, the country's economic model has shared many of the features found in other emerging economies. But it has its individual peculiarities. The government retains a significant role in the economy. The impact of the powerful energy sector can be seen across the whole economy. At the same time, aspects of Islamic economic principles can still be detected, though only in minor ways. Finally, the country's oil and gas reserves have made it a magnet for foreign investment which has, in turn, encouraged a more open economic model. As a result, in 2018, Azerbaijan was ranked 67th in the Index of Economic Freedom. Its position was dragged down by the weakness of property rights, though it was an improvement on 2013, when it was placed 88th. The Doing Business Report which looks at how favorable conditions for business are—particularly, small and medium-sized firms—Azerbaijan was placed 57th.

A privatization process has given private businesses a significant role in the economy. Between 2009 and 2015, the private sector's share of the economy rose to 80%. Enterprises involved in trade and consumer services were privatized first. The privatization of larger enterprises was more complicated, with government bureaucrats and banks retaining import roles. In the oil and gas industry, and in other key areas of infrastructure—in other words, the main areas of the economy—property remained in the hands of the government.

The government today sees its main challenge to be, not further privatization, but rather expanding the private sector and improving its effectiveness. The government has sought to simplify registration procedures and the awarding of licenses. In addition, regular credit auctions are held throughout the country to facilitate access to credit. A project to build a new industrial town near Sumgait, with the hope of providing employment for 10,000 people is well under way. An Export and Investment Incentive Public Fund has been set up to improve the quality of smaller businesses and to assist them in accessing international markets. There is also a National Enterprise Support Fund which supports small industrial and agricultural producers.

Private ownership has become predominant in the agricultural sector. All kolkhozes and sovkhozes have been closed down. Only a handful of breeding and crop farms remain in public ownership. Various types of cooperative have been created, sharing credit and marketing. This has enabled farmers to remain significant players in agricultural production.

The black economy has been significant in Azerbaijan, though it is shrinking rapidly. According to international estimates, it made up around 90% of GDP in the late 1990s, but declined to 40–60% by 2010.

A feature particular to Azerbaijan has been the emergence in recent years of so-called 'Islamic' businesses. The banking sector actively implements Islamic conduct-of-business rules which cater for the increasing numbers of people adhering to Sharia Law which prohibits the earning of interest. There is, for example, an Islamic corporation for financing private business. There is as yet no formal legal framework for this kind of ownership or activity—known as a 'waqf'—but it is becoming increasingly common. A waqf is funded through donations from members of the Islamic community in a version of 'Islamic community capitalism'. A waqf's activities can be educational or commercial. But they must be set up as a charity.

Table 23.1 — GDP in Azerbaijan

	2000	2005	2012	2014	2015	2016	2017*	2020**
GDP, US$ bn	4.9	12.6	68.7	75.2	54.1	37.9		
Gross national income, PPP per capita, US$	3,340	6,280	14,870	16,920	16,910	16130		
GDP growth, %	9.2	26.4	2.2	1.1	-3.8	-3.1	-1,4	2,6

*Estimates of the International Monetary Fund

**Forecast

Source: World Bank. Indicators; World Bank. Global Economic Prospects 2018.

IMF. World Economic Outlook. 2015, p.174; Azerbaijan in Figures, 2016.

Azerbaijan's Economy

In terms of economy and population, Azerbaijan is the largest country in Transcaucasia. In 2016, its population was 9.7 million. In 2000, it accounted for 50% of the region's GDP. By 2015, thanks to the development of the oil and gas sector, this had risen to 78%.

Since 1998, Azerbaijan has seen some of the highest GDP growth rates in the world. The main driver of this has been the growth of the oil and gas sector, helped by rising international prices for energy. The earnings from the export of oil and gas have stimulated the growth of other sectors of the economy, in particular construction and infrastructure. This has enabled the country to weather the storms of the global financial crisis and the decline in oil prices in 2013 and 2014 – though the dependence on oil and gas remains important. Thus, the sharp decline in GDP growth rates—growth in 2012 was just one-sixth of its 2011 level—was largely the result of the reduction in oil extraction is the largest Azeri-Chirag-Guinishli fields. The main operator of this field is British Petroleum. But a sharp decline in oil and gas prices in 2014 led to negative GDP growth in 2015 and 2016.

Investment activity has been strong in recent years. The rate of gross capital formation was 27% of GDP in 2007, increasing to 29% by 2015. After 2007, domestic investment was larger than foreign. In 2015, foreign direct investment accounted for 29% of all gross fixed capital formation.

The structure of GDP is characterized by the predominance of the secondary sector. The primary sector accounts for just 5% of GDP and the tertiary sector 31%. The secondary sector takes up 63%. The industrial make-up of GDP is dominated by the oil and gas sector which provides two-thirds of the total. It also provides over 50% of the national budget and more than 80% of exports. Construction, both large-scale projects and housing, is also important. In the services sector, the opening of domestic and export pipelines has also make an important contribution to the economy, especially after the opening of the Baku–Tbilisi–Ceyhan oil pipeline and the Baku–Tbilisi–Erzurum gas pipeline.

Economic Policy

In the immediate aftermath of the collapse of the Soviet Union, Azerbaijan faced two economic problems: the economic crisis brought about by the collapse; and the need to transition to a market economy. Privatization was an important element in this and the priority was given to the privatization of small and medium-sized businesses. Agricultural policy was aimed at achieving a radical change in the structure of land ownership and use. More recently, it has also focused on introducing intensive farming methods, improving agribusiness management, and maintaining food security.

During the 1990s the government made it a priority to create a business climate in the country that would be attractive to foreign investment. Nowadays, the emphasis has shifted to encouraging involvement from domestic, mainly private, sources of capital in the national economy. This is combined with an acceptance that it is right for the public purse to finance large infrastructure projects of strategic importance that may be less attractive an investment to the private sector. Today, there is also an increasing focus on encourage Azerbaijani capital to seek investment opportunities abroad.

Human Capital

Azerbaijan is the only country in Transcaucasia that has maintained a positive rate of population growth between 1990 and 2010. Between 2000 and 2012, the population grew by an annual average of 1%, taking the total to 9.7 million by 2016. However, over this period, estimates suggest that immigration added twice as much to the population as the natural rate of growth among the native population. The conflict with Armenia was a major cause of immigration. However, there is a paucity of accurate data and record-keeping in relation to migration.

The services sector is the largest employer, with 49% of the workforce. In 2016 agriculture employed 36% of the workforce; while industry employed just 12% despite accounting for 50% of GDP. The oil industry employs just 38,000 people.

The economically active population is reckoned to be 5.8 million. Official statistics put the unemployment rate at 1%, though the real rate is likely to be several times higher, probably at least 6%. About 1.8 million people are non-registered unemployed. The situation is aggravated by the presence of nearly 1 million refugees and forced migrants from Nagorno-Karabakh.

Azerbaijan's rate of literacy is 99%. Education was made compulsory for eight years during the Soviet era. Almost all cities have a university, the largest of which is Baku State University. In recent years the number of Islamic schools—madrassas—has begun to grow.

Today the number of mobile phone accounts in the country exceeds the population, while Internet users now number more than 7 million. Azerbaijan has two of its own communications satellites.

The Real Sector

The main aims of Azerbaijan's food policy are the maintenance of food security and improvement in the living standards of the rural population. After the closure of the kolkhozes and sovkhozes, the majority of agricultural producers are small individual households. They receive substantial support from the government to raise their productivity. Since 2007, a program to provide microcredits from the state budget, redistributed through the National Entrepreneur Support Fund and the State Agency on Agricultural Credit has been implemented. 'Agroleasing', a publicly owned company, provides leasing services for the provision of agricultural equipment at preferential rates. In addition, they can purchase fuel and mineral fertilizers at discount prices.

To encourage greater wheat harvests, farmers receive ₼40 (manat – about US$50) per hectare of crops. In 2012, about 60% of all crops were wheat. This support saw wheat harvests rise from 2.4 to 2.9 million tons between 2008 and 2013. In addition to wheat, rice, cotton, tobacco, vegetables, horticulture, and vines are grown. The subtropical zone of Lankaran is a center of the country's agricultural sector. As well as the cultivation of various crops, there is well-developed cattle farming and fishing (mainly of sturgeon for the production of black caviar). Preferential credits are available to promote poultry facilities, cold storage warehouses, and grain elevators. About 300 km of irrigation canals have been built. Despite all this, there is still significant dependence on food imports. The value of food imports was almost equal to that of imports of equipment for the oil and gas industry.

Oil and gas are the foundations on which the Azerbaijani economy is built. In the Soviet era, up to the 1960s, oil from Baku was the main source for the domestic market. However, by the time the Soviet Union collapsed, the share of the Soviet Union's energy balance taken by Azerbaijani oil was less than 2%. Many of the country's oil fields were decommissioned, to be revived in the post-Soviet period, mainly at the expense of the shelf (coastal zone) of the Caspian Sea. The country now exports 88% of its oil production.

Estimates of Azerbaijan's oil and gas reserves vary. Between 1995 and 2015, proven reserves increased from 660 million tons to 1 bn tons (still only 0.4% of the world's oil reserves). Over the same period, gas reserves increased from 320 bn cubic meters to 1.1 trn (0.6% of the world's reserves). The country expects its current reserves to last for 25–30 years, taking into account both exports and the growth of domestic usage.

The routes along with Azerbaijan exports its oil to the outside world have taken on special significance in recent years, both from a purely domestic view of Azerbaijan's own economic interests, and from the perspective of Europe's desire to diversify its sources of energy supply. The coming on stream of the Azeri-Chirag-Gunashli field has seen the country increase its level of oil extraction. These reserves now make up the bulk of the country's output. The building of the Baku–Tbilisi–Ceyhan pipeline was a major reason for the increase in extraction from this field. The field can now be reckoned to be operating at full capacity. Data on the presence of deep-water layers of oil, including some under the Azeri-Chirag-Gunashli field, hold out the prospect of doubling the output of oil in the long term.

Oil production in Azerbaijan is controlled by the State Oil Company of the Azerbaijan Republic (SOCAR) which can develop reserves itself, or empower foreign companies to develop them subject to a sharing agreement. As a rule, firms are offered deals lasting 30 years. Foreign companies are exempt from customs duties, including those on imported equipment. SOCAR is also active in oil processing, the product of which is also exported. The gasoline, engine oil, diesel fuel, fuel oil, and kerosene produced are mainly exported to neighboring countries, including Russia which is a major buyer of aviation kerosene, and some European countries.

In recent years, the role of the fuel and energy complex, and gas production has increased and predictive estimates of trends in production are positive. Once a net importer of Russian gas, since 2007, it has been an exporter. The state-owned company 'Azerigas' is the industry leader in gas production. The development of Azerbaijan's gas industry has had greater international importance than that of its oil industry. The bulk of the gas reserves are in the Shah Deniz field operated by British Petroleum. The gas from the first stage of the project has filled the capacity of the Baku–Tbilisi–Erzurum pipeline. That from the second stage will require a number of new pipelines for which the Azerbaijanis are lobbying European governments. The projects most likely to come to fruition are the TANAP and TAP. The current level of oil and gas production, and the likely future production taking into account proven reserves, is unlikely to fill the capacity of all projected pipelines. There is, therefore, a move to identify new deposits and also attempts to attract neighboring countries to use the pipelines for their own production. This puts Azerbaijan in competition with Russia.

Electricity is another important part of the country's energy mix. This is controlled by 'Azerenergy', another state-owned organization. In 2016, electricity generation totaled 23.3 bn kWh, with consumption at 20.3 bn kWh. Azerbaijan has signed an electricity exchange agreement with Russia and Iran. In addition, a project known as 'Energy Bridge' is being implemented providing for the creation of a single regional model of a high-voltage power network, combining the power grids of Azerbaijan, Georgia, and Turkey. While Azerbaijan is an exporter of electricity, it imports it from Iran to meet the needs of the Nakhchivan Autonomous Republic.

The country's metallurgical complex is made up of several plants working in both ferrous and non-ferrous metals. Between 2000 and 2012, production increased fourfold. The engineering industry focuses on the production of household appliances. In the 2000s, capital inflows, mainly from Turkey, injected growth into this sector. There is a textile industry which specializes in cotton and wool manufacturing. Together with the food-processing industry, it is a major producer of commodities.

A building boom has seen a fivefold growth in the production of construction materials since 2000. Construction comes second only to oil and gas in its contribution to GDP. The building boom was felt throughout the country, but especially in the capital, Baku. The quality of construction work is increasing.

Since the middle of the 1990s, once the country had weather the crisis, economic activity began to grow. The opening of the Baku–Tbilisi–Ceyhan pipeline has made a significant contribution to the country's economy. The pipeline alone accounts for 17% of the country's cargo transport. Further contributions are made by the Baku–Tbilisi–Erzurum, Baku–Supsa, and Baku–Novorossiysk pipelines.

The conflict with Armenia has held back development of the railway system. Routes to Russia, Georgia, and Iran are all well used. Sea transport plays an active role in trade with other Caspian countries. Baku is the country's major port and there are ferry services to Turkembashi (formerly Krasnovodsk) in Turkmenistan.

Internal trade in Azerbaijan takes many forms: from large supermarkets to small shops. Nowadays, Internet shopping is growing in importance. In addition, there are bazaars which combine small-scale retail operations, producers of handicrafts, and large wholesale companies. In rural areas, there are consumer cooperatives.

The Financial Sector

Like other Transcaucasian countries, Azerbaijan has an under-developed financial sector. The level of monetization is low and the mobilization of domestic savings into finance for economic development remains insignificant. This can be partly explained by the existence of the black economy and the high level of dollarization.

The country's banking sector is overseen by the Central Bank of the Republic of Azerbaijan. In addition to its central bank functions, it promotes development of various programs providing credit to the private sector, both small and medium-sized enterprises. In 2007, the Mortgage Fund was set up within the Central Bank to stimulate the provision of mortgage credit. During the 1990s, reforms aimed at creating a two-level banking system were undertaken. Limits on authorized capital stock were increased in order to strengthen the banks. However, some banks went bankrupt as a result. The overall number of banks fell by 75%, but the sector's capital went up fivefold. Today, the banking sector's assets are equivalent to 32% of GDP. There is a high concentration level in the sector: the assets of the top five banks (International Bank, Capital Bank, Bank Standard, Halg Bank, and Pasha Bank) account for 61% of the entire sector's assets and, between them, they provide 58% of bank credit. By contrast, over 61% of bank deposits are held by International Bank, which is state-owned. In 2011, there were 44 private banks in the country, 22 of which had some foreign capital.

The State Oil Fund plays an increasingly important role in the financial system since its assets are as large as the state budget. The fund was established in 1999. Its assets received from oil revenues are intended to be used for future generations and for the implementation of social programs for refugees and forced migrants.

The growth of its oil revenues has enabled Azerbaijan not only to eliminate the state budget's deficit but to increase expenditure consistently, thanks to one of the strongest records of economic growth in the world. Between 2003 and 2013, budget expenditure increased by a factor of 22. In 2013, expenditure was US$27.2 bn, equivalent to 35.5% of GDP.

Azerbaijan enjoys a liberal tax system. There are direct taxes: on personal income on a progressive scale from 12–35%; on legal entities at 20%; and VAT at 18%. A simplified system has been introduced for small businesses. Agricultural producers benefit from exemptions and only pay land tax.

The budget surplus, due to rising oil prices, flowed into the Oil Fund. Oil revenues have enabled the government to increase its own budget expenditures by a factor of 25 since 2003.

Greater expenditure on social projects has led to higher inflation. In 2008, inflation ran at more than 20%. By 2011, this had come down to 1.9% and, further, to 1.4% in 2013. However, a devaluation of the manat has seen it start to rise again, reaching 157% in 2016.

Azerbaijan differs from other regional countries in having a liberal currency system. The convertibility of the manat is maintained by the Interbank Currency Exchange in Baku.

The External Sector

Azerbaijan has had a positive balance of payments since the middle of the 2000s, the only exception being 2015. This has been fueled by large exports of oil. The financial account has mostly been in deficit due to large debt repayments.

Foreign capital reaches Azerbaijan mainly in the form of direct investment. The stock of accumulated direct investment in 2016 amounted to US$22.2 bn. Of this, 83% was in the oil and gas sector. The main investors are: the United Kingdom making 36.5% of the total; the USA, 12%; Norway, 11%; and Japan, 11%.

The law on the protection of foreign investments, adopted in 1992, permits investment from abroad into all sectors of the economy except for defense and national security. Thus, foreign investment is permitted into the oil and gas industry and occurs mostly in the form of production sharing agreements. The share of foreign capital in the insurance industry remains limited.

In 2016, the country's external debt amounted to US$14 bn, equivalent to 37% of GDP and 8,1% of the exports of goods, services and primary incomes. The crisis of 2008 and 2009 saw a reduction in foreign exchange reserves as they were used to support the Azerbaijani currency, the manat, and to prop up the banks. In 2016 external debt exceeded the gold and foreign exchange reserves of US$7.4bn.

The thrust of Azerbaijan's external economic relations is determined by the country's determination to focus on integration into European and Euro-Atlantic structures. The bulk of foreign direct investment into Azerbaijan comes from the USA and the countries of Europe. Direct overseas investment by Azerbaijani companies is mostly directed at Georgia and Turkey, as well as on other countries aiming to join the EU. In 2008, for example, the state-owned Azerbaijani oil company became a major shareholder of the largest Turkish petrochemical company, 'Petkim'. The accumulated total of direct overseas investment by Azerbaijani companies was US$15.4 bn in 2015.

Azerbaijan's development as an exporting country, therefore, heavily depends on the success of its energy sector. Oil accounts of 87% of the country's total exports. By contrast, gas exports represent just 3% of the total. However, there are efforts under way to develop the export potential of the gas industry, all of which will further establish raw materials as the driving force of the Azerbaijani economy. Most of the country's oil exports go to Europe.

94% of exports are made by state-owned enterprises (2012 figures), while in imports, 80% of the total are made by private companies. Russia is the main source of Azerbaijani imports, accounting for 14%; Turkey is almost equal, also at 14%; the United Kingdom at 12.5% and Germany at 8% are also significant. Former Soviet countries other than Russia account for less than 7% of the turnover in Azerbaijan's foreign trade.

The development of Azerbaijan's intra-regional relations has focused exclusively on Georgia. In 2008, SOCAR bought a controlling share of the

Poti oil terminal and acquired management rights over 29 gas distribution points in Georgia. Georgia has now become the largest buyer of Azerbaijani energy and the main transit country of its energy resources. Despite international sanctions, Azerbaijan has an active relationship with Iran which is its principal supplier of a number of products, including electricity, to the Nakhchivan Autonomous Republic, an enclave of Azerbaijan that borders Iran.

Economic relations with Russia diminished during the 1990s, began to increase again, but since the middle of the 2000s, have gone into decline again as Russia's share of Azerbaijan's foreign trade has fallen. Azerbaijan supplies Russia with the production of energy and fuel, cotton, and chemical products. The country imports machinery, equipment, and fuel and energy products. Russian capital is gradually playing an increasing role in Azerbaijan, especially in the food-processing industry. The energy sector is also a popular destination for investment.

The development of the energy complex and the transportation of hydrocarbons play an increasingly important role in Azerbaijan's economic relations with Russia. Both are Caspian countries, seeking to address the issues of legal status of the Caspian Sea, problems over which have hindered the development of better regional cooperation among the countries of the region. The delineation of borders and agreement between Russia and Azerbaijan over jurisdictions in the sea, have been achieved with the conclusion of a bilateral agreement. This has clarified each country's positions and has thus provided the legal basis for common projects in the area of the Caspian shelf. The two countries share an interest in increasing their exports of energy resources and participating as transit countries for those resources. Europe and the USA are attracted to the idea of using Azerbaijan and its territory as a counterweight to Russia's influence in energy supplies. The construction of oil and gas pipelines through Georgia and Turkey are testament to this.

The construction of the TANAP and the TAP gas pipelines—plans for which have them coming on stream simultaneously with the 'Turkish Steam'—will enhance competition in the gas market. In particular, this should have a beneficial impact on the price of gas being transported to Turkey which will become a powerful energy hub as a result of these developments. However, Azerbaijan will not have enough gas to make full use of the second line of the Shah Deniz pipeline when it comes on stream; so the line may also carry Turkmen and Iranian gas.

Russia is a major destination of labor migration from Azerbaijan. Large-scale migration from what was then the Azerbaijani Soviet Socialist Republic began in the 1980s. There are currently estimated to be around 1.3 million Azerbaijani labor migrants (without accompanying family members) in Russia, with about half of them in Moscow and Saint Petersburg. At the same time, by the turn of the century, the number of Russians in Azerbaijan had decreased from 393,000 to 142,000. As a percentage of the population, that represents a fall from 5.6% to 1.8%. This trend of a fall in the Russian population in Azerbaijan had been apparent for decades and was not due entirely to the collapse of the USSR. Russians had made up 16.5% of the Azerbaijani population in 1939.

The Social Sector

Despite the high earnings from oil and gas and gross national income on a PPP bases reaching US$16,130 per capita, the living standards of the majority of the population in the country remain low. High property differentiation is a significant factor in this (see Table 7.8). Moreover, it should be noted that the extent of the black economy makes it hard to assess levels of actual income accurately. In 2006, the average monthly salary stood at US$159; in 2008, US$327: and in 2015, US$453. Despite this, in 2008, about 16% of the population was living below the poverty line, in 2015, about 5%.

In 2008, a new program aimed at reducing poverty and ensuring sustainable development had a target to halve the number of poor by 2015. A system of targeted social assistance has also been implemented, under which the range of different forms of assistance will be combined into a single targeted program.

The country's system of social security and medical cover was inherited from the Soviet era. There are over 1.2 million pensioners in Azerbaijan. In 2013, the average pension was $193 a month, but differences between different sections of the population are significant. In recent years the private sector has become more active in the provision of health care.

Conclusion

1. Among the countries of Transcaucasia, Azerbaijan has the greatest economic potential, due mainly to its oil and gas industries. Economically, the oil industry is the most important for the country. It

has grown with a program of both modernizing existing oil fields and developing new ones. There has been increasing focus on gas production, particularly for export. This sector dominates the country's GDP and there is, thus, a risk from over-reliance on this single sector, particularly as oil and gas are subject to fluctuations in international prices. A further risk comes from the heavy dependence on foreign investment and on imports for most consumer goods.

2. Azerbaijan was behind other Transcaucasian countries in embarking on economic liberalization. But the country now has the legal framework necessary for a market-based economy. The agricultural sector has also been radically reformed. In line with wider reforms, the government is using the earnings from oil and gas exports to finance programs of social support and initiatives to promote small businesses.
3. Foreign capital has flowed into the country's oil and gas industry and this has been one of the main drivers of development. In fact, Azerbaijani capital is now being extensively invested in neighboring countries.
4. The country's recovery from the economic crisis of 2008 and 2009, the expansion of its industry, and the measures taken to support private businesses have all seen a marked reduction in emigration of labor. However, there has not yet been a major return of Azerbaijani emigrants from Russia.
5. Azerbaijan's external economic relations are focused around oil and gas and the country's export markets in Europe and Asia. Relations with Russia and other former Soviet countries are recovering after the decline in the 1990s. However, they are still not a priority for the government.
6. Due to the unresolved territorial dispute with Armenia, Azerbaijan's efforts at intra-regional relations focus exclusively on Georgia, through which it has access to both the Black Sea and the Mediterranean for its oil and gas exports.

Questions

1. What impact do its natural and geographical features have on Azerbaijan's economy?
2. What role does oil play in Azerbaijan's economy?
3. Describe the reserves, production and potential of Azerbaijan's gas industry. How will planned developments of transnational gas pipelines improve its scope?
4. What role is played by foreign capital in Azerbaijan?

5. Describe Azerbaijan's external economic relations, in particular those with Russia.

Sources of additional information

Sudin A.V. The Oil and Gas Sector of the Economy of Independent Azerbaijan: results for 20 years. IVRAN, Moscow, 2012 (in Russian).
www.ca-c.org (Caucasian Institute of Strategic Research).
www.eurasianet.org
www.cbar.az. (Central Bank of the Republic of Azerbaijan).
www.stat.gov.az (State Statistical Committee of the Republic of Azerbaijan).

CHAPTER 24

ARMENIA

Armenia's Economic Model

Armenia's history as part of the Russian Empire and the Soviet Union has had a major impact on the evolution of its economic model. During the Soviet era, Armenia was one of the most developed Soviet Republics in terms of industry and science.

However, the collapse of the Soviet Union and the loss of its huge market, coupled with the armed conflict with Azerbaijan over the region of Karabakh, led to a severe economic downturn in Armenia. The absence of diplomatic relations with Turkey has not helped (a protocol on establishing relations was signed in 2009 but has still not been ratified). The conflict with Georgia has exacerbated the country's isolation and largely crippled its industry and transport networks.

Against this backdrop of economic crisis, the country has tried to apply market reforms to its Soviet economy in much the same way as most other former Soviet countries. As in other countries of the CSI, initial efforts at introducing and market economy led to hyperinflation and a freeze of investment activity. It also exposed the lack of competitiveness in Armenian industry. Between 1991 and 1993, the country suffered a catastrophic economic slump: GDP fell by almost 2.5 times and prices rose 1400 times. From 1994 onwards, the government enacted a series of reforms approved by the IMF and designed to reflect the country's specific position as a geographical enclave. In the short term, the reforms carried out in Armenia were more radical than those pursued in its Transcaucasian neighbors.

Today, the Armenian economy has features of a classic market economy, but with its own peculiarities. The real sector, the result of an accelerated program of privatization, suffers from poor productivity (except in the construction of housing) thanks to the limited scope of the internal market, poor natural resources, and a continued transport blockade. As a result, the economy depends very heavily on foreign loans, money transferred home by ex-patriates, and foreign investment. Political factors weigh heavily on the economy and there are strong links between the business and political elites.

The share of the economy accounted for the public sector has decreased steadily. It now employs less than 20% of the working population. The share of the economy accredited to small and medium-sized businesses is 42%. The role of smaller enterprises is most marked in agriculture where 97% of all produce comes from farming households. The picture in relation to larger businesses is more complicated. The ownership of almost all large industries was transferred into the hands of a small group of people closely connected with the country's leadership. Now, 90% of privatized enterprises belong to 8% of the families in the country.

Foreign companies have also established strong positions in the economy. For example, the country's electricity network was almost completely bought out by Unified Energy Systems of Russia (RAO) in 2005.

The black economy is also significant—though probably less so that in Azerbaijan and Georgia. Moreover, its share of the overall economy is decreasing, from an estimated 46% in 2003, to 30% in 2013. The black economy in Nagorno-Karabakh and in some of the regions of Azerbaijan occupied by Armenia has a strong criminal element, largely related to trafficking in drugs and arms.

The country suffers from large disparities in the levels of economic and business development in different regions. The region of Erevan, for example, is home to 35% of the population, but produces more than half of the country's GDP and half of all the industrial output. Around 90% of all construction is concentrated here. The government has initiated programs aimed at supporting small and medium-sized enterprises in the hope of spreading the fruits of economic development more evenly to the other ten marzes (regions).

According to 2018 Doing Business report, Armenia was placed 47th, ahead of most other former Soviet countries.

The Economy of Armenia

Since 1994, Armenia's economic development has kept it ahead of other Transcaucasian and former Soviet countries.

Table 24.1 — GDP in Armenia

	2000	2008	2012	2015	2016	2017*	2020**
GDP, US$ bn	1.9	11.9	10.0	10.5	10.6	-	-
GNI PPP per capita, US$	2,300	7,510	7,740	8,450	9,020	-	-
GDP growth rate, %	5.9	6.8	7.2	3.0	0.2	3.7	4.0

*Estimates
**Forecast

Source: National Statistical Service of the Republic of Armenia, 2016.
World Bank. Global Economic Prospects 2018.
Statistical Yearbook of Armenia 2017.

In the 1990s, average annual rates of GDP growth were negative at -3.1%. Industry saw the biggest drop at -9.0%. Growth rates became positive from 1998 onwards and between 2000 and 2012, the annual average was 7.6% (despite a fall of 14.4% in 2009 in the wake of the financial crisis). More recently, the rate of growth has slowed, but remained positive. A number of factors lay behind the high growth rates: the introduction of market mechanisms in all sectors of the economy; the accelerated development of the construction and financial sectors; an increase in inflows of capital from abroad and the subsequent strengthening of the national currency, the dram; and targeted increases in investment. However, despite the economic growth, since 2008 the share of gross capital formation has fallen from 32% of GDP to 21% in 2016.

The primary sector has a significant share of GDP, accounting for 18% of the total in 2016. Construction alone contributes 10% of GDP which boosts the total for the secondary sector as a whole to 31.5%. Construction is regarded as a 'powerhouse' of the Armenian economy. The sector is dominated by housing construction, especially in Erevan where more than 90% of all construction investment is made. The secondary sector has seen its share of GDP fall from 45% in the Soviet era due to continued stagnation in most branches of industry, including the one important jewelry industry (including diamond cutting).

Economic Policy

After the fall of the Soviet Union, the program of privatization in Armenia focused not just on small and medium-sized industries as in other Transcaucasian countries, but on larger enterprises as well. Foreign capital played an important role in the privatization process. At the same time, radical agrarian reform was undertaken, changing the structure of land ownership and use.

The Index of Economic Freedom endorses the view of Armenia as a country actively pursuing economic liberalization. On the 2018 index, Armenia was placed 44th in the global table, behind more liberal economies but above most other former Soviet countries. The country scores well as a result of its efforts to tackle corruption and the measures it has put in place to develop its financial markets in line with liberal principles. One of the key aims of the country's economic policy is the creation of an investment climate that is attractive to foreign capital, including Armenians living overseas.

Human Capital

After falling in the aftermath of the collapse of the Soviet Union, the population has stabilized at around 3 million people. Low birth rates and emigration have kept any increases in check. In Russia, in 2013, there were between 700,000 and 800,000 migrants from Armenia, mostly labor migrants and their families.

Of the economically active population, 44% work in agriculture and 39% in services. The rate of unemployment rose in the aftermath of the economic crisis of 2008 and 2009 and, by 2016, it exceeded 18%. The unemployment figures are inflated by the presence of refugees and forced migrants from Azerbaijan. There are also high levels of informal employment, more than 46% of the total in 2016.

Erevan University is the largest of the country's 20 universities. Education expenditure represents 3% of GDP, but spending on science remains relatively low. Science in Armenia is largely funded by foreign investment and grants from business.

The number of mobile telephone accounts is larger than the population. Information and Communication services accounted for 3.6% of GDP in 2012/2013.

The Real Sector

The country's agro-industrial complex is under-developed and inefficient. This can be seen in the fact that, while 36% of the working population work in agriculture, they produce just 18% of GDP. Almost everyone working in the sector (99%) are employed in farm households. Like the economy as a whole, agriculture declined in the immediate aftermath of the fall of the Soviet Union, but an active privatization program saw it recover quickly so that, by 2002, its output was already back to the level achieved in 1991. However, the continued predominance of small households in the sector means that its commercialization is limited. The sector itself consumes about half of its own output.

Limitations in land and water resources are the main problems facing the agricultural sector. In addition, the small size of many of the households in the sector is also a drawback. The sector also faces competition from imported products and has poor links to domestic food-processing industry. The level of mechanization and the use of chemicals have both decreased in the sector, leaving the sector more vulnerable to adverse weather. As a result, crop yields fluctuate from year to year. Despite some growth in the sector, half of the country's food is imported.

During the 1990s, there was a major recession in the food-processing industry. Recovery was achieved by focusing on exports to Russia. Production of cognac, wine, and mineral water (from the springs in Jermuk and Arzni) have all increased and, with them, the share of the country's exports taken by the agro-industrial complex has gone up to 27%.

Overall, industrial output has never matched the level it achieved in 1989. Today, it is barely three quarters of what it was in its best years. Many enterprises, even those adopting high-tech equipment and methods, stand idle, including many under the control of Russian companies.

Though small, only 5% of GDP and 2% of the country's workforce, the fuel and energy sector is one of the country's most dynamic. The country produces barely 7% of its own energy requirements and so focuses heavily on efficiency and reducing energy consumption. Foreign investments have also been targeted at programs to develop renewable sources of energy such as rivers, solar, and geothermal.

Armenia generates about 7.5 bn kWh. Of the total, 40% comes from thermal power generation, 25% from hydro-electric plants, and the rest from nuclear power. After the collapse of the Soviet Union, Armenia was the first of the Transcaucasian countries to be able to provide an uninterrupted supply of electricity to its people and businesses. It even created a surplus for export to Nagorno-Karabakh and Georgia. The country exports electricity to Iran in return for supplies of gas. Several initiatives have enabled Armenia to increase its generation of electricity: the construction, with Russian help, of the fifth block in the Hrazdan thermal power plant; the modernization of the North-Hrazdan hydro-electric cascade; planning of a new nuclear power plant; and the bring on stream of new capacity in both the existing nuclear plant and the Erevan thermal plant. The gas for new thermal power plants is imported from Iran through the pipeline constructed in 2007.

Manufacturing is the bedrock of Armenian industry, making up 60% of the sector. A Strategy for Industrial Policy was launched in 2013. This provides for the promotion of 11 different branches of industry: cognac production; diamond cutting; jewelry production; manufacture of watches; textiles; the pharmaceutical and biotechnology sector; canning; wine production; mineral water; production of fruit juices; and precision engineering. The main focus in this program is on efforts to attract investment from the private sector.

One of the leading manufacturing sectors is the metals industry, mainly non-ferrous metallurgy. The sector accounts for 25% of all industrial production. The largest non-ferrous smelter is Zangezur, which operates on the basis of its own deposits of copper and molybdenum. This company is 60% owned by the German company, Cronimet. Another large non-ferrous smelter is Agarak, which is owned by a joint Armenian-Georgian-Russian company. There are large copper mines in Kafan, Kajaran, Agarak, and Akhtala. Another successful company is Armenal which is owned by the Russian company Rusal and produces foil, mostly for the Russian market.

The chemical industry had grown rapidly before the economic crisis of 2008 and 2009. The industry had been an important player during the Soviet era which saw the construction of Nairat, a plant producing synthetic rubber in Erevan and Prometheus-Khimprom, a complex producing synthetic corundum and melamine. Both these plants were privatized, with Nairit now owned by the British firm, Rhinoville Property Limited. The government aims to create a single coherent production network involving a number of chemical, metallurgical, and extractive companies that will be more competitive in international markets.

The engineering industry was among the first to be privatized. Its products are designed mainly for exports and account for 18–25% of the country's overall exports. The engineering sector produces CNC machines, tools using synthetic diamonds and hard metals (at the Aragats, Almaz, and Araks plants supported with Russian capital), and electrical products such as switching equipment, motors, relays, and devices for the electronic control of machines.

The construction boom created the conditions for growth in the wood-processing industry and in the production of concrete and construction equipment. Industries that are more traditional in Armenia are textiles and footwear, both of which suffered badly in the economic crisis, not helped by competition in their domestic market from Turkish and Chinese imports. The jewelry industry has not fully recovered from the downturn. It is heavily focused on exports and is vulnerable to fluctuations in the world market.

Construction, mainly of housing, is one of the country's main industries. However, more than 90% of the total volume is focused on Erevan.

Armenia is heavily dependent on transit of goods through Iran and Georgia. Almost all the country's railway (869 km) is electrified and most of its road network (7,700 km) is paved. But, due to difficulties in relations with Turkey and Azerbaijan, both are underutilized. There is a network of 3,800 km of pipeline. The main pipeline from Iran is now in operation.

Given the difficulties with rail and road transport, air transport assumes greater importance. The country has 12 airports, used for both passengers and cargo. In 2013, a program was adopted to gradually liberalize the cargo traffic and several new companies were created to handle this.

The Financial Sector

With insurance and fund management services both under-developed, the banking system takes a leading role in the country's monetary system. The Stock Market functions largely as a mechanism for redistributing property. The Central Bank of the Republic of Armenia oversees the sector. As well as the Central Bank, there are 21 commercial banks. The sector's total assets as a proportion of GDP are relatively small, but are growing fast. In 2003, the share was 16%; in 2007, 29%; and in 2013, 68%. The banking system suffers from severe shortages of long-term funding and hopes to raise its level of capitalization to deal with this.

A feature of the Armenian banking system that sets it apart from its regional counterparts is the almost total lack of any commercial banks that have state capital (unlike Russia) and the prevalence of foreign banks bringing foreign capital to the system. The banking system revolves around five large banks that, between them, own 50% of the entire sector's assets. They are America Bank, VTB-Armenia Bank (a subsidiary of the Russian VTB Bank), Ardshininvestbank, ACBA-Crédit Agricole (a subsidiary of the French Crédit Agricole), and HSBC Armenia (a subsidiary of the British HSBC).

The country's budget has not been balanced for many years. In 2016, the budget deficit was equivalent to 5.5% of GDP. A law of 2013 reduced the rates of income tax and, thus, the share of direct taxes in the government's budget. Direct taxes contributed 25% of the budget in 2014, while VAT contributed 40%. Tax avoidance is rife.

Nearly a third (29%) of government spending goes on social insurance and social security. Military expenditure remains low at 16%, equivalent to 4.4% of GDP.

The External Sector

In the 2000s, Armenia's current account balance of payments was negative. But the financial account was positive thanks to the large inflows of foreign capital. Money sent home by labor emigrants and the Armenian diaspora makes an important contribution to the balance of payments—about a third of households in the country receive at least some money this way. At the turn of the century, almost half of all direct foreign investment came from the Armenia diaspora. However, this has since reduced.

Armenia is an ally of Russia and receives considerable financial support in the form of direct investment and transfers from members of the Armenian diaspora (more than 90% of the entire Armenian diaspora is in Russia). But the country also makes considerable use of credit and capital from Western nations. However, the amount of accumulated foreign direct investment remains small. In 2016, it stood at US$4.6 bn, just one-fifth of the amount in Azerbaijan, and a third of that in Georgia.

The Armenian unit of currency is the dram (֏) which is freely convertible. Between 2000 and 2013, the nominal value of the dram strengthened, partly as a result of the increasing flow of foreign capital into the country in the form of transfers and direct investments. The strengthening of the dram has a dampening effect on inflation as the internal market of Armenia relies heavily on imported goods. Between 2007 and 2016, external debt more than doubled, reaching US$ 9 bn, equivalent to 92% of GDP, of which 70% is long-term debt.

During the 2000s, the country focused its external policy on efforts to increase exports by seeking to encourage greater industrial diversification in the hope of finding specific areas of economic activity in which Armenia could establish comparative advantage. For Armenia, it is important to maintain close ties with Russia while attempting to integrate into European and Atlantic institutions and structures. For example, Armenia has a system of military and technical cooperation with NATO under the auspices of the US program, 'Millennium Challenges' through which it receives aid for the reconstruction of rural districts. Among the countries of the CIS, Armenia's ties with Russia are the most advanced. In Transcaucasia, relations with Georgia are gradually improving. There is a large enclave of Armenians in the Georgian region of Samtskhe-Javakheti.

Since 2002, Armenia's external trade has been growing faster than GDP. In 2016, the value of external trade was equivalent to 48% of GDP. However, the value of imports is two times that of exports, giving the country a significant negative trade balance. In 2016, exports were worth US$1.8 bn, while the value of imports was US$3.3 bn. The trade deficit is thus equivalent to 14% of GDP. More than 70% of exports are ores, precious stones, and metals. The country's exports are heavily concentrated in certain commodity groups which leaves it vulnerable to fluctuations in world markets.

The CIS countries (in particular Russia) account for 30% of the value of Armenia's external turnover. However, the EU now accounts for 28%, a proportion that has been steadily increasing. Armenia's largest trading partner is Russia, which takes 23% of exports and provides 25% of imports. China is also beginning to be a player of note both in terms of trade and economic cooperation (where it is now Armenia's second most important partner after Russia). Iran and Turkey are also worthy of note, the latter in particular as an exporter of goods to Armenia despite not having diplomatic relations.

In terms of relations with its neighbors in Transcaucasia, Armenia only has ties with Georgia. The country uses transport routes and gas pipelines through Georgia to connect with Russia. Armenia supplies electricity to Georgia, mainly to the regions with significant Armenian populations.

Russia remains Armenia's main foreign investment partner. By the beginning of 2014, total Russian investment in Armenia totaled US$3.3 bn, of which US$2.5 bn was Russian direct investment. In other words, over half of all accumulated foreign investment in the country was Russian. Of all enterprises with foreign capital, 28% had some Russian investment. Among joint economic projects, the most successful were in the field of mobile communications. Two large companies belong to Russian companies: "ArmenTel" to "VimpelCom" (since 2009 part of VEON) and "K-Telecom" to "MTS". A joint bank was founded, VTB-Armenia Bank. At the same time, Gazprombank purchased 80% of the stock of Arekimbank. A project to modernize the North-Hrazdan cascade is being carried out. Rusal Armenal, one of the largest manufacturing enterprises in Armenia and the only manufacturer of aluminum foil in the Caucasus, is wholly owned by Russian capital. In 2011, A Russian company, Neva-Rus—using 100% Russian capital—built a mining and concentrating plant near the Armanin polymetallic deposits. 'Russian Railways' won the concession to manage 'Armenian Railways'. The participation of Russian companies in the construction of new nuclear power plants and in the development of uranium deposits is well established. The joint Armenian-Russian Mining Company has been set up for this purpose.

In 2016, the volume of trade between Armenia and Russia exceeded US$1.6 bn. Armenia exports beverages, both alcoholic and non-alcoholic (which make up more than 50% of all the country's exports), cultured pearls (12%) and fruit. Russian exports to Armenia are dominated by fuel (5% of Armenia's total imports), crops, transport vehicles, machinery, and equipment.

As noted, Russia is the main destination for Armenian migrants. Of all emigrants, 90% go to Russia. Money sent home by emigrants (70% of which comes from Russia) amount to at least three times as much as all incoming foreign direct investment.

Armenia's accession to the Eurasian Economic Union in 2015 has increased the potential for the country to develop economic ties with Russia and other members of the Union.

The Social Sector

Despite some success in its economic reforms, a majority of Armenia's people still endure low living standards. In 2015, the average monthly nominal wage per employee was $359. At the end of the previous decade, the bottom decile of the population by income took 3.7% of all earnings, while the top decile took 25.4%. Even so, the Gini coefficient is low and even declining.

The system of social security and health care remains largely as inherited from the Soviet era. However, in recent years, the private sector has taken a more active role in the provision of health care services. The average pension is equivalent to less than 17% of the average nominal wage. In 2014, the country began to transfer people to a compulsory defined contribution pension system. Pension funds are required to invest at least 40% of their assets in foreign stocks.

Conclusion

1. Armenia's economic strategy has focused on accelerating the implementation of a modern market economy. Currently, private business is the bedrock of the economy. In agriculture, small businesses predominate. But in industry, while there is a large number of smaller enterprises, large companies with foreign capital prevail.
2. Armenia's complicated geographical setting and its lack of sea ports have made the country heavily dependent on maintaining good relationships with its neighbors. However, despite ending of the conflict in Nagorno-Karabakh, focusing on better relations with the EU, and improving the prospects of better transport connections, actual results have been few and far between. Russia plays an important role in the Armenian economy and its continued relationship with Iran has given Armenia the opportunity to expand its transport links through Iran, including the building of a gas pipeline.
3. In recent years, construction has been the most dynamic sector of the Armenian economy, along with metals and mining, energy, and the production of wines and cognacs. Armenia is becoming an exporter of electricity to its region, thanks mainly to significant purchases of primary energy resources.
4. Foreign capital, in the form of direct investment, has focused on the mining, energy, and banking sectors. This should offer the country major scope for economic development, but so far there has been little success.
5. In its external economic relations, the EU is gradually closing the gap on the countries of the CIS which have been Armenia's main economic partners in the past. Armenia's accession to the Eurasian Economic

Union in 2015 may reverse this trend. Russia remains Armenia's main trading partner, for both imports and exports. The conflict over Karabakh means that intra-regional relations focus exclusively on Georgia.

Questions

1. What influence do its natural and geographical features have on the industrial and economic structure of Armenia?
2. What role is played by foreign capital in the economy of Armenia?
3. What are the particular features of the reform program under way in Armenia?
4. Describe the business climate in Armenia.
5. Describe Armenia's external economic relations, including those with Russia.

Sources of additional information

Vardomsky L.B., Pylin A.G. and Sokolova T.V. Countries of Southern Caucasus. Moscow, 2014 (in Russian).

Socioeconomic Situation of the Republic of Armenia in January–December of 2014. Erevan, 2015.

www.armstat.am (National Statistics Service of the Republic of Armenia).

www.ved.gov.ru (Ministry of Economic Development of the Russian Federation).

CHAPTER 25

GEORGIA

The Economic Model

The years of development following the fall of the Soviet Union have shaped in different ways of the formation of Georgia's economic model. During the 1990s, the loss of the huge market that had existed in the Soviet Union had a major impact on Georgia. This was compounded by the political and military conflict with Abkhazia and South Ossetia and the break in economic relations with Russia. In more recent years, the greater focus on developing relations with the USA, the EU, and NATO have also shaped Georgia's policies. Georgia is less politically stable than Azerbaijan and Armenia who signed a ceasefire in 1994. This has held back the country's development.

The country's economy shows some of the certain features of a market model. But it also has certain characteristics of its own. After the 'Rose Revolution' in 2004, one of the main features of Georgia's approach was its desire to align itself more closely with European and Atlantic institutions. The use of foreign capital has also become widespread in the economy. The country has also been a significant recipient of foreign aid, which has led to the heavily subsidized nature of the economy. There has been an increase in the inequality of income distribution, leading to greater social tension. This led to the 'Georgia Dream' coalition coming to power in 2013, promising a more balanced approach to the country's external relations. However, hopes of significant changes in policy and the structure of the economy were not fulfilled.

Georgia's Economy

Georgia was one of the most prosperous republics of the Soviet Union. The eventual rupture in its relations with Russia had its roots in the final years of the Soviet Union and, when the Soviet Union collapsed, the economic slowdown in Georgia was worse than in any other of the former Soviet countries. In 1993, Georgia's GDP was just one-third of what it had been in 1990. Signs of stabilization were not seen until the second half of the 1990s. But such was the depth of the recession that had afflicted the country that, even in 2007, GDP was still only half what it had been during the Soviet era.

Table 25.1 — GDP in Georgia

	2000	2005	2012	2013	2015	2016	2017*	2020**
GDP, US$ bn	3.0	6.4	15.8	16.0	14.0	14.4	-	--
GNI PPP per capita, US$	2,690	4,240	6,780	7,020	7,510	9510	-	--
GDP growth, %	4.0	9.6	6.4	3.4	2.8	2.8	4.3	5.0

*Estimate
** Forecast

Source: World Bank. Indicators.
World Bank. Global Economic Prospects 2018.
IMF, World Economic Outlook. April 2015, pp. 173.
Statistical Yearbook of Georgia 2017.

Between 2000 and 2007, the average annual growth rate for GDP was 8.3%. But from 2008, it went into decline, largely as a result of the military campaign against South Ossetia which saw significant military losses. This situation was, of course, aggravated by the economic crisis of 2008 and 2009, as the Georgian economy relied heavily on Western credit and aid. The country returned to growth after 2010. The influx of foreign funds has enable Georgia to maintain a high level of gross capital formation. It grew from 23% in 2012 to 33% in 2016.

The services sector makes up the bulk of Georgia's GDP, 67–79% in 2012/2013. The share accounted for by the secondary sector increased to 24%, due largely to construction of both housing and infrastructure e.g. pipelines and rail routes from Azerbaijan to Turkey. Between 2000 and 2015, the contribution of the primary sector to GDP declined from 22% to 9%, despite its employing more than half of the working population.

Economic Policy

Georgia's program to transform itself into a market economy saw small and medium-sized enterprises privatized first. However, such firms only make up a small part of the economy—around 10%. The Saakashvili government which came to power in 2004, placed the emphasis on privatizing larger enterprises such as the iron and steel company 'Rustavi,' the Georgian Ocean Company and the copper concentrate plant 'Madneuli.' Foreign capital played an active role in the process. The country's roads, the postal service, and major pipelines remain in state hands.

During the 1990s, the country's agricultural policy brought about a radical change in the structure of land ownership and use. Kolkhozes and sovkhozes were replaced with small farms, some of which combined to form cooperatives. Some state farms continue to operate, but more than 90% of agricultural output is now produced by the private sector.

A principal aim of economic policy has been the creation of an investment climate that is attractive to foreign companies. Overseas investors have taken a particular interest in Georgia's potential as a focus for the transport of cargo and raw materials, e.g., energy and other natural resources from around the Caspian region, Russia, and Iran, as well as other cargoes such as Kazakhstani corn which is shipped through Georgia's ports.

It is now possible to conclude that the first stage of Georgia's structural reforms is complete given that the key mechanisms of a market economy are in place, large-scale privatizations have been completed, and the role of the state in entrepreneurship and economic management has been significantly limited. In this respect, Georgia was ahead of its Transcaucasian neighbors. In 2018, the Index of Economic Freedom placed Georgia 16th in the world, alongside the group of countries with predominantly free economies. The Doing Business Report which looks at how favorable the conditions for doing business in a country are, Georgia was ranked 9th in 2018.

Georgia has now embarked on the second stage of reforms in which it plans to develop a competitive economy and a state administration of high quality, with the aim of improving the living standards of the population, reducing corruption, and providing a trustworthy legal system. The Worldwide Competitiveness Index moved Georgia up to 67th place in 2017–2018.

Overall, the share of economic activity undertaken by the public sector has decreased, while those sectors in which the private sector plays an important role, e.g., services, financial, food, and hospitality, have seen rapid growth. As noted above, much of the country's infrastructure remains in state hands, but parts of this are being privatized. For example, the management of the railways was transferred to the British company, Parkfield Investments, for a period of 89 years. As such, the role played by the private sector in the country's economy has become predominant.

Large businesses have been attracted to roles involving infrastructure, especially transportation through the ports of Batumi, Poti, and Supsa.

However, the hidden economy still accounts for between 40% and 50% of economic activity. For years, corruption was a drag on the country's business development. In 2005, Georgia was reckoned to be one of the most corrupt countries in the world, ranking 130th out of 160. However, thanks to the government's efforts to tackle corruption, by 2017, the country had risen to 46th place out of 175 countries.

Human Capital

Over the last 25 years, Georgia's population has declined from 5.5 to 3.7 million, largely due to emigration. Until the end of the 1980s, migration flows were insignificant. Between 1979 and 1988, the number of people emigrating was just 1% of the population. However, between 1989 and 1995, this increased to 11.1%, a much larger proportion than those seen in Azerbaijan (3.8%) and Armenia (1.6%). More recently, this rate of emigration has dropped markedly and the country has even begun to see net immigration.

There is no reliable data on labor migration. However, some estimates put the number of Georgians who have emigrated in search of work at around 1 million. This seems a very high estimate as the country's entire population of working age is reckoned to be 2 million (2011). Of those leaving to find work elsewhere, 90% are heading to Russia.

Unemployment remains high. The official rate is 12–14%, but the real rate is likely to be much higher, probably 20–25%. In particular, hidden unemployment is high, especially in rural areas where there are half a million small farm households and a rural population of 2 million.

The Real Sector

Of all people employed in Georgia, more than 55% work in agriculture. For this reason, the health of the agro-industrial complex has a big influence on the overall state of the economy. In 1993 and 1994, during a severe economic crisis, agricultural output fell to just one-third of the level achieved in 1987.

After the closure of the kolkhozes and sovkhozes and the distribution of land into private ownership, problems arose over how land should be managed, specifically how small holdings might be parceled up into larger units. More than 40% of farms were of less than a single hectare. Most of the farming households on this land were using natural methods of production. Virtually all the corn, grapes, vegetables and citrus fruit produced, as well as 95% of cattle breeding, was being done by family or individual farms. Large-scale operations focused mainly on tea, wheat, and poultry.

The rural population moved to producing just what they needed themselves, leaving the urban population in need of basic commodities. This led to radical changes in the structure of the agricultural industry. During the 1990s, many farms began to focus on grains, mainly corn. As a result, the production of fruit (including citrus) halved, and grapes cultivation reduced even more. Production of tea, which had been a staple crop during the Soviet era, fell by 95%. Grains were the only crop to see the production increase.

Agriculture has traditionally been the main manufacturing industry in Georgia. In recent years, many aspects of the food industry have adapted to an agricultural sector based on small farms. The food industry accounts for 35% of the country's overall industrial output, and employs 38% of all industrial workers. The main products are wines and cognacs, tea, tobacco, mineral water, canned vegetables, and fruit.

The most important branch of the fuel and energy sector is the electrical power industry. Georgia has experiences shortages of electricity since the late 1980s. It lacks the resources to increase its capacity to increase power generation. Only thermal generation power plants rely on domestic raw material, black coal.

Georgia imports gas from various sources. In the late 1950s and early 1960s, the main gas pipelines from Baku and Vladikavkaz were built and throughout the 1970s all the republics of Transcaucasia used mainly

Iranian gas. More recently, Russia has been the main supplier of gas to Georgia. But the construction of the Baku–Tbilisi–Erzurum pipeline has opened the way for Azerbaijani gas to supplant the role previously played by Russia. Under an agreement with Azerbaijan, Georgia takes 5% of all the gas pumped through the pipeline from the Shah Deniz field. Georgia also uses some gas imported from Iran.

As well as its problems with supplying sufficient fuel to its power plants, there were also difficulties with the electrical supply networks, some of which are in the territory of Abkhazia and South Ossetia. As a result, incidences of power cuts increased. The state stepped in to rehabilitate a number of thermal power plants, supply networks, and the Inguri hydro-power plant. At the same time, a number of power facilities have been privatized, including about 30 hydro-power plants and a significant proportion of the distribution companies. As a result, the country now exports twice as much electricity as it imports. Georgia's problems with the supply of electricity are largely a thing of the past.

In the early 1960s, coal mining, one of the sources of raw material for power generation, was a high priority for Georgia as it was the only country in Transcaucasia to have its own coal resources, enough to meet its energy needs. During the Soviet era, the main mining regions were Tkibuli (which produced about 70% of the country's coal) and Tkvarcheli in Abkhazia (producing the other 30%). But in the 1990s, coal mining virtually stopped and, to this day, the industry remains largely inactive.

Despite only having small reserves of oil, an oil industry was developed during the Soviet era, centered on the Batumi oil refinery that refined both domestic and imported oil. Today, the country's oil and gas reserves are largely depleted with oil extraction a mere fraction of what it was in 1990.

Georgia's metal industry has recovered well from earlier declines. The major producers are the metal plant at Rustavi, the ferroalloy plant at Zestafoni (which provides about a fifth of the country's entire exports), the manganese plant at Chiatura, and the copper plant at Madneuli. They mostly use domestic raw materials.

Most engineering companies in Georgia operate at reduced capacity. There is production of electric locomotives and machine tools in Tbilisi and Batumi. The chemical industry is recovering its production capacity. It mainly produces fertilizers, synthetic fibers, paints, and household chemicals. The increase in production in metallurgy and chemicals has been the main factor in the overall rapid increase in manufacturing in recent years. The average annual growth was about 15% between 2000 and 2013. Much of this increase came from large factories that are owned by foreign investors.

Given its level of unemployment, especially hidden rural unemployment, most international analysts believe that Georgia's best chance for development lies in the small and medium-sized enterprises.

As in other countries of Transcaucasia, construction has become one of the fastest growing sectors of the economy. In Georgia's case, this can be attributed to the development of the country's role as a transport corridor between Europe and Asia. In addition to its pipeline projects, Georgia has seen other high-profile transport-related projects, e.g., TRACECA (The Europe–Caucasus–Asia International Transport Corridor). Georgia is also a member of the Organization of the Black Sea Economic Cooperation (BSEC), under whose auspices the modernization of the country's transport infrastructure and the construction of new roads is being financed. The expansion of housing construction has come about largely to meet the need to house refugees from Abkhazia and South Ossetia.

With Georgia's development as a transport corridor, the volume of transit traffic trebled between 2000 and 2013. The traffic flowing from Asia to Europe has enhanced the important of transport in the economy, although traffic volumes of both cargo and passengers are barely a fifth of what they were during the Soviet era. Many local transport links—road and rail—are closed due to the continuing conflicts with Abkhazia and South Ossetia.

Georgia's rail system was electrified during the Soviet era and was connected with those of Armenia, Azerbaijan, and Russia. In 2009, work began on a project, with Turkish financing, to build a rail link from Baku, through Tbilisi and Akhalkalaki to Kars in Turkey. In Akhalkalaki, a station is being built to enable trains to transfer to a European gage.

The country's road network is in a poor state of repair. As such, and given its mountainous landscape, the country relies heavily on air transport. Tbilisi International Airport handles 98% of all air transport. At the same time, Batumi International Airport is being modernized, again with Turkish participation. Oil and oil products are shipped from the port at Batumi to Azerbaijan and Kazakhstan. There are direct rail-ferry services from the port of Poti to Illichivsk in Ukraine, Varna in Bulgaria, and

Kavkaz in Russia. There is also a car-ferry service to Novorossiysk in Russia, Burgas in Bulgaria, and Rise in Turkey.

Pipelines have come to play an increasingly important role in Georgia's transport system. The major pipelines were built during the Soviet era, from Baku (the Baku–Supsa oil pipeline) and a gas pipeline from Vladikavkaz. The construction of pipelines to carry Caspian oil and gas which bypass Russia and Iran has had an important political and economic impact. In 2006 the Baku–Tbilisi–Ceyhan oil pipeline and the Baku–Tbilisi–Erzurum gas pipeline were put into operation and the revenue from them has become an important element in Georgia's economy. In addition, the TANAP project to construct a gas pipeline through Georgia to carry gas from Azerbaijan to Turkey will also be important.

The Financial Sector

Inflation peaked in 2008 at 10% and fell to a negative figure in 2012/2013. Thereafter, it rose again and between 2014 and 2019, it is estimated that the average annual growth rate will be 3%.

During the 2000s, Georgia's banking system has recovered and developed. There are 17 commercial banks, 14 of which have some element of foreign capital from international organizations or foreign banks, e.g., the Russian bank, VTB. This foreign involvement is usually in the form of absolute or majority ownership. These 14 banks now control 80% of the assets of the entire banking sector. The National Bank of Georgia oversees the banking sector. The country also has 38 microcredit institutions, five insurance companies, and two credit unions. However, despite the growth of the banking system, its high costs mean that credit remains prohibitively expensive for most entrepreneurs. More than half of the credit that is issued is used in trade. Georgia has a stock market. But, as in other countries of Transcaucasia, its capital markets are embryonic.

Greater economic stability and GDP growth have enabled the government to raise more money from taxation for the budget. Between 1996 and 2002, state budget revenues did not exceed 16% of GDP. In 2013, they amounted to the equivalent of 28%. The measures to crack down on corruption and the hidden economy have contributed to this. The new tax law, enacted in 2005, also played an important role in increasing the government's tax revenues. It reduced the number of different taxes from 21 to seven, and reduced tax rates as well. Georgia now has seven taxes: income tax at 20%; a tax on profits at 15%; VAT at 18%; real estate tax at a maximum of 1%; import tax at 0%, 5% or 12%; dividend tax at 5%; and excise duty which depends on the type of product. An additional measure is intended to promote the growth of investment by granting businesses a remission of profit taxes for five years if they make additional investments in production.

The government has succeeded in making huge reductions in its budget deficit. By 2017, it was equivalent to 3.9% of GDP. Even so, persistent budget deficits have led to the accumulation of a large government debt. In 2016, the total was equivalent to 44% of GDP, three-quarters of which was external. Since 2006, the budget deficit has been covered with assets allocated by the USA under various aid programs.

The External Sector

Georgia receives a large amount of foreign capital. In addition to foreign direct investments, it receives aid and credits from international financial organizations. In terms of the volume of aid received from the USA, between 2005 and 2008, Georgia was second only to Israel. The financial account and the balance of payments are characterized by significant inflow of foreign capital, especially in the form of direct investment into projects in transport and energy. Between 2010 and 2013, the foreign direct investment was equivalent to, on average, 6.3% of GDP. This was US$1 bn a year, more than 40% of which came from EU countries, and less than 15% from other former Soviet countries. By 2016, the volume of accumulated foreign direct investment amounted to US$14.1 bn. Currency assets were in the form of money transfers from Georgians working overseas and the wider diaspora, mostly in the USA and Russia.

Since the second half of the 1990s, the current account deficit has been falling. This was partly due to the transition in 1998 to a floating exchange rate for the national currency (the Georgian lari, ₾) which led to a gradual decline in the actual exchange rate of the lari, enabling exports to grow rapidly.

In recent years, the country's external debt has been equivalent to four or five times the value of exports, which has severely restricted the ability to service the foreign debt.

Attracting foreign capital is at the core of Georgia's strategic external economic policy. The USA and the EU are principal targets as they account for more than 40% of all foreign direct investment. International financial organizations such as the World Bank and the IMF are also in the frame. Today, the United Arab Emirates, Azerbaijan, Turkey, and Japan are also among the largest of Georgia's creditors.

In 2016, the value of Georgia's imports was US$6.6 bn and its exports were US$2.8 bn. This deficit was covered with external credits. The most important of Georgia's exports are metals (including scrap). Ferrous metals account for over 15% of the total, and non-ferrous over 10%. Other significant exports are concrete, fruit, wine, and mineral water. Fertilizers are also beginning to be an important export commodity. Of the country's imports, fuel is the largest, accounting for over 12% of the total. Automobiles account for 9%. Georgia also imports wheat and flour.

The trading landscape in the Transcaucasian region is changing. Russia is gradually losing its position among Georgia's trading partners. In 2016, Turkey was Georgia's largest trading partner with over 16% of total turnover; Russia was second, and Azerbaijan third. China has been growing in importance among the country's trading relationships. In terms of Georgia's imports and exports, 28% of the overall value is attributed to the EU. The country has now signed an association agreement with the EU which should see trade increase still further in the future.

Georgia is an important player in international labor migration. Money transfers into Georgia from its citizens working overseas continue to be an important factor in the country's balance of payments. In 2007, such transfers were equivalent to 9% of GDP. Various estimates suggest that the amount of such transfers coming from Russia alone amounted to US$1 bn.

Economic relations between Russia and Georgia are influenced by their political relationship. Georgia's conflicts with Abkhazia and South Ossetia led to the country's withdrawal from the CIS and affected relations with Russia. From time to time, Russia has imposed bans on certain Georgian imports and on movements of workers. Relations reached a low point in 2008 as a result of, on the one hand, Georgia's military operations in South Ossetia, and on the other, by Russia's recognition of the independence of Abkhazia and South Ossetia. Even so, as noted above, Russia remains an important trading partner for Georgia, buying mining products, citrus fruits, and chemical products. Russian business is represented in the Georgian banking and energy sectors. However, political differences make these relationships unstable.

The Social Sector

Living standards in Georgia are lower than in Azerbaijan and Armenia. Of course, the size of the hidden economy suggests that real conditions are probably better than official figures suggest. But, nonetheless, raising its citizens' living standards remains Georgia's key economic development challenge. At the beginning of the current decade, about a third of the Georgian population was living below the poverty line, with an income of less than $2 a day (2010). In 2007, the average monthly salary was $210. By 2013, this had risen to $510. The Gini coefficient, with regard to incomes, was 0.460 in 2011 and 0.420 in 2013. The bottom decile of the population by income has just 2% of the wealth while the top decile has 31%.

Standards of education and health care are relatively high in Georgia. The number of universities is growing. There is a particular focus on training specialists in the field of humanities.

Conclusion

1. The country's economy shows some of the certain features characteristic of a market model. But it also has certain characteristics of its own. After the 'Rose Revolution' in 2004, one of the main features of Georgia's approach was its desire to align itself more closely with European and Atlantic institutions. The use of foreign capital has also become widespread in the economy. The country has also been a significant recipient of foreign aid, which has led to the heavily subsidized nature of the economy. There has been an increase in the inequality of income distribution, leading to greater social tension. This led to the 'Georgia Dream' coalition coming to power in 2013, promising a more balanced approach to the country's external relations. However, hopes of significant changes in policy and the structure of the economy were not fulfilled.

2. It is now possible to conclude that the first stage of Georgia's structural reforms is complete given that the key mechanisms of a market economy are in place, large-scale privatizations have been completed, and the role of the state in entrepreneurship and economic management has been significantly limited. In this respect, Georgia was ahead of its Transcaucasian neighbors. In 2014, the Index of Economic Freedom placed Georgia 22nd in the world, alongside the group of countries with predominantly free economies. The Doing Business Report which

looks at how favorable the conditions for doing business in a country are, Georgia was ranked 16th in 2016. Georgia has now embarked on the second stage of reforms in which it plans to develop a competitive economy and a state administration of high quality, with the aim of improving the living standards of the population, reducing corruption, and providing a trustworthy legal system. The Worldwide Competitiveness Index moved Georgia up to 72nd place in 2014.

3. Inflation peaked in 2008 at 10% and fell to a negative figure in 2012/2013. Thereafter, it rose again and between 2014 and 2019, it is estimated that the average annual growth rate will be 3%. During the 2000s, Georgia's banking system was stiffened. There are 17 commercial banks, 14 of whom have some element of foreign capital from international organizations or foreign banks, e.g., the Russian bank, VTB. This foreign involvement is usually in the form of absolute or majority ownership. These 14 banks now control 80% of the assets of the entire banking sector.

4. Georgia receives a large amount of foreign capital. In addition to foreign direct investments, it receives aid and credits from international financial organizations.

Questions

1. Why did Georgia withdraw from the CIS?
2. How successful have Georgia's economic reforms been?
3. Describe the state of Georgia's agricultural sector.
4. Does Russia need economic relations with Georgia?

Sources of additional information

Statistical Yearbook of Georgia 2017. National Statistics Office of Georgia. 2014. Website: www.geostat.ge

State Strategy for Regional Development of Georgia. USAID Caucasus 2013-2017. July 2012.

www.ca-c.org (Caucasian Institute of Strategic Research).

www.eurasianet.org.

www.nbg.gov. ge (National Bank of Georgia).

CHAPTER 26

SOUTH OSSETIA

South Ossetia declared independence from Georgia in 1991. This led to a military conflict. In 2008, Russia recognized South Ossetia's independence.

The conflict which has involved a blockade lasting 20 years has resulted in extensive emigration of the population. At the beginning of 1985, the population was 99,000. Estimates in 2012 put the figure now as low as 52,000, more than half of whom live in the capital, Tskhinvali. This new country, the Republic of South Ossetia, is small with an area of just 4,000 square kilometers. It does not have a reliable statistical service, so much of the information about it is based on estimates.

South Ossetia has reserves of non-ferrous metals, mineral water, and wood. Most of the minerals are found in the Dzau district. The Kvaisa area there has one of the largest deposits of zinc-lead in Transcaucasia. The country also has unspoiled scenery and a mild climate which give it the potential to develop a tourist industry.

The Economic Model

During the Soviet era, South Ossetia was known for its extractive industry, focused on its non-ferrous metal ores. There were also engineering activities and food processing (producing mineral water, wine, beer, fruit juices, meat products and more). However, most of the country's industrial capacity is currently lying idle having been closed, or even destroyed, in the military conflict.

It is difficult to classify the economic model currently in operation in South Ossetia. It is isolated from other former Soviet countries that have all followed the path to developing market instruments for their economies. By contrast, South Ossetia has largely maintained the features of central planning and active state participation in its economy. The public sector accounts for 70% of all employment in the country.

However, the maintenance of extensive state control has not prevented the country from making some moves toward reform of economic management. A process of privatization has started. But in the absence of a clear legislative framework, implementation has been piecemeal and beset by problems. For example, there are unresolved questions over the ownership of the Kvaisa deposits and its associated ore mining and processing, the plant 'Stroyprofress' that should be handling it, remains idle despite a modernization program. With industry largely at a standstill, those people not employed by the state mainly survive by farming.

Economic Policy

Because of the on-going military conflict, economic policy in South Ossetia has focused on centralizing to the extent possible the assets necessary to provide basic supplies to the population and thus ensure its survival. Resources are also dedicated to law enforcement and defense. With these priorities taking precedence, the government has done little to promote private business, despite the passage of laws to support the private sector. All large enterprises remain in state ownership and use out-of-date equipment and technology. The level of qualification among employees has declined. As a result, most of these enterprises are losing money. The system of secondary and specialist profession education is virtually non-existent.

A recovery began in 2008, with Russia providing some basic assistance. In 2014, Russian aid amounted to ₽5.6 bn.

The Real Sector

In South Ossetia cattle breeding is the dominant form of agriculture. However, the sector lacks the tools and resources to match the levels of development seen elsewhere. There is a general acceptance of the need for land reform which would see ownership of land transferred to farmers. The country's farms are also in need of modernization. The development of relations with Russia has raised hopes of a new export market for agricultural produce, especially bioproducts from its Alpine regions. There is fledgling reform process under way in the agricultural sector and more market-oriented dairy farms are emerging in the mountain villages. Cheese production is also rising. The main crops cultivated are wheat, corn, and vegetables. Horticulture and vineyards are also growing in importance.

The reconstruction of the country's industry is another major challenge. During the Soviet era, South Ossetia had several small hydro-electric plants, some of which powered the mines in Kvaisa and Tskhinvali. But today, all the country's electricity comes from Russia. South Ossetia's main industries today are mining and associated engineering, wood processing, the production of construction materials, food processing, and consumer goods. There is a brewery, 'Aluton' in Leningor, another, along with a bakery in Tskhinvali. Thanks to private Russian investment, a clothes factory, 'BTK-4', in Tskhinvali has resumed production. The majority of enterprises, however, still lie idle. In seeking to get the country working again, the government is keen to support small and medium-sized businesses.

The country's transport infrastructure is of a poor standard. The automobile is the main form of transport and the main highway is the Transcaucasian road that connects so with Russia. Roads to Georgia are closed. With the help of the Russian firm, Gazprom, the Dzuarikau–Tskhvali pipeline, built in high mountains, was put into operation and has enabled the country to dispense with gas supplies from Georgia. In 2013, the country began a gasification plan.

Mobile communications are reasonably well developed. In 2009, the Russian company, 'MegaFon' acquired 49% of the stock of the domestic telecommunications company, 'Ostelecom.'

The Financial Sector

South Ossetia's financial situation depends heavily on revenues earned from the transit of Russian goods to Georgia: oil, gas, consumer goods, and commodities. The country also receives aid from Russia. Russian aid includes not just loans and investments, but also direct payments to the citizens of South Ossetia, 99% of whom are also Russian citizens, and thus entitled to the social benefits paid to their counterparts in Russia itself.

Financial aid from Russia makes up the bulk of the state budget. Local revenues come mainly from income tax and customs duties levied on goods in transit, which together account for 90% of domestically raised funds. A further 10% comes from VAT.

The External Sector

South Ossetia receives all the energy resources it needs from Russia: gas, fuel, electricity. All other goods to meet the demands of consumers and businesses come from Russia as well. Finally, all exports from South Ossetia go to Russia. The Russian ruble is the country's unit of currency.

In 2015, an alliance agreement on integration was signed by South Ossetia and Russia. As part of this agreement, Russia ensures that its aid is sufficient to enable the South Ossetian government to bring pension payments to its citizens up to the levels enjoyed elsewhere in the North Caucasian region. Under the agreement, Russia also guarantees the security of South Ossetia and its borders.

Conclusion

1. South Ossetia is a small country in terms of both size and population. It remained largely isolated following its declaration of independence from Georgia in 1991. More than other countries in the region, its economy retains many features of the Soviet era, e.g., a significant role for the public sector in economic management.

2. The country has limited mineral resources. It also faces major challenges in trying to improve the efficiency of its agricultural sector and to create conditions conducive to entrepreneurship in both industry and services.

3. Implementation of the government's social policies depends heavily on financial assistance from Russia. Almost all South Ossetians have Russian citizenship. The main source of earnings for the South Ossetia government is the transit of Russian goods through the country.

Questions

1. How would you describe the economic situation of South Ossetia?

2. Which sectors of the economy are the most promising in the development of the country's economy?

3. What role does Russia play in South Ossetia's social and economic development?

Sources of additional information

www.presidentruo.org. (President of the Republic of South Ossetia).
www. Ossetia.ru (News of North and South Ossetia).

UNIT V

THE ECONOMIC MODELS OF CENTRAL ASIA

CHAPTER 27

SIMILARITIES AND DIFFERENCES IN THE ECONOMIES OF CENTRAL ASIAN COUNTRIES

Kazakhstan, Kyrgyzstan, Tajikistan, Turkmenistan, and Uzbekistan together form a separate region—or, more precisely, a sub-region—in area of the former Soviet Union. As well as a shared geographical location, when it comes to historical development and aspects of civilization, these countries have much in common. In the past, they have been influenced by Iranian, Mongolian, Arabic, and Turkic cultures, with different groupings and state formations emerging over time. By the time these territories joined the Russian Empire in the 19th century, the dominant religion among their populations was Sunni Islam. From a cultural point of view, Kazakhstan is more heterogeneous than the others since, during its formation as a republic of the Soviet Union, the northern regions attached to it in the 1930s were predominantly populated by Russians.

In economic terms, the Russian Empire regarded Central Asia as its colonial outskirts and a source of raw materials for the central regions of the country. Despite huge investment during the Soviet period, modernization was slow. The heavy influence of clans, family groups, and religions has meant that these societies have remained socially conservative, with many local traditions surviving despite changes in education and forms of ownership.

A distinctive feature of the region is the huge differences in the various countries' endowments of natural resources. Almost all the region's reserves of organic fuel are concentrated in Kazakhstan, Turkmenistan, and Uzbekistan. While Uzbekistan largely supplies its domestic market, for Kazakhstan and Turkmenistan, oil and gas are major exports. By contrast, Kyrgyzstan and Tajikistan are wholly dependent on imports of oil and gas. Moreover, these two countries have limited arable land, even though they possess 90% of the region's water resources.

A lack of suitable water to support use of the land has been a growing problem in recent years. All countries of the region are agro-industrial in which the importance of the agricultural sector is determined not by its efficiency but by the number of people who work in it. Kazakhstan, Turkmenistan, and Uzbekistan have sufficient land resources to satisfy their needs. But there is pressure on land resources in Kyrgyzstan and Tajikistan. The climate in Central Asia means that agriculture needs irrigation, with the exception of the northern and central regions of Kazakhstan. Moreover, Kazakhstan, Uzbekistan, and Turkmenistan need significant amounts of water for industrial purposes. But, as noted, the bulk of the region's surface water resources are found in Kyrgyzstan and Tajikistan. This leads to problems over cross-border usage of water.

Similarities and Differences in Economic Models

In comparison with former Soviet countries in East Europe and the Transcaucasus, those in Central Asia experienced greater political and economic authoritarianism, in least in the initial period after the demise of the Soviet Union. This partly explains why state capitalism (which is common in Asian countries) developed in Central Asia. The features of state capitalism were particularly striking in the Turkmen model, noticeable also in the Tajik and Uzbek economies, but less striking in the Kazakhstani case, though in the latter case there are still some obvious features of state capitalism such as strong links between state bodies and businesses. Kyrgyzstan has the most liberal model of all the countries.

Common to all of the countries in the region are the size of the black economy, corruption, and low living standards experienced by the bulk of the population. These countries' economies have also shared a tendency to centripetal, rather than centrifugal, characteristics such that they focus more on relations with countries outside their own region, than with their neighbors.

Similarities and Differences Potential, Proportions, and Dynamics

In the immediate aftermath of their independence, all the countries of Central Asia saw a sharp decline in their economic potential. Tajikistan had the most severe economic shrinkage as a result of its civil war. In 1995, its GDP was equivalent to just 40% of its 1990 level. In Kyrgyzstan, the figure was 52%; Kazakhstan, about 60%; and Turkmenistan, 64%.

Uzbekistan fared the best of all the countries with its 1995 GDP at 83% of the 1990 level. The region saw the lowest point of the economic crisis during the second half of the 1990s. Kazakhstan's GDP growth recovered in 1998 and Kyrgyzstan's in 2002. Growth rates in all countries of the sub-region suffered during the economic crisis that began in 2008, but actual negative growth was only seen in Kyrgyzstan in 2010 and 2012.

Table 27.1 — Some macroeconomic indicators of the Central Asian countries in 2016

	Kazakhstan	Kyrgyzstan	Tajikistan	Turkmenistan	Uzbekistan
Population, million people	17.8	6.1	8.7	5.7	31.8
GDP, US$ bn	137.3	6.6	7.0	36.2	67.2
GNI PPP per capita, US$	22,930	3,410	3,500	16,060	6,640
Average annual rate of growth between 2009 and 2016, %	4.8	3.8	6.9	10.1	8.1

Sources: Interstate Statistical Committee of the Commonwealth of Independent States (http//www.cisstat.org).
World Development Indicators 2017.
World Bank. The Global Economic Prospects Jan. 2018.

At the present time, Central Asia taken as a whole is one of the most economically dynamic regions in the world. Each country has an annual average growth rate that exceeds the global average. Moreover, the short-term forecast envisages average growth of 6% by 2019.

However, with the exception of Kazakhstan, none of the countries in the sub-region have returned to the level of gross national income achieved during the Soviet era. The problem is particularly acute in the GDP growth rates of Tajikistan, Kyrgyzstan, and Uzbekistan.

The economies of Central Asia have generally maintained the focus on agriculture and raw materials that emerged during the Soviet era. The relative growth of the share of GDP accounted for by fuel, energy, agriculture, and services was not due to any increase in output, but rather to the demise of the countries' manufacturing industries. Moreover, the increased share taken by agriculture and services came about as a result of greater activity among the smallest economic players: farm households and small-scale retailing. In many countries, a focus on raw materials acts as a break on better development in agriculture and manufacturing. It also has the effect of strengthening the family and clan system that is a feature of the state capitalism. Such a system is unlikely to be stable over the long term as it can create problems in the distribution of property and also lead to political problems.

Similarities and Differences in Economic Policy

The countries of the Central Asian region have adopted a variety of economic approaches. The speed and extent of market reforms have depended on the nature of each country's political regime, the degree of authoritarianism, the readiness of the population to accept reforms, and the orientation of the country's external policy.

Kazakhstan and Kyrgyzstan have seen the most radical market reforms. Both have been actively implementing programs recommended by the IMF, privatizing state enterprises and attracting foreign aid and investment. In Kyrgyzstan, radical liberalization led to a sharp decrease in revenues, a suppression of demand, and emigration. But these effects were mitigated to some extent by foreign aid. The focus of the country's current economic policy is less on market reforms and more on reviving the industry and reducing poverty. Kazakhstan used its revenues from the oil and gas industry—a major recipient of foreign investment—to conduct market reforms.

As early as 1991, Uzbekistan embarked on a course of gradual privatization and liberalization of prices. It also sought to develop greater external economic activity. With economic growth producing positive outcomes and with the political situation stabilizing, in the middle of the last decade, the process of reform was speeded up.

In Tajikistan, political instability and in-fighting acted as a block to market reforms until the late 1990s. Their progress remains slow by grinding poverty and the increasing emigration of the working-age population. But it was in Turkmenistan where the totalitarian nature of the regime led to the slowest economic reform program in the sub-region. Economic liberalization has only been pursued in earnest since 2006, but, even then, not as wholeheartedly as elsewhere.

In 2018, the Doing Business Report assesses the business conditions in these countries very poorly. Tajikistan, for example, was ranked 128th and Uzbekistan 74th. In the ranking for economic freedom, in 2014, Kyrgyzstan was 67th, Tajikistan 139th, Uzbekistan 163rd, and Turkmenistan 171st.

Region-wide Economic Problems

Poor levels of economic development remain the region's main problem. Only Kazakhstan seems to have conquered the issue.

When it comes to economic management, all countries of the region share the need to get away from state monopolism which has stifled the creation and development of small and medium-sized businesses. This problem is linked to another, the authoritarian nature of the ruling elites which slow down both political and economic democratization. However, it should be noted that, in some countries, Kazakhstan for example, the authoritarian regime has supported reform, while in others, such as Turkmenistan, it has slowed reform down.

One of the problems affecting the whole region and influencing economic policy has been the emergence of Islamic movement, and especially their more radical elements. The Uzbek government, in particular, has taken a cautious approach to reform in the face of growing Islamic extremism.

The lack of close cooperation between the countries of Central Asia during the Soviet era continued after the demise of the Soviet Union and was, in fact, exacerbated, firstly by the different economic policies adopted by the various countries, and also by political tensions and ethnic conflicts in Tajikistan, Uzbekistan, and Kyrgyzstan. Each country forged its own economic path with little or no regard for regional cooperation. National strategies focused on achieving self-sufficiency, which lessens the need for integration and can also blunt the effectiveness of development. For example, with no effective regional cooperation, the countries of the region have no way of considering what might be an optimal distribution of energy, water, and labor resources.

Table 27.2 — Rates of growth of consumer prices in the countries of Central Asia, in percent

	2007	2008	2009	2010	2011	2012	2013	2014	2015	2016*
Kazakhstan	10.8	17.1	7.3	7.1	8.3	5.1	5.8	6.7	6.5	8.5
Kyrgyzstan	10.2	24.5	6.8	7.8	16.6	2.8	6.6	7.5	6.5	-0.5
Tajikistan	13.2	20.4	6.5	6.5	12.4	5.8	5.0	6.1	5.8	6.1
Turkmenistan	6.3	14.5	-2.7	4.4	5.3	5.3	6.8	6.0	5.8	6.1
Uzbekistan	12.3	12.7	14.1	9.4	12.8	12.1	11.7	9.1	8.5	5.7

*Estimates

Sources: Interstate Statistical Committee of the Commonwealth of Independent States (http//www.cisstat.org). IMF. World Economic Outlook. October 2016, p. 237.

The region would undoubtedly benefit from the development of an integrated transport system or a unified electrical power system, both of which would make the region more attractive to foreign investment. Historically, the Great Silk Road passed through this region which acted as a bridge between Europe and Asia. This underlines the importance of the transport infrastructure if the region is to achieve integration.

Regardless of the orientation of their external policy—toward Russia, the West, Turkey, or China—, all countries of the region are keen to attract foreign investment. But a common problem is high inflation. This fell after the turn of the century, but rose again after 2008. Kyrgyzstan and Tajikistan, in particular, saw high inflation from 2007 onwards in the context of the international financial crisis.

Economic Cooperation in the Region

Although all countries in the region have chosen to prioritize exports in their economic plans, the uniformity of their economies, with a focus on agriculture and raw materials, has meant that economic relations between the countries have remained very limited. Of their total turnover of foreign trade, intraregional trade accounts for just 5–7%.

The level of complementarity of the countries of the region should be sufficient to enable the development of regional cooperation. For example, exchanges of energy and water resources should be possible. However, as noted above, political and ethnic conflicts have put serious barriers in the way of serious cooperation. This is unlikely to change in the short or medium term. The Eurasian Economic Union may act as a forum to encourage greater cooperation between the countries in the region; Kazakhstan and Kyrgyzstan are already members.

Common External Economic Problems

Relationships with countries outside the sub-region dominate the external economic of the countries within the region, especially for those with important raw material exports.

Table 27.3 —Asian countries in Indicators of external economic relations of the Central Asian countries in 2016

	Merchandize trade as % of GDP	External debt as % of GGP	Accumulated foreign direct investments, US$ bn
Kazakhstan	46.0	89..3	129.8
Kyrgyzstan	83.0	118.6	5.1
Tajikistan	38.0	54.4	2.1
Turkmenistan	50.0	1.1	32.1
Uzbekistan	32.0	21.8	9.9

Sources: World Bank. World Development Indicators. Country Profile 2017; UNCTAD. World Investment Report 2017.

In general, the region's degree of openness—as the ratio of external trade to GDP—was 67.7% in 2012,45% in 2016. The ratio of external debt to GDP was about 50%. Most of the external trade is with Russia or the EU. However, in recent years, trade with Turkey and China has been growing in importance.

A problem common to all countries in the region is the black economy. This is prevalent both in trade between the countries of the region and in their trade with other countries. The greatest problem is with drug trafficking, involving drugs produced in the region as well as those supplied from Afghanistan. The Central Asian region has become a main transit route for Afghan opium being transported to Russia and then on to Europe.

Problems with the Transport of Caspian Oil

The energy resources of the Central Asian region are illustrated in Table 27.4.

With their large reserves of oil and gas, Kazakhstan and Turkmenistan now find themselves in competition to supply oil to oil-importing countries like Turkey and China. They are also in competition with other oil exporters like Russia and Iran. The USA and EU have also taken an interest in the resources of Kazakhstan and Turkmenistan as they can offer deliveries of energy resources with no involvement from Russia or Iran.

Table 27.4 — Indicators of the energy potential of the Central Asian countries in 2016

	Proven oil reserves, billion tons	Oil production, million tons	Consumption, million tons	Natural gas proven reserves, trillion cubic meters	Natural gas production, billion cubic meters	Natural gas consumption, billion cubic meters
Kazakhstan	3.7	79.3	12.7	0.9	19.9	13.4
Turkmenistan	0.1	12.7	6.4	17.5	66.8	29.5
Uzbekistan	0.1	2.6	2.8	1.1	62.8	51.4

Source: BP Statistical Review of World Energy June 2017.

In 2007, Turkmenistan signed an agreement with China on the development of one of its most promising gas fields, the South Yolotan-Osman field (which has the fourth or fifth largest reserves in the world), and on the construction of a gas pipeline to China. Kazakhstan has now joined this arrangement to extend the pipeline to the Beyneu field in the west of the country. The pipeline, taking gas from Turkmenistan through Uzbekistan and Kazakhstan and on to China, opened at the end of 2009. In 2013, exports of Turkmen natural gas to China amounted to 27 bn cubic meters, with 9 bn cubic meters doing to Iran. With a network of eight gas pipelines, Turkmenistan hopes to see its exports to China rise to 230 bn cubic meters by 2030. The Uzbek section of the Central Asia–China gas pipeline came into operation in 2014. A fourth branch of this pipeline is planned and will be located in Tajikistan and Kyrgyzstan.

The USA has lobbied for the Trans-Caspian gas pipeline (which goes under the Caspian Sea) to be connected to the existing Baku–Tbilisi–Erzurum pipeline which is expected to be extended to Europe under the TANAP project. In view of the economic sanctions on Iran (which is involved in the construction of a gas pipeline to Pakistan and India), the USA has also lobbied for the Trans-Afghan (TAPI) project to supply gas from the Turken Dauletabad field to India, Pakistan, and Afghanistan.

The Region's Economic Relations with Russia

The region's economic ties with Russia declined after the 1990s. The USA and the EU saw an opportunity to usurp Russian influence in the region and focused in particular on energy projects. Despite this, the countries of Central Asia have continued to invest in developing their relationships with Russia. They remain interested in Russian transport and energy systems and industrial technologies. They also enjoy Russian consumer goods. Russia accounts for 20% of the total turnover of the region's external trade and remains an important economic partner.

Russia is particularly keen to promote the Eurasian Economic Union in the region. Kazakhstan and Kyrgyzstan are already members and Tajikistan is expected to join in the near future. It is still unclear whether Uzbekistan will join and it seems unlikely that Turkmenistan will do so.

Region-wide Social Problems

Unemployment is the region's biggest social problem, affecting all countries, with only Kazakhstan avoiding its worst effects. In the case of Turkmenistan, there is a lack of accurate data, but some indications are that more than half of the adult population is unemployed. Official data in 2015 put the level of unemployment in Kazakhstan at 5.0%; in Kyrgyzstan at 7.6%; Tajikistan at 11.5%; and in Uzbekistan at 5.1% (2014). However, the real rates of unemployment will certainly be higher. The estimate for Uzbekistan is no less than 20%.

The region suffers from significant emigration. Though exacerbated by the creation of the new states in the region, the problem was already apparent in the final years of the Soviet era. Between 1979 and 1988, the net migration from Kazakhstan was equivalent to 5% of its population; for Kyrgyzstan, it was 4.4%; for Uzbekistan, 3.3%; and Turkmenistan, 3%. The most obvious feature of this trend was the outflow of the ethnic Russian population, which led to the national ethnic groups accounting for a greater proportion of the population across the region. The highest levels of emigration were seen in the years of crisis from 1989 to 1995. During this period, net migration from Kazakhstan was 1.2 million people, 7.8% of the population; in Kyrgyzstan it was 8.4%; Tajikistan, 7.0%; and Uzbekistan, 3.1%. At this stage, emigration from Turkmenistan has begun to decline and the same occurred in the other countries by the end of the last decade.

Most of this emigration is people looking for work. In Kyrgyzstan and Tajikistan up to a third of the economically active population has emigrated. The majority go to Russia. But, in recent years, Kazakhstan has been attracting migrants, although estimates of how many migrant laborers there are in the country vary greatly, from 200,000 to 1 million.

In Russia, between 80 and 85% of all immigrants have come from Kyrgyzstan, Tajikistan, and Uzbekistan. Money transferred home from Russia by these migrants play a significant role in the economic development of the countries of the region. It is, for example, one of the main sources of income for the population in Kyrgyz and Tajikistan. Between 2013 and 2015, due to the economic recession and the fall in value of the ruble, the flow of migrants from Central Asia decreased. However, its own demographic problems leave Russia still needing a flow of immigration which is only likely to grow as the country continues to recover from the recession.

Corruption is another problem that affects the entire region. It affects both economic and political stability. The Corruption Perception Index puts all the countries in the region near the bottom of its standings. The problem is exacerbated by the extent of the black economy which, according to some estimates, ranges from 20% of GDP in Kazakhstan to 50–60% in Kyrgyzstan and Tajikistan.

The Human Development Index has Kazakhstan at a relatively high position of 70th, reflecting the high per capita GDP and the quality of the health care and education systems which have survived from the Soviet era. The other regional countries are much lower down the list: Turkmenistan is 103rd; Uzbekistan, 116th; Kyrgyzstan, 125th; and Tajikistan, 133rd.

Even toward the end of the Soviet era, Central Asia was suffering severe socio-ecological problems, the most obvious of which was the pollution in the Aral Sea. This has been a serious drag on the economies of Kazakhstan and Uzbekistan.

With the exception of Kazakhstan, the countries of the region suffered disproportionately from the economic crisis of the 1990s. Despite improvements in GDP growth rates, the levels of socio-economic development of the countries of Central Asia continue to be lowest among all former Soviet countries.

Conclusion

1. In the Central Asian sub-region, not single entity has been formed to develop economic cooperation. The countries involved are, in fact, more distant from each other in terms of economic relations than they were in the Soviet era. Despite some participation in regional initiatives, including in organizations of which Russia and China were also members, there has been little progress toward regional integration. The economic structure, a hang-over from the Soviet era, and other political factors have combined to hold back integration.

2. Some common trends can be seen in the economic policies of the countries of the region, such as the creation of market structures. In addition, the principles of state capitalism are commonly observed, with some national variations.

3. Low standards of living are the most acute problem faced by the region. Unemployment also blights the lives of many in the region. A failure to capitalize on the region's potential during the Soviet era, coupled with a focus since independence on less labor-intensive industries in the energy and fuel and gas sectors, have exacerbated the unemployment situation. Few small or medium-sized businesses have been formed. Finally, inflation has also hindered economic development.

4. All countries in the region have pursued economic policies aimed at increasing their integration into global trade and economic systems. The regions relative isolation from many of the traditional centers of trade has hampered these efforts. But its close proximity to the growing economy of China is beginning to be an important beneficial factor.

5. The countries of the region have adopted open approaches to economic policy. External relations play an important role in their economic development. Economic relations with the West have expanded and the USA and the EU have been attracted by the opportunity to usurp the position of Russia in the region. However, the countries of the region have maintained a keen interest in relations with Russia, especially for access to its transport and energy systems. At the same time, China's influence has been growing, spurred on by its interest in the region's energy resources and its transport infrastructure.

Questions

1. How are the economies of the Central Asian region affected by their geographical location and by the differences in access to natural resources?

2. Assess the participation of the different countries of Central Asia in the exploitation of the energy resources of the Caspian.

3. What factors militate against integration in Central Asia?

4. What has been the impact of emigration on the economies of the region and on that of Russia?

5. Which of the Central Asian economies are the most attractive to foreign and Russian investment, and why?

Sources of additional information

The Commonwealth of Independent States. Short Digest. Moscow, 2015.

National Accounts of Countries of the Commonwealth of Independent States 2000–2013. International Statistical Committee of the Commonwealth of Independent States. 2016 (in Russian).

Olkott, Marta. Tajikistan: difficult path of development. Vremya. Moscow, 2014.

Central Asia: Role in Restructuring of World Oil and Natural Gas Markets. M. IMEMO, 2014 (in Russian).

Post-Soviet States: 25 years of Independent Development. Vol.1.Western Flank of the CIS. Central Asia. M. IMEMO, 2017.

www.eurasianet.org

www.cisstat.com (Interstate Statistical Committee of the Commonwealth of Independent States).

www.centrasia.ru

CHAPTER 28

KAZAKHSTAN

The Economic Model

Kazakhstan is the largest and most developed country in the Central Asian sub-region. During the Soviet era, it was the center of the Soviet non-ferrous metallurgy industry. It also had a developed coal-mining sector and provided the Soviet Union with a fifth of its grain. Among the Soviet republics, it was the second largest producer of wool and third in meat production.

Like all other former Soviet countries, Kazakhstan suffered a severe economic downturn after the demise of the Soviet Union. It was one of the first countries in Central Asia to embark on market reforms, taking as its model Russia's 'shock therapy.' A huge program of denationalization and privatization was begun in 1993. The privatization of small and medium-sized businesses proceeded quickly and was generally successful. The raw material industries were in crisis but were returned to growth by the sale of the leading enterprises to foreign investors between 1995 and 1997. Foreign investors purchased both ferrous and non-ferrous enterprises along with the major oil fields, Tengiz and Kumkol. In total, around 50 leading firms in the oil, metallurgy, mining, and energy sectors were sold. As a result, almost all of Kazakhstan's export capacity is in foreign hands. The privatization was conducted in a way that respected the clan traditions of the country. This resulted in a merging of private and foreign capital in the upper echelons of central and provincial bureaucracies.

Despite its weak democracy and the disadvantageous results of the privatization process, Kazakhstan has remained firmly on the road to economic liberalization and has protected the private sector from state dominance of the economy. Kazakhstan's economic model is less 'eastern' than those of the other countries in the region, probably because Russians have historically made up a higher proportion of the country's population. The private sector produces more than 90% of the country's GDP. Almost all key sectors of the economy, including energy, housing, and public services are in private hands. The government only maintains a monopoly transport. It also retains a significant role in the oil and gas industry. According to the index of global economic competitiveness, between 2013 and 2016, Kazakhstan ranked 53rd in the world; among other CIS countries, it ranked behind only to Russia and Azerbaijan.

Kazakhstan's main vulnerability from an economic perspective is its reliance on raw materials which leaves it at the mercy of world prices for its raw materials, mainly oil. Its heavy dependence on foreign investment is also a potential weakness. Moreover, many sectors of the economy remain underdeveloped, e.g., agriculture and manufacturing.

Focusing an economic model on the oil and gas sector has proved an efficient approach in some oil-exporting countries in the Persian Gulf and North Africa. But in the case of Kazakhstan, the country's large population and the resulting smaller share of rental payment per capita can act over time to slow down the modernization of the economy. Besides, Kazakhstan does not have hydrocarbon reserves to match those of the Gulf states and most of the oil it produces is in the hands of foreign firms.

The Potential and Size of the Economy

The rapid development of its economy, thanks largely to the oil and gas industry, has taken Kazakhstan's share of the GDP of the Central Asian region to almost 70%

Table 28.1 — GDP in Kazakhstan

	2000	2008	2012	2015	2016	2018*	2020*
GDP, US$ bn	18.3	135.0	203.5	184.4	137.3	…	…
GNI PPP per capita, US$	7,170	15,440	18,870	25,055	22,930	…	…
GDP growth, %	10.1	3.3	5.0	0.3	1.0	2.6	3.0

* Estimates

Sources: World Bank. World Development Indicators 2017.
World Bank. The Global Economic Prospects, Jan. 2018.

Between 2001 and 2007, Kazakhstan's average annual rate of GDP growth was 10%, the highest in the region. The increase in gross national income per capita to US$19,000 put Kazakhstan among the group of countries with incomes above the world average. All this led to talk of the 'Kazakhstani Economic Miracle.' However, the country's focus on raw materials production meant that, in the ensuing period of low world energy prices, its growth slowed significantly.

The active development of the country's oil and gas resources stimulated a process of investment: in 2007, the ratio of gross capital formation reached 31% of GDP which was one of the factors that prevented a more serious decline in the years of crisis. However, in the subsequent decade, the ratio fell to 23–25%, mainly as a result of a reduction in the growth of private and foreign investment. By the beginning of this decade, the share of private sector in the gross capital formation had decreased from 57 to 48%; the share of foreign capital had increased to 30% and the government's share had also gone up to 22%.

The economic structure of Kazakhstan is characterized by the extraordinary share of the secondary sector which accounts for 39% of the total. The primary sector's share is 5%, and that of the tertiary sector is 56%. Industry is dominated by the mining industry and energy (mainly oil and gas, metal ore and coal production). These account for 70% of industrial production in the country.

Official estimates of the non-observed economy put it at no more than 20% of GDP. In truth, it is more than 30%, most significantly in agriculture (60% of production), the hotel sector (as much as 50%), construction, and trade and commerce.

Economic Policy

One of the country's priorities in its economic policy is to create a climate that is attractive to foreign investors who control the most promising and profitable enterprises in the raw materials sector. In 2015, the total amount of accumulated foreign direct investment in Kazakhstan stood at US$ 120 bn, i.e., about 80% of all accumulated foreign investment in Central Asia. However, during the current decade, the flow of foreign direct investment has begun to decrease. In response, the mobilization of internal sources of finance has become a key plank of economic policy. To achieve this, the tax burden on sectors other than raw materials has been lowered since 2009, while taxes on raw materials have been raised. In 2012, a strategy named 'Kazakhstan 2050' was adopted, the main purpose being to move toward a developed economy and to see Kazakhstan in top thirty most developed countries in the world. It embodies seven long-term priorities for the country, including full support for private business.

Before the global economic crisis, the public sector's share of GDP was declining: in 2003, it accounted for 10.6% of GDP; in 2007, it stood at 8.4%. However, this tendency was altered by more active state intervention in the economy. This was managed through the creation of new holding companies to manage the funds. With foreign capital reducing its involvement as a result of the crisis, these funds began to buy shares of the largest enterprises, mainly in the mining sector. As an example, using the state-owned shares in strategically important enterprises, the sustainable development fund 'Samruk-Kazyna Trust' was created. In 2008, the government decided to reopen the National Oil Fund of Kazakhstan. US$10 bn was transferred from this to the Samruk-Kazyna Trust, mainly for the purpose of managing blocks of shares in the four major banks and a number of large industrial companies. In this way, all the economic resources of the public sector have been concentrated into the Samruk-Kazyna Trust. This includes: shares in private companies; government pension funds; assets in the oil and gas, electric power, and metallurgy industries; transport; and communications.

However, the private sector continues to play a leading role in the economy. In 2013, its share of GDP was 79%, compared to just 9% for the public sector 12% attributable to foreign companies. The private sector is dominated by small businesses, many of whom only employ, on average, two people. The self-employed sector is the least productive. Even in cities this sector can account for as many as 24% of the population, mainly employed in trade and the hotel and catering sector. In agriculture, following the demise of the kolkhozes and sovkhozes, small households became the main commercial entities in the sector, undertaking traditional farming, often only at subsistence levels. In such households, as many as 55% of those working are classed as self-employed. Across the country as a whole, household business, urban and rural, produce 20% of GDP.

Large businesses produce 40% of GDP and this share is rising. In 2006, a new law, 'On Concessions,' was adopted allowing private businesses (domestic and foreign) to invest in priority sectors through partnerships with the state. As a result, the national private business sector has strengthened. However, most large companies are, in fact, joint ventures with foreign capital. Virtually all large businesses are involved in industry, transport, energy, and the modern services sector (banks and telecommunications). The number of large agro-industrial companies is very small.

Human Capital

By the end of the 1980s on the eve of the demise of the Soviet Union, immigrants (including some forced immigrants) made up 60% of the Kazakh population. However, in 1990, something of an exodus of non-Kazakhs began resulting in a change in the ethnic structure with ethnic Kazakhs again dominating. Between 1989 and 1999, more than three million people left the country. The ethnic Russian population almost halved. In 2009, it stood at 3.8 million. As a result, Kazakhstan avoided the serious ethnic and political conflicts seen in other former Soviet countries.

At the same time as non-Kazakhs were leaving in large numbers, up to a million ethnic Kazakhs returned home from other countries. Nonetheless, between 1991 and 2001, the population declined by an average of 0.9% a year, seeing the population fall from 16.9 to 14.9 million. After 2001, the population began to grow again, reaching 17.2 million. This came about as a result of organic increases of between 0.5 and 1.5% a year, combined with immigration from the rest of Central Asia. Since the turn of the century, average earnings in Kazakhstan have been four or five times higher than those of Kyrgyzstan and Uzbekistan, and as much as nine or ten times higher than those of Tajikistan. The existence of Uzbek communities in the Chimkent region of Kazakhstan has encouraged greater immigration from Uzbekistan. Up to 400,000 seasonal workers come to Kazakhstan every year from Tajikistan.

However, despite the economic recovery that began in the second half of the 1990s, the employment landscape has seen regressive changes. Indeed, there has been negative development with the share of people employed in agriculture increasing from 22 to 24% (2013), while the proportion of people employed in industry went down from 17 to 12%. It should also be noted that out of an employed population of 9 million people, about 3 million are self-employed, working mainly on small plots of land. Around 2 million people are employed in small enterprises. These statistics highlight the existence of a large traditional sector which, despite all the progress toward modernization, still employs the majority of the population.

In 2015, the level of unemployment was estimated to be 5%. This was highest in the 15–24 age group and the government decided to make a reduction of this youth unemployment one of its priorities in social and economic policy.

Compared with the rest of the region, Kazakhstan has high literacy rates. A program to improve the education system with the gradual introduction of Western methods of teaching has been established. Internet coverage is improving with 96% of schools now on-line.

Almost all the country's major cities have a university, the largest of which is the Abai National Pedagogical University in Almaty. In recent years there has been an increase in the number of Islamic educational institutions, including an Islamic University.

Expenditure on R&D remains low at just 0.3% of GDP. As a result, the country's scientific sector is ill-equipped to cope with modern market condition. However, a number of funds have been set up specifically to finance and implement scientific innovation. Technology parks are also being constructed.

The Real Sector

During the Soviet era, there was massive development of virgin and fallow agricultural land. This saw the northern regions of Kazakhstan transformed into a center for the production of grain crops. But after 1991, and especially following the dissolution of the kolkhozes and sovkhozes and the redistribution of land, agricultural production fell sharply: from 30 million tons in 1992 to 6 million tons in 1998. Thereafter, production stabilized and began to rise again, reaching 13 million tons in 2014, 6 million tons of which was exported. A large proportion, 70%, of the wheat crop was produced on large-scale farms which occupy 36% of plowed land. While the large farms produce the bulk of the grain crops, the small household farms produce more than 90% of the country's cotton and over 60% of the beets and sunflowers. A system of insurance for harvest has been developed and it now covers 80% of all sewn land.

The 1990s saw a particularly harsh recession in the cattle sector. The cattle stock fell to 60% of its 1990 level; sheep and goats fell to less than 50%; pigs to 42%; and poultry 50%. None of these has returned to its pre-1990 level. In an attempt to help the sector recover, a program to create large dairy companies and increase the number of breeding stock has been implemented. The informal sector, which is particularly important in livestock, accounts for up to 60% of the overall agricultural output.

The fishing industry in Kazakhstan has been affected by the problems in the Aral Sea. Measures are being taken to revive the Northern Aral, which lies within the territory of Kazakhstan. A dam, constructed in 2005, combined with new water development facilities on the Syr Darya river have succeeded in producing a 50% increase in the water surface of the Northern Aral. This has enabled a revival of fishing and fish farming.

Agricultural productivity remains low despite the introduction in recent years of modern technologies and advanced methods. Yields of wheat are less than 1,350–1,400kg per hectare. A state holding company, 'KazAgro,' was established in 2007 to finance and implement initiatives to introduce modern agricultural technologies.

In addition to the natural environment that is suitable for agriculture, Kazakhstan is rich in natural resources for industry. The country has the 13th largest oil reserves in the world. Inland oil reserves are estimated at 4 bn tons and shelf reserves at 15 bn tons. In terms of gas reserves, the country is 12th in the world with 1.3–1.8 trn cubic meters. These oil and gas reserves are concentrated in a small number of fields; almost 90% of exploitable resources are found in 12 fields, the largest of which is the Tengiz (Tengiz-Korolev) and Karachaganak fields.

Kazakhstan has the world's largest confirmed reserves of zinc, tungsten, barites and uranium. It has the second largest reserves of lead, silver, and chrome; the third largest reserves of copper and manganese; and the fourth largest reserves of molybdenum. It is in the world's top ten for reserves of gold. Kazakhstan has almost 8% of the world's reserves of iron ore and about 25% of all reserves of uranium. The country also has large coal reserves of varying quality.

The fuel and energy complex is the cornerstone of Kazakhstani industry. In 2016, the country's oil production was three times what it had been in 1991, totaling 84 million tons (1.7 million barrels a day), or about 2% of world production. Over the same period, natural gas production almost quadrupled to stand as 20 billion cubic meters in 2016. The fuel and energy complex is dominated by foreign companies, e.g., Lukoil, ENI, Total, ExxonMobil, Royal Dutch Shell, Conoco Phillips, Inpex, CNPC, and others. However, in recent years, the Kazakhstani public sector has increased its involvement by purchasing shares in some of these companies. The leading state-owned company is KaxMunayGas, which has licenses for 15 oil and gas fields. It controls about 7% of the country's oil production and owns three oil-processing plants. At the end of 2008, the state took control of the largest coal deposit, Bogatyr. The state company Kazatomprom controls the production of uranium which, at 22,600 tons, is the largest in the world, accounting for 37% of total global production.

The state has also been growing its influence in the power-generation industry, especially through the Samruk-Kaznya Trust, a state-owned entity which took over the state's holdings in the largest power plants. In 2016, electricity generation amounted to 94.5 billion kWh. More than 85% of this electricity is produced by thermal power plants using coal. Only about 5% is produced by plants using gas turbines. Kazakhstan is almost self-sufficient in power generation and trades in electricity with its neighbors.

Manufacturing is mainly represented by the metal industry, which benefits from having its own raw materials. It produces 37% of all the country's production and is an active exporter. Engineering accounts for 12% of manufacturing output, mainly transportation vehicles, electrical equipment, and optical devices.

One problem facing the country is the underdeveloped nature of the consumer goods industry. It produces mostly textiles and footwear. This accounts for less than 1% of total manufacturing output and meets no more than 10% of domestic demand.

In general, the manufacturing industry is characterized by low productivity and is, thus, not attractive to investors. Its best prospects from growth come from increasing production to meet the needs of the oil and gas complex.

Construction saw many years of significant growth and its share of GDP rose accordingly, mainly driven by extensive spending on construction of homes and new government buildings in the country's new capital (Astana).

Kazakhstan is a large country and the development of its transport infrastructure is thus a priority. The road network dominates, carrying 99.8% of all passenger journeys and 78.5% of all cargo. The rail network carries just 12% of all cargo and virtually no passenger transport. In recent years, attention has focused on the development of the local road network, as well as the construction and modernization of international transit corridors. The largest project is the 'TRACECA,' which from its inception in 1993 has counted on the involvement of other Transcaucasian and Central Asian countries. This project follows the route of the Great Silk Road and seeks to integrate all modes of transport. In Kazakhstan and Central Asian countries the particular emphasis is on rail transport.

Until the 1990s, rail transport connecting the east and west of the Eurasian continent was dominated by the Trans-Siberian railway. However, in 1990, the connection between Druzhba in Kazakhstan and Alashankou in China was established and the Trans-Asian Railway came into being to offer the Trans-Siberian route some competition. Moreover, the completion in 2007 of a 235-kilometer section of the Khromtau-Altynsarin line finally enabled travel between the west of the country and the northern and central regions without the need to rely on Russian railways. By 2013, there were more than 15,000 km of railway in Kazakhstan, though only 4,000 km of this are electrified. The road network has 97,400 km of which more than 87,000 are paved.

There are two large oil terminal ports on the Caspian Sea at Aktau (Shevchenko) and Atyrau (Guryev).

In general, however, the quality of the transport infrastructure is very low. It does not match the level that might be expected in view of the country's economic and trade relations, both domestic and with its neighbors. The road network fails to provide suitable links between centers of production, centers of trade, and the ports.

Pipeline transportation is vital for Kazakhstan, although the pipelines' share of overall cargo turnover is relatively low at just 11%. The country has an extensive network of gas and oil pipelines, with a total length of over 24,000 km. Turkmen gas is also carried on Kazakhstan's network. Kazakhstani oil uses a diverse range of transportation methods. For example, in 2001, the Caspian Pipeline Consortium (CPC) which is 44% owned by Russian companies, opened its pipeline connecting the western regions of Kazakhstan with Novorossiysk and carrying 40% of the country's oil for export. The Atyrau-Samara oil pipeline which was constructed during the Soviet era now carries 22% of the country's exports. The oil from Tengiz is transported by tanker from Aktau to Baku, and from there by rail to Batumi. From 2008, it has also been carried by the Baku–Tbilisi–Ceyhan pipeline. At the end of 2005, the eastern section of the main Atasu–Alanshankou pipeline to China was opened. A second stage of this pipeline from Kenyiak to Kumol, was opened in 2009, bringing its total length to more than 700 km. It now carries 16% of the country's oil and it offers the Russians serious competition in the supply of oil to China. Kazakhstan also exports oil in the form of 'swap supplies' through Iran: when oil is delivered by tankers from Kazakhstan to the north of Iran, a corresponding volume is exported through the ports of the Persian Gulf.

The routes and pipelines used for gas are still in flux. A project for a Caspian Coastal Pipeline, to carry both Kazakh and Turkmen gas along the eastern shore of the Caspian linking up to the Russian pipeline system, with a capacity of 20 million cubic meters a year, has failed to materialize. A proposed Trans-Caspian gas pipeline under the Caspian Sea offering an alternative to the Caspian Coastal Pipeline has also failed to see the light of day. In addition to the northern route through Russia, Kazakhstan also supplies gas to China through the Central Asia–China pipeline.

Kazakhstan's communications systems are well developed. In recent years, particular attention has been paid to projects to develop satellite communications, digital communications and infrastructure, and the extension of telecommunications networks to rural areas. As part of this effort, in 2007, the first national broadcasting communication satellite 'Kazsat' was launched from the Baikonur space center. In 2007, the company Kazakhtelecom completed construction of the main ring of a national information superhighway which has put 14 large cities, 116 small towns, regional centers, and rural villages on a single digital ring. The country now has full independence in terms of its telecommunications infrastructure and can offer the shorted telecommunications bridge between Europe and the countries of South East Asia.

The Financial Sector

In its scope, Kazakhstan's banking sector is on a par with many European countries. In 2013, banking assets in the country amounted to the equivalent of 43% of GDP. Due to the world economic crisis, there were serious problems with liquidity and threats of defaults on foreign loans by major banks. However, operations have been largely stabilized. Both before and after the crisis, the banking sector's growth has been largely thanks to foreign capital. The banking sector has two levels: it is overseen by the National Bank of Kazakhstan (the central bank), under which there are 38 commercial and investment banks, 19 of which are banks with foreign capital involvement.

The banking system is characterized by a high level of concentration of assets. The largest banks are Kazkommertsbank and Halyak Bank. In 2015, these two accounted for 30% of the banking system's total assets. The top five banks—the two listed above along with Turan Alem, Tsesnabank, and Sberbank—control 53% of the system's assets. In addition to the National Bank of Kazakhstan, there are two further state-owned banks, the Development Bank of Kazakhstan and the mortgage credit and lending bank Zhilstroybank that was transferred to the national holding company, Baiterek, in 2013. This latter institution and Samruk-Kazyna are the country's two largest holding companies. They receive funds from the National Oil Fund.

Greater competition and the growth in demand for deposits have pushed the major Kazakh banks to enter neighboring markets. For example, Turan Alem has subsidiaries in Russia, Armenia, Georgia, Belarus, and Ukraine.

One of the key objectives of the country's economic policy has been the control of inflation. This fell to 6–8% during the 2000s, but rose to over 18% in 2007. It has since fallen back to the 6–8% level.

The stock market remains underdeveloped. The Kazakhstan Stock Exchange (KASE) has a low level of capitalization, equivalent to barely 5% of GDP.

In 1991, the national budget expenditure amounted to the equivalent of 17% of GDP. This has rised to 22%. The consolidated budget is made up of local budgets and the national budget which takes about 77% of budgetary revenues. The bulk of the revenues come from the taxes applied to companies in the raw materials industry. From 2007 onwards, the revenue from the sale of oil, has been channeled into the National Oil Fund which led to the budget being increasingly dependent on 'oil money.'

In 2008, a new tax code was adopted. The mining sector saw a major change with the introduction of higher mineral extraction taxes, along with export duties on oil and gas products. During to rising prices for energy, the development of the fuel and energy complex, and greater activity on the part of small businesses, the budget revenues have exceeded expenditures in recent years, despite repayments of foreign debt. But subsequent falls in the oil price have prompted a decision to transfer to the budget, US$3 bn a year from the National Oil Fund. The bulk of the budget goes on social expenditure, with investment in transport and communications also benefiting.

In 1993, Kazakhstan introduced its own currency, the tenge (₸). In 1999, a free-floating exchange rate was implemented. The restriction which required exporters to sell 50% of their hard currency earnings was lifted.

The External Sector

The export of energy resources mean that the value of the country's exports is almost double that of its imports, a very positive trade balance. As a result, even taking into account large repatriation of profits by foreign investors, the current account balance has been generally positive with a few exceptions (2009, 2015, and 2016).

The financial account is also positive. Kazakhstan has attracted more foreign direct investment than most of the other former Soviet countries. In 2015, the volume of accumulated foreign direct investment amounted to US$120 bn. The main source of this foreign direct investment has been the Netherlands with 28%, followed by the USA, China, Switzerland, Russia, France, Belgium, the United Kingdom, and the British Virgin Islands. About 40% of foreign direct investment is aimed at geological survey activity; 30% goes into mining; and 10% goes to the manufacturing industry.

At the same time, foreign loans have poured in, taking the external debt to US$154 bn at the end of 2015. However, the assets of the National Oil Fund and the county's international reserves together far exceed the country's short-term debt.

With significant revenue earned from its exports, Kazakhstan has seen an increase in its own overseas investment activity and a resulting rise in its external trade turnover. KazMunayGas purchased a 75% share of the stock of the large Romanian company, Rompetrol Group TRG, two oil-processing plants in Romania, and 630 fuel stations in several other European countries.

Kazakhstan has been an active player in the integration process among former Soviet countries in the post-Soviet era. The country's leadership announced long ago an initiative to create the Eurasian Economic Union (EEU). Moreover, Kazakhstan is keen to pursue integration beyond the economic sphere and include, for example, greater coordination in the area of defense.

Kazakhstan seeks to adopt a multi-vector approach to its external economic relationships. It is thus actively involved in regional and sub-regional economic organizations and initiatives, while at the same time pursuing better bilateral relations with the countries of Europe, Asia, and the Americas. This approach has enabled the country to make the most of its existing ties to Russia at the same time which have acted as a counterweight to the expansion of China. It has established new routes for its energy exports and been able to attract foreign investment from a number of different countries to finance its development. The country is an active participant in the CIS, the Collective Security Treaty Organization, the Economic Cooperation Organization, the Shanghai Cooperation Organization, and the Eurasian Economic Union. In 2015, it joined the World Trade Organization.

In 2015, Kazakhstan's merchandize exports totaled US$46 bn, equivalent to 38% of its GDP. Minerals form the largest component of these exports, at 49% of the total. Metals and related products are another important element with 21% of the total. Exports of agricultural production and the output of other branches of the manufacturing industry are insignificant. On the import side, cars and related equipment are the largest single sector with 28% of the total.

Kazakhstan's important trading partners are the countries of the EU. They take almost 60% of the country's exports and are the main purchasers of Kazakhstani oil and metals. However, only about 26% of the country's imports are from the EU. In 2015, the countries of the CIS accounted for about 20% of Kazakhstan's external trade turnover (17% of exports and 43% of imports). Russia took the lion's share of this trade. The share attributable to the other Central Asian countries is small, and is mostly concentrated on Uzbekistan.

Despite the low level of trade with the countries of Central Asia, Kazakhstan still has a significant impact on the commodity markets in Kyrgyzstan, Tajikistan, Turkmenistan, and Uzbekistan which is growing as a result of its investment activity. Kyrgyzstan has seen the most notable economic penetration from Kazakhstan which has antagonized the local elite. One of Kyrgyz's most important projects, worth US$3 bn, is the construction of the cascade of the Kambartinsk hydro-electric power plants. This is being financed with Kazakhstani help in the form of a joint company of which Russia and Kazakhstan each hold 33% of the shares, while Kyrgyzstan has 34%. What looks like Kazakhstani ambitions for economic dominance of the region have not been welcome in Uzbekistan which has similar ambitions toward regional leadership.

Russia and Kazakhstan are strategic partners. Their history dictates the need to maintain their economic relationship. However, Kazakhstan's efforts to export its oil and gas have been a source of tension between the two. Kazakhstan seeks to use Russian transit routes while targeting wider world markets. The Trans-Caspian pipeline system and the Atyrau-Samara oil pipeline are used in tandem. A system of mutual gas supply has been developed under which gas from the Karachaganak field is supplied to the Russian pipeline system while an equivalent amount of Russian gas is supplied to the Kostanay and Aktobe regions. Russia and Kazakhstan were the first countries on the Caspian Sea to agree a division of the coastal shelf and joint use of the Caspian fields, including the Kashgan field. Russia continues to use the Baikour space complex under a long-term lease.

Russia is an active investor in the Kazakhstani coal industry and in the development of its uranium deposits. It controls up to 20% of the reserves of uranium ore as stockholder of uranium extraction companies such as Zarechnoe, Akbastau, and Karatau.

Many Kazakhstani companies, especially those in the northern regions that have high Russian populations, tend to focus on trade with the neighboring regions of Russia. Kazakhstan imports coal, electricity, gas, oil and oil products, and vehicles from Russia.

Russia and Kazakhstan both support the integration among the former Soviet countries in the framework of regional organizations, especially the Eurasian Economic Union.

The Social Sphere

Although poverty rates (income of less than US$2 a day) fell dramatically between 2000 and 2010, from 47 to 6.5%, the living standards of most of the population remain low. At the same time, social stratification is a significant problem. At the beginning of the present decade, the share of national income taken by the lowest income decile as 3.9%, while the top decile took 23.7%. Also, there continues to be a gap between the living standards of the urban and rural populations: the poverty rate in the cities is less than 5%, but double that in rural areas.

The extent of the unofficial economy, which is estimated to be equivalent to 25–30% of GDP, and the high number of self-employed people make it hard to determine accurately the real value of incomes in the population. In 2015, the monthly average salary was estimated to be around US$568.

Kazakhstan differed from most other former Soviet countries in the way it dismantled its Soviet social security and health care systems in the early 1990s. A new combined system of social security services was formed to offer basic pensions for 1.7 million pensioners and a defined contribution system for 4.5 million people in work; this did not include the self-employed. About 30% of the population receives some form of social assistance from both government and non-state funds.

In 2013, expenditure on social security was equivalent to 2.2% of GDP, education was 3.1%, and health care 1.8%. In other words, despite its oil wealth, Kazakhstan's expenditure in these areas was proportionately lower than in some other former Soviet countries.

Conclusion

1. Kazakhstan has the greatest economic potential of all the countries of Central Asia, thanks largely to its energy resources. Currently, the oil industry dominates, thanks both to the development of existing deposits and the discovery of new ones. The development of the fuel and energy complex has been the main driver of growth in the economy and the focus of the country's exports. However, the dominance of this one sector leaves Kazakhstan vulnerable to fluctuations in prices on world energy markets. In response to this, the country's industrial profile is changing, but mainly with the development of industries that service the fuel and energy complex and the expansion of its infrastructure, all of which only increases the country's dependence on imports, both of consumer goods and investment.

2. The growth of the fuel and energy complex has not been matched by adequate growth in manufacturing. Only the mining sector has seen any diversification of industrial production. Uranium is a promising sector for Kazakhstan as the country has a quarter of all world reserves of the mineral.

3. The country has laid the foundations for a market economy. The national currency is convertible. Market reforms have been supported by improvements in the legal system.

4. Since the middle of the 1990s, efforts to develop a new economic model have relied heavily on attracting foreign capital. Between 1995 and 1997, the country's leading enterprises were sold to foreign investors. These included enterprises involved in ferrous and non-ferrous metallurgy along with the richest oil fields at Tengiz and Kumkol. Currently, almost the entire export potential is in foreign hands.

5. The country's economic growth, bringing expansion of industry and government measures to support small entrepreneurship have combined to reduce the level of emigration from the country. Indeed, they have encouraged a rise in immigration into the country from its Central Asian neighbors.

6. As a landlocked country, Kazakhstan's external activities require good economic relationships with its neighbors, especially for the transshipment of oil and gas. Export activity is largely focused on Russia, the EU, China, and Japan.

7. Relations with Russia and other former Soviet countries remain a priority for Kazakhstan and do not conflict with its ambitions to develop relationships with countries further afield as part of its multi-vector approach to its external economic policy. Kazakhstan takes an active interest in its regional relationships, especially with Uzbekistan whose economic potential is on a par with its own. The country is actively involved in all regional organizations and has ambitions to be the regional leader.

Questions

1. What is the role of oil in the Kazakhstani economy?

2. Describe the country's economic model and the influence of the family and clan structures.

3. Describe the main characteristics of Kazakhstan's external economic relations.

4. Describe Kazakhstan's relations with Russia.

Sources of additional information

The Commonwealth of Independent States in 2000–2014. Short digest. Moscow, 2015.

National Accounts of Countries of the Commonwealth of Independent States 2000–2013. International Statistical Committee of the Commonwealth of Independent States. 2016.

Report on the Economy of Kazakhstan. 2014. World Bank.

Development of Industry in the Republic of Kazakhstan. Astana, September 2013.

Post-Soviet States: 25 years of Independent Development. Vol. 1. Western Flank of the CIS. Central Asia. M. IMEMO, 2017.

www.stat.org.kz.(Statistical Agency of the Republic of Kazakhstan).

www.nationalbank.kz (National Bank of Kazakhstan).

www.rdb.rz (Development Bank of Kazakhstan).

www.eurasianet.org.

www.kisi.kz (Kazakhstan Institute for Strategic Studies under the President of the Republic of Kazakhstan).

CHAPTER 29

KYRGYZSTAN

The Economic Model

Kyrgyzstan had been a recipient of considerable resources from the central budget of the Soviet Union and it saw its GDP almost halved in the early years of its independence. Faced with hyperinflation, poverty, and unemployment, the country's leadership opted for the 'shock therapy' of economic liberalization. One factor militating in favor of this approach was that Kyrgyzstan, unlike many other former Soviet countries, has no significant natural resources (apart from water and gold). It is also isolated from important transport arteries and has only a small domestic market. This pushed Kyrgyzstan to be one of the first of the former Soviet countries to embark on market-oriented reforms. The country was the first in Central Asia to implement IMF recommendations, the first to have a convertible national currency, and the first to join the WTO.

Its rapid economic liberalization helped the country out of a crisis. It conquered hyperinflation and set it on course for economic growth from 1996 onwards. However, the country remained heavily dependent on external aid—more than any other country in the region—and this has left it vulnerable to economic fluctuations.

The apparent weakness of Kyrgyz's economic potential, especially for exports, has gradually deterred foreign investors. Rather than stimulate the creations of competing companies, the open market reforms only laid the foundations for more informal and traditional enterprises, in which the majority of the population work. The new economy has only pockets of what would be recognized as modern elsewhere. This has led to a strengthening of economic and social disparities in the country, and a widening of the gap between the better-off north and the poorer south. The country's economic model cannot therefore be deemed a success, nor has it met the needs of its people.

The National Economy

Just a short distance behind Turkmenistan, Kyrgyz has the smallest GDP among all the former Soviet countries. In 2016, it accounted for just 2.6% of the GDP of the Central Asian sub-region (Tajikistan produced 2.8%). This despite having 8.7% of the sub-region's population. The country has enjoyed economic growth since 1996 with an average annual growth rate between 2000 and 2016 of 4.7%. But this growth has been unstable. The GNI PPP per head of population in 2010-2016 more than double.

During the 2000s, economic growth was driven by a gradual increase in investment activity, which provided an inflow of capital for housing construction, transport, communication, and also to the energy sector and other branches of industry. However, growth was erratic, as demonstrated by the fluctuation in the gross fixed capital formation rate between 14 and 25%, as well as changes in the level of gold production and fluctuations in the world price for the precious metal.

There have been significant changes in the structure of the country's economy: the share contributed by the primary sector has reduced (though it has remained large, at 21%), while the secondary sector has increased and now stands at 34%. The tertiary sector accounts for the remaining 45%. The tertiary sector is mainly made up of trade, with re-exports of Chinese goods to neighboring countries playing a key role. Gold mining in Kumtor has been the main driver of growth in the secondary sector. Gold production feeds through to the economy as a whole: if production falls, GDP falls with it; if production and prices rise, GDP growth accelerates accordingly.

Estimates of the size of the unofficial economy vary from 17 to 60% of GDP. It is most prevalent in agriculture, construction, and the retail trade. Kyrgyzstan has become an important transit route for Afghan drugs being trafficked into Russia.

Table 29.1 — GDP in Kyrgyz

	2000	2005	2008	2012	2013	2015	2016	2018*	2020*
Population, millions	5.0	5.0	5.0	5.6	5.7	6.0	6.08	-	-
GDP, US$ bn	1.3	2.4	5.05	6.6	7.2	6.6	6,55		
CNI PPP per capita, US$	1,550*	2,030*	2,570*	2,830*	3,080*	3,434	3410		
GDP rate of growth, %	5.4	-0.2	7.6	-0.9	6.6	6.5	-0.1	4.2	4.6

*Estimate

Sources: Interstate Statistical Committee of the Commonwealth of Independent States (http//www.cisstat.org).
World Bank. World Development Indicators 2017.
World Bank. The Global Economic Prospects. Jan. 2018.
Social and economic situation of Kyrgyz Republic. January–December 2014. Bishkek. 2015.

Economic Policy

Along with liberalization, the government has made the use of foreign aid, foreign loans, and foreign direct investment a key plank of its economic policy. During the first ten years of independence, the focus was on foreign capital in particular.

Despite active implementation of programs recommended by the IMF and the World Bank, the economy that has emerged still has significant features of 'family' or 'crony' capitalism. This lay behind the moves to complement market reforms with property redistribution and attempts to create conditions conducive to wider business activity. For the future, the country is looking to develop manufacturing, agriculture, and power generation in the southern regions, while the north becomes the focus for mining (including gold) and tourism.

In 2007, the government adopted a three-year development strategy to run until 2010. But the global economic crisis and the country's huge foreign debts stopped the plan in its tracks. Diversion of financial assistance and outright corruption have also held the country back. This led to social upheaval in 2010 and a transfer of power. In 2013, a Transition Program and Plan for Kyrgyzstan was adopted to run from 2013 to 2017. This sought to stimulate the development of the private sector, including small businesses, and the agricultural sector. It also had plans to implement investment projects in the energy and mining industries, and in agricultural product processing.

During the reforms of the 1990s, the vast majority of enterprises in Kyrgyzstan were passed into the private sector. The 27 largest enterprises were privatized, with the assistance of the World Bank which provided most of the financing for their restructuring. However, a large part of the public property portfolio ended up in the hands of a small group of families.

By 2015, most economic entities in the country belonged to individual entrepreneurs or farm households, either small companies or small farms. These provide work for most of the population and are the bedrock of the unofficial economy. Retail markets are important in the country's economic life, to the extent that the struggle to control them can sometimes lead to armed conflict.

The public sector remains a player in the mining, energy, and transport industries, mainly in the form of its holdings in joint enterprises that also involve foreign capital. A key characteristic of the business landscape in Kyrgyzstan, just as in Kazakhstan, is the importance of clans, and the way in with the families of the political elite retain control over the economy.

Human Capital

Kyrgyzstan's population grew at an average annual rate of 1.2% during the 1990s and by 1.6% during the 2000s. By 2016, the total stood at 6.1 million. Two-thirds of the population (66%) live in the countryside. Over 60% of the population (3.5 million) are of working age but only 2.3 million are actually working—70% of whom do so in the information economy. The official unemployment rate of 7.7% substantially understates the reality. Agriculture's share of employment has decreased gradually, while those of construction and the service industries have grown.

The Real Sector

A large proportion of Kyrgyzstan is mountainous—only 7% of the land is cultivated. A recession in agriculture was overcome with land reforms, but the sector has continued to see sluggish growth rates in its production. Animal husbandry is a popular traditional occupation. However, the number of livestock fell during the crisis of the 1990s. Most of the crops that make up the bulk of agricultural output, have seen their production falling in recent years. This is largely due to the poor state of irrigation facilities that has left farmers more vulnerable to weather conditions. The amount of land under cultivation has fallen as a result.

With 55% of its food being imported, the country faces a threat to its food security. To address this, since the second half of the 2000s, the government has been developing measures involving state support to increase the amount of land under cultivation by improving existing irrigation systems and building new systems to increase the land area served.

The process of agricultural and animal products is the basis of the sector's manufacturing, covering meat processing, dairy, flour, grains, and soft drinks. Environmentally friendly agricultural products are exported to Russia, Kazakhstan, China, and other countries.

Kyrgyzstan has only limited reserves of oil and gas, but it benefits from extensive water resources thanks to its many mountains and rivers. Among former Soviet countries, only Russia and Tajikistan have larger water resources. The country has two thermal and 17 hydro power plants. The largest power plant is the Toktogulsky Hydro plant which accounts for about 40% of all electricity generated in the country. It supplies all of the south of the country and also exports power to Uzbekistan and Kazakhstan.

However, a drop in the level of water in the Toktogulsky reservoir has caused considerable problems as it also feeds the Naryn River on which there are five further hydro power plants. This has led to a fall in power-generation capacity and large-scale outages of power. The reservoir was constructed during the Soviet era with the goal of supplying the sub-region with both a water supply and the capacity to generate power. Kyrgyzstan and Tajikistan have a greater interest in the power generation, while Kazakhstan and Uzbekistan are more concerned with the irrigation. Since 1993, the operation of the Toktogulsky cascade has concentrated on power generation which requires large increases in the accumulated water during the summer and floods in winter. Problems have thus arisen in the Syr Darya basin, with disagreements between the countries of Central Asia and competition over the water resources. Kyrgyzstan and Tajikistan have the rivers flowing through their territories and so have sought to treat the water as a good for export.

Kyrgyz's electric power system is connected to the systems of Tajikistan, Uzbekistan, Turkmenistan, and South Kazakhstan. The country generates about 15–16 bn kWh, of which about 6–7 bn kWh is exported to Kazakhstan, Uzbekistan, China, and Russia. Because of the increase in power consumption thanks to cheaper rates over recent years coupled with the fall in the reservoir levels described above and the impact on hydro generating capacity (hydro plants generate 80% of the country's total), Kyrgyzstan has gone from being a country with energy surpluses three years ago to one that today suffers shortages. Projects have been implemented to introduce new generating capacity, firstly at the Kambartinshy hydro plant on the River Naryn, construction of which began in the 1980s. Construction of the largest element of this, Kambartinskaya-1, is being undertaken with Russian assistance. Construction of the Upper Naryn cascade hydro station, also under an agreement with Russia, is showing promise. China is also interested in the construction of coal thermal plants. Kyrgyzstan has the third largest coal reserves among former Soviet countries.

Looking at non-energy natural resources, the most important one in terms of market value is gold. The country has 12 large deposits of gold, including Kumtor, which is among the largest ten deposits in the world. In addition, there are at Dzheruy and Taldy-Bulak. There are also significant deposits of mercury, of which Kyrgyzstan has 20% of global reserves. There are also reserves of non-ferrous and rare-earth metals such as platinum and uranium at Kok-Moynok.

Gold mining and non-ferrous metals are the backbone of Kyrgyzstan industry. Operations at the Kumtor gold mine are carried out by a joint Kyrgyz-Canadian company, Centerra, of which the state in Kyrgyzstan holds a 70% stake. The Dzheruy deposit is worked by a joint Kyrgyz-Austrian company of which 40% belongs to the state. Finally, the Taldy-Bulak field is exploited by a Kyrgyz-Kazakh company. The Kumtor mine produces 95% of the country's gold, an amount equivalent to 7–10% of GDP.

In 2007, the Russian company Renova acquitted a majority stake in the Kara-Baltinsky mining company. This processes raw uranium ore imported from Kazakhstan. There is, as yet, no industrial production of uranium.

The textile industry has been developing slowly, focusing on sewing, the manual production of carpets and felt products.

A building boom in the 2000s was centered on house building, though expenditure and work on the construction of irrigation systems was also considerable. There has also been work on a holiday resort on Issyk Kul Lake with foreign—mainly Kazakh—money.

All normal types of transport operate in the country. But networks and vehicles are in a poor state of repair. As Kyrgyzstan acts as a conduit between China and Central Asia, transport projects have been financed by the Asian Development Bank. The country has a relatively small 470km of railway tracks. The main rail center is Bishkek which is connected to the Russian rail network through Uzbekistan and Kazakhstan. The Bishkek–Torugart highway is being modernized as part of the highway connecting Central Asia to China. The country's pipeline system, stretching 480km, mostly transports gas.

Given the country's mountainous terrain making many areas remote and hard to reach, the development of communications is of primary importance. There are about half a million users of landlines. In addition, the country's mobile network is well developed, with the number of lines exceeding the population. Internet use has been growing rapidly.

The Financial Sector

Kyrgyz's monetary and credit system relies on 26 commercial banks, overseen by the National Bank of the Kyrgyz Republic. The main source of assets for Kyrgyzstan banks has been money borrowed from abroad. This, coupled with the small size and open nature of the economy which foment instability in the demand of credit, the world economic crisis hit Kyrgyzstan hard. Five banks have had to close since 2008. With interests in 14 banks, foreign capital, including that from Russia and Kazakhstan, is well represented in the banking system. The four largest banks control 52% of the entire sector's assets.

In general, the country's banking system is not well developed. Banks only offer a limited range of services. The volume of credit supplied by the banks to the private sector does not exceed the equivalent of 23% of GDP (2015). Only 6% of the population has a bank account.

Eco Islamic Bank (which has some Russian backing) has been licensed to conduct Islamic finance operations. There is also widespread use of non-bank financial credit institutions, mostly in the form of credit unions and microfinance organizations. The non-bank sector is reckoned to have about 19% of the assets of the whole financial sector.

There is a stock exchange, but its total capitalization is equivalent to just 2.5% of GDP.

The state budget has two parts: the republican and the local budgets. The government has been focusing on reforming the tax system, seeking to reduce VAT and simplify the overall number of taxes. However, even after the reduction in VAT, indirect taxes (VAT and excise duties) still bring in about 58% of tax revenues. As the major component of the government's tax earnings, VAT is targeted mostly at imported goods. In addition, over 16% of tax revenues come from goods in transit (equivalent to 3.3% of GDP). Government expenditure has pensions and benefits as the largest single element of the overall budget, taking 20.5% in 2014. Education accounted for 18.5% (equivalent to 5.5% of GDP); health care, 10.2% (3% of GDP); and defense and public order, 11.2% (3.3% of GDP). In recent years the budget has been in surplus. In 2014 this was equivalent to 1.2% of GDP.

The External Sector

Kyrgyzstan balance of payments is characterized by a large current account deficit (equivalent to 15% of GDP), as the revenues from exports and from money transfers do not match expenditure on imports and on payments to non-residents for loans and other forms of financial support.

The gap is plugged by inflows of foreign capital, with the majority being in the form of foreign direct investment and loans from foreign governments. In 2015, the stock of accumulated foreign direct investment was US$3.9 bn, equivalent to more than 50% of GDP. After 2008, the amount of foreign direct investment coming from other former Soviet countries fell dramatically. Having stood at 45% of the total in 2007, it was just 13% in 2013. Russia and Kazakhstan were the main sources. In 2014, about 80% of foreign investment was aimed at mining and geological exploration.

Transfers of money from Kyrgyzstan migrants working overseas are an important element in the country's finances. Almost one-fifth of the working population works in Russia. In 2013, they transferred more than US$2.1 bn back to Kyrgyzstan, that is more than the foreign direct investment from the previous four years.

The use of foreign credit and aid has led to the accumulation of considerable external debt. By 2014, this had increased to US$3.9 bn, equivalent to 55% of GDP.

Kyrgyzstan is a member of the WTO, and its economy is becoming increasingly open. The national currency (the som, c) has a floating rate.

The ratio of foreign trade turnover to GDP is 107%. The balance of trade in goods is permanently negative since imports exceed exports many times over.

In 2008, more than half of the turnover of foreign trade was to and from other CIS countries. In 2014, this had decreased to 48%. The country's main imports are mineral fuel, equipment, vehicles, and metal ware. Imports of food items such as wheat and vegetable oil have increased. Kyrgyzstan exports gold and precious and semiprecious stones which make up 40% of all exports. In addition, mineral products, agricultural items (cotton, sugar, tobacco), and animal husbandry products are exported. The main destinations for Kyrgyzstan products are Switzerland (33%) which buys mostly gold, Russia (about 20%), Uzbekistan (14.5%), and Kazakhstan (about 12%). The main sources of imports are Russia (36%), China (18%), Kazakhstan (9%), and Uzbekistan (about 4%).

Kyrgyzstan was a main transit route for Chinese goods getting into the Soviet Union. There are no exact figures for the illegal trade, only estimates. But Kyrgyz is undoubtedly one of the largest ‘holes’ among the former Soviet countries. Joining the Eurasian Economic Union with its common customs regime presents Kyrgyz with a problem of how to close this ‘hole.’ It is attempting to solve the problem by increasing the processing of some imported goods within the country, taking into account the existence of five functioning free economic zones: Bishkek (the capital); Klarakol, on the cost of the Issyk Kul Lake; Maymak, on the border with Kazakhstan; Naryn, on the border with China; and Ley-Lek, created in 2011 to help develop the tourism industry.

Kyrgyzstan’s priority remains its economic relations with Russia, especially after joining the EEU. Those relations take a number of forms: investment and credit, trade, and labor migration. Russia is the largest source of imports into Kyrgyzstan and it is also one of the country’s largest investors. Kyrgyzstan and Russia jointly built the Kambartinsky hydro power plant 1 and signed an agreement worth US$1.7 bn for the construction of the second phase in 2009. In addition, Russia is the main shareholder in several defense companies (which were established during the Soviet era) as well as in the Kara-Baltinsky mining company and the Kadamzhaysky company that produces antimony metal. A number of Russian companies, e.g., Inter RAO, RusHydro, Gazprom, and Rosneft are active in the Kyrgyzstan market.

The Social Sector

Kyrgyz is one of the most backward of the former Soviet countries when it comes to GDP per capita. At the turn of the century, the average monthly salary was just US$25–30. By 2015, this had risen to US$209.

Income inequality is very marked. In 2013, the top decile was as much as ten times richer than the bottom decile. However between 2004 and 2013, the number of people regarded as poor fell from 50% of the population to 37%.

Levels of literacy and social security have fallen since the demise of the Soviet Union, though they are average when compared to other developing countries.

Conclusion

1. Just a short distance behind Turkmenistan, Kyrgyzstan has the smallest GDP among all the former Soviet countries, as well as in Central Asia. Its economic weakness stems from its isolated geographical location, its poor levels of natural resources, and the difficulties it faces in maintaining traditional social and economic relations. The collapse of relations between the former Soviet countries after the demise of the Soviet Union saw Kyrgyzstan suffer the largest drop in production. To recover, the country embarked on a strategy which saw the fastest transition to a market economy among former Soviet countries.

2. When developing its new economic model, Kyrgyzstan has made foreign investment its priority. After privatization, the largest companies in the mining industry along with the most significant gold deposits were in the hands of Western countries. Foreign investment and loans continue to play an important role in the country.

3. After the demise of the Soviet Union, food security worsened. Food processing industries have taken until recent years to return to full production. One of the main reasons for this was competition from imported goods, a situation which was exacerbated by the country joining the WTO.

4. Despite economic growth during the 2000s, Kyrgyzstan still has one of the lowest standards of living among the former Soviet countries. Labor migration remains high, with Russia as the most popular destination.

5. Without access to a sea port, Kyrgyzstan must rely on good relations with its immediate neighbors in order to develop economic ties with countries further afield. Lacking major economic potential, the country has sought to develop build strong trading links with its neighbors in Central Asia. However, in more recent years, its role as a transit route for Chinese goods (in both formal and 'informal' trade) has come to the fore. Kyrgyzstan participates in all regional organizations, seeking to use its membership to access funding for large-scale projects such as those in the power and transport sectors.

6. Relations with other former Soviet countries, especially Russia, remain a priority for Kyrgyzstan. Russia is the main source of imports into the country and is also a major investor.

7. Kyrgyz's economy is heavily dependent on the fluctuating price of gold on world markets. It can also be affected adversely by changes in the prices of food products. As a small country, it is also vulnerable to the ups and downs of the economies of its large neighbors; Russia, Kazakhstan, and China.

Questions

1. How do natural and geographical factors affect the sectoral make-up of the economy of Kyrgyzstan?
2. How do the family and clan system affect the economy of Kyrgyzstan?
3. What role is played by foreign capital in the economy?
4. Describe Kyrgyzstan's foreign relationships, especially that with Russia.

Sources of additional information

Years that have changed Central Asia. Ed. by I.Zvyagelskaya. Moscow, 2009 (in Russian)

The Commonwealth of Independent States in 2008–2012. Quick reference book of preliminary statistic results. Moscow, 2014.

Social and economic status of the Kyrgyz Republic. January–December 2014. Bishkek. 2015 (in Russian).

Social standard of living of population of the Kyrgyz Republic, 2009–2013. National Statistical Committee of the Kyrgyz Republic. Bishkek, 2014 (in Russian).

Informal employment in Kyrgyzstan. Strategic Research National Institute. Bishkek 2014 (in Russian).

The Kyrgyz Republic finance sector stability report. Bishkek, 2013 (in Russian).

Post-Soviet States: 25 years of Independent Development. Vol. 1. Western Flank of the CIS. Central Asia. M. IMEMO, 2017. (in Russian)

www.nbkr.kg (National Bank of the Kyrgyz Republic)

www.stat.kg (National Statistical Committee of the Kyrgyz Republic)

CHAPTER 30

TAJIKISTAN

The demise of the Soviet Union, the destabilization in neighboring Afghanistan, and its own long-running civil war (1992–1997) combined to leave Tajikistan mired in crisis at the end of the 1990s. The war saw up to 100,000 people lose their lives and left nearly half a million as refugees. It left the economy in tatters and put the very existence of the state at risk. Although a coalition government came to power in 1996, it was not until the beginning of the next decade that it was able to set the country on the road to peaceful development.

The Economic Model

The building of a new economic model for the country began despite there being no agreement between the former Soviet elite and the regional clans who were reasserting themselves. Although market reforms followed the pattern seen elsewhere in the former Soviet countries—price liberalization, privatization, support for private businesses, encouragement of foreign investment—in Tajikistan, they began late and proceeded only slowly.

By 2007, all small enterprises and most of the larger ones had been privatized. Most agricultural land had been divided among farmers; just 24% remained in the hands of former collective and state farms. The agro-industrial complex with numerous ginnery and other processing enterprises, forms the backbone of the national economy. It is now largely in private hands with only 6% of its gross output coming from public sector enterprises.

However, a significant level of government intervention in the economy remains a characteristic of Tajikistan, as does the low standard of living endured by the majority of the population. Other important features of the country are the size of the informal economy, its dependence on foreign sources of credit, and the importance of the money sent home by labor emigrants.

The National Economy

Tajikistan is responsible for just 2.8% of the sub-region's total GDP even though it has 12.4% of the population.

Although market reforms in Tajikistan have brought about an economic recovery, by 2013, production of GNI per capita was just 11% above its level in 1990, according to the World Bank. The economy only began to grow in 1997. Between 2000 and 2016, average annual growth was 7.6%. But in 2015–2016 annual growth was negative.

Substantial economic growth during the 2000s was driven by the increase in the ratio of gross capital formation to GDP: from 9.3% in 2000 to 20.7% in 2103, and 29% in 2014. This was largely down to the growth of both state and foreign investment into the power industry and construction sector. The share of national private investments in the country's GDP is less than 10%, the lowest among former Soviet countries.

At 23%, the primary sector maintains a significant part in the sectoral make-up of the economy. The secondary sector's share is relatively small at 35%, and the tertiary sector has 42%. The division of employment among the three sectors differs: 47% in the primary sector, 11% in the secondary, and 42% in the tertiary.

The non-observed or informal economy is large; according to the Shark National Research Center, it exceeded 60% of GDP at the end of the last decade. A significant portion of this is connected to the trafficking of drugs from Afghanistan.

Table 30.1 — GDP in Tajikistan

	2000	2008	2012	2013	2015	2016	2018*	2020*
GDP, US$ bn	1.0	4.8	7.6	8.5	7.9	7.0	-	-
GNI PPP per capita, US$	900**	1,900**	2,350**	2,500**	2,834	3500	-	-
GDP rate of growth, %	9.5	7.9	7.5	7.4	6.0	6.0	5.0	5.7

* Estimate

Sources: Interstate Statistical Committee of the Commonwealth of Independent States (http//www.cisstat.org).
World Bank. World Development Indcators 2017.
World Bank. The Global Economic Prospects. Jan. 2018.
Agency of Statistics under the President of Republic of Tajikistan, 2014.

Economic Policy

An almost decade-long period of post-war economic recovery came to an end in 2007. The ruling elite had managed to eliminate the Islamic opposition and from 2006/2007 were able to exercise greater control over the country's economic development, with a long-term goal of accelerating growth and promoting development.

However, Tajikistan's economy sits permanently on the edge of imbalance. As such, the conduct of economic policy is a constant process of fire-fighting as new problems constantly arise such as interruptions in the power supply in fall and winter (causing annual losses of the equivalent of 3% of GDP), falls in the supply of Uzbek gas, negotiations with hedge funds over purchases of agricultural production (the funds buy mostly cotton before it is harvested) which has become one of the main causes of the crisis in agriculture.

To address its problems, the government have embarked on reforms aimed at creating conditions favorable to the development of the private sector—small and medium businesses—and favorable to investment, both domestic and foreign. In 2004, a Strategy for the National Development of Tajikistan was adopted. This ran until 2015, when it was succeeded by the Strategy for the National Development of Tajikistan. The plan regards it as a reasonable goal to aim to restore the country's industry along the lines of the same structural make-up that existed during the Soviet era. The economic policy also aims to increase employment and wages and to decrease wage inequality. It also hopes to implement social assistance to support the poorer sectors of society. However, even despite positive macroeconomic indicators, Tajikistan still lags behind its Central Asian neighbors when it comes to the creation of business opportunities.

Most large industrial enterprises, along with the social infrastructure, remain in state ownership. However, by the end of the last decade, the proportion of the total workforce employed by the state has fallen to 15.5%.

The private sector consists mainly of micro, small and medium-sized enterprises and provides the majority of the country's employment. However, the profitability of these firms remains low. It also fails to attract worthwhile amounts of investment into its fixed capital, receiving just 15% of the national total.

The public sector produces 39% of GDP and employs 25% of all workers. This sector includes a variety of enterprises: from joint stock companies to collective farms. There are also religious forms of business: funds and waqfs. There are a large number of foreign companies who have positions in both the private and public sectors.

Just as in other countries of Central Asia, the clan system in Tajikistan has a major bearing on the way business operates, with the main economic positions being dominated by groups with ties of family, religion, or place of origin. In the 2016 Index of Economic Freedom, Tajikistan was in 149th place and 132nd in the 2018 Doing Business Report.

Human Capital

Despite the civil war and the large-scale emigration, the birth rate has continued to grow by a relatively high 2.7% a year, which has seen the population increase by an average of 1.4% a year. Since 1991, the population has grown by almost a third to 7.9 million in 2015. Most of the population—75%—live in villages.

The working-age population makes up 57.7% of the total. Of the population, 2.4 million are economically active, of whom 2.3 million are working. Official statistics put unemployment at 2.5%. In reality it is much higher; the World Bank estimates it to be as high as 30%. The situation in the agricultural sector is particularly difficult. However, the country does not have a defined concept of what constitutes employment, still less any clear mechanism for measuring it.

One serious problem is continuous emigration. The mass emigration of the Russian-speaking population began during the civil war. Estimates vary, but some suggest as many as 90% of Russian speakers left. There was also an outflow of Uzbeks. Thereafter, the high levels of unemployment encouraged further emigration.

The annual number of labor emigrants reached as high as 650,000, meaning that as many as 30% of the male working-age population—both unskilled and educated—were working in other countries, between 80 and 85% of them in Russia. Though Tajik workers tend to earn low wages in other CIS countries, the money they transfer home is still equivalent to between 21 and 40% of GDP. This trend has led to a lack of qualified laborers in Tajikistan.

The education sector has also faced a crisis. The level of literacy, remains high at 99.5%, despite having fallen in recent years. There is a lack of teachers. There are also many religious schools financed by foreign Islamic funds. The system of vocational education has suffered more than most.

The Real Sector

As was the case in the Soviet era, agriculture is the backbone of the Tajik economy. About 70% of everyone employed in the country works in agriculture. The sector has managed to accommodate some of those made redundant by the fall in industrial production. However, the lack of land resources places a limit on the sector's ability to grow. With labor productivity very low, the sector also struggles to benefit from greater efficiency. In rural areas, there is only 0.2 hectares of land per person, with between 0.12 and 0.15 of this being irrigated. To make matters worse, over 80% of land has suffered some degree of land erosion.

Despite the privatization process, the state has maintained its role in agriculture, with more than 24% of all land under crops and 27% of irrigated land. The state continues to support the private sector with a system to supply seeds and offer preferential credit terms. The state is also responsible for the maintenance of the irrigation system (67% of all cultivated land in Tajikistan is irrigated). At the same time, in the private sector, access to land is restricted by the system based on political and family connections. The state offers both employment to workers on its land and leases to people wishing to farm.

About 40% of the land is sown with grain crops, especially wheat and barley intended for domestic consumption. Cotton, the country's main agricultural export, is grown on 30% of the land. There is a semi-compulsory scheme to use school pupils and students to pick the cotton. They are paid around 4¢ for every kilogram of cotton picked. Cotton is the largest crop and nearly half of all agricultural workers are involved in its cultivation. About 90% of the cotton fiber produced is exported, with 10% of the earnings going to the state budget.

The government faces a dilemma in that it needs the earnings from the export of cotton, but faces demands to increase the amount of land being used for other crops to supply growing demands for food. However, the production of cotton is beset by low productivity so its share of exports is decreasing anyway.

Light industry is also recovering on the basis of agricultural production, mainly products for the textile industry (cotton, silk-weaving, and garment and carpet production) as well as food (especially canned food and processed fruits and nuts). In 2014, the food industry accounts for more than 48% of the country's overall industrial production, a high figure compared with other countries.

Tajikistan has excellent natural water resources which give it significant potential to generate power. It has 77% of Central Asia's water resources. But, despite this, the fuel and energy complex is in crisis. The industry is able to generate 4.5 million kW of power. There are five hydro power plants in operation. The largest is Nurek on the Vakhsh River. With the power to generate 3 million kW, it is one of the 30 largest plants in the world. At the end of the Soviet era, construction began on two further large hydro plants on the Vakhsh, Rogun and Sangtuda which have been completed only recently. The construction of Sangtuda-1 was carried out jointly with Russia (which has a 75% share in this 670 MW project). Sangtuda-2 was built with Iran. A project to work with Russia on building one of the world's largest hydro power plants (3.6 million kW) at Rogun ran into difficulties with the construction of a 335m dam. Specifically, Tajikistan wanted to increase the height of the dam, making it the highest in the world. In response, Russia raised concerns that this would drain too much water from the Vakhsh and would thus need to be agreed by all the countries in the Amu Darya basin, mainly Uzbekistan. In 2012, Russia withdrew from the project. Although the project was subsequently approved and authorized in 2014 by an expert commission of the World Bank, construction remains stalled due to a lack of finance.

Up to 2010, Tajikistan's power supply networks were part of the Central Asian network. But with Kazakhstan and Uzbekistan withdrawing, the system ceased to operate. Tajikistan now has three separate power networks, though the country remains keen to explore exchange of power with its neighbors, especially to enable it to purchase more power during the winter months. The country is also prepared to purchase surplus power during the summer, but Uzbekistan has denied it the use of its networks. Bringing the Sangtuda power plants on stream has improved the situation and enabled the country to begin exporting power to neighboring countries.

The breakdown of USSR-wide communication networks, coupled with the civil war in Tajikistan, hit the mining and manufacturing industries particularly hard. Most enterprises either reduced operations or came to a complete standstill. The average depreciation of industrial assets reached 80–90%. Subsequently, over the last two decades, industry's growth rates have outstripped that of GDP as a whole. But the country's industry remains in crisis and has yet to return to the levels of production seen in 1990.

The mineral resources in Tajikistan that have industrial value include zinc, lead, silver, uranium, gold, tungsten, antimony, table, salt, coal, and precious stones. There are only small deposits of oil and gas and these are very deep. The largest single sector of the country's industry is non-ferrous metals which accounts for 40% of the total industrial output. An aluminum plant constructed during the Soviet era near the border with Uzbekistan is an important part of the industry. Work on the hydro plants has also been key to the country's industrial strategy. However, it should be noted that a key contributor to earnings is the role played by intermediary companies under foreign ownership. Gold mining is largely undertaken thanks to foreign investment. Uranium is mined by a Russian-Tajik company which has resumed operations. The chemical industry continues to face difficulties. The largest enterprises in this sector are the Vakhsh nitrogen-mineral fertilizer plant and the Yavensk chemical plant which focuses on the processing of imported raw materials. Neither plant is operating at full capacity.

Tajikistan's low standard of living means that the construction industry is not as active as in other former Soviet countries. The sector is also held back by a lack of investment, foreign or domestic. The roads that connect Tajikistan to China have been built with Chinese credit.

Roads provide the main means of transport, carrying about 90% of all passenger and freight traffic. But there is no single unified national network of roads. Connections between the rural south and the industrial north are complicated by mountains. During the winter months, the easiest way to get from one to the other is via Uzbekistan. Transport independence is thus a key plank of the government plans for economic development. To achieve this Tajikistan has borrowed money from China for the construction of two tunnels: 'Shakhristan' to the north of Dushanbe, and 'Shar-Shar' to the southeast.

The country has 28,000 km of roads and only 482 km of railways which are divided into northern and southern section with the largest junction at Dushanbe. China has plans to forge a rail network reaching Iran, passing through Kyrgyzstan, Tajikistan, and Afghanistan. Tajikistan's pipeline network is small with just 38 km of oil pipelines and 680 km of gas pipeline which brings gas from Uzbekistan.

The country's telephone infrastructure is underdeveloped, though the number of mobile users has grown rapidly and now includes 90% of the population. The number of people connected to the Internet has also risen rapidly and now stands at 700,000.

The Financial Sector

The National Bank of Tajikistan oversees the country's banking system which comprises 16 commercial banks, one non-bank credit organization, and 124 micro-financial organizations. Apart from the central bank, all banks are private and the five largest control 70% of the country's bank assets.

The amount of credit extended to the private sector in 2015 was equivalent to 23% of GDP. The cotton sector took half of all this credit. The activity of commercial banks is generally limited to the provision of short-term credit. The money transferred home by labor emigrants is an important part of the country's financial position. A major area of banking activity is dealing in foreign exchange connected with these transfers from migrants. This area has grown significantly following the cancellation of a 30% tax on transfers of foreign currency.

A stock exchange was established in 1994 but does not operate. Although there is some trading in stocks, there is no organized secondary securities market. Volumes of over-the-counter trades are insignificant and the market in debt instruments has yet to develop.

Inflation began to rise in 2006 and, by 2008, had reached an annual level of 20%. By 2016 it fell to 5.3%, producing a stable exchange rate and lower increases in food prices.

Following independence, the country's currency was the Tajik ruble, which was tied to the Russian ruble. But in 2000, a new national currency, the somoni, was issued.

The budget revenue share of GDP increased from 14% in 2000 to 26% in 2014. The main contributor to tax is VAT, making up 55% of the total. Income tax on individuals and legal entities contributes 15% of the total. Other revenue comes from various fines and penalties as well as external credit.

Through the adoption of a strict tax and budgetary policy, the government of Tajikistan has managed in some years to achieve a surplus on the state budget. However, such years are the exception as reductions in the country's external income in other years has created huge burdens on the state budget, forcing the reduction of economic and social programs.

The External Sector

The dependence of Tajikistan's on external aid is illustrated by the constant deficit in the current balance of payments which was equivalent to 5% of GDP in 2015. A key factor in this is the fact that the imports of goods exceed exports: in 2014, imports were worth US$4.3 bn while exports just US$1 bn.

The floating exchange rate for the somoni functions well enough, but a lack of official reserves limits the central bank's ability to support the currency. Reserves are valued at US$1.1 bn which is less than 30% of the annual value of imported goods. Falls in the amount of foreign aid also limit the scope for action to tackle the problem. In 2014, foreign aid totaled US$38 million, more than half of which came from the USA.

This context—deficits and falling aid receipts—illustrates why the transfers of money from labor emigrants play such an important part in the country's economy. However, slowing economic activity in the countries to which Tajik emigrants travel has seen a corresponding fall of 30–40% in these transfers.

Tajikistan's economic strategy is based on a twin approach of maintaining strong economic relations with Russia while still trying to secure financial aid from further afield. The country receives aid from many international organizations and seeks to be an active participant in all regional projects with external financing, for example, the development of the Silk Road. It also has a long-term goal to join the Eurasian Economic Union.

In 2015, the total amount of accumulated foreign direct investment in Tajikistan was just US$2.1 bn. Given the lack of a well-developed stock market, there is little or no effective portfolio investment. Western investors are mainly interested in the country's raw materials. Russia has shown interest in energy projects. Iran has taken an interest in both energy and transport. China and Kazakhstan have taken a wider interest across the country's industrial landscape.

Tajikistan follows a liberal trade policy with a relatively free regime. Between 2000 and 2014, the turnover of foreign trade grew by 260%. However, the deficit in foreign trade also grew, worsening the balance of payments and increasing the country's dependence on foreign aid and investment. In 2016, the main export items were cotton (25% of the total), aluminum (also 24%), and fruit and textile products mainly destined for the EU and Turkey. Imports are mostly raw materials for the productions of aluminum (19.3%), oil products (14.7% of the total), cars and related equipment (22.7%), and food (6.7%).

The destinations for Tajikistan's exports in 2015 were Switzerland (17%), Turkey (26%), Kazakhstan (10%), Iran (13%), Uzbekistan (6%), Russia (6%), Afghanistan (5%), and China (7%). Imports came from Russia (17%), China (47%), Kazakhstan (11%), Turkey (5%). Trade credits from China have seen the trade volumes with that country grow especially quickly.

Tajikistan places particular importance on its cooperation with Russia, seeking in particular to attract Russian investment into construction and the operation of the hydro power plants at Rogun and Sangtuda-1. Russia have written off some of Tajikistan's debts and, in an effort to secure further concessions, Tajikistan has transferred to Russia shares of certain large enterprises (e.g., a 50% stake in the Nurrek hydro power plant) along with a number of textile enterprises that focus on the Russian market.

The Social Sector

In terms of GDP per capita, Tajikistan is the poorest country in the sub-region. The percentage of the population living below the poverty line has been falling but remains at a relatively high 26% (2013). There is also a large disparity of income. The lowest decile earns just 3.3% of the nation's income, while the top decile takes 25.6%. The average monthly salary was US$143 in 2015.

Poverty is the main destabilizing factor in the population and is thus the focus for humanitarian aid entering the country. The health system is largely moribund and the prevalence of infectious diseases has been increasing. Life expectancy is a relatively low 65 years.

Conclusion

1. Tajikistan has the weakest economy among the Central Asian countries. Like Kyrgyzstan, it suffers as a result of its geographic isolation, meager natural resources, and the continuation of traditional social and economic customs. The civil war and the resulting emigration have a particularly negative impact on the country. Many enterprises were left in ruins. As a result of its civil war, Tajikistan was some years behind other Central Asian countries in being able to embark on real recovery.

2. Despite growth in its GDP over the last two decades, Tajikistan remains heavily dependent on two key factors: the production of aluminum (which requires imported raw materials), and money transferred back to the country by labor emigrants. A genuine transition to a market economy is still at a formative stage. Privatization of land, industrial property, and some success in attracting foreign investment have not yet produced any noticeable improvement in the living standards of the majority of the population.

3. Problems of food and energy security have worsened. Projects to build the hydro power facilities are capital intensive and have required foreign investment. The creation of a unified national transport network is a key challenge for the government. This will also require foreign investment.

4. There is only limited interest in Tajikistan from foreign investors and the amount of investments made is correspondingly small. Proximity to Afghanistan, social problems, and drug trafficking are all factors deterring foreign investors. However, they help the country attract aid in the form of gifts, grants, and soft loans both from countries as well as from humanitarian and international organizations and Islamic funds.

5. Tajikistan is keen to maintain thriving relationships with its neighbors involving investment and trade cooperation. It is also keen to play an active part in regional organizations, seeking to benefit with support for large-scale economic projects such a power plants and its transport infrastructure.

6. Economic ties with Russia and other former Soviet countries are important. Russia is the priority as it is seen as a potential investor in

the country's large energy projects, some of which date from the Soviet era.

Questions

1. What are the peculiar features of the sectoral make-up of Tajikistan's economy?
2. What particular problems does Tajikistan face in the area of energy?
3. Describe the state of the country's agro-industrial sector, in particular cotton growing.
4. What role does foreign capital play in the economy of Tajikistan?
5. Describe Tajikistan's foreign economic relationships, especially that with Russia.

Sources of additional information

The Social and Economic Situation of the Republic of Tajikistan. January–February. Agency on Statistics under President of the Republic of Tajikistan. 2014.

Martha Olcott. Tajikistan. Difficult development path. Moscow, Time. 2014 (in Russian).

The Commonwealth of Independent States in 2016. Moscow.2017.

Years that have changed Central Asia. Ed. by I. Zvyagelskaya. Moscow, 2009 (in Russian).

Post-Soviet States: 25 years of Independent Development. Vol. 1. Western Flank of the CIS. Central Asia. M. IMEMO, 2017 (in Russian).

www.eurasianet.org

www.nbt.tj (National Bank of Tajikistan).

www.stat.tj (Agency on Statistics under President of the Republic of Tajikistan).

CHAPTER 31

TURKMENISTAN

During the Soviet era Turkmenistan made considerable strides in transforming itself from a tribal way of life to a modern agro-industrial society. Even so, as the beginning of the 1990s, natural resources was still the dominant force in the country's economy and the general level of development in the industrial, agricultural, and financial sectors was low. As a result, the demise of the Soviet Union appeared to leave Turkmenistan in crisis, made worse by the departure of many of the country's Russian-speaking population who made a significant proportion of the qualified personnel. The new regime was formed along the traditional lines of focusing on strong individual power. This dominated the public sector and led to poor economic management. Poor management was also a feature of the public statistical service and, as a result, serious analysis of the country's economy during this period is difficult due to a lack of reliable official data, often conflicting with other evidence. This situation continued until 2007. All statistics cited on Turkmenistan should, therefore, be regarded as estimates.

The Economic Model

From the very beginning of the 1990s, Turkmenistan set about forming an economic model that differed from all other former Soviet countries. Its long-term goal was to create a market economy. But the early priority was to help the country make the social and psychological adjustment to the principles of private property, an idea which had historically not been a feature of Turkmen society. The public sector assumed a leadership role in bringing this transformation about, leading to the emergence of state paternalism.

Up to 2007, the Turkmen economic model was a curious mixture of Soviet, Uzbek, and Iranian characteristics. In particular, it borrowed from Iran a strong form of populism (these were also the early days in the formation of the Iranian model). But, in contrast with Uzbekistan and Iran, Turkmenistan began to adopt a more rigid enforced centralized economy, in which populist measures became less and less relevant to the emerging market framework (e.g., free electricity, gas, and water). As part of the transition to the new market model, the state set about liberalizing prices, and privatizing state assets in a bid to attract foreign investment. In seeking to attract foreign business and investment, the government professed itself to be guided by a principle of 'limited protectionism.'

A feature of the Turkmen model was said to be the formation of various forms of ownership. Land and subsoil resources remained in state hands, but there was a lack of clarity over rules for land use and whether land occupied by privatized entities belonged to them or not. In other countries of Central Asia, the early stages in the formation of new economic models put an emphasis on support for private business. By contract, this was not a priority for Turkmenistan, especially in the industrial sector.

New market institutions such as banks and a stock exchange were formally established. At the same time privatized enterprises were not granted economic independence. Indeed, privatization was only effective in agriculture, trade, and other branches of the services sector. In agriculture, agricultural workers were granted homesteads and they began to create private farms on what had been collective farm lands.

Efforts to attract foreign capital were made largely according to the whim and personal preferences of the country's leaders with a focus on friendly countries and companies. Nonetheless, the country's highly promising energy resources proved a considerable draw for foreign investors and the inflows of their capital sparked economic recovery and high rates of growth.

In 2003, Turkmenistan signed up to the Millennium Development Goals Declaration (first adopted by the United Nations in 2000) as part of its 'Strategy for Economic, Political, and Cultural Development in Turkmenistan up to 2020' which emphasized an increase in living standards and improving the country's standing on the human development index.

However, the reality fell short of the promises. The political leadership was unable to overcome the country's systemic crisis, even despite high growth rates. Following the death of President Niyazov in 2006, there was an easing of the authoritarian approach to power and a strengthening of economic liberalization, especially in relation to small businesses. Various stock exchanges, including currency exchanges, were set up and this made the national currency, the manat (T), more convertible. A new national program of economic development running from 2011 to 2030 was adopted with an emphasis on increasing the efficiency of the private sector and attracting more foreign investment and business people.

It is true that the country's economic model remains generally very centralized, with excessive state regulation and a significant amount of state ownership. But, seen in the context of the traditional approaches to economic life, the progress made in 20 years to transform the country from a centralized planned model to a market-oriented economy is impressive, especially as it has been achieved largely without the social and political conflicts seen in other former Soviet countries.

The National Economy

According to national statistics, GDP in 1995 was half what it had been in 1991. Recovery with high growth rates kicked in after 1998. Between 2000 and 2015, the average annual rate of growth was 8.8%. During the global crisis of 2008 and 2009, GDP fell, but returned to growth in 2010.

Table 31.1 — GDP in Turkmenistan

	2000	2008	2012	2013	2015	2016	2018*	2020*
GDP, US$ bn	4.4	28.8	35.2	41.9	35.9	36.2	-	-
GNI PPP per capita, US$	3,900	8,070	11,050	12,920	16,533	16060	-	-
GDP rate of growth, %	18.6	14.7	11.1	10.2	6.5	6.2	6.3	6.3

*Estimate

Sources: Interstate Statistical Committee of the Commonwealth of Independent States (http//www.cisstat.org).
World Bank. World Development Indicators 2017.
World Bank. The Global Economic Prospects. Jan. 2018.
State Statistics Committee of Turkmenistan (www.stat.gov.tm).

Turkmenistan's economic prospects rest largely on its gas industry which, in turn, depends heavily on world energy markets. In fact, Turkmenistan's vulnerability to world markets is higher than in other former Soviet countries. The fuel and energy complex provides 35% of GDP (70% of the country's industrial production and 15% of employment). In fact, the real contribution may well be higher than these statistics suggest.

Economic Policy

As noted, after the change of leadership in 2006, the country embarked on a policy to accelerate economic reforms and see the country more integrated into the world economy. To achieve this, between 2008 and 2015, particular effort was made to establishing a legal basis for business, both domestic and foreign. The state adopted a program to support small and medium-sized businesses between 2011 and 2015. This gave considerable tax breaks and other forms of assistance to businesses. A new law on foreign direct investment came into force in 2008. Measures were enacted to reform the financial sector and increase the external activities of the country's enterprises. A unified rate of exchange was also introduced.

However, the transition to market disciplines of management has progressed very slowly; in 2016, Turkmenistan was placed 174st on the Index of Economic Freedom. The economic strategy hopes to transform the country into a transit hub in Central Asia, along with the development of the energy sector.

The state has maintained complete control over key industries in the economy such as oil and gas, energy, and finance. State-owned industries account for 80% of GDP, about half of which is fuel and energy. Certain other sectors have as much as 56% in private hands which government development programs expect to rise to 70% by 2020 (though this will not include oil and gas).

In 2011, in conjunction with the Union of Industrialists and Entrepreneurs of Turkmenistan, a commercial bank, Rysgal, was set up to provide support for individual entrepreneurs. From 2012, soft loans have been available to small and medium-sized businesses at 5% interest for a guaranteed period of 10 years, the number of entrepreneurs in this economic sector has been growing. A new law on microfinancing was adopted in 2011 to support smaller businesses.

The issue of the private ownership of land remains unresolved. The process of granting land to rural residents (up to 50 hectares of land and up to 500 hectares in long-term rent) has been rolled out gradually. So far, foreign investors have only been able to rent land. Until 2007, foreign investors had to form a joint venture to invest. Since that date, they have been permitted to form independent companies.

Like all countries of Central Asia, Turkmenistan has a large informal economy, made worse by the low level of economic freedom and the high level of government corruption. Turkmenistan finds itself near the bottom of the global Corruption Perception Index. The smuggling of Afghan drugs is a particularly profitable area of illegal trade. Turkmenistan has become one of the main transit routes for drugs between Russia and Europe. A wide range of people and organizations, including governmental, are involved in the trade.

Human Capital

During the 1990s, Turkmenistan's population grew by an annual average of 2.8% but thereafter the growth rate more than halved and stood at 1.1% in 2014. The 1995 census put the population at 4.5 million. Estimates for 2014 have it at 5.2 million. The rural population, which makes up 50.3% of the total, is concentrated on oases along the rivers; the vast Kara Kum Desert region is sparsely populated. In 1989 there was estimated to be 336,000 Russians in Turkmenistan, but this fell dramatically to 100,000 by the turn of the century. The population of working age is about 70% of the total, 3.6 million, with no more than 2.5 million in employment. Official statistics put the unemployment rate at 3–5%, but in reality it is likely to be as much as 10 times higher.

The literacy level in Turkmenistan is over 99%, but the level of those who have at least an elementary education is relatively low at 85%. In recent years, investment in education has increased; in 2014, it stood at 4.3% of GDP. The time spent in school has increased. There are more than 20 universities, all of them public. The largest is the Turkmen State University.

The Real Sector

Agriculture contributes less than 8% of GDP, some estimates suggest it employs about half of the population. The main crop is cotton; Turkmenistan is among the world's top ten cotton growers by size of crop. After cotton the main crops are grains: wheat, barley, corn, and rice.

The level of state intervention in agriculture remains high. The government sets agricultural prices, oversees the use of water resources, and even directs the times of sowing. There is a system to recruit school pupils and university students as unpaid labor at harvest time. In addition, private producers of cotton and grain can access soft loans from the state and be exempt from income tax. Finally, the state will pay up to 50% of the cost of seeds, mineral fertilizers, chemicals, and technical services.

In more recent years, the state has reduced its intervention in the sector, but increased its investment in its infrastructure (roads, irrigation etc.). This includes the social infrastructure. Land tax is charged at nominal rates and farms can be exempt from other taxes. Moreover, electricity, gasoline, and diesel are provided free of charge.

The Tajik food industry is dominated by flour and feed milling, as well as meat packing. Up to half of all food consumed in prepared within domestic households.

The largest contribution to GDP comes from the energy and fuel complex, though the sector only employs 15% of the working population. The sector is dominated by the gas industry which was established during the 1960s and 1970s. During the 1990s, production fell sharply, but recovered once deliveries to Russia started again. The start of the production of liquefied gas at Turkmenbashi (Krasnovodsk) has also boosted the sector.

At 17.5 trillion cubic meters, Turkmenistan's gas reserves are among the largest in the world. Of the reserves, 6 trillion cubic meters are on the Caspian Sea shelf. One of the largest gas fields is at Galkynysh. The fields at Southern Iolotan, Minara, and others were combined into Galkynysh in 2011. Oil reserves are much smaller, estimated at 100 million tons.

Gas production has grown and now stands at 70 billion cubic meters a year, only 20 billion of which is consumed in the country. Gas exports have traditionally gone to Russia, but in recent years Iran and China have also been taking Turkmen imports. Gas production is currently managed as a monopoly by Turkmengaz, a state holding company. The opening of the Galkynysh field in 2001, has strengthened the position of Turkmenistan in world markets.

Oil production, in 2015, totaled 13 million tons, compared with the 15 million tons achieved during the Soviet era. The country's oil production is facing the problems depleting reserves, outdated equipment, and insufficient geological prospecting data. Much of the country's oil and gas reserves are buried very deep, more than 3.5 km down, requiring special equipment to be extracted. In addition, many of the deposits have a high concentration of hydrogen sulfide (1% and above) that requires additional processing. Oil production remains largely under the control of the state, with foreign companies producing less than a quarter of the total.

With a greater focus on the export of refined rather than crude oil, Turkmenistan has made large investments in oil refining and petrochemical production. The reconstructed Turkmenbashi oil refinery is the country's largest. Both this, and the second largest refinery at Seidinsky, have become modern facilities with high value-added production. In 2007, Dragon Oil brought on stream the first refinery under foreign ownership. Agreements to build further petrochemical facilities have been signed with Japanese firms.

Electricity generation in Turkmenistan is based largely on thermal power plants using gas. About 20 bn kWh is produced, with just 17 bn kWh being used and the excess being exported. Over half of it goes to Iran and the rest to Afghanistan and Turkey.

The country's chemical industry operates mostly on domestic raw materials, for example, the glauber salt, mirabilite, found in the Kara-Bogaz-Gol Gulf is known around the world. Successful operations include the production of mirabilite (by the Karabogazsulfat Company) and iodine, while the refining of oil and gas to remove sulfur impurities is also developing well. Other products include sulfates of sodium, potassium, magnesium, iodine compounds (at the Chelikentsky and Nebitdagsky plants), technical carbon, plastics, and mineral fertilizers. There is a large nitrogen fertilizer plant in Chardzhou.

The mechanical engineering sector is dominated by small firms, as was the case during the Soviet era, producing equipment for the oil refining industry, pumps, cables, and other equipment for light industry.

There is a significant textile industry, 90% of which is owned by Turkish investors. Thirteen large textile complexes have been built since 1991. Turkish-style traditional handmade carpets are popular around the world.

The development of the construction industry has relied heavily on public investment. The capacity to produce materials for the construction industry has increased. Cement is produced in Bezmein, glass in Ashgabat, reinforced concrete in Mary and Bezmein. A plant to make rolled iron has opened in Ovadandep with Turkish investment. In other former Soviet countries, it was the construction of new houses that drove growth in the construction industry. In Turkmenistan's case it was driven more by a series of ambitious projects developed by the country's former leaders. For example, in 2000, work began to construct the Altyn Asyr reservoir, a unique hydro-technical project, at Kara Kum. Its stated aim was to address the problem of soil salination in bog soils and irrigation systems, but it had wider propaganda purposes as did the construction of grandiose buildings and monuments in the country's capital. Since 2007, the largest construction projects have been cotton mills, new power lines, gas pipelines (one connecting the country with Uzbekistan, Kazakhstan, and China and another, Dovletabad–Searkhs–Hangeran with come into operation in 2010), social infrastructure, and the construction of the Olympic complex in Ashgabat.

The country's cargo is mostly carried by rail. The southern part of the country is crossed by the Trans-Caspian railroad (Turkmenbashi–Ashgabat–Samarkand). The Chardzhou–Tashauz–Makat line gives Turkmenistan access to Russia. In 1996, the Serakhs–Mashhad line gave Turkmenistan access to the Iranian rail network and, through that, to the Indian Ocean and the Persian Gulf. During the 2000s, a rail line was built through the country's central region (Ashgabat–Kara Kum–Dashoguz). This 900 km line would connect Turkmenistan with Iran, Kazakhstan, and Russia.

The country's main highways are generally paved and follow similar routes to the railways, forming part of the international transport corridor that crosses Turkmenistan from north to south. Ferry traffic is also important; there are two sea crossings from Turkmenbashi to Makhachkala and to Baku. The Karakum irrigation canal and the Amu Darya river are used for inland navigation.

Pipelines play an important role, carrying about a half of the country's exports. There are 7,500 km of pipelines for gas and 1,500 km for oil. The main pipeline is the Central Asia–Center gas pipeline to Iran. Construction of a major pipeline to China has been completed and, in 2015, a Declaration on Energy Cooperation was signed between Turkmenistan, Turkey, Azerbaijan, and the EU. This has again generated interest in the idea of a Trans-Caspian gas pipeline along the seas-bed to Azerbaijan. Turkmenistan has repeatedly expressed its willingness to participate in implementing the project known at TAPI (Turkmenistan–Afghanistan–Pakistan–India).

In recent years, the use of mobile communications has increased. In 2012, the number of people using mobile devices stood at 4 million, compared with the country's 460,000 fixed phone lines. The Russian MTS company has a major stake in this sector alongside domestic suppliers. Internet use is growing but still lags behind other countries. Turkmenistan did not see its first Internet café until 2007.

The Financial Sector

The banking system remains under strict control by the state. The Central Bank of Turkmenistan oversees the system which has five state banks: Vnesheconombank (the country's largest commercial bank), Turkmenistan Bank, Turkmenbashi Bank, Daykhanbank, and Halkbank. There are also four private banks, including the Turkish-Turkmen Agricultural (Ziraat) Rysgal.

The state distributes money equivalent to just 17% of GDP (2014 figures). Budget receipts come mainly from the oil and gas sectors. The state budget is made up of the central budget (93% of the total) and local budgets (e.g., the budgets of Ashgabat and Velayats). There are a wide variety of different state funds which complicates the exercise of control over the budget. Until 2008, most of the money from the oil and gas sector (about 80%) was channeled into the Foreign Exchange Reserve Fund (FERF), which was under the direct supervision of the former state president. Money from this fund was spent on grandiose schemes mention above such as the construction of the Kara Kum reservoir, dredging the river in Ashgabat, construction of a large mosque in the home village of President Niyazov (at a cost of US$100 million), and the construction of five-star hotels and opulent government buildings in the capital. In 2008, the Stabilization Fund of Turkmenistan was set up based on the budget surplus. Its objective was to fund projects that would help reduce the country's vulnerability to fluctuations in world energy prices. Between 2000 and 2014, the country ran a budget surplus, equivalent to more than 1% of GDP. Sources of income other than oil and gas are relatively small. The level of taxation is moderate. VAT is charged at between 0 and 15%. Individual income and corporation tax are both levied at 10%. Foreign companies face 20% tax.

More than half of the state budget goes on social spending. Transport, fuel, and utilities are subsidized. Spending on education is equivalent to 4.3% of GDP, while that on health care is equivalent to 1.1%.

Official statistics only included inflation for the first time in 2007 when it measured 6%. In 2008, it reached 18%. Between 2013 and 2016, consumer price inflation was estimated to be 5–6% a year and is forecast to remain at that level until 2020.

The External Sector

Turkmenistan's official statistics do not include data about the country's trade balance or the balance of payments. High prices for energy products, the export of which provides the government with 90% of its revenues, produced a positive balance during the 2000s which led to growth in the official reserves. By the start of 2014, they were estimated to be US$22.35 bn. External debt, estimated in 2012 to be US$0.4 bn, was equivalent to just 1.2% of GDP.

Turkmenistan left the ruble zone in 1993 and established its own currency, the manat. The exchange rate at which Turkmen companies were obliged to see most of their foreign currency was fixed. At the same time, any purchases of currency at the fixed rate to repay currency credits, to repatriate the profits of foreign investors, or to pay for imports was only possible with the personal permission of the president. The exchange rate was allowed to float in 2008 but was fixed again from 2009. The currency was redenominated and the exchange rate of US$1/T2.85 was set and remains in place.

After independence Turkmenistan's external policy has as its main aim to reduce the country's dependence on Russia, to expand relations with Turkey and Iran, to establish relations with the former Soviet countries in Central Asia, and to develop trade, economic, and investment relationships with the EU and the USA. In foreign and economic relations, Turkmenistan adopted a neutral stance and a resolution on the permanent neutrality of Turkmenistan was adopted by the United Nations General Assembly in 1995. In 2005, Turkmenistan withdrew from permanent membership of the CIS, becoming instead an associate member. Since 2007, the country has been actively trying to improve its international image. To do this, it has increased its activity in international and regional economic organizations and in international energy and transport initiatives in the hope of capitalizing as much as possible on its potential in these areas. In 2013, a special commission was established to look into the issues surrounding the country's eventual entry into the WTO.

One of the main objectives of the country's foreign economic policy is to diversify the range of markets to which it exports gas. It hopes to capitalize on the desire in Europe and the USA to reduce their dependence on imports of gas from Russia. In addition, Turkmenistan has focused efforts on exporting gas to Iran and China. In 2006, Turkmenistan and China signed an agreement to construct a pipeline to China capable of carrying 30 billion cubic meters of gas. A number of subsequent agreements were signed and the first phase of the pipeline came on stream in 2009, with the second following at the end of 2010. Since 2011, China has become Turkmenistan's largest market for gas, taking 51% of the country's exports. In 2013, around 27 billion cubic meters were exported to China and nine million to Iran. Russia no longer figures as a market for Turkmenistan.

Foreign credit and direct investments are both significant features of the country's capital inflows. Direct investment has been coming into Turkmenistan since the early 1990s. By 2015, the volume of accumulated foreign direct investment stood at US$32.1 bn, up from less than US$1 bn prior to 2000. This provided between 31 and 47% of all investment into fixed assets. Foreign investment was generally targeted at the fuel industry, but also into communications and data transmission (with the Russian company MTS and other Chinese companies involved) and the textile industry (with the involvement of Turkish companies).

While not restricting foreign capital, the Turkmen leadership still seeks to maintain administrative and financial control over foreign companies. Foreign exchange transactions have to be conducted through authorized banks with a license from the central bank. There is no limit on the import or export of foreign currency. Foreign companies operate without a clear definition of their legal status, and that status can often change. Many companies making large investments have now withdrawn from the market, and those companies that have managed to gain a foothold in Turkmenistan have to operate almost behind closed doors. For foreign companies, direct contacts with the former president were the key to success. The new leadership initiated new laws on foreign investment and the exploitation of hydrocarbon resources in 2008 which brought the country more into line with international practice. Under this new regime, foreign investors gained the right to set up wholly owned enterprises, not just joint ventures. They are now also able to acquire movable and real estate assets. There is a light-touch regulatory regime for foreign exchange transactions for those investors participating in the oil and gas sectors. As a result, the large international oil companies have stepped up their work in the country.

The turnover of foreign trade is equivalent to about 50% of GDP (2016). Between 2000 and 2014, the turnover increased by 750%, giving the country a large positive balance in its foreign trade. In 2014, the value of exports was US$19.8 bn compared with US$16.6 bn of imports. The list of items exported is relatively short with energy resources accounting for about 90% of the total in 2012 (gas alone is more than 65%; crude oil, 7%; and oil products 17.5%). The only other export item of any note is cotton, with 5% of the total. In the case of imports, 80% of the total is accounted for my equipment and semi-finished products for industry. Consumer goods make up the remaining 20%.

Turkmenistan's largest trade partners are China, Russia, Iran, and Turkey. Between 2007 and 2012, trade with China, which became the main buyer of Turkmen gas, grew almost twentyfold. As well as its major foothold in the gas market, China has also increased its exports to Turkmenistan through the granting of trade loans.

Turkmenistan has a relatively closed economy. So, to expand its foreign economic relations, the country decided to create more than 10 free economic zones. But the only one that has operated effectively is the Avaza tourist zone in Turkmenbashi which, in its role as a center for tourism and leisure, has helped improve economic relations with the other Caspian states.

An early goal for Turkmenistan following its independence, was to achieve economic independence from Russia. However, much of its gas was exported through the Russian Central Asian system. But, between 2012 and 2015, as China became the major buyer of Turkmen gas and deliveries to Iran also increased, Russia's purchases of gas and oil from Turkmenistan decreased. Even so, Russia remains second behind China in Turkmenistan's foreign trade turnover, accounting for 15% of the total in 2013. Nearly half, 44%, of Russian exports to Turkmenistan are equipment and vehicles. Metals and metal ware make up 30%. Russia imports polypropylene and textiles. In fact, it takes 70% of all Turkmenistan's textile exports.

The Social Sector

The population of Turkmenistan suffers a generally low standard of living. This is despite low prices (one liter of gasoline costing just 2¢) and largely free utilities in municipal housing. Between 2007 and 2013, the average salary of workers almost trebled to stand at approximately US$288 a month. But about 58% of the population lives below the poverty line, with rural areas suffering particularly hard. For example, even bread supplies can sometimes be interrupted despite official statistics showing growing crops of grain.

Between 1990 and 2007, the number of educational and health care institutions actually fell. But a series of educational reforms were begun in 2007 and, since then, investment into equipment for schools has increased, and children must now spend 10 years in school.

Conclusion

1. Oil and gas dominate Turkmenistan's economy. The economy's sectoral structure is focused on exploiting the country's raw materials.

2. Turkmenistan's economic model has been formed in the context of the authoritarian character of political power. Up until 2007, the country pursued a peculiar model which combined rigid state regulation with widely populist measures. This was accompanied by a stage-by-stage approach to privatization where the emphasis was placed on attracting foreign investment and the establishment of institutions that, while based on those found in more open markets, were not able to operate in the same way. Economic reform has accelerated since 2007 across all industries. However, the country continues to operate a very centralized economy, with excessive state regulation and significant public ownership.

3. Turkmenistan's external economic relations are defined by its political choice to remain neutral and maintain good relations with its principal trading partners. Relying as it does on making the most of its gas resources, Turkmenistan has a keen interest in the development of regional transport and pipeline networks. For this reason, it seeks to play an active role in economic regional organizations.

4. Turkmenistan's relations with Russia now center on the coordination of gas transportation routes, on the import of Russian industrial products, and on working together in regional economic organizations.

Questions

1. What are the main drivers of Turkmenistan's economic development?
2. Describe the potential for growth of the country's oil and gas industry. What role has Turkmenistan played in the implementation of projects related to energy resources on the Caspian Sea?
3. Describe the level of state intervention in the Turkmen economy.
4. What position does foreign capital enjoy in the Turkmen economy?
5. Describe Turkmenistan's foreign economic relations, in particular those with Russia.

Sources of additional information

Years that have changed Central Asia. Ed. by I. Zvyagelskaya. Moscow. 2009 (in Russian).

Dzhumaev. I. The Foreign Trade of Turkmenistan: trends, problems and prospects. University of Central Asia. Ashkhabad, 2012.

Turkmenistan economy: thorny way to market. The Public Finance Monitoring Center. Baku. 2010.

The Statistical Yearbook of Turkmenistan 2012. The State Statistics Committee of Turkmenistan

The Central Asia: role in the restructuring of oil and natural gas world markets. 2014 (in Russian).

Turkmenistan. Diversifying The Turkmen Economy. Document of the World Bank. August, 2014

Post-Soviet States:25 years of Independent Development. Vol.1. Western Flank of the CIS. Central Asia. M. IMEMO, 2017

www.stat.gov.tm (State Statistics Committee of Turkmenistan).

www.cbt.tm (Central Bank of Turkmenistan).

www.Turkmenistan.ru.

CHAPTER 32

UZBEKISTAN

Uzbekistan's Economic Model

Uzbekistan developed considerable economic potential during the Soviet era thanks to targeted inflows of resources from the federal center. By the end of the 1980s, direct subsidies made up 20% of its GDP. This does not take into account hidden subsidization of the prices of energy resources and industrial inputs.

Uzbekistan's economy was well integrated into the union-wide economy of the Soviet Union. But, it still had a plentiful domestic market which was one of the reasons that Uzbekistan saw a lower fall in GDP—18%—than other former Soviet countries after the demise of the Soviet Union.

The country set about creating a new economic model, built on the country's traditional features of management and entrepreneurship. The new state maintained an authoritarian form of government and chose to embark on a process of gradual economic reform. In the initial stages, the state maintained a significant role in both economic and social life.

Uzbekistan followed the Chinese experience, especially at the initial stage of reform, by placing emphasis on shifting the public sector to a more market-oriented model, while at the same time encouraging the private sector to develop. This Uzbek model represents a peculiarly eastern form of state capitalism in which the state remains the main initiator and guarantor of reforms. At the same time a number of financially powerful families or clans (between three and seven) retain substantial influence on economic policy.

Ministries and state departments were transformed into state holdings, owning the country's strategically important economic entities. At the same time, state and collective farms were privatized along with small and medium-sized enterprises, while the state set about giving large-scale support to the newly created class of owners, businessmen who had been able to acquire leases on state property.

The reorganization of state and collective farms was an example of this model of privatization. State farms were transformed into joint stock companies to carry out commercial farming. But the land was divided and assigned to the families working on it. Collective farms were turned into shirkatas (partnerships). The land was assigned to the shirkata in perpetuity, with each member (being a family) allocated a certain section of the land each year for a designated crop. Part of the land that had belonged to the collective farms was allocated to the formation of dehkan (farm) holdings which led to the growth of more market-oriented farms. They were given land on long-term leases and this set-up became profitable. For the purposes of official statistics, they are classed as belonging to the private sector. They now account for 85% of all land under cultivation, 94% of all agricultural production and 99% of the main crop, cotton.

The gradual saturation of the domestic market and the introduction of a new national currency in 1994 reduced the level of state intervention in pricing and accelerated the formation of national businesses. But, at the same time, these changes strengthened the state's control over the currency market. The acceleration of economic liberalism has been more noticeable since 2001, including in the area of currency markets. The process has seen greater privatization of state medium and large-scale enterprises and has involved measures to reduce dramatically the level of administrative regulation of the economy. As a result, by 2014, the state was responsible for just 17.1% of GDP.

Official accounts of Uzbekistan's transition highlight five principles: 'de-ideologization' and pragmatism of economic policy; the importance of the state's role as the main instigator of reform; the supremacy of law; strong social policy; and a gradual approach to staging the reform process. The ultimate goal is a diversified economy, fundamentally changing its structure, and the formation of new, export-oriented industries, along with modern market infrastructure.

The National Economy

In terms of economic potential, Uzbekistan comes second to Kazakhstan in Central Asia. Although it has the larger population (the third largest among former Soviet countries) its GDP lags far behind as does its low level of GNI per capita.

Uzbekistan was one of the first former Soviet countries to overcome the economic recession that followed independence. Economic growth began in earnest in 1996. Between 2000 and 2016, average annual growth in GDP was 7.5%. The country also fared better than the other Central Asian countries in the last economic crisis, demonstrating that it is one of the most dynamic countries among those of the former Soviet Union.

Table 32.1 — GDP in Uzbekistan

	2000	2008	2012	2013	2015	2016	2018*	2020*
GDP, US$ bn	13.5	26.6	51.2	55.2	66.7	67.2	-	-
GNI PPP per capita, US$	1,940	3,870	4,910	5,290	6,087	6640	-	-
GDP rate of growth, %	3.8	9.0	8.2	8.0	8.0	7.8	5.6	6.5

*Estimate

Sources: Interstate Statistical Committee of the Commonwealth of Independent States (http//www.cisstat.org).
World Bank. World Development Indicators 2017.
World Bank. Global Economy Prospects. Jan. 2018.
Major indicators of social and economic development of the Republic of Uzbekistan during 2011–2013, 2014 (www.stat.uz).

Relatively high levels of investment into fixed assets have been one of the main drivers of growth. In 2015, the ratio of gross capital formation to GDP exceeded 24%. Inflows of foreign capital have played a part in this.

Between 1991 and 2013, the country's economy underwent considerable structural changes. The share taken by the primary sector decreased to 18%; the secondary sector grew to 30% as a result of industrialization. But the tertiary sector grew to 52% largely thanks to the development of modern services such as banking, insurance, and communications.

The country's economic policy had as its main aim the recovery from recession and the building of a modern market economy. This was to be achieved in a gradual way, under state control. The approach proved to be generally productive; Uzbekistan achieved a measure of macroeconomic stability and was able to carry out the important transformation of ownership structures.

Since the middle of the 2000s, the country's economic policy has had a number of key objectives: deeper structural transformation; further rowing back of the state's participation in the economy; modernization and reform of the financial sector; and the achievement of greater balance between relations with Russia and the West. Despite all this, in 2016, Uzbekistan was ranked 87th in the Doing Business list of countries according to how favorable they are to business.

The public sector still has a noticeable share of the economy: 17% in 2014. The state sector also controls about 7% of industry and 65% of transport.

State support for small businesses in the wake of the financial crisis of 2008 has seen this sector increase its share of GDP from 31% in 2000 to 56% in 2013. Small businesses account for 98% of the agricultural sector, 71.5% of construction, but just 46% of trade, 28% of industry, and 33% of investments. These businesses provide 77% of all employment, mainly in agriculture. They receive tax support, with their main tax rate cut from 15.2% to 6%, and soft loans.

Joint ventures, set up with foreign investment, have been playing an increasing role in the economy. In 2015, Uzbekistan had over 4,000 companies with investment from over 90 different countries. However, the data available on large businesses is highly inconsistent.

The black or unobserved economy, according to official estimates employs about 20% of the available workforce. Unofficial estimates put its share of the national economy at somewhere between 40 and 60%.

Human Capital

Uzbekistan has the largest population among the countries of the region, 31.3 million (2016). Moreover, its share of the regional population is increasing as the annual rate of growth in the population (1.7% in 2015) is beaten only by Kyrgyzstan (2.1%) and Tajikistan (2.2%). However, between 2013 and 2015, national statistics show a 1% decrease in the population, with the urban population overtaking the rural.

Of the 17 million people in the workforce, 26% work in agriculture, 13% in industry and construction, and 61% in services. Real employment is high (more than 20%), though official figures put it at 4.8% (2015).

Official Russian data suggest that, measured in 2015, 2.2 million Uzbek citizens were working in Russia. Other estimates suggest the figure could be higher, up to 5 million. This represents a third of the working-age population of Uzbekistan. In addition, between 100,000 and 200,000 Uzbek migrants work on Kazakhstan and the border regions of Kyrgyzstan.

The level of literacy in Uzbekistan is relatively high at more than 99%. There is a well-developed system of higher education with more than 30 state universities, the largest being Tashkent State University. Recently, the government has been seeking to increase the number of vocational schools. The country is also home to some madrasah (Islamic religious schools) and religious higher education establishments.

The Real Sector

The private sector dominates agriculture, with a mix of 'dehkan' (farming households) and farms. In 2014, the dehkan households accounted for 65% of overall production, with farms providing 33% and other agricultural enterprises 2%. However, it should be noted that farms produce 99% of raw cotton and about 80% of grain.

One of the main problems facing the agricultural sector is land parceling, the way in which land is divided into small plots. At the initial stage of the reform of the state farms, the small plots allocated to dekhans and farms have proved to be a limiting factor on attempts to improve efficiency in agricultural production. The state started to address this issue in 2013 by increasing the average size of the plots allocated to farms producing cotton and grain from 37 to 94 hectares.

Arable farming consists of two main crops: grain (48%), the majority of which is wheat, and cotton (36%). In 2014, Uzbekistan was the world's sixth largest producer of cotton, and the fifth largest exporter. However, in recent decades, the structure of agricultural production has been shifting to include more food crops, with wheat predominating. This has seen production of grain crops increase from less than 1 million to more than 8 million tons. Of the total cost of agricultural production, about 9% is spent on cotton, 9% on grain, 42% on vegetables and grapes, and 40% on animal husbandry. A large proportion of the crops is bought by the state: 40% of the grain harvest and 100% of the cotton. During the 2000s, Uzbekistan was among the world's top ten exporters of fruit and vegetables.

The country now faces a problem in the need to modernize the way in which the ecological equilibrium of the land is maintained. This is particularly the case for land used to grow cotton which has become saturated by chemical fertilizers. There will be no solution to this problem without state intervention.

Uzbekistan's food industry has developed using the country's own agricultural raw materials and now accounts for 16% of the all industrial output. The textile industry accounts for 14%, which includes cotton fiber, cotton yarn, fabrics (including natural silks), knitted goods, and carpets. A large proportion of the textile industry is operated by the Uzbekendgilsanoat state group which owns 305 enterprises, 253 of which are small private businesses. Textiles products go both to the domestic market as well as to export, thus reducing the exports of raw cotton. The percentage of cotton fiber that is processed locally increased from 7% in 1991 to 44% in 2014.

Uzbekistan's proven oil reserves total 100 million tons. The largest deposit, Kokdumalakskoye, provides about 70% of current production. However, most of the 85 oil fields have only small reserves. The proven reserves of gas total 1.1 trillion cubic meters. Most of the gas extracted, 95%, comes from the three largest fields at Gazli, Shurtanskoye, and Alanskoye. In the case of Gazli, new fields were opened there in 2013 and 2014. Uzbekistan is only the 20th largest in the world in terms of gas reserves. Moreover, most of the country's gas has a high sulfur content and needs additional processing to clean it. Industry efficiency also suffers from having a large number of small fields scattered around the country. At 1.9 billion tons, coal reserves are substantial. The largest deposits (of brown coal) are in the Angrensky field. In addition, Uzbekistan has the world's 7th largest reserves of uranium, with the Uchkuduksk field being the largest. There is also considerable potential for hydro power on the Chirchik, Sur-handarya, Angren, and a number of other small rivers. As such, the country has a strong natural base from which to develop its fuel and energy complex, which already makes up 20% of industrial output.

Uzbekistan is among the world's top 20 producers of natural gas. In 2015, natural gas production was 58 billion cubic meters, about 50 billion of which was used in the country, with the rest exported to Russia, Kazakhstan, Tajikistan, and China. The country's gas needs to be processed to remove impurities and there are several plants where this is performed. A new gas-chemical complex is being developed at Ust-Yurtovsk which will be the largest in Central Asia. Uzbekistan's oil and gas industry is controlled by the Uzbekneftegaz holding company which owns six joint stock companies engaged all stages of the industry: from geological exploration to the processing of oil and gas.

The current situation with regard to oil production is more difficult. Firstly, the key operating fields have been largely exhausted. But, while the production of oil and gas condensate has gradually declined (down to 3 million tons in 2015), consumption has been growing (reaching 2.8 million tons in 2015). The oil refineries at Fergana, the modernization of which was completed in 2000 with Japanese investment, and Bukhara are working with domestically produced oil and gas condensate. The Navoi mining and smelting complex in Uchkuduk which is state-owned has a monopoly on the production of uranium. It produces low-enriched uranium all of which is exported as Uzbekistan does not have a domestic nuclear industry.

Non-ferrous metals also have an important role in the economy, accounting for 9% of industrial output. This involves the production and processing of gold, silver, and polymetallic ores. With an annual production of 80 tons, Uzbekistan ranks among the world's largest 10 producers of gold. The Navoi complex produces 70% of the country's gold (2014) and, with modernization, plans to increase its production by developing gold fields in the Kyzyl Kum Desert. The Almalik mining and smelting plant produces 20% of the country's gold, 90% of its silver; it is the only producer of copper and also processes zinc and lead.

Engineering accounts for 20% of the country's output. At the start of the 1990s, the first automobile assembly plant in the country was developed with participation from the South Korean firm Daewoo and the US firm General Motors. Subsequently, the Japanese firm Isuzu was involved in the creation of SamAuto which produces buses and trucks. There are also Russian investors involved in the industry. In 2014, more than 250,000 cars, trucks, and buses rolled off the production line in Uzbekistan. Of these, more than 55,000 were exported—38,000 to Russia.

Plants surviving from the Soviet era continue to produce tractors, tractor cultivators, refrigerators, and deep freezers. In 2013/2014, the Artel company introduced new technologies to improve the production of refrigerators and cell phones.

Construction is carried on by both private and state enterprises. Over the last three years, the construction of gas pipelines has been a dominant feature of the sector. These pipelines follow routes through Uzbekistan and Kazakhstan to China.

Motor transport dominates the country's cargo transport sector, accounting for 91% of the total. Rail transport and pipelines have 4.5% each. In the case of passenger transport, roads dominate the sector with 99% of the total. A unique, two-tunnel highway through the Kamchik pass connecting the Fergana Valley with the central part of the country has been opened.

In developing the transport sector, the country has placed particular importance on integrating its networks into international transport corridors. There are now more than 20 international corridors passing through Uzbekistan, including three rail services, connecting 18 countries in Europe and Asia.

With about 14,000 km, Uzbekistan's pipeline network is long and extensive. In addition, there are 944 km of oil pipelines. There are eight main gas pipelines passing through Uzbekistan, including the international Central Asia–Center pipeline providing gas to Russia. There are also pipelines to Kazakhstan, Kyrgyzstan, Tajikistan, and, via these, China.

The information infrastructure is being upgraded and extended. Though the number of landline users has barely changed in recent years, the number of users of mobile telephone has multiplied many times over and stood at 20.4 million in 2013. The number of Internet users has grown to 4.7 million.

The Financial Sector

The state continues to play an important role in Uzbekistan's financial sector. An independent monetary policy was introduced in 1993 when the country launched its own national currency, the som. Much of the 1990s, as well as the early 2000s, were characterized by high inflation, a depreciation of the som, the introduction of various exchange rates, and rigid controls over currency transactions. The country's financial system was left in a critical condition, with the most serious issue being the backward nature of credit systems leaving many enterprises unpaid. During the 2000s, the situation stabilized, with the government making the stability of the national currency the main objective of its monetary policy. As part of this, an exchange rate permitted to float within a targeted corridor was established. By 2016, inflation had come down to 5.7%.

Since 2005, the government has been actively working to develop the banking system. A key element in this was the expansion of the network of private commercial banks. From 2008, the commercial banks set about buying up shares of enterprises experiencing financial difficulties. State banks also undertook such purchases, leading to an increase in the stock of state property. In an attempt to further strengthen the banking system during the financial crisis of 2008, measures were taken to increase the capital of the leading banks, in particular Asaka, Gallabank, Uzpromstroybank, Pakhtabank, and Mikrocreditbank (specializing in financing small businesses).

In 2014, the country had 30 commercial banks: three state banks, 13 with a majority state holding, nine private banks, and five with some foreign participation. The banking system—and the state banks, in particular—play a role in supporting small businesses and funding export activity with soft loans.

There is a stock exchange in operation. Over-the-counter trading accounts for 4% of the total. Prior to 2008, there was a great deal of secondary market trading. But this fell to just 47% of the total in 2011 and 2012.

The amount of financial resources distributed through the state budget in 2014 was equivalent to 26% of GDP. The consolidated budget consists of the state budget and the off-budget special purpose funds that cover schools, pensions, roads, employment assistance, reconstruction and development, and public property. Over half of tax revenues come from indirect taxes, including: VAT (48%), excise duties (26%). The share provided by direct taxation is less than 26%. The government's tax policy has sought both to unify tax rates and to see them come down. As part of this, between 1994 and 2014, the rate of corporation tax was lowered from 45 to 9%; the uniform social tax from 40 to 24%; the unified tax for farmers and small businesses was introduced with a maximum rate of 6%; and individual tax rates were lowered to 7.5%. The rate of VAT is 20%.

In 2014, the budget was allocated as follows: 59% to social expenses, including education which accounted for 30%; 11.5% to health care; over 20% to investments and other expenses; and a rather high proportion of 6% went on defense.

The lowering of corporate tax rates led to an increase in business activity and, with it, an increase in the amount of tax collected. This, in turn, has enabled the budget to be operated at a surplus. In 2013/2014, the surplus was equivalent to 0.2–0.3% of GDP.

The External Sector

In the 2000s, a combination of factors produced a current account surplus in Uzbekistan: the improvement in world markets for the country's main exported goods; a devaluation of the Uzbek currency; and an increase in the transfers of money from Uzbeks working abroad. The latter element, the transfers of money from overseas by Uzbek migrant workers are an important part of the equation; in 2014 they were equivalent to about 10.5% of GDP. Uzbekistan receives the largest amount of such transfers from Russia—more than US$6 bn in 2014. This has contributed to an increase in Uzbekistan's official reserves from US$10 bn at the beginning of 2009, to US$17 bn by the beginning of 2014.

External debt had climbed to the equivalent of 40% of GDP in 2003 but fell to 23% by 2015, or US$14.8 bn, a level which is not overly onerous for an economy whose exports considerably exceed the level of its debt.

The inflow of foreign investment is an important element in Uzbekistan's economy. They have been pivotal in the creation of new sectors of industry and communication facilities. In the 1990s, loans were the principal form of foreign investment, but there is now greater direct investment. In recent years, the annual inflow of FDI has been about US$0.5–0.6 bn a year. By 2016, the accumulated total of FDI had reached US$9 bn. However, this represents just 7% of the total FDI in all the countries of Central Asia. Uzbekistan still lags far behind Turkmenistan and Kazakhstan. Most of the FDI coming into Uzbekistan goes into the fuel and energy complex, including support for the construction of the main gas pipelines. Gold and rare-metal mining are also important recipients. Three special economic zones have been created to attract FDI: Navoi, Angren, and Jizzakh.

Since the 2000s, the country has enjoyed a positive trade balance, which has allowed imports to grow to about US$14 bn despite a significant level of protectionism in the import regime. Russia is the country's main trading partner, though its importance has been falling; it accounted for 22% of Uzbekistan's trade turnover in 2014. By contrast, China's importance is growing, with 17% of turnover. Kazakhstan with 13% and South Korea with 7% are also important.

Energy and oil, with 26% of the total, were Uzbekistan's main exports in 2014. Service accounted for 21.5%; food products 12%; and cotton with just 7%, a considerable reduction on previous levels. In 2014,

Uzbekistan's main imports were cars and related equipment (40% of the total), chemical products (16%), food products (11%), and ferrous and non-ferrous metals (8%).

As noted, Russia remains Uzbekistan's main economic partner even though its share of Uzbekistan's trade has declined. The total trade turnover in 2014 was US$6.1 bn, of which exports to Russia totaled US$3.2 bn and imports from Russia, US$0.9 bn. Russian exports to Uzbekistan include engineering products, metals, wood, microbiological products, and food. It imports mainly cars (28% of imports), fruit, cotton, and natural gas.

According to Uzbek statistics, between 2008 and 2012, direct Russian investment into Uzbekistan amounted to US$5.5 bn. At the start of 2013, there were 902 companies in Uzbekistan with Russian capital. Of there, 150 were 100% Russian owned. The Russian firms Lukoil and Gazprom work with Uzbekneftegaz. At the end of 2014 the company MTS returned to the Uzbek market. About 75% of Russian FDI in Uzbekistan goes into the fuel and energy complex; the communications sector takes most of the rest. The two countries share an interest in developing new gas fields in Uzbekistan and in expanding the capacity of the Central Asia–Center gas pipeline. At the same time, there are now 489 companies with Uzbek capital operating in Russia.

Russia is home to about 80% of Uzbekistan's emigrant workers. The two countries cooperate in education; the Russian Plekhanov Academy of Economists, MSU, and the Gubkin Russian State University of Oil and Gas have branches in Uzbekistan. As well as their bilateral ties, the two countries work together in regional organizations.

The Social Sector

The majority of the Uzbek population still endure a relatively low standard of living. Unemployment remains a major problem for the country. A third of the rural population lives below the poverty line. There is also significant inequality. See the Gini index figures in Table 7.8. In 2015, the average monthly salary was equal to US$353, though other estimates put it as low as US$232.

The government's main objective in its social programs is to boost employment by, for example, providing work in towns and villages, or providing poor families with cattle.

Conclusion

1. Among the states of Central Asia, Uzbekistan has considerable potential. It has rich natural resources, able to meet its own needs and drive exports. It is well placed to become a regional leader.

2. Uzbekistan has benefited from its own particular model of economic development, combining traditional, Soviet, and market elements. Faced with demographic challenges, the country has prioritized the development of small businesses in all sectors of the economy in order to transform itself into a fully modern economy.

3. The state has controlled economic reform and remained an active player in the country's business activity. The public sector is more prevalent than in other regional countries, though at the same time, the traditional clan structures continue to have an important role. The state has encouraged the use of foreign investment, focusing on Russia and the West, and, more recently, on China.

4. Uzbekistan has sought to diversify its foreign economic relations, looking beyond its immediate region and neighbors. Nonetheless, it continues to maintain close relations with its neighbors, capitalizing on good transport and pipeline communications. Its regional partners, including Russia, will continue to be important to its national interests.

Questions

1. Describe the role of the state in Uzbekistan's economy.

2. What is the potential of the country's oil and gas sector? What role does Uzbekistan play in projects to develop Kazakh and Turkmen energy resources?

3. What are the main challenges facing Uzbekistan's agricultural sector and how are these being addressed?

4. What role does foreign investment play in Uzbekistan?

5. How would you characterize Uzbekistan's foreign economic relations, including those with Russia?

Sources of additional information

Years that have changed Central Asia. Ed. by I. Zvyagelskaya. Moscow. 2009 (in Russian).

Review of the Economic Conditions and Main Directions of Foreign Economic Activity of the Republic of Uzbekistan. The Trade Mission of the Russian Federation in the Republic of Uzbekistan. Tashkent, 2015 (in Russian).

Central Asia: a role in reorganization of the world markets of oil and natural gas. Moscow. IMEMO. 2014 (in Russian).

A. Malashenko. A. Uzbekistan: transit isn't visible yet. Moscow, 2014 (in Russian).

Post-Soviet States: 25 years of Independent Development. Vol. 1. Western Flank of the CIS. Central Asia. M. IMEMO, 2017.

www.cbu.uz(Central Bank of the Republic of Uzbekistan).

www.stat.uz (State Statistics Committee of Uzbekistan).

www.imf/org/external/country/UZB/ (website of IMF of Uzbekistan).

www.investuzbekistan.uz

www.gov.uz (Government of Uzbekistan).

UNIT VI

THE BALTIC STATES: CHARACTERISTICS OF ECONOMIC MODELS

CHAPTER 33

SIMILARITIES AND DIFFERENCES IN THE ECONOMIES OF THE BALTIC COUNTRIES

The Baltics comprise Latvia, Lithuania, and Estonia, three former republics of the Soviet Union. Due to their geographical proximity, as well as similarities in cultural traditions, lifestyle, and economies, the three have always been thought of as a coherent unit. They have usually been regarded as part of Western civilization, both during the Russian empire and the Soviet era and their links to the West have enabled them to profit from the transit of freight and goods between East and West, despite Russia's success in building routs to bypass them.

The Baltic nations have much in common. Their histories all feature the fight to preserve national identity through resistance to aggressors who have threatened them over the centuries. Another common feature is that all three were admitted to NATO and the European Union in 2004. They have all faced similar problems adapting to the EU.

Similarities and Differences in Economic Models and Policy

Before the demise of the Soviet Union, the Baltics were known for well-developed mechanical and radio engineering, high-tech chemistry, a diversified timber industry, the production of high-quality construction materials, textiles and food, and the most efficient meat and dairy production in the Soviet Union. The three countries spent over 10 years on difficult reforms after independence, mainly required for their accession to the EU. Above all, they needed to align their own systems with the EU's legal and economic standards. The main elements of the reform process were the establishment of national currencies (later replaced by the euro), the denationalization of state enterprises (usually conducted through auctions), the restitution or return of property to its former owners, and finally the complete restructuring of the tax and budgetary systems to reduce the tax burden on producers.

Estonia led the way in the creation of a market economy. First of all, many state enterprises were allowed to go bankrupt under a strict, transparent, and uncompromising system. They were left with a start choice between privatization and closure. This approach proved effective in attracting foreign partners to set up joint ventures. Today, almost all large companies and banks belong to foreign investors. Latvia followed a similar approach but did so more slowly. Lithuania did not make use of forced bankruptcies in the same way, but sought to restructure state enterprises. As a result, it has attracted less foreign investment than the other two. This difference of approach can also be seen in the way the three countries set about reforming their rural economies: in Estonia, it was allowed to fail; in Latvia, it suffered major difficulties; while in Lithuania, it was propped up by the government.

The reform process in the Baltic States were made easier by the relatively small size of the economies, by national unity and way the population generally trusted the political elites, and by the fact that the structure of their industries was generally more modern than other former Soviet countries. Moreover, their privatization processes were more measured and, above all, avoided the 'capture' of property by small groups of people. For example, in Lithuania, privatization certificates were distributed equally to all adults in the country. These enabled people to participate in the initial stage of privatizations with the result that over two-thirds of workers ended up owning shares in formerly state enterprises. In Latvia, one-third of workers were able to buy shares, while in Estonia, less than a quarter did.

Agrarian reforms focused on the privatization of rural enterprises and on improving the tax system as it applied to farmland. Collective and state farms were abolished and privatized, creating in the process a more traditional model of farms of between 1 and 20 hectares. Most farms were also given forest lands which soon became assets to buy and sell. The transition period in the Baltic States during the 1990s, produced a situation not seen before in Europe: large-scale, highly productive rural enterprises being turned back into semi-natural, small-scale operations capable of more modest production. Today, production for market is an important feature of the agricultural sectors in these three countries.

The demise of the Soviet Union also had an important impact on the Baltic States in that they looked west for new markets and faced the need to adapt to higher standards than they had been used to when selling to the less sophisticated Russian market. To compete in European markets, the Baltic States had to capitalize on their strengths, such as cheap and high-quality construction materials, chemicals, and some timber products. Many leading enterprises either changed their business models or closed down. Some sectors survived from the Soviet era and remain important, such as freight transport, tourism, foods, and light industry. However, plans to develop their high-tech industries, attempting to recreate what they had during the Soviet era, have proved less successful.

The impact of the economic transformation was significant in all three Baltic countries. In the first five or six years after independence, GDP fell by 51% in Latvia, 44% in Lithuania, and by 35% in Estonia. Along with other former Soviet countries, the extent and duration of these falls were worse than in Eastern European countries.

However, healthy economic growth returned toward the end of the 1990s and lasted for 10 years. Between 1997 and 2007, across the region, the average annual GDP growth was 7.5–8%. Even allowing for the decline during the economic crisis of 2008 and 2009 when GDP fell by around 3% a year, the long-term growth of the Baltic States is still more than double that of other eurozone countries. Economic growth has been driven partly by effective strategies of product specialization, but also by low costs made possible by inexpensive labor and low taxes (in the Baltic States, tax expenditure is equivalent to about 30% of GDP, compared with around 45% in other leading EU countries). These circumstances have been key in attracting greater inflows of foreign investment.

It is important to note that, despite the economic, social, and political difficulties faces during the transition period that followed the demise of the Soviet Union, the Baltic States have been much more successful than other former Soviet countries in making the transition. The reform programs of the 1990s, strengthened the private sector, created favorable macroeconomic conditions for economic development, improved the atmosphere for businesses, increased the inflow of foreign investment, and promoted gradual modernization of the economies. With much investment going into real estate as well as trade and other services, what the Baltic States did, in effect, was to deindustrialize their economies.

Table 33.1 — GDP in the Baltic States in 2016

	Latvia	Lithuania	Estonia
GDP, US$ bn	27.6	42.8	23.3
GDP PPP per capita, US$	25,587	29,862	29,843
GDP rate of growth in 2017, %	4.5	3.8	4.9

Sources: World Bank. Indicators; IMF. World Economic Outlook. April 2018. p. 241

Region-wide Economic Problems

The markets in the Baltic States are now dominated by European companies and banks. Duty-free imports of European goods resulted not only in poor current balance of payments (in all three countries, imports exceed exports, even of food), but also to pressure on local producers. Cheap loans from European banks were most used to purchase real estate which became the first main engine of economic growth but ran out of steam at the start of the world economic crisis.

The region as a whole faces difficulties in the agricultural sector. The European Union subsidizes the Baltic States to encourage their farmers not to plant crops but to develop 'landscape tourism' instead. Funds are thus invested in projects to protect the environment.

The low taxes in the Baltic States are a source of friction with the rest of the European Union. Some EU member states believe that the Baltics use the system of low taxes to benefit their citizens unfairly and to achieve smaller payments to the EU's central budget.

The recent economic slowdown across the Baltics is the result of the wider European situation. The recession has affected all member states, but had a particular impact on the smaller countries. Increases in production have slowed across Europe. This means dwindling order books for companies in the Baltic States and falling production as a result. This hits many companies in the region particularly hard as their domestic markets, with falling purchasing power, are small. The sanctions imposed by the EU and Russia on each other have also make life difficult.

Labor productivity in the Baltic States still lags behind the levels seen in Central Europe. In Latvia, for example, productivity is 46% of the EU average; in Lithuania it is 52%; and in Estonia 56%. Moreover, wages growth has exceeded growth in productivity.

Economic Cooperation in the Baltic Region

While there have never been any conflicts between the Baltic States, there have not been any alliances either. The three countries have been integrated into the economic sphere of Russia, then the Soviet Union and finally the EU, and always as three separate entities. The economic relations between them have never been particularly strong such that we cannot think of the region as an economic cluster. In fact, they compete with each other for foreign trade.

However, the Western banks and companies that are now active in the Baltics do tend to regard the three countries and a single region. That, coupled with the introduction in all three of the euro and greater differentiation of their production specialities, has led to a strengthening of relations.

Economic Relations with Russia

Although good economic relations between the Baltic States and Russia would be in the interests of all sides, ties over the last two decades have been strained, as ideology and politics have trumped economic reality. The elites in the Baltic societies have made Russophobia a new ideology, supported by the West. The Baltics are now seen as an outpost of NATO.

For this reason, Russia has been in no hurry to develop fuller cooperation with its former allies from the Soviet era. If there is to be progress, Baltic chauvinism in relation to Russians will need to be overcome (see below) as the status of Russian living in the Baltics is the most pressing issues in relations between Russia and the Baltic States.

Moscow has adopted a consistently hard line on the rerouting freight traffic had the desired effect when the Baltics lowered transit and related duties. As a result, transit through the Baltic ports, especially those in Latvia, has been able to continue.

Table 33.2 — Baltics exports to Russia, %

	Latvia	Lithuania	Estonia
Food stuffs and agricultural raw materials	9.5	11.8	5.0
Alcohol and tobacco goods	2.7	1.6	1.6
Mineral products	19.1	4.7	9.0
Fuel	5.2	23.8	15.1
Products of animal and vegetable origin	0.2	0.2	0.3
Chemical products	7.9	9.2	5.4
Manufacturing industry products	25.8	10.9	16.7
Machines, equipment and transport vehicles	16.6	22.1	30.9
Others	13.0	15.6	15.6

Source: Custom Statistics of the Russian Federation

In 2014, Latvia sent 15% of its exports to Russia. For Lithuania the figure was 21%, and for Estonia, 7%. The restrictions imposed by Russia on food imports from Europe in 2014 had a big impact on Lithuania for whom the value of exports in the products affected was equivalent to 2.5% of GDP.

Region-wide Social Problems

The region faces demographic challenges as a result of the negative natural growth of the population couple with migration. These issues are compounded by the issues surrounding the status of the Russian-speaking minorities.

Table 33.3 — Demographic and social indicators in the Baltic States

	Population in 2016, millions	Population growth in 2016, %	Human Development Index (HDI) in 2015
Latvia	2.0	-0.9	0.830
Lithuania	2.9	-1.3	0.848
Estonia	1.3	0.0	0.865

Source: http://ec.europa.eu/eurostat/data/database

The negative natural growth of the population in the Baltics was caused by a fall in the birth rate and a sharp rise in the number of people of retirement age.

There has also been considerable emigration by people seeking a better life elsewhere. Moreover, it is often the most able members of society and the workforce who move away. After joining the EU, more than 10% of the population left Lithuania (500,000 people). Latvia lost 200,000 and Estonia 30,000. As a result, since independence, the population of Latvia has reduced by 26%, that of Lithuania by 21%, and Estonia by 18%.

There have been Russians living in the Baltics since the Great Northern War, initially as representatives of the Imperial administration. A significant wave of immigration by Russian-speaking people followed the Second World War when the Baltics pursued active industrialization policies. Skilled workers, engineers, teachers, doctors, and scientists moved from Russia. There was also a large number of Russian-speaking military personnel stationed in the Baltic military district. There were generally officer class, with secondary education or higher.

By independence, there were 1,122,000 Russian speakers in Latvia, representing 34% of the population. In Estonia, 475,000 represented 30.3% of the population; and, in Lithuania, the 344,000 Russian speakers made up 9.4% of the population. In some of the large cities, the Russian speakers were in the majority. This remains the case today, for example, in Riga, the largest city in the region. This is a constant irritant to local nationalists who would like to see the Russians squeezed out. Lithuania adopted a different approach, offering citizenship to all residents at the time of independence. Although Lithuania has thus avoided some of the ethnic tensions seen in Latvia and Estonia, it is not without difficulties in areas such as education in Russian language, employment, and social security.

Although the population of ethnic Russians has fallen around 1 million, this is still a significant proportion of the people and continues to be a cause of concern for civil authorities and military strategists who fear any strengthening of Russian influence. Estimates suggest that Russians now make up 33% of the population in Latvia, 26% in Estonia, and 6% in Lithuania.

In general, the Russian populations show loyalty to the new states, reflecting the fact that a large proportion of the commercial world in the

Baltic States is in the hands of the Russian diaspora; its hold on finance and economics in Latvia is particularly marked where it controls over half of business activity. In Estonia Russians control around 20%, and in Lithuania around 8%. Many Russians living in the Baltic States, hope to gain citizenship there as this will give them the rights of EU citizens, enabling them to live and travel freely throughout the EU. Many predict significant migration of Russians from the Baltics to the rest of the EU.

Conclusion

1. In the quarter-century that has passed since their independence, the Baltic States have conducted programs of fundamental social and economic reform. Among former Soviet countries, the three Baltic countries had the most suitable conditions for enacting market reforms in a short space of time. Above all, they only had a relatively short socialist history which enabled them to return many business resources to previous owners. In addition, they had a cheap but well qualified workforce, comparatively well-developed infrastructure, a convenient geographical location, industries focused on export markets, and generous aid from Western countries.

2. Extensive liberalization in both economic activity and foreign trade was undertaken. Most state enterprises were privatized. Large-scale structural reform was achieved in the key industries and modern market institutions were created. Privatizations were carried out by selling company shares to strategic investors. Foreign investors enjoyed open access to all areas of the economies, including the financial sectors.

3. The Baltic States were able to integrate themselves quickly into the economic system of Western Europe. Today, their main socioeconomic challenge is emigration.

Questions

1. What special features of economic policy do the Baltic States share?

2. Evaluate the potential of the Baltic States to act as transit countries.

3. What competitive advantages do the Baltic States enjoy?

4. Why are membership of the EU and NATO so attractive to the Baltic States?

Sources of additional information

Business & Baltics (Baltic business newspaper, http://www.dd.lv).
BaltInfo (http://www.baltinfo.ru/news).
Eurostat (http://epp.eurostat.ec.europa).
Custom Statistics of the Russian Federation (http://ctu.customs.ru/ru/statistics).

CHAPTER 34

LATVIA

Latvia's Economic Model

During the Soviet era, Latvia's economic circumstances were characterized by its highly qualified workforce (including ethnic Russians), relatively few natural resources, and its advantageous geographic position. The reforms of the 1990s were aimed at making the transition to a market economy to enable the country to join the European Union. The reforms included privatization; price liberalization; fundamental reorganization of the tax, banking, and budgetary systems; and the creation of the market mechanisms necessary to support foreign trade.

The privatization process started in 1994. More than half of the country's inhabitants received privatization certificates with which they were able to open privatization accounts. But the mechanisms for their use were not well established and the certificates depreciated in value. The privatization process saw state enterprises transformed into joint-stock companies. In many cases employees were able to buy shares in their own companies. There were also sales at auction, which were open to foreign investors. More than 700 state enterprises were transferred to private ownership while 38 went into liquidation.

However, the economic model that arose during the 1990s was based largely on cheap labor and failed to capitalize on new technologies. As such, it proved to be a poor choice for a country lacking in natural resources. To address this, a National Program of Innovation was established to try and increase the proportion of the country's manufacturing that used knowledge-intensive forms of production from 6 to 25%. The European average is 30% and about 10% of the workforce work in the high-tech sector. In Latvia that figure is just 4%. State spending on scientific development in Latvia is just one-third of the European average. The number of people employed in the sciences has fallen from 31,000 to just 4,000. Moreover, the private sector has failed to engage in research and development.

Latvia has also failed to find a credible niche for itself in the division of labor around Europe. Its agriculture and textile production is of good quality, but struggles to distinguish itself in international markets, even given the advantage of cheap labor. The same goes for the machine-building sector. As a result, a number of large companies have disappeared. Among them were RAF (manufacturing mini-buses), VEF (radios), Kommutator (telephones and exchange equipment), and Radiotechnika. The company RVR which was the largest manufacturer of electric trains in the Soviet era now focuses only on repair. The same goes for a major plant that once produced trams.

The National Economy

Although Latvia had the highest rate of growth in the EU between 2000 and 2007, the country only restored its pre-reform level of GDP in 2005. Both GDP and employment peaked in 2008. Growth was strongest in construction, the retail trade and financial intermediation. It was weakest in manufacturing. The high growth came on the back of rapid wage increases that led to a consumer boom which was felt most noticeably in trade and the building of new homes. At the same time, the inflows of foreign capital into the banking sector led to a boom in credit, both consumer and mortgage lending.

It is thus not surprising that, in the years immediately following the global financial crisis, Latvia—along with the other Baltic States—had one of the world's sharpest falls in GDP. During the current decade, growth rates have been steady at 2–3%, and are forecasted to remain at the same level.

Table 34.1 — GDP in Latvia

	2000	2006	2008	2009	2011	2013	2016
GDP PPP, US$ bn	17.1	34.4	37.9	32.1	35.4	47.7	50.9
GDP PPP per capita, US$	6.96	15.5	16.7	14.6	17.1	23.5	25.6
GDP dynamics, %	6.9	12.2	-4.6	-18	5.5	4.2	2.2

Sources: World Development Report 2010. N.Y. p.388.
IMF. World Economic Outlook. April 2010.P.159.
Eurostat //www.eep.eurostat.cec.eu.int; https://www.cia.gov/index.html.

Looking at the industrial structure of GDP in Latvia, the primary sector accounts for just 3%; the secondary sector, 23%; and the tertiary sector, 74% (partially at the expense of transit of goods via Latvian ports). About 9% of the workforce is engaged in agriculture and 24% in industry.

Today, Latvia is still living with the consequences of errors made at the beginning of the 1990s when almost all manufacturing in the country was closed down and the country harbored the illusion that it would be possible to create a strong economic base, able to withstand external crises and internal problems, without domestic manufacturing, a sound skills base, and a recognizable niche in world markets. The country placed too much faith in the EU providing both a source of income and a fair division of labor. Today, 75% of the economy is in foreign hands and 75% of consumption is provided by imports. As such, Latvians have lost a measure of the autonomy necessary to decide their own economic future, at least in relation to those industries that produce the most income: finance, real estate, and retail.

Economic Policy

Like its Baltic neighbors, Latvia must, to some extent, live according to edicts from the European Commission. However, in 2007, the country adopted a 20-year development plan which marked a return to medium and long-term economic planning. The plan identifies clearly which industries are successful and thus worthy of support. The priorities are construction, energy, metal and timber, pharmaceuticals, and tourism. Much is expected of investment funds from the EU to support the plan.

Human Capital

For many Latvians, joining the EU offered a chance to move and earn more money. There has been significant emigration from the country. This, coupled with a low birth rate, has led to a fall in the working-age population. The birth rate was at its lowest in the early 1990s, so as the cohort of people born then has been entering the workforce, the impact has been at its height. The greatest shortage is among those taking low-skilled jobs.

The Real Sector

The process of reform and privatization in the agricultural sector saw a reduction of 40% in the amount of land under cultivation. This was caused in part by the system of restitution whereby was returned to former owners, some of whom were either unwilling or unable to cultivate the land. The average size of plots in Latvia is less than 20 hectares. But, given the soil and climate, a farmer needs at least 100 hectares for a business to be viable. The large farms of the Soviet era have been divided into smaller enterprises.

Latvian agriculture runs on a quota system according to the recommendations of the EU on what should be produced, when, and in what volume. Farmers have been encouraged to reduce their production and invest in rural tourism instead. For this they receive compensation from the EU.

The amount of fish being caught and processed is barely a third of what it used to be. In the food sector, the success of small enterprises depends on their ability to produce a product that is exclusive or of high quality. There is only one successful large food company, Latviyas Balzamx, which produces alcoholic drinks. It has achieved steady sales and is among the country's largest three taxpayers.

Of Latvia's energy, 67% is generated by hydroelectric power stations, with the rest coming from thermal stations. However, as the country is relatively flat, the hydro capacity is limited. There are only meager domestic resources for the development of thermal stations. There is only peat, with reserves estimated to be 530 million tons. This is used at the Riga power station. Estimates suggest that there may be up to 30 million tons of oil deposits on the Baltic Sea shelf. Domestic electricity generation produces only 3.3 billion kWh, only half of the country's requirements. The shortfall is met by power imported from Lithuania, Estonia, and Russia.

Mechanical engineering provides 20% of the country's manufacturing output and 30% of the exports of finished products. The sector is made up largely of small and medium-sized companies focused on small quantities of niche products.

Timber processing is an important part of Latvian exports. There are large companies in the cities, with small concerns in rural areas. The textile industry is made up of about 60 companies, the largest of which are able to compete with traditional European suppliers. They are focused almost exclusively on exports. Raw materials for these sectors are imported from Russia, Ukraine, Belarus, and Uzbekistan.

As a proportion of GDP, Latvia's transport sector is the largest in the Baltics, based on large-scale freight. Freight transit contributes 30% of the government's budget revenues and up to 27% of export of goods and services. However, the Soviet era oil terminal at Ventspils no longer receives supplies of crude oil from Russia, placing its future in doubt.

The Financial Sector

The banking sector is made up of 23 commercial banks and 10 credit unions. The share of foreign capital in the sector exceeds 70%. Shares in Latvian banks are held by investors from Sweden, Germany, Finland, Estonia, Russia, and the European Bank of Reconstruction and Development. A group was formed of banks operating with foreign investment, including Russian. The banks in the group were more profitable than domestic banks. The banking sector plays an important role in managing the flow of money back and forth with Russia. Inflation has been kept under control and has averaged 1% a year, with deflation in some years.

There are just 17 listed companies on the stock market. Riga could be said to have the potential to become a regional financial center thanks to its advantageous geographical position and its historically strong links with eastern neighbors as well as Western Europe.

The financial crisis saw Latvia's fiscal budget surpluses become deficits. Under pressure from the EU, the government was forced to achieve a sharp reduction in the deficit. This even required reductions in pensions. The fiscal deficit caused substantial public debt. In 2016, the debt was equivalent to more than 38% of GDP. In more recent years, a return to surpluses has brought this under control.

The External Sector

Deficits in the balance of payments have been another feature of the Latvian economy. The same is true for the other Baltic States. This is a logical consequence of the inflows of foreign capital which provide the surplus on the financial balance and finance the preference for imports over exports. Foreign capital has also been responsible for 40% of all the investment into fixed assets. All of this had meant that Latvian foreign trade has developed with persistent negative balances, equivalent to about 30% of GDP.

The country's external economic policy has been directly toward greater integration into the European structures. However, recently there has been a more balanced approach with attempts to be more even-handed, especially when it comes to Russia. Latvia's EU partners have taken 65–70% of the country's exports and supply 75% of its imports. The most important single partner is Lithuania which takes 15% of Latvia's exports and supplies 19% of its imports. Germany, Sweden, and Estonia are also significant markets. The CIS accounts for 16% of Latvia's foreign trade, but nearly all (15%) of this is trade with Russia.

In 2016, the accumulated foreign direct investment in Latvia had reached nearly US$14.5 bn, a high figure for such a small country. Along with the inflows of private capital, significant funds have also come from EU bodies, which provided €4 bn between 2007 and 2013. Investments were aimed at the development and effective use of human resources, increasing competitiveness in enterprises, and at reconstructing the country's infrastructure.

The large inflows of private foreign investment have created the current situation in which two-thirds of the country's fixed assets now belong to foreigners. This is particularly true in the finance, real estate, and trade sectors. Latvian law provides favorable terms for foreign investors and allows ample freedom to conduct currency transactions. Entities in north European countries own 35% of the foreign investment in Latvia. A further 12% is held by institutions in Estonia, but many of these are in fact the Estonian branches of foreign banks and companies.

Latvia's external debt in 2000 was US$2.7 bn, equivalent to 37% of GDP. But by 2016, this had grown to US$39.9 bn, equivalent to 106% of GDP.

Latvia's economic relationship with Russia is defined first and foremost by the situation as neighbors and, secondly, by Russia's interest in freight through Latvian territory. After joining the EU and NATO, the Latvian leadership sought to minimize their economic ties with Russia. At the same time, the Russian State Duma recommended to the Russian government that any further development of trade and economic relations with Latvia should depend on how the Latvian government treated the native Russian population in the country.

The two countries did not sign a formal border agreement until as late as 2007. Latvia was forced to make certain concessions over the Pytalovo area in the Pskov region. This agreement improved the atmosphere in bilateral relations and saw an increase in trade. By 2013, Russia was Latvia's second largest trade partner, taking 18.2% of its exports and supplying 9.2% of its imports. However, the subsequent imposition of sanctions on both sides saw trade in both directions decrease slightly. By 2015, Russia was taking 15% of Latvia's exports.

Russia is the fifth largest investor in Latvia, behind Sweden, Germany, Estonia, and Denmark. The largest Russian investor is Gazprom which owns 34% of the national gas company, Latvijas Gaze. In addition, Transnefteproduct is involved in the Latrostrans joint venture. In 2003, the Latvian Trade Bank became the first subsidiary of the Russian MDM Bank. Around 1,000 companies in Latvia have some level of Russian investment. About 4% of the accumulated FDI in Latvia is Russian.

Russian business interests in Latvia have focused on the power industry, as well as transport and finance. In Pskov and Novgorod there are several Latvian-owned companies producing plywood.

The Social Sector

Latvia has seen its population fall by between 1 and 2% a year over the last 10 years as a result of a falling birth rate and emigration from both the Latvian and Russian populations. Between 2008 and 2016, the population fell by about 7%. This has brought about a decrease in the population of working age.

The issue of the declining population is aggravated by the problem of way in which the Russian-speaking population suffers discrimination. The proportion of the overall population that are Russian speakers is not great with its increasing as a result of greater emigration by Latvians. At the moment, the population of the country is about 2 million. The proportion made up by native Latvians has fallen to 55%, while that made up of Russian speakers has increased to 37%. Belarussians account for 4% and Ukrainians 3%.

The standard of living in Latvia is, on average, just 27% of the EU average. In 2000, unemployment stood at 14%. By 2008, this had fallen to 5.6%, but then rose dramatically to 18% as a result of the global economic crisis. Between 2008 and 2012, about 5% of the population emigrated and unemployment fell to 14% in 2013, and to 9% in 2015 2017.

The real income of the population is high when compared to other former Soviet countries. The average monthly salary, after tax, is €620. However, inflation remains a problem, especially for goods and services, and housing. In terms of income, the top decile earns 10 times as much as the lowest decile.

Conclusion

1. Latvia's economic reforms have been aimed at making the transition to a market economy to enable the country to join the EU. The main goals of the reforms were privatization; price liberalization; new taxation and budgetary systems; monetary and credit reforms and the creation of a new banking system; the creation of market mechanisms for foreign trade; and a reform of the country currency. The IMF played an important role in preparing and implementing measures to bring about economic stabilization. It oversaw the first stage of reforms which began the process of joining the EU.

2. However, business activity remains generally low, despite the government's efforts to reduce the bureaucratic burden on small and medium businesses. The lack of large investment projects is also holding the country back.

3. Thanks to the country's role as a major transit route between Russia and Western Europe, Riga and Ventspils have become the two largest cities in the Baltics. The country's economic prosperity in the future will depend largely on how it can capitalize on these advantages.

Questions

1. What are the main similarities and differences, both demographic, and social and economic, between Latvia and its Baltic neighbors?

2. What changes have been experienced by Latvian industry since the demise of the Soviet Union?

3. Describe Latvia's agro-industrial complex.

4. How have Latvia's foreign economic relations developed in recent years?

Sources of additional information

"Business&Baltic" (Baltic daily business newspaper, http://www.bb.lv).
Economic Development of Latvia Report. Ministry of Economy Republic of Latvia.
www.lda.gov.lv (official gazette).
www.csb.lv (Central Statistical Office).
www.icc-info.lv (information bulletin).

CHAPTER 35

LITHUANIA

The Economic Model

Lithuania is the only Baltic country that can claim to have a long history of national statehood. However, as a result of its largely agricultural character and lack of large cities, its economic development has lagged behind that of its neighbors. In the early 1950s, the urban population was only 22%, with the bulk of the rest of the population scattered among 250,000 farms. Today, two-thirds of the population are city dwellers.

During the Soviet era, industries such as mechanical engineering, shipbuilding, instrument engineering, electric engine building, electronic and radio engineering, chemical and oil refining, microbiological, and construction material construction. In total, over 200 large industrial plants were built.

It is worth noting that after independence, while other Baltic States closed many enterprises that had survived from the Soviet era, Lithuania took a more cautious approach and maintained much of its productive capacity.

The National Economy and Economic Policy

After the collapse of the Soviet Union, Lithuania embarked on a process of transformation which began with a fall in national output, exacerbated by the breakdown of economic relationships with former Soviet partners, which lasted until 2000. Thereafter, average annual growth rates exceeded 7% until the start of the global financial crisis in 2008. The strongest growth was seen in manufacturing, construction, retail, transport, and utilities. Between 2011 and 2016, average annual growth was just 2.6% and the IMF forecasts that, by the middle of the next century, it will be at the same level.

Today, the private sector is responsible for more than 90% of GDP. The main goal of the government's economic policy is the creation of an atmosphere that will attract foreign investment. Foreign owners are already in control of many of the country's most profitable companies.

In recent years, economic development has focused mainly on the capital and the fast-developing seaport of Klaipeda which has developed into an important transit point for freight from throughout the former Soviet Union, including Central Asia. A free economic zone has been set up in the port. This has seen the construction of a container terminal and an increase in the amount of oil being handled. The port's easy access to European markets has made it an attractive target for foreign investors, like the German electro-technical company Siemens, the Danish brewer Karlsburg, and the U.S. tobacco company, Philip Morris. To attract foreign investment, commercial advantages have been made available, such as the waiver of taxes on land and real estate.

Human Capital

Lithuania's population has fallen from 3.7 million in 1991 to 2.9 million in 2017 and it continues to fall by 20,000 a year. However, its population remains the largest among the Baltic States.

Today, Lithuania has the largest level of emigration of any EU member state. The main destinations for Lithuanians are the United Kingdom, Ireland, and Norway. The mass outflows of workers have produced labor shortages, especially of builders. To fill the gap, workers have been recruited from Belarus, Moldova, and especially Ukraine.

Native Lithuanians make up 83% of the population, with Poles at 7%, Russians 6% and Belarussians 2%. About 300,000 Lithuanians live overseas, about 70,000 of them in Russia.

The Real Sector

Since the demise of the Soviet Union, Lithuania's industrial structure has changed considerably. The share taken by the primary sector as fallen to 4%, the share of the service sector has grown to 63%, while the share accounted for by industry has remained at 33%. In industry, emphasis was placed on food and textile companies using local resources.

Lithuania has better conditions for agriculture than Estonia or Latvia. Almost the entire country is relatively flat, the climate is good, and the soil fertile enabling the cultivation of a many different crops. However, during the first half of the 1990s, agricultural production fell dramatically to half its 1989 level. A number of measures enabled the sector to recover quickly: privatizations; the restoration of the rights of former land owners; and the formation of family farms. However, the sector, especially livestock farmers, faced stiff competition from large producers in Europe.

Fisheries are also important for Lithuania. However, the country's ocean-going fleet was largely sold off after the demise of the Soviet Union, and what it left tends not to venture beyond the Baltic Sea. The activities of fishing boats are supplemented by trout and salmon farming. The food industry accounts for 30% of industrial output and has traditionally produced meat, dairy, butter, cheese, and fish (although, the latter is in decline due to falling stocks).

Fuel and energy requirements are generally met with imports from Russia and Norway. The EU insisted on the closure of the Ignalina nuclear power plant for environmental reasons, paying Lithuania €220 million compensation. The country generates about 4 bn kWh, which represents just one-quarter of its needs. The shortfall is imported, mainly from Sweden along an underwater cable. The government plans to reduce energy consumption by 20% and produce a quarter of power needs from renewable sources by 2020.

Lithuania is home to the only oil refinery in the Baltics, the plant at Mazeikiai was constructed during the Soviet era and produced 12 million tons a year, contributing 10% of the country's GDP and 20% of tax revenues. The refinery has recently been acquired by the Polish company, PKN ORLEN. Lithuania has been attempting to develop its own oil extraction on the sea shelf but, so far, volumes have not reached 100,000 tons.

In 2011, the government adopted a law on natural gas which requires that the supply and transfer of fuel must be carried out by operators independent of each other. In 2014, Lithuania turned down an opportunity to purchase gas from Russia, preferring instead to buy from Norway even thought this cost twice as much. Lithuania consumes 3 bn cubic meters of gas each year.

The chemical industry produces phosphoric and nitrogen fertilizers which are exported due to a lack of domestic demand. In addition, there are companies producing both synthetic and cellulose-based fibers for the textile industry. The pharmaceutical industry produces mainly liquid medicines. The production of plywood, construction materials, and furniture takes place across the country. The country's output of paper has reduced sharply.

Mechanical engineering, which produces 17% of total output, turns out metal-cutting machines, electrical equipment, refrigerators, TV sets, components, computers and other devices, along with agricultural machinery. However, output is barely a quarter of what it was in 1990. There are about 130 companies that have survived since the Soviet era without significant restructuring that produce cars, equipment, and other metal products. There are large-scale machine-tool enterprises operating to a European standard, Zalgiris in Kaunas producing heavy machinery and drills, and Shilyalis which is engaged in R&D and produces TVs and other radio and electronic equipment.

Another significant sector is textiles which accounts for 20% of industrial production. This sector has seen significant upgrading to European standards and is one of the sectors of the Lithuanian economy that is able to attract substantial levels of foreign investment. In Panevezhis and Plunge, traditional production of linen fabrics based on local raw materials supports a diversified textile industry. Unique arts and crafts made from amber and ceramics are exported around the world.

For a long time, Lithuania has served as a transit corridor between Russia and the West. Today, the transit of freight and passengers to and from Kaliningrad has become an important additional function. This has led to the development of the transit sector along with various supporting activities. A raft of new opportunities may open up with the opening of the system of trans-European railways, the Rail Baltica, connecting Helsinki, Tallinn, Riga, Kaunas, Warsaw, and Berlin.

Unlike its Baltic neighbors, Lithuania is keen to encourage tourism from the East, with low fees and streamlined bureaucracy. The country's resorts welcome over 100,000 Russians every year.

The Financial Sector

Lithuania has 10 commercial banks, three affiliates of foreign banks, the Central Credit Union of Lithuania, and several other credit unions. Nordic banks have played a particularly important role in the privatization of the state banks. For example, Vilniaus Banka, the largest commercial bank which controls 40% of the Lithuanian financial market, was sold to the Swedish Skandinaviska Enskilda Banken. The Estonian banking group Hansabank (which belongs to the Swedish Swedbank) bought 91% of the shares in the Lithuanian state savings bank. The Latvian Pareks Bank bought the local Industrial Bank. The German Nord B bought the Agricultural Bank, the second largest bank in Lithuania. There is a significant network of local branches of other European banks in Vilnius and other cities. The Lithuanian Development Bank was founded to finance investment projects, with 36% of its shares belonging to the EBRD and the remainder staying with the Lithuanian government.

Inflation fell sharply after 2000 (in 2003, there was even deflation) but rose after the financial crisis in 2008. It has since fallen back again to between 1.5 and 3.5% a year.

There is a budget deficit which has caused an increase in national debt which has been equivalent to around 45% of GDP (42% in 2016).

The External Sector

Like its Baltic neighbors, Lithuania's balance of payments is characterized by a negative current balance of payments and a positive financial account. This reflects the large inflows of foreign investment and the opportunity for some of this to be spent on imported goods.

Lithuania adopted an external economic policy that is more reasonable and pragmatic than those of its neighbors. Even though it is now an EU member, the country has maintained its relationships with its partners to the East and they continue to account for a substantial part of its foreign trade turnover. When animosity between Estonia and Russia rose at the beginning of 2007 and the transit of Russian goods through Estonia fell by a half, Lithuania seized the opportunity to attract more Russian freight to transit through its territory. A majority of Lithuania's exports now go to EU markets and over 40% of its imports come from there.

Accumulated foreign direct investment in Lithuania now exceeds US$14 bn. Nearly 40% of foreign investment goes into manufacturing, unlike in Latvia and Estonia where the bulk of it is targeted at the financial services industry. The largest investors are in Denmark which accounts for 15% of all accumulated FDI; Sweden has 14%, Russia 13%, and Germany 12%. Russian FDI is focused on telecommunications, the food industry, and banking.

Economic Relations with Russia

As political tensions with Russia have worsened, the Lithuanian government suspended purchases of Russian gas. The Russian government responded by stopping imports of Lithuanian food. In 2014, Lithuanian exports to Russia fell to just one-third of their previous level. In 2015, just 15% of the country's exports went to Russia.

As a member of the EU, Lithuania has sought to use the Kaliningrad special economic zone as a platform to the CIS markets. In pursuit of this objective, the country quickly developed a network of joint ventures in Kaliningrad which facilitate trade to Russia under preferential tariff arrangements. Lithuanian FDI in Kaliningrad, however, is still less than US$150 million.

The Social Sector

Unemployment is an increasing problem. It rose from 5.7% in 2008 to 7.1% in 2017. The average monthly salary in 2014 exceeded €900, but the average old-age pension was the lowest in the EU and just €100 a month.

Conclusion

1. Lithuania has given the impression of being more tolerant than its neighbors toward its ethnic minorities as well as to its erstwhile partners to the east. Unlike Latvia and Estonia, it managed to establish healthy economic relations with Russia that promoted and enhanced economic cooperation. Trade between the two grew for some years, with Lithuania capitalizing on its position as a conduit between East and West. However, with Russia and the EU now imposing sanctions on each other, the economic ties have inevitably been affected.

2. Most of the reform program that followed the demise of the Soviet Union has focused on giving every possible support to business initiatives and improving the functioning of the market. Lithuania has the largest market in the region along with the most reliable infrastructure. Its economy has the highest growth rates in the Baltics. Low inflation has also been a major factor in the country becoming the regional leader in attracting foreign investment.

3. Economic policy has been designed around the country's membership of the EU but with features unique to itself. Its priorities have been the formation of a modern economy with a market infrastructure adapted to Western Europe. It has also sought to encourage industry to become more export oriented.

Questions

1. What economic, geographic and geopolitical advantages does Lithuania possess?

2. What industries prospered in the country when it was part of the Soviet Union?

3. What changes have been seen in the country's economic structure during the years of independent development?

4. What are the main characteristics of Lithuania's foreign economic policy?

5. Assess the prospects for trade and economic relations between Lithuania and Russia.

Sources of additional information

"BalticTimes" (weekly newspaper).
«Lietuvos rytas» and "Echo of Lithuania" (daily newspaper).
http://www.stat.gov.lt (state paper).
http://epp.eurostat.ec.europa.eu (EU statistical bulletin).
www.baltic-course.com (Quarterly analytical journal "Baltic course").

CHAPTER 36

ESTONIA

The Economic Model

Of the three Baltic States, Estonia has had the strongest record in establishing a market economy. Unprofitable state enterprises were forced in bankruptcy, with the legal regime around bankruptcy being the most transparent, rigid, and uncompromising: firms were either forced to close or to go for privatization, usually in the hands of foreign business interests. This proved effective in attracting foreign investment so that, today, almost all large firms and banks belong to foreign investors.

After the demise of the Soviet Union, almost all industry created during the Soviet era was abolished and the economy reconstructed along market principles and reoriented toward the West.

The National Economy

In common with the other Baltic States, Estonia experienced a deep recession before achieving high rates of GDP growth. That growth was driven largely by inflows of foreign capital, financing cheap credit, including house building.

However, the 2008 global financial crisis hit the Estonian economy hard; GDP fell by over 19%; unemployment grew to 18%; and real incomes fell by 11%. After the crisis, growth rates did not match their pre-crisis levels and for the second half of the current decade, they are forecast to average between 2.5% and 3.5% a year. Currently, GDP by PPP in Estonia is the highest among former Soviet countries but is still only 65% of the Central European average. Labor productivity is also one-third lower than the EU average.

Since independence, Estonia's economy has undergone fundamental change. In 1991 about 12% of GDP could be attributed to the primary sector and 52% to the secondary. By 2018, this had fallen to 3% and 27% respectively. At the same time, the services sector grew to 70%.

Estonian economic policy has been focused mainly on adapting the country to the EU market. Enterprises and even whole industries that had previously been designed around integration with neighbors to the east, were either sharply reduced or abolished altogether. The main focus now is on export-oriented sectors involved in the processing of local raw materials. The government aims to foment the conditions most favorable to the private sector to enable it to attract foreign investment and drive the internationalization of companies. The EU's support plan for Estonia, which ran from 2007 to 2013, provided more than US$4 bn a year. Between 2004 and 2006, the country received three times as much back from the EU than it paid into the central budget. Between 2007 and 2013, it was three-and-a-half times as much.

Today, only Tallinn port, the railways, the energy industry, and the postal service remain in public ownership. The state follows strict and consistent policy of non-interference in the private sector. It maintained this stance, even during the last financial crisis.

Most Estonian companies, 97%, are small. In terms of commercial management in all its aspect, e.g., liquidity, cash flow, etc., large companies in Estonia face more difficulties that smaller ones. Many Estonian analysts see specialization as the way forward and so expect to see many larger companies being split up into smaller units in the future.

Estonia is in for a period of restructuring. The government envisages a support program for small and medium businesses focused on improving export performance. This will target companies with annual sales of no more than US$50 million and a maximum of 250 employees. This support will be in the form of credits rather than subsidies.

Human Capital

Between 2000 and 2014, the population shrank by 0.4% a year as a result of a falling birth rate and emigration. Today, it stands at 1.3 million people. In the quarter-century since independence, the population has fallen by about 20%. At the same time, the urban lifestyle has become more popular and there has been internal migration into the cities. For example, nearly a third of the entire population lives in the capital and this is expected to rise to a half by 2030. Ethnic Estonians make up 68% of the population while Russians make up 26%.

The number of people in work has fallen to 650,000. The number of people working in agriculture, chemicals, and food halved, while the numbers in construction and trade doubled.

The level of educational achievement among the Estonian population is high, maintained by a network of institutions of higher education. There are 35 universities and other institutions attended by about 70,000 students, i.e., about 65% of the relevant age group is still in full-time education, one of the highest levels among former Soviet countries.

There are a total of 69 scientific research bodies. Before the economic crisis of 2008, spending on science was equivalent to 1% of GDP, putting Estonia second only to Russia among former Soviet countries. But in terms of information resources, Estonia is the undisputed leader; it is the most computerized country in Europe and among the world leaders in terms of mobile phone ownership and access to the Internet.

The Real Sector

Estonia's agricultural sector continues to focus on dairy and meat production along with pig breeding. A third of its production is exported. Under pressure from the EU, the number of cattle and pigs has been reduced by two-thirds. European experts claim these results from the high costs of handling the animals. At the same time, quotas for the export of the sector's produce to Europe have been heavily reduced. It is worth noting that the cost of milk production in Estonia is one-third higher than in Latvia and Lithuania. For this reason, Estonian producers tend to use raw materials from their neighbors. Sheep breeding is growing in popularity.

EU policies that aim to encourage large farms have led to the almost complete elimination of small farms and producers. In 2001, there were 65,000 farms; today there are no more than 20,000 left. The number of people employed in agriculture has fallen from 140,000 to 73,000 and as much as a third of farmland has been taken out of cultivation.

Estonia's food industry is broadly able to meet domestic needs and is able to export more than a third of its production. But, even here, there have been major changes. When the country entered the EU, more than 130 meat and dairy companies had to be closed down as they did not conform to EU standards.

The fuel and energy sector is largely based on the use of combustible shale (with production of 13 million tons a year) and peat. However, burning these fuels leads to high carbon dioxide emissions. There are two power stations, Baltic and Estonian, producing 12 bn kWh a year while domestic demand is just 7.4 bn kWh.

The EU is conscious of the importance of shale to the Estonian economy and has not sought to force the closure of the shale mines or the redesign of the power stations. However, it has made clear that this situation is only temporary. The production of biofuels is growing, with five enterprises already active.

The metal industry is dominated by a large plant producing steel tape (3 million tons a year) constructed by the American firm, Galvex. Like the power industry, the chemical sector relies heavily on shale. It should be noted that the technologies used in the chemical processing of shale were developed during the Soviet era and are unique to Estonia. They are not used anywhere else in the world. The country also has chemical plants producing nitrogen fertilizers, phenols, dyes, and pitches. In addition, there is production of plastics, household products, and pharmaceuticals.

The timber processing industry employs 5% of the active workforce in the country, produces 20% of all industrial output and provides 7% of export revenues. Half of the raw materials for the timber, pulp, and paper industry is imported from Russia as the country does not have sufficient domestic supply of wood that is of the requisite quality. Wood processing produces office furniture, plywood, and matches. A Norwegian company has built a large pulp plant.

The mechanical engineering sector has moved to forms of engineering and electronics that use less metal. This industry relies almost exclusively on orders from overseas for devices and components to be used in vessels, electric motors, excavators, radio equipment, and farming machinery. The Norma company supplies metal and plastic components to the Volga and Gorkovskiy automobile plants in Russia, as well as to the Opel plants. Plants belonging to the Finnish holding group PKC produce electrical fittings for trucks and tractors, along with telecommunications cables. The German company, Trinon Titanium, has opened a plant in Narva to produce unique titanium products for medical and electro-technical uses.

Demand for these is growing around the world. The Finnish company Elcoteq employs more than 3,000 people at its branch in Tallinn, specializing in the assemble of telecommunications equipment. The company, Ecometal reprocesses old automobile accumulators, thousands of tons of which come from Sweden and Finland. The pure lead is extracted from them and sold to German and Polish companies. A plant in Sillamae, which has operated since the Soviet era, processes rare earth ores imported from the Murmansk region of Russia. There is a plant producing heat pumps which can accumulate and use natural energy from the sun and soil as well as heat produced as a by-product of production processes. It also produces a third of global production of generators for wind turbines. The Baltic ship yard has suffered difficult times but has recovered and it now among the largest in the Baltics. Bulk carriers are being constructed at the Tallinn shipyard with technical assistance from a Dutch shipbuilding company.

In the textile industry, it is worth highlighting the story of Krengolmsky Manufactory in Narva. In 1994, it was on the verge of bankruptcy when it was purchased by the Swedish firm, Boras Wafveri AB. It was extensively modernized and emerged in 2007 as one of the largest producers of textiles in Europe. The Baltika and Marat factories also produce ready-to-wear clothes.

The road and rail networks carry the bulk of the country's freight. The railway company was sold in 2001 to Baltic Rail Services, an international consortium. However, having seen it fall into serious disrepair, the state was forced to renationalize it in 2007 but had to pay three-and-a-half times the price it had received in 2001.

Tallinn and Ventspils in Latvia are the two major ports in the Baltics. Tallinn can process up to 40 million tons of freight a year. A total of 24 million tons of oil products pass through the port of Muuga. As well as Tallinn, several small privatized ports operate with a total goods turnover of 6 million tons.

Tourism accounts for 8% of GDP with about 4 million visitors a year, 17% of them from Finland and 6% from Russia.

The Financial Sector

Two Swedish banks, Swedbank and SEB, control 85% of bank assets in Estonia. In total, there are seven commercial banks, seven affiliates of foreign banks and three insurance companies operating in the country.

By international standards, Estonia has a low rate of corporation tax at 21%, but this is higher than Lithuania and Latvia where it is just 15%. This has resulted in the main tax burden shifting on to salaries. The amount of tax levied on labor is equivalent to about 20% of GDP. It is worth noting that it is a cornerstone of Estonia tax policy that direct taxes remain constant. However, there is no such restriction on indirect taxes such as those on fuel, power, heating, tobacco, and alcohol. Estonia's national debt is relatively small. At the equivalent of 10% of GDP, it is the lowest in the Eurozone.

The External Sector

A number of factors have combined to make Estonia an attractive destination for foreign investment: a favorable investment climate; the abolition in 2000 of the tax on reinvestment of profits; and the competitive cost of labor. Annual foreign direct investment has provided up to half of all capital investment. The bulk of FDI comes from Sweden (40%), Finland (25%), and the USA (9%). In 2016, accumulated FDI reached US$19 bn. This is higher than Latvia and Lithuania.

Overseas investments by the Estonia branches of foreign multinational corporations have exceeded US$7 bn. Nearly half of these investments was directed at Lithuania and a third to Latvia.

The basic principles behind the country's external economic policy—both before and since the transition period—have been a fixed currency rate, a liberal regime, the free floating of capital, and equal conditions for domestic and overseas investors.

In terms of foreign trade, Estonia's exports to former Soviet countries have fallen to 10–12% of total exports. Imports from former Soviet countries amount to 14% of total imports. The reorientation of exports toward the West has posed marketing problems as Western consumers remain suspicious about the quality of Estonian goods. A solution has been identified in the promotion, for example, of textile products under other brand names. The country's trade balance is in deficit.

Free economic zones operate in Muuga, Sillamae, and Valga which, between them, play host to 470 enterprises. There is a technology park at the Technology University in Tallinn, considered to be a leading institution in its field within the Baltics.

Economic Relations with Russia

Estonian radicals are among the most vociferously anti-Russian in the world. Tensions came to a head on 9 May 2007 when, on the anniversary of the victory over fascism, the Estonian authorities demolished a monument to the soldiers who liberated Estonia. It was seen by many as an act of defiance. In May 2009, publications printed in Russian ceased along with Russian language TV broadcasts. The events in Ukraine in 2014 have seen political tension rise even further.

Russia has not gone beyond the sanctions on food from the EU and has sought to bring about a cooling of the tension. The amount of Russian freight traffic passing through Estonia fell dramatically and many Russian companies, e.g., Severstal ceased activities in the country. But this trend did not last long and, by 2013, the share of Estonia exports going to Russia was 7% and Russia was responsible for 6% of Estonia's imports. Estonia's main exports to Russia are metalware, and its traditional textiles and food.

In Estonia, the sanctions imposed by Russia on imports of European food had the biggest impact on dairy products which made up 24% of all food exports to Russia. The resulting surpluses of milk and related products were diverted to Lithuania, Latvia, Finland, and Germany. However, the oversupply meant that the Lithuanians who were under sanctions themselves would only pay €243 for a ton of raw milk, compared to the earlier price of €410.

There has been almost a complete stop to Russian tourists visiting Estonia. In May 2015, the Estonian rail company, GoRail, started to suffer losses because of the reduced traffic and was eventually forced to end its service from Tallinn to Moscow.

The Social Sector

Between 2008 and 2013, according to official statistics, the number of available jobs in Estonia fell by more than 100,000. The biggest fall was seen in construction, manufacturing, and trade, both retail and wholesale.

The rate of unemployment increased from 4.7% in 2007 to 10.9% in 2013 and 6.8 in 2017, despite the reduction in the population of working age.

There is no officially established living wage in Estonia. The minimum wage was raised from €290 in 2012 to €320 in 2013. The average monthly salary in 2015 was €836. Income inequality is not high. The Gini index has fallen from 0.37 in 1990 to 0.21 today.

Conclusion

1. Since independence Estonia has made progress in creating a market economy, achieving macroeconomic stability and growth, restructuring the country's enterprises, and carrying out structural reforms. The country has achieved an open economy, an acceptable level of competitiveness, a transparent tax system, and a legal framework that encourages investment. This has enabled the free circulation of goods, free movement of citizens, and free exchange of services and capital. Foreign investment and the active involvement of foreign companies, both alone and in joint ventures, have led to an inflow of new equipment and technologies.

2. However, the global financial crisis has exposed the reality of a number of problems that have yet to be addressed. There is still work to be done on the sectoral structure of the economy to make it able to take advantage of new economic condition. At the same time, there are difficulties in achieving the levels of sales that will enable industries to maintain former levels of production. This has led to the country's GDP now being more oriented toward the services sector which has become a key component in the economy. Some industries have been nimble in responding to the changes quickly, for example, financial services, trade, freight transit, and foreign tourism.

3. The current deficit in the balance of payments is covered by inflows of private and foreign investment that speak to a level of confidence in the Estonian economy. However, the increasing dependence on foreign direct investment leaves the economy vulnerable. The growth of credit offering by banks also poses a risk to the balanced development of the banking sector.

Questions

1. Assess Estonia's economic potential.
2. Evaluate the results of Estonia's economic reforms.
3. What are the prospects for real regional cooperation between the Baltic States?
4. How do you judge the current state and likely future prospects for economic relations between Russia and Estonia?

Sources of additional information

Estonian Statistical Office (statistical yearbook).
«Business journal » (economic weekly paper).
«Postimees» (daily newspaper).
http://www.mineco.ee (website of Ministry of Economy).
http://www.stat.ee/.
http://www.ee/epbe (websites of the Estonian Bank).
http://www.estonica.org/ru/ (Encyclopedia of Estonia).